THE LETTERS OF

Charles and Mary Anne Lamb

Volume III • 1809–1817

CHARLES LAMB AT FORTY-FOUR.
From a watercolor by George Francis Joseph (1764–1846).
Courtesy of The British Museum, London.

THE LETTERS OF

Charles and Mary Anne Lamb

Volume III • 1809–1817

EDITED BY EDWIN W. MARRS, JR.

CORNELL UNIVERSITY PRESS

ITHACA AND LONDON

1978

First published 1978 by Cornell University Press.
Published in the United Kingdom by Cornell University Press Ltd.,
2-4 Brook Street, London W1Y 1AA.

International Standard Book Number 0-8014-1129-7
Library of Congress Catalog Card Number 75-8436
Printed in the United States of America by York Composition Co., Inc.

CONTENTS

ILLUSTRATIONS

ABBREVIATIONS

Ainger (1888)   Alfred Ainger, ed. *The Letters of Charles Lamb: Newly Arranged, with Additions.* 2 vols. London and New York: Macmillan, 1888.

Ainger (1900)   Alfred Ainger, ed. *The Letters of Charles Lamb: Newly Arranged, with Additions,* Vols. I–IV. Vols. IX–XII of *The Life and Works of Charles Lamb.* 12 vols. London: Macmillan, 1899–1900.

Ainger (1904)   Alfred Ainger, ed. *The Letters of Charles Lamb: Newly Arranged, with Additions.* 2 vols. London and New York: Macmillan, 1904.

At the Shrine of St. Charles   E. V. Lucas. *At the Shrine of St. Charles: Stray Papers on Lamb Brought Together for the Centenary of His Death in 1834.* London: Methuen, 1934.

C. L.   Charles Lamb.

CLSB   *Charles Lamb Society Bulletin.* Retitled *Charles Lamb Bulletin* January 1973.

Coleridge's Letters   Earl Leslie Griggs, ed. *Collected Letters of Samuel Taylor Coleridge.* 6 vols. Oxford: Clarendon Press, 1956–1971.

Coleridge's Poetical Works (1912)   Ernest Hartley Coleridge, ed. *The Complete Poetical Works of Samuel Taylor Coleridge, Including Poems and Versions of Poems Now Published for the First Time.* 2 vols. Oxford: Clarendon Press, 1912.

Coleridge's Shakespearean Criticism   Thomas Middleton Raysor, ed. *Samuel Taylor Coleridge: Shakespearean Criticism.* 2d ed. 2 vols. 1960. Rpt. London: Dent; New York: Dutton, 1967.

De Quincey's Writings   David Masson, ed. *The Collected Writings of Thomas De Quincey.* 14 vols. London: Black, 1896–1897.

DNB   *Dictionary of National Biography.*

Fate of the Fenwicks, The   A. F. Wedd, ed. *The Fate of the Fenwicks: Letters to Mary Hays (1798–1828).* London: Methuen, 1927.

Fitzgerald   Percy Fitzgerald, ed. *The Life, Letters and Writings of Charles Lamb.* 6 vols. London: Moxon, 1876.

Friend, The, ed. Barbara Rooke   Barbara E. Rooke, ed. *The Friend, I* [and *II*], in *The Collected Works of Samuel Taylor Coleridge,* ed. Kathleen Coburn and Bart Winer. Vol. IV, Parts 1 and 2. London: Routledge & Kegan Paul; Princeton: Princeton University Press, 1969.

Godwin   C. Kegan Paul. *William Godwin: His Friends and Contemporaries.* 2 vols. London: King, 1876.

Harper   Henry H. Harper [and Richard Garnett], eds. *The Letters of Charles Lamb: In Which Many Mutilated Words and Passages Have Been Restored to Their Original Form; with Letters Never before Published and Facsimiles of Original MS Letters and Poems.* 5 vols. Boston: Bibliophile Society, 1905.

Hartley Coleridge   Earl Leslie Griggs. *Hartley Coleridge: His Life and Work.* London: University of London Press, 1929.

Haydon's Diary   Willard Bissell Pope, ed. *The Diary of Benjamin Robert Haydon.* 5 vols. Cambridge, Mass.: Harvard University Press, 1960–1963.

Hazlitt   W[illiam] Carew Hazlitt, ed. *Letters of Charles Lamb: With Some Account of the Writer, His Friends and Correspondents, and Explanatory Notes. By the Late Thomas Noon Talfourd, D.C.L., One of His Executors. An Entirely New Edition, Carefully Revised and Greatly Enlarged.* 2 vols. London: Bell, 1886.

Hazlitt   Herschel Baker. *William Hazlitt.* Cambridge, Mass.: Harvard University Press, 1962.

Hazlitt's Works   P. P. Howe, ed. *The Complete Works of William Hazlitt. After the Edition of A. R. Waller and Arnold Glover.* 21 vols. London and Toronto: Dent, 1930–1934.

H. C. R. on Books and Writers   Edith J. Morley, ed. *Henry Crabb Robinson on Books and Their Writers.* 3 vols. London: Dent, 1938.

H. C. R.'s Correspondence with the Wordsworth Circle   Edith J. Morley, ed. *The Correspondence of Henry Crabb Robinson with the Wordsworth Circle (1808–1866), the Greater Part Now for the First Time Printed from the Originals in Dr. Williams's Library, London. Chronologically Arranged and Edited with Introduction, Notes and Index.* 2 vols. Oxford: Clarendon Press, 1927.

H. C. R.'s Diary   Thomas Sadler, ed. *Diary, Reminiscences, and Correspondence of Henry Crabb Robinson, Barrister-at-Law, F.S.A.* 2 vols. Boston: Fields, Osgood, 1870.

Holcroft   Elbridge Colby, ed. *The Life of Thomas Holcroft: Written by Himself, Continued to the Time of His Death from His Diary*

Notes & Other Papers by William Hazlitt, and Now Newly Edited with Introduction and Notes. 2 vols. London: Constable, 1925.

House of Letters, A   Ernest Betham, ed. *A House of Letters: Being Excerpts from the Correspondence of Miss Charlotte Jerningham (the Honble. Lady Bedingfeld), Lady Jerningham, Coleridge, Lamb, Southey, Bernard and Lucy Barton, and Others, with [Mary] Matilda Betham; and from Diaries and Various Sources; and a Chapter upon Landor's Quarrel with Charles Betham at Llanthony. Also Notes of Some Phases in the Evolution of an English Family.* New ed. London: Jarrolds [1905].

Hunt's Autobiography   Roger Ingpen, ed. *The Autobiography of Leigh Hunt: With Reminiscences of Friends and Contemporaries, and with Thornton Hunt's Introduction and Postscript.* 2 vols. New York: Dutton, 1903.

Hunt's "Reflector"   Kenneth E. Kendall. *Leigh Hunt's "Reflector."* The Hague and Paris: Mouton, 1971.

Lamb and Hazlitt   William Carew Hazlitt, ed. *Lamb and Hazlitt: Further Letters and Records Hitherto Unpublished.* New York: Dodd, Mead, 1899.

Lamb and His Hertfordshire   Reginald L. Hine. *Charles Lamb and His Hertfordshire.* London: Dent, 1949.

Lamb and the Lloyds   E. V. Lucas, ed. *Charles Lamb and the Lloyds.* London: Smith, Elder, 1898.

Lambs, The   William Carew Hazlitt. *The Lambs: Their Lives, Their Friends, and Their Correspondence. New Particulars and New Material.* London: Mathews; New York: Scribner's, 1897.

Life of Lamb, The   E. V. Lucas. *The Life of Charles Lamb.* 2 vols. London: Methuen, 1905.

Lloyd-Manning Letters   Frederick L. Beaty, ed. *The Lloyd-Manning Letters.* Bloomington: Indiana University Press, 1957.

Lucas (1905)   E. V. Lucas, ed. *The Works of Charles and Mary Lamb.* 7 vols. New York: Putnam's; London: Methuen, 1903–1905.

Lucas (1912)   E. V. Lucas, ed. *The Letters of Charles and Mary Lamb, 1796–1820* [and *1821–1842*]. Vols. V–VI of *The Works of Charles and Mary Lamb.* 6 vols. London: Methuen, 1912.

Lucas (1935)   E. V. Lucas, ed. *The Letters of Charles Lamb: To Which Are Added Those of His Sister, Mary Lamb.* 3 vols. London: Dent and Methuen (copublishers), 1935.

Macdonald   William Macdonald, ed. *Letters of Charles Lamb,* Vols. I–II. Vols. XI–XII of *The Works of Charles Lamb.* Large-paper Edition. 12 vols. London: Dent; New York: Dutton, 1903.

M. A. L.   Mary Anne Lamb.

Manning-Lamb Letters   G. A. Anderson [and P. P. Howe], eds. *The Letters of Thomas Manning to Charles Lamb*. London: Secker, 1925.

Mary Shelley's Letters   Frederick L. Jones, ed. *The Letters of Mary W. Shelley*. 2 vols. Norman: University of Oklahoma Press, 1944.

New Southey Letters   Kenneth Curry, ed. *New Letters of Robert Southey*. 2 vols. New York and London: Columbia University Press, 1965.

Purnell   Thomas Purnell, ed. *The Complete Correspondence and Works of Charles Lamb*. 4 vols. London: Moxon, 1870.

Sala   George Augustus Sala, ed. *The Complete Correspondence and Works of Charles Lamb*. London: Moxon, 1868.

Sara Hutchinson's Letters   Kathleen Coburn, ed. *The Letters of Sara Hutchinson from 1800 to 1835*. Toronto: University of Toronto Press, 1954.

Shelley and His Circle   Kenneth Neill Cameron and Donald H. Reiman, eds. *Shelley and His Circle: 1773–1822*. 6 vols. Cambridge, Mass.: Harvard University Press, 1961–1973.

Six Life Studies of Famous Women   M. Betham-Edwards. *Six Life Studies of Famous Women*. London: Griffith and Farran; New York: Dutton, 1880.

Southey's Correspondence   Charles Cuthbert Southey, ed. *The Life and Correspondence of Robert Southey*. 6 vols. 1849–1850. Rpt. St. Clair Shores, Mich.: Scholarly Press [1968].

Talfourd (1837)   Thomas Noon Talfourd, ed. *The Letters of Charles Lamb, with a Sketch of His Life*. 2 vols. London: Moxon, 1837.

Talfourd (1848)   Thomas Noon Talfourd, ed. *Final Memorials of Charles Lamb; Consisting Chiefly of His Letters Not before Published, with Sketches of Some of His Companions*. 2 vols. London: Moxon, 1848.

TLS   *Times Literary Supplement* (London).

Wordsworths' Letters   Ernest de Selincourt, ed. *The Letters of William and Dorothy Wordsworth*. 6 vols. Oxford: Clarendon Press, 1935–1939. 2d ed.: Vol. I, rev. Chester L. Shaver (1967); Vol. II, rev. Mary Moorman (1969); Vol. III, rev. Mary Moorman and Alan G. Hill (1970).

Wordsworth's Poetical Works (1940–1949)   E[rnest] de Selincourt and Helen Darbishire, eds. *The Poetical Works of William Wordsworth*. 5 vols. Oxford: Clarendon Press, 1940–1949.

Wordsworth's Prose Works   Alexander B. Grosart, ed. *The Prose Works of William Wordsworth. For the First Time Collected, with Additions from Unpublished Manuscripts. Edited, with Preface, Notes and Illustrations.* 3 vols. London: Moxon, 1876.

Works   E. V. Lucas, ed. *The Works of Charles and Mary Lamb.* 7 vols. New York: Putnam's; London: Methuen, 1903–1905.

Works (1818)   *The Works of Charles Lamb.* 2 vols. London: Ollier, 1818.

The act, scene, and line numbers locating the passages from Shakespeare correspond to those in *The Riverside Shakespeare,* ed. G. Blakemore Evans *et al.* (Boston: Houghton Mifflin, 1974).

LIST OF LETTERS

PART VII

Letters 232–276
34 Southampton Buildings, Chancery Lane, Holborn
and 4 Inner Temple Lane, Inner Temple
March 29, 1809 — Spring 1814?

232.   *Charles Lamb to Thomas Manning*

[Wednesday,] 28 [29] Mar 1809

Dear Manning,

I sent you a long letter[1] by the ships which sailed the beginning of last month, accompanied with books &c. I do not know whether you will receive that or this first. Since I wrote, Holcroft is dead. He died on Thursday last, and is not yet buried. He has been opened by Carlisle, and his heart was found completely ossified. He has had a long and severe illness. He seemed very willing to live, and to the last acted upon his favorite principle of the power of the will to overcome disease. I believe his strong faith in that power kept him alive long after another person would have given up. The physicians all concurred in positively saying he would not live a week, many weeks before he died. The family are as well as could be expected. I told you something about Mrs. Holcroft's plans. Since his death there has been a meeting of his friends, and a subscription has been mentioned. I have no doubt that she will be set agoing, and that she will be fully competent to the scheme which she proposes. Fanny[2] bears it much better than I could have supposed.

So there is one of your friends whom you will never see again. Perhaps the next fleet may bring you a Letter from Martin Burney, to say that he writes by desire of Miss Lamb who is not well enough to write herself, to inform you that her brother died on Thursday last 14 June &c.— But I hope *not*. I should be sorry to give occasion to open a correspondence between Martin and you. This letter must be short, for I have driven it off to the very moment of doing up the packets, and besides, that which I refer to above, is a very long one, and if you have received my books, you will have enough to do to read them. While I think on it, let me tell you, we are moved. Do'nt come any more to Mitre Court Buildings. We are at 34 Southamptn. Buildgs. Chancy. Lane, and shall be here till about the end of May, then we re-move to No 2[3] Inner Temple Lane, where I mean to live and die; for I have such horror of moving, that I would not take a

benefice from the King, if I was not indulged with non residence.
What a dislocation of comfort is comprized in that word **moving!**—
Such a heap of little nasty things, after you think all is got into the
cart, old drudging boxes, worn out brushes, gallipots, vials, things that
it is impossible the most necessitous person can ever want, but which
the Women, who preside on these occasions, will not leave behind if
it was to save your soul, they'd keep the cart ten minutes to stow in
dirty pipes and broken matches, to shew their economy. Then you can
find nothing you want for many days after you get into your new
lodgings. You must comb your hair with your fingers, wash your
hands without soap, go about in dirty gaiters, was I Diogenes[4] I would
not move out of a kilderkin into a hogshead though the first had had
nothing but small beer in it, and the second reeked Claret. Our
place of final destination, I dont mean the grave, but No 2 Inner
Temple Lane, looks out upon a gloomy churchyard like Court, call'd
Hare Court, with three trees and a Pump in it. Do you know it? I
was born near it, and used to drink at that Pump when I was a
Rechabite of six years old.

If you see newspapers you will read about Mrs. **Clarke.**[5] The
sensation in London about this nonsensical business is marvellous.
I remember nothing in my life like it. Thousands of ballads, caricatures, lives of Mrs. Clarke, in every blind alley. Yet in the midst of this
stir a sublime abstracted Dancing Master who attends a family we
know in Kensington, being asked a question about the progress of the
examinations in the house, **enquired** who Mrs. Clarke was? he had
heard nothing of it. He had evaded this omnipresence by utter in-
significancy. The Duke should make that man his confidential valet. I
proposed locking him up, barring him the use of his fiddle and red
pumps, until he had minutely perused and committed to memory the
whole body of the examinations which employ'd the House of Commons a fortnight—to teach him to be more attentive to what concerns
the Public.

I think I told you of Godwin's little book,[6] and of Coleridge's
Prospectus, in my last; if I did not, remind me of it, and I will send
you them or an account of them next fleet. I have no conveniency of
doing it by this. **Mrs. ——** grows every day in disfavour with God and
Man. I will be buried with this inscription over me, Here lies C L the
Woman Hater: I mean, that hated **one woman.** For the rest, God

bless them, and when he makes any more, make 'em prettier. How do you like the Mandarinesses? are you on some little footing with any of them? This is Wednesday. On Wednesdays is my Levee. The Captain, Martin, Phillips (not the Sheriff) Rickman,[7] & some more are constant attendants, besides stray visitors: we play at whist, eat cold meat and hot potatoes, and any Gentleman that chuses **smokes—**. Why do *you never* drop in? You'll come some day, w'ont you?

C Lamb &c.

MS: Henry E. Huntington Library; by permission of The Huntington Library, San Marino, Calif. Pub.: Talfourd (1837), I, 309–312; Sala, I, 403–405; Purnell, I, 403–405; Fitzgerald, II, 236–238; Hazlitt, I, 395–398; Ainger (1888), I, 249–251; Ainger (1900), II, 166–169; Macdonald, I, 311–313; Ainger (1904), I, 302–304; Harper, III, 278–283; Lucas (1905), VI, 395–397, and VII, 971; Lucas (1912), V, 416–418; Lucas (1935), II, 68–70. Address: T. Manning Esqr./ Canton. Lamb gives the day on which he is writing near the end of the letter.

1. Unrecovered. In his letter to Lamb of March 1, 1809 (*Manning-Lamb Letters*, p. 111), Manning remarked that the last letter he had from Lamb is that dated February 26, 1808 (in my Vol. II, Letter 222). The dramatist Thomas Holcroft, of whom Lamb writes below, had died in his residence, in Clipstone Street, Marylebone, on Thursday, March 23, 1809, and was buried in the larger parish cemetery in Paddington Street, Marylebone, on April 1. The physicians who performed the autopsy and wrote the "*Statement of the Anatomical Inspection . . . ,*" published in *Holcroft*, II, 312–313, were Anthony Carlisle (see my Vol. I, Introduction, p. xxxi) and Alexander Peter Buchan (1764–1824). Holcroft and Godwin, who had been estranged since their misunderstanding over the failure of Godwin's "Faulkener, a Tragedy in Prose" (discussed in Vol. II, Letter 216, note 4), were reconciled on the Sunday and Monday before Holcroft died. It was probably Godwin, moved as he was by his reconciliation with Holcroft and by Holcroft's death, who was primarily responsible for obtaining a subscription of one thousand pounds for Mrs. Louisa Holcroft (identified in Vol. II, Letter 133, note 7) and a commission for Hazlitt to prepare some of the letters and the (uncompleted) memoirs of Holcroft for publication. Hazlitt completed his work in January 1810. But objections of Godwin, George Leman Tuthill (see Vol. II, Letter 208, note 1), and another member of the Godwin-Holcroft circle— the inventor and scientific writer William Nicholson (1753–1815)—to Hazlitt's verbatim inclusion of Holcroft's diary delayed until 1816 the appearance of *Memoirs of the Late Thomas Holcroft, Written by Himself, and Continued to the Time of His Death, from His Diary, Notes, and Other Papers*. More on the matter is given in *Hazlitt*, pp. 177–181.

2. Fanny Holcroft. See Vol. II, Letter 133, note 7.

3. Properly Number 4. What follows becomes a familiar complaint of Lamb, one he made not only in other letters (see, for example, Letter 236, at the reference to note 3, and Letter 244, last paragraph) but also, in 1821, in "New Year's Eve" (*Works*, II, 29): "I am content to stand still at the age to which I am arrived; I, and my friends: to be no younger, no richer, no handsomer. I do not want to be weaned by age; or drop, like mellow fruit, as they say, into the grave.—Any alteration, on this earth of mine, in diet or in lodging, puzzles and discomposes me. My household-gods plant a terrible fixed foot, and are not rooted up without blood."

4. The Greek Cynic philosopher Diogenes (412? B.C.–323 B.C.), who once lived

in a tub to toughen himself to the changes in the weather. "Rechabite," as Lamb uses the term near the end of his paragraph, denotes an abstainer from intoxicating liquors.

5. Mary Anne Clarke (1776–1852), born Thompson. She was married to the stonemason Clarke in 1794, left him when he went bankrupt, became an actress, and became in 1803 the mistress of Frederick Augustus, Duke of York and Albany (1763–1827), the second son of George III. Her acceptance of bribes from various military, civil, and clerical promotion seekers in return for her attempts to influence the duke in their behalf had just been exposed in Parliament. She was examined by the House of Commons and tried for libel in 1809, was imprisoned on that charge in 1813, and in about 1816 moved to Paris with cash and a pension from the duke as her price for not publishing his letters to her. He was removed as commander-in-chief of the army, a post he had held since 1798, but was reinstated in it in 1811. Neither the dancing master, mentioned below, nor the Kensington family he attended has been identified.

6. Probably *An Essay on Sepulchres.* (See Vol. II, Letter 228, note 2.) But there also appeared in 1809 Godwin's *The History of Rome* and "A New Guide to the English Tongue," both under the pseudonym Edward Baldwin, Esq. Godwin's *Lives of Edward and John Philips, Nephews and Pupils of Milton* may have appeared in 1809. (See Letter 296, note 10.) "A New Guide to the English Tongue" was issued first in the Godwins' Juvenile Library publication of the second edition of *Mylius's School Dictionary of the English Language. . . . To Which Is Prefixed, A New Guide to the English Tongue* (1st ed., September 1809; 2d ed., November 1809) and issued next in the Godwins' Juvenile Library publication of Hazlitt's *A New and Improved Grammar of the English Tongue. . . . To Which Is Added, A New Guide to the English Tongue, in a Letter to Mr. W. F. Mylius, Author of the School Dictionary* (published November 1809; dated 1810). (See Letter 245, note 10.) William Frederick Mylius (1776–1863) was the principal, perhaps the founder, of a Catholic academy for boys that operated in Red Lion Square, High Holborn, from 1801 to 1812; as Bornhem House Academy, Carshalton, Surrey, from 1812 to 1829; and as The Manor House Collegiate School, in Cheyne Walk, Chelsea, from 1829 to 1853. Then the institution was closed. Besides the second edition of *Mylius's School Dictionary,* Mylius was the author and the Godwins were the publishers of *Mylius's Junior Class-book* (1809), which contains portions of the Lambs' *Tales from Shakespear* and of Lamb's *The Adventures of Ulysses;* and *Mylius's Poetical Class-book* (1809) and *The First Book of Poetry* (issued November 1810; dated, according to the British Museum and Library of Congress catalogues, 1811), in both of which are poems from the Lambs' *Poetry for Children.* (See Letter 236, note 4.) Mylius was also the author of *An Abridged History of England, Designed Principally for the Use of Catholic Seminaries* (1817). (For further information about him—about his family and particularly about those of his works that hold selections from the Lambs' works—see Cyril C. Hussey's "Fresh Light on the Poems of Mary Lamb," which is published as a supplement to the *CLSB* of January 1972; see also the observations of Annette Park in the *CLSB* of the same date and the letters from Bertram R. Davis and Cyril C. Hussey in the *CLSB* of April 1972.) For information about Coleridge's Prospectus for *The Friend,* the prospectus Lamb mentions following, see my Vol. II, Letter 228, note 4. Below, the locution with the dash is a reference to Mrs. Godwin.

7. Mentioned in addition to Martin Burney and John Rickman are Martin's father, James; and Edward Phillips, not the author and publisher Sir Richard Phillips. (See Vol. II, Letter 198, note 1; and Vol. I, Letter 29, note 2.) Sir Richard had been elected sheriff of London in 1807 and knighted in 1808.

233.   *Mary Anne Lamb and C. L. to Louisa Martin, with two*
       postscripts from M. A. L.
                                   [Wednesday,] March 28 [29, 1809]
Dear Louisa,

I promised never to let a letter of yours remain unanswered one
week, if I have exceeded the time a few days you will not be surprized
when I tell you we have been removing from our dear old dirty
chambers into lodgings, which has been great labour, and pain, and
grief to me. I had persuaded myself that I should be glad to quit
them but when the time came you cannot imagine what I felt when
they were clean swept out and I was about to lock the door & leave
them.

We are in Hazlitts old lodgings,[1] and I believe must remain here at
least two months before our new Chambers are ready for us.

Charles is now sitting by me writing to Manning, if you have any
message to send to him now is your time to speak.

Poor Holcroft died last thursday. Mrs Reynolds is very ill. I am
almost afraid she will never recover, her complaint seems to have fallen
upon her lungs. Hazlitt has been in town, and is just gone back again.
His child is expected to die.[2]

We were pleased to see by your specimen of law-hand, that you
have not quite forgotten old times, but we met with an instance
yesterday of a still longer memory than yours. A Mr Lloyd who we
have not seen since we lived at Islington dined with us; we had boiled
pork and he waited some time with the meat on his plate till Emily
brought up the mustard, and he confessed afterwards that he could
not eat his dinner because the mustard was in a different mustard pot
to what he had been used to see at Islington.

Poor Nurse, about a week before we left the Temple, fell down &
hurt her hip. She is now in the Westminster Infirmary, and is not expected ever to be able to walk again.[3] I think I have nothing but
dismal news to send you.

We left the carpet, the beautiful carpet Sarah and you so much admired, and which I hear you make frequent enquiries after in your
letters to Hannah, we left it behind us with the deepest regret.

We have bought some very fine chairs & window curtains and we intend almost to ruin ourselves, in various other articles of expensive furniture—. And we have hired a maid[4] too, you will find strange alterations at your next hollidays.

This is wednesday which I am very glad of for it will make the place seem more like a home to me, at present I feel quite unsettled and un-homed.

Mary[5] is suddenly snatch'd away (not by Death) and has left her letter open, which I am tempted to fill up. Some odd things have occurred since you went away. Dawe the Painter has painted a Picture of the Princess Charlotte of Wales, which pleased the King so much, that he knighted him. He is now Sir George Dawe. Mary told you about Nurse. I was wishing her to die, and how lucky things fall out! J. Hazlitt's child died of swallowing a bag of white paint, which the poor little innocent thing mistook for sugar candy. It told its mother just two hours before it died, that it did not like soft sugarcandy, and so it came out, which was not before suspected. When it was opened several other things were found in it, particularly a small hearth brush, two golden pippins, and a letter which I had written to Hazlitt from Bath. The letter had nothing remarkable in it. Martin Burney has displeased his family by marrying. You know the person, Miss Winter that used to come for work to our house. It [w]as there they contrived to meet. We suspected nothing. My brother John said in a public coffee house the other day, that his brother [Cha]rles (meaning me) had the best heart of anybody he knew. An eminent Merchant in consequence took it up very warmly, and promised his interest at the next election of Governors for Bartholomew Hospital, to make me a Governor. Those institutions require humane people to have the superintendance of them. Why dont you *mind* your spelling better? in your last letter you spelt finish, **finnish**, with two n's. When you a'nt quite sure of a word, write it at full length on three sorts of paper, or as many as you think it may be spelt ways, then throw them up the chimney, the smoke will carry them up, and watch on the outside till they come down, and that that's most smoked is the right way of spelling it. They always do so in Wales. But their chimneys are lower. Your sister Hannah spoke 34750 words in twenty or one & twenty minutes last Saturday. There was a man with me who took them down; an amazing instance of the rapidity and volubility of some people's way of speaking.

Let[6] us hear from you soon. Farewell

I am yours affectionately

M Lamb

He has only left room for me to say I hope it is true that you do not show your friends nonsensical letters to your Governess.

I have not seen your mother since the moving day, nor Hannah for several weeks. Sarah seems to succeed admirably.

MS: Huntington Library. Pub.: Lucas (1912), V, viii; Lucas (1935), II, 65–68. Address: Miss L. Martin/Mrs. Howell's School, Watford,/Herts. Postmark: March 29, 1809. Louisa Martin is identified in my Vol. II, Letter 185, note 2. Mary Lamb begins this letter.

1. Those formerly of William Hazlitt. (See Vol. II, Letter 231, note 3.) Referred to in the second paragraph below is Mrs. Elizabeth Reynolds. See Vol. I, Introduction, pp. xxviii–xxix.

2. The William Hazlitts' first child, William, had been born on January 15 and would die on July 5, 1809. The Lloyd referred to in the next paragraph is Robert. (See Vol. II, Letter 231.) Emily may have been a Buffam. It seems to have been from a Mrs. Buffam, whose name is associated with Hazlitt's in Letter 245, near the reference to note 13, that the Lambs, and Hazlitt before them, rented the rooms in Southampton Buildings. (Mrs. Buffam is identified in Purnell, I, 410, as the "landlady at No. 9, Southampton Buildings." It is indicated in Fitzgerald, II, 243, note, that the identification was first made by William Carew Hazlitt.) The Misses Buffam became the Lambs' landladies when the Lambs returned to 34 Southampton Buildings in 1830.

3. It is recorded in Lucas (1935), II, 87, that the minutes of Westminster Hospital for October 11, 1809, show that Mary Grant, aged sixty-nine, was then admitted as a patient to its establishment for incurables. (See my Vol. II, Letter 165, note 7.) Sarah and Hannah, named in the next paragraph, are Louisa Martin's sisters. See Vol. II, Letter 185, note 2.

4. Probably the Jane mentioned in Letter 235, at the reference to note 1, and Letter 243, in the paragraph below the reference to note 5.

5. This paragraph is from Lamb. All that he writes is nonsense except the one fact that George Dawe did paint, apparently at about this time, a portrait of Princess Charlotte Augusta. (See Letter 321, near the reference to note 3.) The National Portrait Gallery, London, purchased it in 1858, and it is reproduced in *The National Portrait Gallery,* ed. Lionel Cust (London and New York: Cassell, 1902–1904), II, 118, Plate 51.

6. From Mary. Louisa Martin's governess, whom Mary mentions in her first postscript, has not been identified. Mary may mean Mrs. Howell, named in the address of this letter as the mistress of the school Louisa is attending.

234.   *C. L. to Henry Crabb Robinson*

[May 1809]

Dear Sir,

Would you be so kind as when you go to the Times office to see about an Advertisemt. which My Landlady's Daughter left for insertion about ten days since & has not appeared, for a Governesses Place? The references are to Thorpe & Graves[1] 18 Lower Holborn & to M B 115 Oxford St.— Though not anxious about attitudes, she pines for a situation. I got home tolerably well, as I hear, the other evening. It may be a warning to any one in future to ask me to a dinner party. I always disgrace myself. I floated up stairs on the Coachman's back, like **Ariel**; "On a bat's back I do fly, After Sunset merrily"— —[2]

In sobriety
I am yours truly
C Lamb

MS: Dr. Williams's Library, London. Pub.: Harper, III, 284; Lucas (1905), VI, 398; Lucas (1912), V, 419; Lucas (1935), II, 71. Address: H. Robinson Esqr/56 Hatton Garden. Date, by Robinson: May 1809.

1. Listed as Thorpe and Greaves, or Greaves and Thorpe, linen drapers, in the London directories for 1808–1810. *The Post-office Annual Directory* for 1810 gives Greaves's Christian name as Curtis. "M B" (below) has not been identified.

2. *The Tempest*, V, i, 91–92. Lamb will use the passage again, in a letter of probably 1830 (in my Vol. VI) to Dr. J. Vale Asbury of Enfield and, in part, in "Rejoicings upon the New Year's Coming of Age" (*Works*, II, 239).

235.   *M. A. L. to Sarah Stoddart Hazlitt, with a paragraph from Martin Charles Burney to M. A. L.*

Saturday [Friday, June 2, 1809]

⟨I am sorry I could not bring the Ticket sooner I left with Jane.⟩[1] You may write to Hazlitt that I will *certainly* go to Winterslough as my Father has agreed to give me £5 to bear my expences & has given leave that I may stop till that is spent leaving enough to defray my Carriage on the 14*th* July

So far Martin has written, but farther than that I can give you no intelligence for I do not yet know Phillips' intentions nor can I tell you the exact time when we can come. Nor can I positively say we shall come at all, for we have scruples of conscience about there being so many of us. Martin says if you can borrow a blanket or two he can sleep on the floor without either bed or matress which would save his expences at the Hut,[2] for if Phillips breakfasts there he must do so too which would swallow up all his money. And he and I have calculated that if he has no Inn-expences he may as well spare that money, to give you for a part of his roast beef. We can spare you also just five pounds. You are not to say this to Hazlitt lest his delicacy should be alarmed, but I tell you what Martin and I have planned that if you happen to be empty pursed at this time you may think it as well to make him up a bed in the best kitchen. I think it very probable that Phillips will come, and if you do not like such a croud of us, for they both talk of staying a whole month, tell me so and we will put off our visit till next summer.

The 14th of July is the day Martin has fixt for *coming.*

I should have written before if I could have got a positive answer from them.

Thank you very much for the good work you have done for me. Mrs Stoddart[3] also thanks you for the gloves. How often must I tell you never to do any needle work for any body but me.

Martin Burney has been very ill, and still is very weak & pale. Mrs Holcroft & all her children and all her scholars have had the measles. Your old friend Mrs Fenwick is in town.

We are going to see Mrs Martin and her daughter Mrs Fulton (Sarah Martin) and I expect to see there the future husband[4] of Louisa. It will be a charming evening doubtless.

I cannot write any more, for we have got a noble Life of Lord Nelson lent us for a short time by my poor relation the book binder and I want to read as much of it as I can.

Yours affectionately
M Lamb

on reading Martins note over again we guess the Captain means him to stay only a fortnight. it is most likely we shall come the beginning of July.

MS: Henry W. and Albert A. Berg Collection, The New York Public Library, Astor, Lenox and Tilden Foundations. Pub.: Lucas (1905), VI, 398–399; Lucas (1912), V, 419–420; Lucas (1935), II, 72–73. Address: Mrs Hazlitt/Winterslow/near Salisbury. Watermark: 1808. Postmark: June 2 [1809]. The letter is for the most part taken up with the Lambs' plans to spend July with the Hazlitts at Winterslow and either to take Martin Burney and Edward Phillips with them or to have Burney and Phillips join them there later. But because Mary fell ill on Monday, June 5, and had to be confined for approximately six weeks, the outing had to be postponed until October. The opening paragraph is Burney's.

1. See Letter 233, note 4.

2. The inn, called The Pheasant as well as The Hut, at Winterslow.

3. Isabella (the younger Mrs. John) Stoddart. (See Vol. I, Letter 3, note 28.) One of Mrs. Louisa Holcroft's scholars, mentioned in the next paragraph, was Barbara Betham. (See Letter 282, near the reference to and note 1, and Vol. II, Letter 222, note 13.) About Eliza (Mrs. John) Fenwick see Vol. II, Letter 108, note 1.

4. Unidentified. Louisa Martin, so far as is known, was never married. The biography of Nelson mentioned in the next paragraph is probably that by James Stanier Clarke (1765?–1834) and John McArthur, or MacArthur (1755–1840)— *The Life of Admiral Lord Nelson, K.B., from His Lordship's Manuscripts* (1809)— which was the best and fullest account of Nelson then published. About the Lambs' relation Charles Lovekin the bookbinder see my Vol. II, Letter 215, note 2.

236. *C. L. to Samuel Taylor Coleridge*

[Wednesday, June 7, 1809]

Dear Coleridge,

I congratulate you on the appearance of the Friend.[1] Your first number promises well, and I have no doubt the succeeding numbers will fulfil the promise. I had a kind Letter from you some time since which I have left unanswered. I am also obliged to you I believe for a Review in the Annual, am I not?— The monthly Review sneers at me and asks if Comus is not *good enough* for Mr Lamb—because I have said no good serious dramas have been written since the death of Chas. the First except Samson Agonistes. So because they do not know or wont remember that Comus was written long before, I am to be set down as an undervaluer of Milton.— O Coleridge, do kill those Reviews, or they will kill us, kill all we like. Be a Friend to all else, but their **Foe**.— I have been turned out of my Chambers in the Temple by a Landlord[2] who wanted them for himself, but I have got other at No. 4 Inner Temple Lane, far more commodious & roomy. I have two rooms on 3d. floor & five rooms above, with an inner staircase to myself, and all new painted &c. and all for £30 a Year. I came into them on Saturday week, and on Monday following Mary was taken ill, with the fatigue of moving, and affected I believe by the novelty of the Home she could not sleep, and I am left alone with a Maid quite a stranger to me, & she has a month or two's sad distraction to go through. What sad large pieces it cuts out of life, out of her life who

XIII. Inner Temple Lane, Inner Temple, in 1855, showing Number 1, where Samuel Johnson lived from 1760 to 1765. From a watercolor by J. Findlay (fl. in London 1825–1857). Courtesy of The British Museum, London.

XIV. Hare Court, Inner Temple, in 1857. From a woodcut. Courtesy of The British Museum, London.

is getting rather old and we may not have many years to live together.
I am weaker & bear it worse than I ever did. But I hope we shall be
comfortable by & bye. The rooms are delicious and the best look backwards into Hare Court where there is a Pump always going. Just now
it is dry. Hare Court Trees come in at the window, [so] that it's like
living in a Garden. I try to persuade myself it is much pleasanter than
Mitre Court—but alas! the Household Gods are slow to come in a new
Mansion, They are in their infancy to me, I do not feel them yet—no
hearth has blazed to them yet—. How I hate and dread **New Places!**.[3]

I was very glad to see Wordsworth's Book advertised, I am to have
it tomorrow lent me, and if W. dont send me an Order for one upon
Longman, I will buy it. It is greatly extolled & liked by all who have
seen it. Let me hear from some of you, for I am desolate.— I shall
have to send you in a week or two two volumes of Juvenile Poetry[4]
done by Mary & me within the last six months, and That Tale in
Prose which Wordsworth so much liked which was published at
Xmas with nine others by us—& has reached a **Second Edition.**
There's for you!— We have almost worked ourselves out of Child's
Work—& I dont know what to do. Sometimes I think of a drama, but
I have no head for play-making, I can do the Dialogue & thats all—.
I am quite aground for a Plan, and I must do something for money.
Not that I have immediate wants, but I have prospective ones. O
money money how blindly thou hast been worshipped, & how stupidly
abused! Thou art health, & liberty, and strength and he that has thee
may rattle his pockets at the Devil. Nevertheless do not understand by
this that I have not quite enough for my occasions for a year or two
to come.— While I think on it, Coleridge, I fetch'd away my books
which you had at the Courier Office & found all but a 3d Vol. of The
Old Plays,[5] containing The White Devil, Green's Tu Quoque, Honest
Whore—perhaps the most valuable volume of them all; *that* I could
not find. Pray, if you can remember what you did with it, or where
you took it out with you a walking perhaps, send me word, for to use
the old Plea, it **spoils** a Set. I found 2 other volumes (you had three)
the Arcadia, & **Daniel** enriched with MSS notes, I wish every book I
have were so noted. They have thoroughly converted me to relish
Daniel, or to say I relish him, for after all I believe I did relish him.
You well call him sober-minded. Your Notes are excellent. Perhaps
you've forgot them.—[6] I have read a Review in the Quarterly by

Southey on the Missionaries, which is most masterly. I only grudge its being there. It is quite beautiful. Do remember my Dodsley, and pray do write or let some of you write. Clarkson tells me you are in a smoky house. Have you cured it? It is hard to cure anything of **smoking**—

Our little poems are but humble, but they have no name, You must read them remembring they were task-work, & perhaps you will admire the number of subjects, all of children, pick'd out by an old Bachelor & an old Maid. Many Parents would not have found so many.— Have you read Cælebs?[7] which has reach'd 8 Editions in so many weeks, yet literally it is one of the very poorest sort of common novels with the drawback of dull religion in it. Had the Religion been high & flavor'd, it would have been something. I borrow'd this **Cælebs** in search of a Wife of a very careful neat Lady, & return'd it with this staff written in the beginning

> If ever I marry a Wife
> I'll marry a Landlord's Daughter,
> For then I may sit in the Bar,
> And drink cold Brandy & Water!—

I dont expect you can find time from your Friend to write to me much but write something. For there has been a long silence. You know Holcroft is dead.— Godwin is well. He has written a very pretty, absurd, book about Sepulchres. He was affronted because I told him it was better than **Harvey,** but not so good as Sir **T. Browne.**—[8] This Letter is all about Books. But my head akes and I hardly know what I write. But I could not let the Friend pass without a congratulatory Epistle. I wont criticise till it comes to a Volume.— Tell me how I shall send my packet to you? by what conveyance? by Longman, Short-man, or how?— — Give my kindest remembrances to the Wordsworths—. Tell him he must give me a Book. My kind love to Mrs. W. & to Dorothy seperately & conjointly. I wish you could all come & see me in my new rooms.— God bless you all

C L

MS: Huntington Library. Pub.: Talfourd (1848), I, 170–175; Sala, I, 149–153; Purnell, I, 149–153; Fitzgerald, II, 3–7; Hazlitt, I, 399–402; Ainger (1888), I, 251–254; Ainger (1900), II, 169–174; Macdonald, I, 313–316; Ainger (1904),

I, 304–307; Harper, I, facsimile, and III, 284–289; Lucas (1905), VI, 400–402; Lucas (1912), V, 421–423; Lucas (1935), II, 73–76. Address: Mr Coleridge/ Grasmere/near Kendal/Westmorland. Postmark: June 7, 1809.

1. *The Friend; a Literary, Moral, and Political Weekly Paper, Excluding Personal and Party Politics, and the Events of the Day,* whose first number is dated Thursday, June 1, 1809. The (unsigned) reviews referred to below, of Lamb's *Specimens of English Dramatic Poets, Who Lived about the Time of Shakspeare: With Notes,* are in the *Annual Review,* 7 (1808), 562–570, and in the *Monthly Review,* 58 (April 1809), 349–356. See my Vol. II, Letter 211, note 1.

2. Unidentified.

3. See Letter 232, note 3. Wordsworth's book, properly pamphlet, referred to near the beginning of the next paragraph, is *Concerning the Relations of Great Britain, Spain, and Portugal, to Each Other, and to the Common Enemy, at This Crisis; and Specifically as Affected by the Convention of Cintra: The Whole Brought to the Test of Those Principles, by Which Alone the Independence and Freedom of Nations Can Be Preserved or Recovered.* Daniel Stuart and Thomas De Quincey saw it through the press; Stuart advertised it in *The Courier* of May 27 and 29 and June 1, 1809; and the firm of Longman, Hurst, Rees, and Orme published it in June 1809. The pamphlet was first printed with the title *Concerning the Convention of Cintra, in Relation to the Principles by Which the Independence of Nations Must Be Preserved or Recovered,* but the present title was substituted for it before the work was issued. Two installments, with which Coleridge assisted, appear in *The Courier* of December 27, 1808, and January 13, 1809, under the title "Concerning the Convention of Cintra, in Reference to the Principles by Which the Independence and Freedom of Nations Must Be Preserved or Recovered." The convention, or treaty, of August 30, 1808, though negotiated in Cintra, Portugal, was signed in Lisbon. It stipulated that the French forces that the British had defeated and the French arms and artillery that the British had captured at Vimierio on August 21 were to be transported in British ships back to France and released to Napoleon in return for the evacuation of the French from Portugal. Portugal, clear of the French, could consequently be freely used by the British for future military operations. When the news of the substance of the treaty reached England, there arose a public outcry against the British generals who devised it, because of their leniency toward the French and their indifference to the Portuguese. Wordsworth and, of Wordsworth's friends, Southey especially, were among the most outraged.

4. *Poetry for Children, Entirely Original* (2 vols.; London: M. J. Godwin, 1809). It is stated in Lucas (1935), II, 76, that the tale referred to below as a favorite of Wordsworth, the tale from Lamb and Mary's *Mrs. Leicester's School: Or, the History of Several Young Ladies, Related by Themselves* (London: M. J. Godwin, 1809), was Lamb's "Arabella Hardy: The Sea Voyage" (*Works,* III, 331–335). The second edition of the book had just appeared. The first edition, though published (according to Lamb here) at Christmas 1808, is dated 1809.

5. Apparently the first edition of Robert Dodsley's *A Select Collection of Old Plays* (12 vols.; 1744): *The White Devil* (1612), by John Webster; *Green's Tu Quoque; or, the City Gallant. A Comedy* (1614), by Jo. Cooke (fl. 1614); and *The Honest Whore. A Comedy* (1604) and *The Second Part of the Honest Whore* (1630), both by Thomas Dekker (ca. 1570–1632), are in separate volumes in the second (1780) edition of Dodsley's collection. The first and second editions of that work were the only ones available when Lamb compiled *Specimens of English Dramatic Poets,* in which he included extracts from the four plays mentioned. For those extracts see *Works,* IV, 181–193, 47, and 54–56.

6. "Reader," Elia implores in "The Two Races of Men" (*Works,* II, 26–27), "if haply thou art blessed with a moderate collection, be shy of showing it; or if

thy heart overfloweth to lend them, lend thy books; but let it be to such a one as S. T. C.—he will return them (generally anticipating the time appointed) with usury; enriched with annotations, tripling their value. I have had experience. Many are these precious MSS. of his—(in *matter* oftentimes, and almost in *quantity* not unfrequently, vying with the originals)—in no very clerkly hand— legible in my Daniel. . . . I counsel thee, shut not thy heart, nor thy library, against S. T. C." Lamb's copy of Sir Philip Sidney's *Arcadia* is not known. Lamb's copy of Samuel Daniel's *Poetical Works* (2 vols.; London, 1718) is in the Harvard College Library. Written on the flyleaves of the second volume are two letters from Coleridge to Lamb dated February 9, 1808, in the second of which Coleridge calls Daniel "Gravely sober in all ordinary affairs, & not easily excited by any" (*Coleridge's Letters*, III, 55). There are annotations by Lamb in both volumes, and by Coleridge in the second volume. Some of Lamb's and all of Coleridge's are published in Cecil C. Seronsy's "Coleridge Marginalia in Lamb's Copy of Daniel's *Poetical Works*," *Harvard Library Bulletin*, 7 (Winter 1953), 105–112. (A good discussion of Coleridge marginalia in Lamb's books generally is George Whalley's "Lend Your Books to Such a One," in the *CLSB* of April/July 1975, pp. 55–60.) Southey's review, referred to next, of *Periodical Accounts Relative to the Baptist Missionary Society* (6 vols.; 1800–1817), is in the *Quarterly Review*, 1 (February 1809), 193–226. Concerning Lamb's grudging "its being there" (below) see Letter 287, source note. The Clarkson mentioned near the end of Lamb's para- graph is Thomas. The house mentioned there is Allan Bank, about whose smoke and soot Dorothy Wordsworth had complained to Catherine Clarkson, Thomas' wife, in a letter of December 8, 1808. (See *Wordsworths' Letters*, II, 281–282.) Coleridge had departed from Allan Bank on February 27, 1809, chiefly for Penrith to look after the printing of *The Friend* (see Letter 241, source note) and for Keswick. He arrived back at Allan Bank on June 14.

7. *Cœlebs in Search of a Wife*, by the religious writer Hannah More (1745– 1833). The novel was published and reached twelve editions in 1809. The lady, mentioned below, whose copy of the book Lamb had borrowed has not been identified, and her copy has not been recovered. Lamb's "staff," or "stave," is not in *Works*.

8. Godwin's *An Essay on Sepulchres* is better, that is, than "Meditations among the Tombs," the first part of *Meditations and Contemplations* (1746–1747), by the devotional writer James Hervey (1714–1758), but not so good as Sir Thomas Browne's *Hydriotaphia, or Urn-burial* (1658).

237. C. L. to Charles Lloyd, the elder

Temple

13 June, 09

Dear Sir,—

I received with great pleasure the mark of your remembrance which you were pleased to send me, the Translation from Homer.[1] You desire my opinion of it. I think it is plainer and more to the pur- pose than Pope's, though it may want some of his Splendour and some of his Sound. Yet I do not remember in any part of his translation a series of more manly versification than the conference of Priam with

Hermes in your translation (Lines 499 to 530),[2] or than that part of the reply of Achilles to Priam, beginning with the fable of the Two Urns (in page 24); or than the Story of Niobe which follows a little after. I do not retain enough of my Greek (to my shame I say it) to venture at an opinion of the correctness of your version. What I seem to miss, and what certainly everybody misses in Pope, is a certain savage-like plainness of speaking in Achilles—a sort of indelicacy—the heroes in Homer are not half civilised, they utter all the cruel, all the selfish, all the *mean thoughts* even of their nature, which it is the fashion of our great men to keep in. I cannot, in lack of Greek, point to any one place—but I remember the general feature as I read him at school. But your principles and turn of mind would, I have no doubt, lead you to *civilize* his phrases, and sometimes to *half christen* them.

I have marked a few verbal slips, the doing of which cannot be called criticism, or it is as if a Reviewer being taken ill, his printer's Compositor or Reader were called to supply his place.

[. . .][3]

Lines 243, 244, 245 are the flattest lines in the whole:

But now *be open,* and *declare thy mind,*
For I *confess I feel myself inclined,*
Indeed impell'd by Jove's command to go,
And face the man the cause of all our woe—

is the cool language of a Man and his Wife upon ordinary occurrences over a peaceable fireside—not the waverings of a divinely-impelled, humanly-shrinking, Priam striving to bolster up his own half-doubting inspirations by infusing a courage which he does not feel into the aged partner of his throne, that she may give it back to him. I should not have exprest myself thus petulantly, if there were many more, or indeed any more such Lines in the Translation, but they stopt the current of my feeling in the place, and I hope you will pardon my expressions.

[. . .]

I don't know Homer's word,[4] not having my books about me, but surely in English, Priam would have said the *Slayer* of my *Son,* not call'd Achilles *murderer,* at such a time. That is rather too plain for the homely-speaking Homeric Heroes.

[. . .]

Tumulus[5] is too much like *making Homer talk Latin*. Tumulus is always spoken by an English mouth with a consciousness of *scientific attainment*. Priam and his People were no scholars—plain downright fighting men.

[. . .]

Minstrels,[6] I suspect to be a word bringing merely English or English ballad feelings to the Mind. It expresses the thing and something more, as to say Sarpedon was a Gentleman, or as somebody translated Paul's address, "Ye men of Athens," "Gentlemen of Athens."

[. . .]

I am sure I ought to make many apologies for the freedom I have taken, but it will at least convince you that I have read the Book—which I have twice, and the last time with more pleasure, because more at leisure. I wish you Joy of an Amusement which I somehow seem to have done with. Excepting some Things for Children, I have scarce chimed ten couplets in the last as many years. Be pleased to give my most kind remembrances to Mrs. Lloyd; and please to tell Robert that my Sister is getting well, and I hope will soon be able to take pleasure in his affectionate Epistle. My Love also to Charles, when you write.

I am, Sir, with the greatest [. . .][7]

Robert will have told you how pleased I was with your truly Horatian Epistle in the "Gent. Mag."

MS: unrecovered. Text: *Lamb and the Lloyds,* pp. 199–204, here reconstructed. Also pub.: Harper, III, 289–292; Lucas (1935), II, 76–79.

1. The senior Charles Lloyd's *A Translation of the Twenty-fourth Book of the Iliad of Homer,* which Robert Lloyd had printed, privately in Birmingham under his imprint Knott and Lloyd, in 1807. He reprinted it in 1810, probably with his father's revisions. I have not seen the 1810 edition.

2. Homer's lines 405–431. The "fable of the Two Urns," praised below, is told by Lloyd in lines 661–684 and by Homer in lines 527–551. The "Story of Niobe" as translated by Lloyd in lines 748–772 from Homer's lines 602–620 reads so:

> For fair-hair'd Niobe did not forsake
> Her food, and who more reason to complain?
> She had twelve children all together slain,
> Six lovely daughters and six blooming boys,
> Apollo's silver bow all these destroys;
> (Angry with Niobe) Diana's dart
> Pierc'd the six lovely daughters to the heart,
> Because their mother with the flaxen hair,
> Had offer'd insult to Latona fair,
> Saying, To me are many children born,

But to Latona two. This taunting scorn
Caus'd the two angry deities to slay
Her sons and daughters in a single day.
Nine days they lay in heaps, besmear'd with gore,
And no man to their grave their bodies bore
(For Jove had froze the people into stones).
On the tenth day the gods interr'd their bones;
And Niobe, tho' almost dead with grief,
Scorn'd not of food the nourishing relief;
And now among the rocks in desert cell,
In Sypilus, where wood-nymphs love to dwell
(Nymphs who about fam'd Achelous sing,
In choral dances round the mystic ring)
There, tho' a rock, she cherishes her woe,
Tears from her eyes continue still to flow.

3. This and the bracketed ellipses below replace passages of Lamb's criticisms that Lucas believed too slight to be published in *Lamb and the Lloyds*. The other texts of this letter were derived from that text. Lines 243–246 in Lloyd's work, which Lamb quotes below, are translations of Homer's lines 197–199:

ἀλλ' ἄγε μοι τόδε εἰπέ, τί τοι φρεσὶν εἴδεται εἶναι;
αἰνῶς γάρ μ' αὐτόν γε μένος καὶ θυμὸς ἄνωγε
κεῖσ' ἰέναι ἐπὶ νῆας ἔσω στρατὸν εὐρὺν Ἀχαιῶν.

[*Homer: Iliad, Books XIII–XXIV*, ed. D. B. Monro (4th ed., rev., 1897; rpt. Oxford: Clarendon Press, 1968), p. 243]

4. The word παιδοφόνοιο in Homer's line 506. Lloyd had translated it as "murderer" in his line 628.

5. The Latin word current in English since 1686—to mean a mound of earth, especially over a grave; a barrow—that Lloyd had employed in his lines 832, 1011, and 1015 for τύμβον in Homer's line 666, for σῆμ' in Homer's line 799, and for σῆμα in Homer's line 801.

6. In Lloyd's line 907 for ἀοιδοὺς in Homer's line 720. The translation, below, of the opening of Paul's address to the Athenians (Acts 17:22–31) is, presumably, a part of some (unidentified) life and collection of epistles of the apostle.

7. It is noted in *Lamb and the Lloyds*, p. 204, that "the last few words, including signature, have been cut away." Lloyd's translation "Horace. Book I. Epistle I. To Mæcenas," mentioned below, appears in the *Gentleman's Magazine*, 79 (March 1809), 255–256. See Letter 268 and its notes for information on Lloyd's other translations from Latin, from and of the *Epistles* of Horace.

238. *C. L. to Charles Lloyd, the elder*

Temple
19 June, 09

Dear Sir,—

I can only say that I shall be most happy to see anything that you can send me at any time that has reference to your newly taken up pursuits. I will faithfully return the Manuscript[1] with such observations as a mere acquaintance with English, and with English Poetry, may suggest. I dare not dictate in Greek. I am *Homo unius linguæ—*

your vindication of the Lines which I had objected to makes me ashamed of the unimportance of my remarks: they were not worth confuting. Only on Line 33, Page 4, I still retain my opinion that it[2] should be "were made."

> All seem'd to wish that such attempt were made,
> Save Juno, Neptune, and the blue-ey'd maid.

I am glad to see you venture *made* and *maid* for rhymes. 'Tis true their sound is the same. But the mind occupied in revolving the different meaning of two words so literally the same, is diverted from the objection which the mere Ear would make, and to the mind it is rhyme enough. I had not noticed it till this moment of transcribing the couplet. A timidity of Rhyming, whether of bringing together sounds too near, or too remote to each other, is a fault of the present day. The old English poets were richer in their diction, as they were less scrupulous. I shall expect your MS. with curiosity.

I am, Sir,

Yours with great respect,

C. Lamb

My kind remembrances to Robert. I shall soon have a little parcel[3] to send him. I am very sorry to hear of the ill-health of Sophia.

MS: unrecovered. Text: *Lamb and the Lloyds,* pp. 205–206. Also pub.: Harper, III, 292–293; Lucas (1935), II, 79–80.

1. Of the senior Charles Lloyd's translation of the first two books of the *Odyssey.* Lloyd completed translating its twenty-four books in 1816, but had printed, privately in Birmingham by Knott and Lloyd, in 1810, only *A Translation of the First Seven Books of the Odyssey of Homer.* (See the next letter, Letter 249, and *Lamb and the Lloyds,* pp. 221–222.) After the Latin, below, which translates as "a man of one tongue," Lamb reverts to Lloyd's *A Translation of the Twenty-fourth Book of the Iliad of Homer.*

2. Lloyd's "be made." Lloyd's lines 33–34—"All seem'd to wish that such attempt be made, / Save Juno, Neptune, and the blue-ey'd maid"—are a translation of Homer's lines 25–26: "ἔνθ' ἄλλοις μὲν πᾶσιν ἐήνδανεν, οὐδέ ποθ' Ἥρῃ / οὐδὲ Ποσειδάων' οὐδὲ γλαυκώπιδι κούρῃ."

3. Containing *Poetry for Children.* (See the next letter.) Sophia, named at the end of this letter, is the wife of the younger Charles Lloyd. See Vol. I, Letter 10, note 4.

239. *C. L. to Robert Lloyd and Charles Lloyd, the elder*
[Late June to mid-July 1809]

Dear Robert,—

Make my apologies to your father for not returning his "Odyssey" sooner, but I lent it to a friend[1] who is a better Grecian than me, to make remarks on, and he has been so busied (he is a Doctor of Laws) that I have rescued the MSS. from him at last by force. He has written a few observations. I send you our poems. All mine are marked $\sqrt{}$ in the contents. The rest are Mary's, all but the "Beggar Man,"[2] which is my brother's. The farce is not at home, but you shall have it ere long.— What follows is for your Father to see.— Mary desires her remembrances.

Dear Sir,—

A friend who has kept your MS. unreasonably long has ventured a few remarks on the first Book. And I have twice read thro' both with care, and can only reprehend a few trifling expressions with my scanty knowledge of Greek. I thank you for the reading of them, and assure you they read to me beautifully simple and in the manner of the original as far as I understand it.

Yours truly,
C. L.

My kind respects to Mrs. Lloyd.

[. . .][3]

Oxen of the Sun, I conjure. Bullocks is too Smithfield and sublunary a Word. Oxen of the Sun, or of Apollo, but in any case not Bullocks.

[. . .]

"The Cyclops' Eye still rankles in his Breast."[4] Here is an unlucky confusion of literal with figurative language. One Man's *Eye* rankles in another *Breast*. "Cyclops' wrongs" would do better.

[. . .]

These[5] sound too modern-kitchenish. One might be called an officer or servitor, the other a server. Milton speaks of these things as the office mean "of sewer and seneschall." Perhaps sewer is too old. But Cook and Butler are too like modern Establishments.

[. . .]

Unaffected[6] Grace. Is there any word in Homer to express *affectation?* I think not. Then certainly he has no such idea as *unaffected.* [. . .]

MS: unrecovered. Text: *Lamb and the Lloyds,* pp. 207–210, here reconstructed. Also pub.: Harper, III, 296–297; Lucas (1935), II, 80–81.

1. That he is "a Doctor of Laws" (see below) indicates that he is John Stoddart.

2. "The Beggar-man," in *Poetry for Children* (*Works,* III, 395). The farce, mentioned below, is, presumably, "Mr. H———."

3. This and the bracketed ellipses below replace passages of Lamb's criticisms that Lucas believed too slight, it would seem, to be published in *Lamb and the Lloyds.* The other texts of this letter were derived from that text. "Bullocks of the Sun" (see below), according to *Lamb and the Lloyds,* p. 208, appears in Lloyd's (original) translation of the first book of the *Odyssey.* It is Lloyd's rendering of Βοῦς Ὑπερίονος Ἠελίοιο, in Homer's line 8. Lloyd's *A Translation of the First Seven Books of the Odyssey of Homer* (1810), Book I, line 10, reads, "On oxen sacred to Apollo fed." From early times to 1855 Smithfield was the site of the central cattle and hay markets of London.

4. In part for "ἀλλὰ Ποσειδάων γαιήοχος ἀσκελὲς αἰὲν / Κύκλωπος κεχόλωται, ὃν ὀφθαλμοῦ ἀλάωσεν," in Homer's Book I, lines 68–69 (quoted from *Homer's Odyssey,* ed. W. Walter Merry and James Riddell [2d ed., rev.; Oxford: Clarendon Press, 1886], I, 9). Lloyd's 1810 translation—Book I, lines 81–82—of that passage reads so: "By Neptune's wrath the hero is distress'd, / The Cyclops' wrong still rankles in his breast."

5. The titles "cook" and "butler" for δαιτρὸς and κῆρυξ in Homer's Book I, lines 141 and 143, respectively. Lloyd's 1810 translation, Book I, lines 175 and 177, has "sewer" and "servitor." Lamb below partly paraphrases and partly misquotes *Paradise Lost,* IX, 38–39.

6. Lloyd's interpolation from Homer's Book I, lines 334–336:

ἄντα παρειάων σχομένη λιπαρὰ κρήδεμνα·
ἀμφίπολος δ' ἄρα οἱ κεδνὴ ἑκάτερθε παρέστη·
δακρύσασα δ' ἔπειτα προσηύδα θεῖον ἀοιδόν.

Lloyd's 1810 translation—Book I, lines 411–414—of that passage reads so:
        A light thin veil flow'd loosely o'er her face,
        And standing at the door with *pensive* grace,
        The master of the song she thus address'd,
        In words which told the anguish of her breast. [My italics]

240.   *C. L. to Charles Lloyd, the elder*

July 31, 1809

Dear Sir,—

The general impression made by your Translation on the mind of my friend who kept your MS. so unreasonably long, as well as on another friend[1] who read over a good part of it with me, was that it gave a great deal more of the sense of Homer than either of his two great modern Translators have done. In several expressions which they at first objected to, on turning to the Greek they found it completely warranted you in the use of them; and they were even surprised that you could combine so much fidelity with so much of the turn of the best modern improvements in the Couplet versification. I think of the two, I rather prefer the Book of the Iliad which you sent me, for the sound of the verse; but the difference of subject almost involuntarily modifies verse. I find Cowper is a favourite with nobody. His injudicious use of the stately slow Miltonic verse in a subject so very different, has given a distaste. Nothing can be more unlike to my fancy than Homer and Milton. Homer is perfect prattle, tho' exquisite prattle, compared to the deep oracular voice of Milton. In Milton you love to stop, and saturate your mind with every great image or sentiment; in Homer you want to go on, to have more of his agreeable narrative. Cowper delays you as much, walking over a Bowling Green, as the other does, travelling over steep Alpine heights, where the labour enters into and makes a part of the pleasure. From what I have seen, I would certainly be glad to hear that you continued your employment quite through the Poem: that is, for an agreeable and honourable recreation to yourself; though I should scarce think that (Pope having got the ground) a translation in Pope's Couplet versification would ever supersede his to the public, however faithfuller or in some respects better. Pitt's Virgil[2] is not much read, I believe, though nearer to the Original than Dryden's. Perhaps it is, that people do not like two Homers or Virgils—there is a sort of confusion in it to an English reader, who has not a centre of reference in the Original: when Tate and Brady's Psalms[3] came out in our Churches, many pious people would not substitute them in the room of David's, as they call'd Sternhold and Hopkins's. But if you write for a relaxation from other sort of occupations I can only congratulate you, Sir, on the noble choice, as it seems to me, which you have made, and express my wonder at the facility which you suddenly have arrived at, if (as I suspect) these are indeed the first specimens of this sort which you have produced. But I cannot help thinking that you betray a more practised gait than a late beginner could so soon acquire. Perhaps you have only resumed, what you had formerly laid aside as interrupting more necessary avocations.

I need not add how happy I shall be to see at any time what you may please to send me. In particular, I should be glad to see that you had taken up Horace,[4] which I think you enter into as much as any man that was not born in his days, and in the *Via Longa* or *Flaminia,* or near the *Forum.*

With many apologies for keeping your MS. so long, which my friend's engagements in business must excuse,

I remain,

Dear Sir, yours truly,

C. L.

My kind respects to Mrs. Ll., and my remembrances to Robert, &c., &c.

MS: unrecovered. Text: *Lamb and the Lloyds,* pp. 210–213. Also pub.: Ainger (1900), II, 174–176; Ainger (1904), I, 307–309; Harper, III, 293–296; Lucas (1935), II, 81–83.

1. Unidentified. Lamb soon makes clear that Homer's "two great modern Translators" (below) are Pope and Cowper.

2. The translation of the *Aeneid,* published in 1740, by the poet Christopher Pitt (1699–1748).

3. *A New Version of the Psalms of David,* by Nahum Tate (see Vol. II, Letter 135, note 2) and the divine and poet Nicholas Brady (1659–1726). It was published in 1696 and its use then sanctioned in all churches, chapels, and congregations by William III. The "Old Version" of the Psalms was begun by Thomas Sternhold (d. 1549), a member of the household of Henry VIII and possibly of Edward VI. It appeared sometime between 1547 and 1549, as *Certayne Psalmes Chosē out of the Psalter of Dauid and Drawē into Englishē Metre by Thomas Sternhold, Grome of Ye Kynges Maiesties Roobes.* Additional psalms were added and revised editions issued by, among others, John Hopkins (d. 1570), a Suffolk schoolmaster and clergyman. The developing Psalter, as it existed at the time, was brought into service on the accession of Elizabeth I, in 1558. The completed "Old Version" first appeared in 1562, as *The Whole Booke of Psalmes, Collected into Englysh Metre by T. Sternhold I. Hopkins & Others: Conferred with the Ebrue, with Apt Notes to Synge Thē Withal, Faithfully Perused and Alowed According to Thordre Appointed in the Quenes Maiesties Iniunctions. Very Mete to Be Vsed of All Sortes of People Priuately for Their Solace & Comfort: Laying Apart All Vngodly Songes and Ballades, Which Tends Only to the Norishing of Vyce, and Corrupting of Youth.*

4. See Letter 237, note 7. The Via Flaminia, mentioned below, was the great north road from Rome to Ariminum. It was constructed principally by the direction of the statesman and general Gaius Flaminius during his censorship (220 B.C.) of Rome.

241. *C. L. to John Brown, with a note, on the verso, from Brown to Coleridge*

Temple
24 August 1809

[I]¹ request you to send the *fourth number* of [the Fr]iend and *all succeeding numbers* to

Mr. Lamb No. 4 Inner Temple Lane, London

and to send the whole from the beginning, and so on,

to
Mr. Rickman, New Palace Yard, Westminster.

&

to
Capt. Burney, 26 James Street, Pimlico.

They have been ordered at Clement's² in the Strand, & Mr. Clement refuses to send them, because he says it is an irregular publication.

Please to observe that *I* want no numbers before the 4th, but the other Gentlemen are to have all——

Your humble Servant
C. Lamb

Sir,

I send you this to know if you think proper to continue Clement as your agent after what Mr Lamb has stated on the other side.————³ The Copy I have on hand will make another Number and about 8 or 9 pages over. There should be another supply of stamps ordered, as what we have on hand will only serve for about 3 Numbers—

Among the names you sent there was ten not in the book.— I have received 16 Names from Longman's.

MS: Wordsworth Library, Grasmere. Pub.: *Coleridge's Letters,* III, 220. Addresses (on separate leaves), by Lamb: Mr. J. Brown/Bookseller/Penrith/Cumberland; by Brown: S. T. Coleridge, Esq./Grasmere/Westmorland. Postmark: August 24, 1809. John Brown, "Printer & Stationer, Penrith" (*Coleridge's Letters,* III, 180), had agreed in mid-February 1809 to print and publish Coleridge's *The Friend.*

1. The corner of the paper is torn away. The fourth number of *The Friend,* requested (with other numbers) following, is dated Thursday, September 7, 1809.

2. The bookshop, at 201 Strand, of William Innell Clement (d. 1852). He and Longman's firm were the London agents for *The Friend.* Clement between 1810 and 1815, according to the *DNB,* became one of the proprietors of the Sunday illustrated paper *The Observer* and from 1821 to 1834 was the proprietor of the *Morning Chronicle.*

3. Coleridge so responded to Brown on September 11: "I assuredly would not have any more [numbers of *The Friend*] sent to Clement, but instead of him to Longman what used to be sent to the former—& an advertisment shall appear to that purport" (*Coleridge's Letters,* III, 220). Clement protested to Coleridge on October 7: it was not Clement but rather his shopman who had asserted that "Mr Coleridge is very irregular with his Friends" (*The Friend,* ed. Barbara Rooke, I, lvi); Clement had always displayed the periodical in his window, and he had advertised its fourth number in *The Courier* and the *Morning Post* on September 12. Coleridge, on the recommendation of Daniel Stuart, reinstated Clement as a London agent of *The Friend* beginning with its ninth number, of October 12, and had Clement's name added to those of Brown and the Longman company on the colophons of numbers 9 through 20 and 22 through 27. See *The Friend,* ed. Barbara Rooke, II, 373–375, for the colophons of the 1809–1810 and 1812 editions, and II, 407–467, for the subscribers (whose names Brown kept in the book, an account book, mentioned below) to the periodical.

242.   *C. L. to Coleridge*

Monday 30th Oct 1809

Dear Coleridge,

I have but this moment received your Letter dated the 9th Inst.!— having just come off a Journey from *Wiltshire,* where I have been with Mary on a visit to Hazlitt. The journey has been of infinite service to her. We have had nothing but sunshiney days & daily walks from 8 to 20 miles a day. Have seen Wilton,[1] Salisbury, Stonehenge &c:— Her illness lasted but 6 weeks, it left her weak, but the Country has made us whole. We came back to our Hogarth Room—. I have made several acqui[s]itions since you saw them—and found Nos. 8. 9. 10 of *the friend.* The account of Luther in the Warteburg[2] is as fine as any thing I ever read. God forbid that a Man who has such things to say should be be silenced for want of £100. This Custom & Duty Age, would have made the **Preacher** on the Mount take out a Licence, and St. Pauls Epistles **not** missible without a stamp. O that you may find means to go on. But alas!— Where is Sir G. Beaumont, Sotheby, What is become of the rich Auditors in albermale Street.?—

Your Letter has saddened me,———— I am so tired with my journey being up all night, I have neither things nor word in my power. I

believe I exprest my admiration of the Pamphlet.[3] Its power over me
was like that which Milton's pamphlets must have had on his contemporaries who were tuned to them. What a piece of prose. Do you
hear if it is read at all? I am out of the world if[4] readers. I hate all
that do read, for they read nothing but reviews & new books. I gather
myse[lf] up unto the old things. I have put up shelve[s.] You never
saw a Book case in more **true** harmony with the contents than what
I've nailed up in a room which though new has more aptitudes for
growing old than you shall often see—as one sometimes gets a friend
in the middle of life who becomes an old friend in a short time.[5]
My rooms are luxurious. One is for prints & one for Books. A Summer & a Winter Parlour. When shall I ever see you in them?—[6]

[. . .] My head is so sore, I writ[e] I know not what. It always
is after [. . .]

MS: Huntington Library. Pub.: Talfourd (1848), I, 176–180; Sala, I, 153–
156; Purnell, I, 153–156; Fitzgerald, II, 7–10; Hazlitt, I, 403–404; Ainger (1888),
I, 254–255; Ainger (1900), II, 176–178; Macdonald, I, 316–317; Ainger (1904),
I, 309–310; Harper, III, 298–299; Lucas (1905), VI, 403–404; Lucas (1912), V,
425; Lucas (1935), II, 83–84. Address: Mr Coleridge/Grasmere/Kendal/Westmor-
land. Postmark: October 30, 1809.
 1. A market and an industrial town known for its carpets; for its having been
a seat of the West Saxon kings; and for Wilton House, the mansion constructed
for Sir William Herbert, first Earl of Pembroke of the second creation (1501?–
1570), and the country home of Mary Herbert, Countess of Pembroke (1561–
1621), the sister of Sir Philip Sidney and the wife of Henry Herbert, second
Earl of Pembroke (1534?–1601). There Sidney wrote the *Arcadia* and there
Shakespeare's company may have performed. Salisbury, mentioned following, is
famous for its Early English cathedral of St. Mary. Hazlitt, in "A Farewell to
Essay-writing," has a sentence on a bit of probably the month in 1809 that the
Lambs spent at Winterslow: "I used to walk out at this time with Mr. and Miss
L—— of an evening, to look at the Claude Lorraine skies over our heads, melting
from azure into purple and gold, and to gather mushrooms, that sprung up at our
feet, to throw into our hashed mutton at supper" (*Hazlitt's Works*, XVII, 319–
320). See Letter 251 and its note 2 about the Lambs' month or so at Winterslow
in 1810 and for what Hazlitt wrote about Lamb concerning probably that time.
The "Hogarth Room," thus designated below, is the room—"my best room"
Lamb calls it in his letter to Manning of January 2, 1810 (Letter 245, near the
beginning)—is the room in the Lambs' apartment at 4 Inner Temple Lane in
which Lamb displayed his collection of William Hogarth's prints. "The furniture
is old-fashioned and worn," reads a part of Thomas Noon Talfourd's description
of that interior; "the ceiling low, and not wholly unstained by traces of 'the
great plant [tobacco],' though now virtuously forborne; but the Hogarths, in
narrow black frames, abounding in infinite thought, humor and pathos, enrich
the walls; and all things wear an air of comfort and hearty English welcome"
(*Literary Sketches and Letters: Being the Final Memorials of Charles Lamb,
Never before Published* [New York: D. Appleton; Philadelphia: Geo. S. Appleton,
1848], p. 231—one of the American editions of the work abbreviated in this

edition of Lamb letters as "Talfourd [1848]"). In her and Charles's letter to
Dorothy Wordsworth of November 21, 1817 (in my Vol. IV, Letter 332), written
shortly after the move from 4 Inner Temple Lane to 20 Russell Street, Covent
Garden, Mary states, in her fifth paragraph, that "Charles has had all his Hogarths
bound in a book, they were sent home yesterday, and now that I have them all together and perceive the advantage of peeping close at them through my spectacles
I am reconciled to the loss of them hanging round the room, which has been a
great mortification to me—in vain I tried to console myself with looking at our
new chairs and carpets." Some bibliographical and other details of Lamb's essay, of
1811, on Hogarth are included in Letter 291, note 3.

2. In *The Friend*, No. 8 (October 5, 1809), 119–127. The matter beginning
with the next sentence bears on the difficulty Coleridge was having in paying
especially for the stamps and paper for *The Friend*. He appealed for financial
assistance neither to Sir George Howland Beaumont nor to William Sotheby
(identified in my Vol. II, Letter 176, note 1, and Vol. I, Letter 16, note 8), both
of whom had helped him in the past. (The "rich Auditors in albermale Street"
[below] were those who had attended Coleridge's lectures on the "Principles of
Poetry," given at the Royal Institution, 21 Albemarle Street, in 1808.) Coleridge
appealed, rather, to his brother George; Thomas Hutchinson; Thomas Poole; and
Richard, "Conversation," Sharp (1759–1835), who was a London businessman
and a member of Parliament, had been Coleridge's correspondent since 1804, and
would become the author of *Letters and Essays in Prose and Verse* (1834). All
except George Coleridge came forward with loans. Daniel Stuart, who had advanced the paper for the first ten numbers of the periodical but had come to
believe he could advance it no longer, unexpectedly and without having been
asked sent a generous new supply. Coleridge was in consequence able to continue
printing stamped numbers of *The Friend* for its subscribers and unstamped
numbers for collection into volumes.

3. Wordsworth's, presumably, on the convention of Cintra. Lamb had mentioned it earlier—in Letter 236, in the paragraph below the reference to note 3.

4. A mistake for "of."

5. Lamb's library, wrote Leigh Hunt in "My Books," in the *Literary Examiner*,
1 (July 5, 1823), 3, "though not abounding in Greek or Latin (which are the
only things to help some persons to an idea of literature) is anything but superficial. The depths of philosophy and poetry are there, the innermost passages of
the human heart. It has some Latin, too. It has also an handsome contempt for
appearance. It looks like what it is, a selection made at precious intervals from the
book-stalls;—now a Chaucer at nine and twopence; now a Montaigne or a Sir
Thomas Brown at two shillings; now a Jeremy Taylor, a Spinoza; an old English
Dramatist, Prior, and Sir Philip Sidney; and the books are 'neat as imported.' The
very perusal of the backs is a 'discipline of humanity.' There Mr. Southey takes
his place again with an old Radical friend: there Jeremy Collier is at peace with
Dryden: there the lion, Martin Luther, lies down with the Quaker lamb, Sewell:
there Guzman d'Alfarache thinks himself fit company for Sir Charles Grandison,
and has his claims admitted. Even the 'high fantastical' Duchess of Newcastle,
with her laurel on her head, is received with grave honours, and not the less
for declining to trouble herself with the constitutions of her maids." (Among
those named in Hunt's passage are the poet and diplomatist Matthew Prior [1664–
1721]; Jeremy Collier [1650–1726], a nonjuror and the author of *Short View
of the Immorality and Profaneness of the English Stage* [1698], *Ecclesiastical History of Great Britain from the First Planting of Christianity to the End of the
Reign of Charles II* [1708–1714], and other works, whom Lamb wrote of in
"[Dryden and Collier]" and mentioned in "The Ass" [*Works*, I, 157–158 and 305];
William Sewel [1654–1720], whose publications include *History of the Rise,
Increase, and Progress of the Christian People Called Quakers* [1722], the transla-

tion by Sewel of his own Low Dutch original, published in 1717; the title character of *Guzmán de Alfarache* [1594 and 1604], a popular picaresque novel [translated into English in 1623] by the Spanish novelist Mateo Alemán [1547–1609?]; the title character of Samuel Richardson's *Sir Charles Grandison* [1753–1754]; and Margaret Cavendish, Duchess of Newcastle [1624?–1674], who wrote a variety of works—verses, plays, essays, an autobiography, a biography of her husband, William Cavendish, Duke of Newcastle [1592–1676]—and whom Lamb praised highly in "The Two Races of Men," "Mackery End, in Hertfordshire," "A Complaint of the Decay of Beggars in the Metropolis," and "Detached Thoughts on Books and Reading" [*Works,* II, 26, 76, 115, and 174].) Another account of Lamb's books, and of Lamb's preferences and range in reading, is in Bryan Waller Procter's "Recollections of Charles Lamb," in *The Athenaeum,* No. 378 (January 24, 1835), 72:

> The books that I have adverted to, as filling his shelves, were mainly English books—the poets, dramatists, divines, essayists, &c.,—ranging from the commencement of the Elizabeth period, down to the times of Addison and Steele. Besides these,—of the earliest writers, Chaucer was there; and, amongst the moderns, Wordsworth, Coleridge, and others, whom he loved.
>
> He had more real knowledge of old English literature than any man whom I ever knew. He was not an antiquarian. He neither hunted after commas, nor scribbled notes which confounded his text. The *Spirit* of the author descended upon him; and he felt it!—With Burton and Fuller, Jeremy Taylor, and Sir Thomas Browne, he was an intimate. The ancient poets—chiefly the dramatic poets—were his especial friends. He knew every point and turn of their wit— all the beauty of their characters; loving each for some one distinguishing particular, and despising none. For absolute contempt is a quality of youth and ignorance—a foppery which a wise man rejects; and *he* rejected it accordingly. If he contemned anything, it was contempt itself. He saw that every one bore some sign or mark (God's gift), for which he ought to be valued by his fellows, and esteemed a man. He could pick out a merit from each author in his turn. He liked Heywood for his simplicity and pathos; Webster for his deep and gloomy insight into the heart; Ben Jonson for his humour; Marlow for his "mighty line"; [John] Fletcher for his wit and flowing sweetness; and Shakspeare for his combination of wonders. He loved Donne too, and [Francis] Quarles, and Marvell, and Sir Philip Sidney, and a long list besides. Setting aside the extreme moderns, he was a Catholic in his worship of books; preferring some assuredly to others—some for their intrinsic excellence—some for their modest half-concealed beauties—and a few because they were robbed, as he thought, of their just fame. No subject deterred him: he read and pondered over histories, poems, sermons, essays, and plays. He traversed all the regions of fiction; from the Elysian fields to the plains of La Mancha—from the transformations of Ovid to the Arabian enchantments. 'Scanderbeg' was not too heavy, nor 'Riquet with the Tuft' too light for him. He loved best, perhaps, the fine gentlemen of the days of Wycherley and Congreve, or the finer race of Elizabethan times, but he could turn aside from these, and go backwards into the heroic ages, and muse upon "the shores of Old Romance."

(Mentioned in Procter's passage are Thomas Fuller [1608–1661], from whose *The History of the Worthies of England* [1662], among others of Fuller's books, Lamb took extracts for inclusion in "Specimens from the Writings of Fuller, the Church Historian" [*Works,* I, 112–118]; Thomas Heywood [d. 1650?], from whose *A Woman Kill'd with Kindness: A Tragedy* [1607], among others of Heywood's plays, Lamb took extracts for inclusion in *Specimens of English Dramatic Poets* [*Works,* IV, 89–94; see also pp. 84–89 and 95–104]; presumably *The Great Scanderbeg, a Novel Done out of the French* [1690 and later], an anonymous translation of Mlle de la Roche-Guilhem's *Le grand Scanderbeg. Nouvelle* [1688], whose subject, also known as Iskender Bey, was an Albanian prince and a national hero actually named Giorgio Castriota [1403–1467]; and the fairy tale "Riquet with the Tuft," from perhaps Robert Samber's translation—*Histories, or Tales of Past Times . . .* [1729]—of *Histoires ou contes du temps passé avec des moralités* [1697], by the critic and poet Charles Perrault [1628–1703]. The haunting, concluding quotation in the passage is from Wordsworth's "A narrow girdle of rough stones and crags," line 38.) *A Descriptive Catalogue of the Library of Charles Lamb* was published in New York by The Dibdin Club in 1897. It contains this introductory statement:

> Charles Lamb at his death bequeathed to his life-long friend, Edward Moxon, the well-known London publisher, his curious collection of books. Moxon, it seems, did not claim his inheritance until after the death of Mary Lamb, during whose last long illness the collection of books, that had formed the solace and delight of her brother's life, had met with neglect and partial dispersion, chiefly among his friends. After her death Moxon selected upwards of sixty volumes from the mass as worthy of presentation because of the notes, etc., which they contained, by Lamb and his friends, and then destroyed the remainder of the library. Charles Welford, then of the firm of Bartlett & Welford, an intimate friend of Moxon's, on learning that the collection was to be sold induced Moxon to let him carry off the prize to America. The books were brought to this country early in 1848, and were placed on exhibition in the store of Bartlett & Welford at Nos. 2 and 4 Barclay Street, in the Astor House, New York. There they were sold piecemeal to the many admirers of the "gentle Elia," who had come from California and Oregon as well as from the Eastern States, and from Labrador to Mexico.

6. Fourteen to eighteen lines of a new paragraph are canceled, and a strip about an inch high has been torn away from across the bottom of the second leaf of Lamb's folio sheet. Canceled lines on the recto and uncanceled lines on the verso went with the torn-away strip.

243.   *M. A. L. to Sarah Stoddart Hazlitt*

Tuesday [November 7, 1809]

My dear Sarah

The dear quiet lazy delicious month we spent with you is remembered by me with such regret that I feel quite discontented & Winterslow-sick. I assure you I never passed such a pleasant time in the countery in my life, both in the house & out of it—the card playing quarrels, and a few gaspings for breath, after your swift footsteps up the high hills excepted, and those drawbacks are not unpleasant in the recollection.— We have got some salt butter, to make our toast seem like yours, and we have tried to eat meat suppers, but that would not do for we left our appetites behind us, and the dry loaf, which offended you, now comes in at night unaccompanied, but, sorry am I to add, it is soon followed by the pipe and the gin bottle.— We smoked the very first night of our arrival.

Great News! I have just been interrupted by Mr Daw who came to tell me he was yesterday elected a **Royal Academician.**[1] He said none of his own friends voted for him, he got it by strangers who were pleased with his picture of Mrs White. Charles says he does not believe Northcote ever voted for the admission of any one. Though a very cold day Daw was in a prodigious sweat for joy at his good fortune. More great News, my beautiful green curtains were put up yesterday, and all the doors listed with green baize, and four new boards put to the coal hole, and fastening hasps put to the windows and my dyed Manning-silk[2] cut out. Yesterday was an eventful day for yesterday too Martin Burney was to be examined by Lord Eldon previous to his being admitted as an Attorney, but he has not yet been here to announce his success.

I carried the baby-caps to Mrs Hazlitt, she was much pleased, and vastly thankful Mr H. got fifty four guineas at Rochester and has now several pictures in hand. He has been very disorderly lately. I am going to tell you a secret for Mrs H says he would be very sorry to have it talked of. One night he came home from the Alehouse, bringing with him a great rough ill-looking fellow whom he introduced to Mrs Hazlitt as Mr Brown a gentleman he had hired as a mad keeper to take care of him at forty pounds a year, being ten pounds under the market price for keepers, which sum Mr Brown had agreed to remit out of pure friendship. It was with great difficulty, and by threatening to call in the aid of watchmen & constables that she could prevail on Mr Brown to leave the house.

We had a good chearful meeting on Wednesday. Much talk of Winterslow, its woods & its sun flowers. I did not so much like Phillips at Winterslow, as I now like him for having been with us at Winterslow. We roasted the last of his "Beach of oily nut prolific"[3] on friday at the Captains. Nurse is now established in Paradise alias the Incurable ward. I have seen her sitting in most superb state, surrounded by her seven Incurable companions. They call each other ladies. Nurse looks as if she would be considered as the first lady in the ward, only one seemed at [all (?)] like to rival her in dignity.

A man in the India House[4] has resigned by which Charles will get twenty pounds a year, and White has prevailed on him to write some more lottery puffs, if that ends in smoke the twenty pounds is a sure card, and has made us very joyful.

I continue very well & return you very sincere thanks for my good health and improved looks which have almost made Mrs Godwin die with envy, She longs to come to Winterslow as much as the spiteful elder sister did to go to the well for a gift to spit diamonds.—⁵

Jane, and I, have agreed to boil a Round of Beef for your suppers when you come to town again. she, Jane, broke two of the Hogarth glasses while we where away, whereat I made a great noise.

Farewel. Love to William, and Charless love and good wishes for the speedy arrival of the Life of Holcroft & the bearer thereof

Yours most affectionately

M Lamb

Charles told Mrs Godwin Hazlitt had found a well in his garden, which, water being scarce in your county, would bring him in two hundred a year, and she came in great haste the next morning to ask me if it were true. Your brother and his &c⁶ are all well.

MS:The Pierpont Morgan Library, New York. Pub.: Talfourd (1848), I, 163–166; Sala, I, 433–436; Purnell, I, 433–436; Lucas (1905), VI, 405–407; Lucas (1912), V, 427–429; Lucas (1935), II, 85–87. Address: Mrs. Hazlitt/Winterslow/near/Salisbury. Postmark: November 7, 1809.

1. Dawe had just been elected an associate member of the Royal Academy. He did not become a full member until 1814, when he submitted as his diploma work "The Demoniac." It is reproduced in G. D. Leslie and Fred. A. Eaton's "The Royal Academy in the Present Century," *Art Journal* (London: H. Virtue, 1899), p. 40. Mentioned below is Dawe's portrait of the wife (who has not been otherwise identified) of Anthony White (1782–1849), a surgeon, at one time an apprentice to Sir Anthony Carlisle. The portrait is dated 1809 in Emmanuel Bénézit's *Dictionnaire critique et documentaire des peintres, sculpteurs, dessinateurs et graveurs* ([Paris:] Gründ, 1903–1955), III, 78, and as having been sold in 1935 for £10 10s. The painter and author James Northcote (1746–1831), whose manner Dawe had attempted to emulate early in his career and who was among Dawe's subjects, had been a member of the Royal Academy since 1787. Northcote and Hazlitt had known each other since at least the early 1800s, and Hazlitt would publish some of Northcote's conversations, serially between 1826 and 1830 (in the *New Monthly Magazine* of 1826 and 1827, the *London Weekly Review* of 1829, *The Atlas* of 1829, and the *Court Journal* of 1830) and as *Conversations of James Northcote, Esq., R.A.* in 1830. Northcote and Lamb were together, with others (see *Hazlitt*, p. 168), at a tea Hazlitt gave in his rooms at 34 Southampton Buildings on March 18, 1808.

2. See Vol. II, Letter 222, near the reference to note 1. Referred to below is John Scott, first Earl of Eldon (1751–1838), lord chancellor of England from 1801 to 1806 and from 1807 to 1827. Martin Burney did qualify as a barrister, with promise of a success he never realized. According to Phyllis G. Mann's "A New Gloss for 'The Wedding,'" in the *CLSB* of March 1963, he was articled to and began his professional life in the law office of the attorney and historian Sharon Turner (1768–1847). But see Letter 250, at the reference to note 4, and Letter 296, at the reference to note 8. Winifred Woodham in her "Martin Charles Burney, 1788–1852," in the *CLSB* of May 1951, mentioned neither

Turner nor the name of any law firm or office with which Burney was associated. Mary Lamb in her next paragraph writes of Mrs. John Hazlitt and her husband. He had, it seems, sold some of his pictures in Rochester, Kent. His friend Brown has not been identified.

3. William Cowper, *The Task,* I, 315–316. About Mary's former nurse Mary Grant see Letter 233, note 3.

4. The man could be the clerk William Evans (identified in Vol. I, Letter 3, note 29), who had left the accountant general's department before the June quarter of 1808; the clerk William Marter (b. 1773?), who had been transferred from that department to the baggage warehouse during the June quarter of 1808 and was retired in 1812; or Richard Le Gros, a clerk considerably Lamb's senior who had been transferred from the accountant general's department to another office in the June quarter of 1809. (The Evans named as though a clerk promoted from the department in Samuel McKechnie's "Charles Lamb of the India House," *Notes and Queries,* 192 [February 8, 1947], 55, is the baggage warehouseman William Evans [d. 1826], more fully identified in Letter 298, note 3.) The India House records do not show any resignations in 1809 or that Lamb succeeded to the higher-salaried position that Le Gros's transfer had opened. But the records do show that Lamb's quarterly gratuity of fifteen pounds was increased to twenty beginning early in the September quarter of 1809. White, mentioned below, is James White. (See Vol. I, Introduction, pp. xxxv–xxxvi.) About the lottery puffs see Vol. II, Letter 185, note 10.

5. An incident in "The Fairy" in Charles Perrault's *The Tales of Mother Goose,* tr. Charles Welsh (Boston: Heath, 1901), pp. 75–79. Mary could have read the story in *Histories, or Tales of Past Times Told by Mother Goose. With Morals,* tr. G[uy] M[ièges] (12th ed.; Salisbury: B. C. Collins, 1802). See Letter 233, note 4, about Jane (referred to in the next paragraph), and Letter 232, note 1, about Hazlitt's *Memoirs of the Late Thomas Holcroft.*

6. The younger John Stoddart and his family. See Vol. I, Letter 3, note 28.

244. *C. L. to Robert Lloyd*

[January 1, 1810]

Dear Robert

In great haste I write. The Turkey is down at the fire, and some pleasant friends are come in, to partake of it. The Sender's Health shall not be forgot.— What you tell me of your Father's perseverance in his honorable task[1] gives me great pleasure. Seven Books are a serious earnest of the whole, which I hope to see finish'd.—

We had a delightful month in Wiltshire, four weeks of uniform fine weather, the only fine days which had been all the Summer, saw Salisbury Cathedral, Stonehenge, Wilton &cc—. Mary is in excellent health, and sends her Love. Accept of mine with my kind respects to Mrs Ll.—and to your father & mother

Coleridge's friend is occasionally sublime—. What do you think of that Decription of Luther in his Study in one of the earlier numbers?[2]

The worst is, he is always promising something which never comes, it is now 18th Number, and continues introductory, the 17th (that stupid long letter) was nothing better than a Prospectus & ought to have preceded the 1st Number. But I rejoice that it lives.—

When you come to London, you find us at **No.** 4 Inner Temple Lane, with a few old Books, a few old Hogarths round the room, and the **Household** Gods at last establish'd. The feeling of **Home,** which has been slow to come, has come at last. May I never **move** again, but may my next Lodging be my **Coffin.**[3]

Yours Truly
C Lamb

MS: Huntington Library. Pub.: Ainger (1900), II, 178–179; Macdonald, I, 318–319; Ainger (1904), I, 310–311; Harper, III, 299–300; Lucas (1935), II, 88. Address: Mr. R. Lloyd/(Messs. Nott & Lloyd)/Birmingham. Postmark: January 1, 1810.
1. Of translating the first seven books of the *Odyssey.* See Letter 238, note 1.
2. **What** Lamb thought of the "Decription" is in Letter 242, especially in the sentence containing the reference to note 2. Number 18 of *The Friend,* referred to below, is dated Thursday, December 21, 1809. Number 17, of December 14, 1809, has on pages 257–268 a letter, signed "MATHETES" ("Learner"), concerning what the writers of the letter conceived to be "the state of many minds, which may derive important advantages" (p. 257) from *The Friend.* The writers were the Wordsworths' neighbor John Wilson, later of *Blackwood's Edinburgh Magazine,* and Wilson's friend Alexander Blair, who in 1825 became a professor of English literature at University College London. On pages 268–272 of Number 17 is the beginning of a reply, which Wordsworth wrote at Coleridge's request. (See *Wordsworths' Letters,* II, 378–379; the information given above about Blair is taken from II, 431.) The ending of Wordsworth's reply, signed "M. M.," is in *The Friend,* No. 20 (January 4, 1810), 305–318.
3. See Letter 232, note 3.

245. *C. L. to Manning*

Jan. 2nd, 1810

Dear Manning,

When I last wrote to you,[1] I was in lodgings. I am now in chambers, No. 4, Inner Temple Lane, where I should be happy to see you any evening. Bring any of your friends, the Mandarins, with you. I have two sitting-rooms: I call them so *par excellence,* for you may stand, or loll, or lean, or try any posture in them; but they are best for sitting; not squatting down Japanese fashion, but the more decorous use of the posteriors which European usage has consecrated. I have two of these rooms on the third floor, and five sleeping, cooking, &c., rooms, on the fourth floor. In my best room is a choice collection of the works of Hogarth, an English painter of some humour. In my next best are shelves containing a small but well-chosen library. My best room commands a court, in which there are trees and a pump, the water of which is excellent—cold with brandy, and not very insipid without. Here I hope to set up my rest, and not quit till Mr. Powell, the undertaker,[2] gives me notice that I may have possession of my last lodging. He lets lodgings for single gentlemen. I sent you a parcel of books by my last, to give you some idea of the state of European literature. There comes with this two volumes, done up as letters, of minor poetry, a sequel to 'Mrs. Leicester'; the best you may suppose mine; the next best are my coadjutor's; you may amuse yourself in guessing them out; but I must tell you mine are but one-third in quantity of the whole. So much for a very delicate subject. It is hard to speak of one's self, &c. Holcroft had finished his life when I wrote to you, and Hazlitt has since finished his life—I do not mean his own life, but he has finished a life of Holcroft, which is going to press.[3] Tuthill is Dr. Tuthill. I continue Mr. Lamb. I have published a little book for children on titles of honour: and to give them some idea of the difference of rank and gradual rising, I have made a little scale, supposing myself to receive the following various accessions of dignity from the king, who is the fountain of honour—As at first, 1, Mr. C. Lamb; 2, C. Lamb, Esq.; 3, Sir C. Lamb, Bart.; 4, Baron Lamb of Stamford;* 5, Viscount Lamb; 6, Earl Lamb; 7, Marquis Lamb; 8, Duke Lamb. It would look like quibbling to carry it on further, and especially as it is not necessary for children to go beyond the ordinary titles of sub-regal dignity in our own country, otherwise I have sometimes in my dreams imagined myself still advancing, as 9th, King Lamb; 10th, Emperor Lamb; 11th, Pope Innocent, higher than which is nothing but the Lamb of God. Puns I have not made many (nor punch much), since the date of my last; one I cannot help relating. A constable in Salisbury Cathedral was telling me that eight people dined at the top of the spire of the cathedral; upon which I remarked, that they must be very sharp-set. But in general I cultivate the reasoning part of my mind more than the imaginative. Do you know Kate *********?[4] I am stuffed out so with eating turkey for dinner, and another turkey for supper yesterday (turkey in Europe and turkey in Asia), that I can't jog on. It is New-Year here. That is, it was New-Year half a-year back, when I was writing this. Nothing puzzles me more than time and space, and yet nothing puzzles me less, for I never think about them.[5] Miss Knap is turned midwife. Never having had a child herself, she can't draw any wrong analogies from her own case. Dr. Stoddart has had Twins. There was five shillings to pay the Nurse. Mrs. Godwin was impannelled on a jury of Matrons last Sessions. She saved a criminal's life by giving it as her opinion that ————. The Judge listened to her with the greatest deference. The Persian ambassador[6] is the principal thing talked of now. I sent some people to see him worship the sun on Primrose Hill at half past six in the morning, 28th November; but he did not come, which makes me think the old fire-worshippers are a sect almost extinct in Persia. Have you trampled on the Cross yet? The Persian ambassador's name is Shaw Ali Mirza. The common people call him Shaw Nonsense. While I think of it, I have put three letters besides my own three into the India post for you, from your brother, sister,[7] and some gentleman whose name I forget. Will they, have they, did they, come safe? The distance you are at, cuts up tenses by the root. I think you said you did not know Kate *********. I express her by nine stars, though she is but one, but if ever one star differed from another in glory——. You must have seen her at her father's. Try and remember her. Coleridge is bringing out a paper in weekly numbers, called the 'Friend,' which I would send, if I could; but the difficulty I had in getting the packets of books out to you before deters me; and you'll want something new to read when you come home. It is chiefly intended to puff off Wordsworth's poetry; but there are some noble things in it by the by. Except Kate, I have had no vision of excellence this year, and she passed by like the queen on her coronation day; you don't know whether you saw her or not. Kate is fifteen: I go about moping, and sing the old pathetic ballad[8] I used to like in my youth—

> She's sweet Fifteen,
> I'm *one year more.*

Mrs. Bland sung it in boy's clothes the first time I heard it. I sometimes think the lower notes in my voice are like Mrs. Bland's. That glorious singer Braham, one of my lights, is fled. He was for a season.

He was a rare composition of the Jew, the gentleman, and the angel, yet all these elements mixed up so kindly in him, that you could not tell which predominated; but he is gone, and one Phillips[9] is engaged instead. Kate is vanished, but Miss B****** is always to be met with!

Queens drop away, while blue-legg'd Maukin thrives;
And courtly Mildred dies while country Madge survives.

That is not my poetry, but Quarles's; but haven't you observed that the rarest things are the least obvious? Don't show anybody the names in this letter. I write confidentially, and wish this letter to be considered as *private*. Hazlitt has written a *grammar*[10] for Godwin; Godwin sells it bound up with a treatise of his own on language, but the *grey mare is the better horse*. I don't allude to Mrs. Godwin, but to the word *grammar*, which comes near to *grey mare*, if you observe, in sound. That figure is called paranomasia[11] in Greek. I am sometimes happy in it. An old woman begged of me for charity. 'Ah! sir,' said she, 'I have seen better days'; So have I, good woman,' I replied; but I meant literally, days not so rainy and overcast as that on which she begged: she meant more prosperous days. Mr. Dawe is made associate of the Royal Academy. By what law of association I can't guess. Mrs. Holcroft, Miss Holcroft,[12] Mr. and Mrs. Godwin, Mr. and Mrs. Hazlitt, Mrs. Martin and Louisa, Mrs. Lum, Capt. Burney, Mrs. Burney, Martin Burney, Mr. Rickman, Mrs. Rickman, Dr. Stoddart, William Dollin, Mr. Thompson, Mr. and Mrs. Norris, Mr. Fenwick, Mrs. Fenwick, Miss Fenwick, a man that saw you at our house one day, and a lady that heard me speak of you; Mrs. Buffam that heard Hazlitt mention you, Dr. Tuthill, Mrs. Tuthill, Colonel Harwood, Mrs. Harwood, Mr. Collier, Mrs. Collier, Mr. Sutton, Nurse, Mr. Fell, Mrs. Fell, Mr. Marshall, are very well, and occasionally inquire after you.[13]

[I remain yours ever,
Ch. Lamb]

Mary sends her love.

* Where my family come from. I have chosen that if ever I should have my choice. [The first sentence in this note may be true: Stamford is in Lincolnshire; Lamb wrote in "Poor Relations" (*Works*, II, 161–162) of Lincoln, of his father as a schoolboy and mountain

climber there, of his aunt as "an old Lincolnian"; Lamb's "Susan
Yates: First Going to Church," in *Mrs. Leicester's School* (*Works,*
III, esp. 326–327), begins, "I was born and brought up, in a house
in which my parents had all their lives resided, which stood in the
midst of that lonely tract of land called the Lincolnshire fens," and
then proceeds to a description of the locality.—Ed.]

MS: unrecovered. Text: Lucas (1935), II, 89–92. Also pub.: Talfourd (1837),
I, 312–318; Sala, I, 405–410; Purnell, I, 405–410; Fitzgerald, II, 238–243; Hazlitt,
I, 404–407; Ainger (1888), I, 255–259; Ainger (1900), II, 179–184; Macdonald,
I, 319–323; Ainger (1904), I, 311–315; Harper, III, 301–306; Lucas (1905), VI,
408–410, and VII, 971–972; Lucas (1912), V, 429–432.

1. On March 29, 1809 (Letter 232).

2. An Edward Powell of that profession, of 41 Joiner Street, is listed in *The
Post-office Annual Directory* for 1810. *Holden's Annual Directory* for 1811 additionally lists George, of 9 Little Carter Lane; James, of 100 Wapping Street; and
John, of 28 Cross Street. The two volumes Lamb writes of below form *Poetry
for Children.*

3. See Letter 232, note 1. Tuthill, mentioned next, had earned his M.A. in
1809; he would not earn his M.D. until 1816. (See Vol. II, Letter 208, note 1.)
Lamb's sentence below regarding the children's book on titles of honor seems, with
what follows, to be an airy invention for Manning's amusement. This note about
it is in Lucas (1935), II, 92: "The circumstance that in 1805 [Richard] Phillips
put forth a little work called *The Book of the Rank and Dignities of British
Society* has, on the strength of Lamb's sentence, led to the association of his name
with it, and there are collectors [see page 230, note 29, of Carl Woodring's article
cited in my next sentence] who boldly ascribe it to him. But, more than doubtful,
I am utterly unconvinced. The evidence of style is against such an ascription; it is
not in the Lamb tradition, which, even when he was being a hack, insisted upon
themes calling for fancy and imagination." Carl Woodring in "Charles Lamb in
the Harvard Library," *Harvard Library Bulletin,* 10 (1956), 230–231, wrote that
the work "is usually called *The Book of the Ranks and Dignities of British Society,*
from a copy reprinted by Clement K. Shorter in 1924. The title-page of the copy
at Harvard reads thus: 'A Book Explaining the Ranks and Dignities of British
Society. Intended Chiefly for the Instruction of Young Persons. . . . London:
Printed for Tabart and Co. at the Juvenile and School Library, 157, New Bond-
Street, by Heney & Haddon, 12, Tabernacle-Walk. . . . 1809.' " Woodring explained that the colored frontispiece has a superscription containing the information "Pub. by Tabart & Co June 4–1805. New Bond St."; that the dedication is
dated November 1805 and signed "by The Author. *London,* Feb. 2, 1809"; that
there is in the book a leaf of advertisements for Richard Phillips; that in 1807 and
1808 the Godwins printed Tabart's name and address on some of their publications for the young; that Benjamin Tabart is listed as at the Juvenile Library in
The Post-office Annual Directory for 1803 and Tabart & Co. is listed as at 85
Piccadilly in *Kent's Directory* for 1817. The association of Godwin and Tabart,
the dates of and in the book, and this letter of Lamb's all hint at Lamb's association with the work. Yet Woodring's conclusion is still the sound one: "We must
reject Lucas' contention that Lamb just would not have written a humorless book
for children, but there is really no reasonable evidence whatsoever that he did
write one."

4. Unidentified. The further remarks about her in this letter intimate that she
too is Lamb's invention.

5. Cf. "Distant Correspondents" (*Works*, II, esp. 104). Miss Knap, mentioned following, has not been identified. About the John Stoddarts' twins see Vol. I, Letter 3, note 28.

6. Haji Mirza Abul Hasan Khan (b. 1776?), formerly the governor of the district of Shushtar, or Shushter, and from 1809 to 1810 the Persian ambassador to the Court of St. James. His portrait by Sir William Beechey (1753–1839) is in the collection of the India Office Library and Records. Haji Mirza was also immortalized by the diplomatist, traveler, and novelist James Justinian Morier (1780?–1849), in *The Adventures of Hajji Baba of Ispahan* (1824) and its sequel, *The Adventures of Hajji Baba of Ispahan in England* (1828). Primrose Hill, named below, is in Regent's Park, London.

7. "Miss F. Manning/Newnham/near/Cambridge" is the address on Lamb's letter to her of June 4, 1813 (Letter 274). Her and Thomas Manning's brother Edward (to whom Lamb here probably refers: see Letter 274, note 1, in the letter there quoted) is mentioned in the *Manning-Lamb Letters,* pp. 103 and 104, as of Lynn, Norfolk, in January 1808. Miss Manning and Edward have not been otherwise identified. Their brother William (1771–1857) was born in Broome, Norfolk, and attended Bury School, Bury St. Edmunds. In 1788 he was admitted to Gonville and Caius College, Cambridge, where he received his B.A. in 1793 and his M.A. in 1796. He was ordained a deacon at Norwich in 1794 and a priest in 1795. He served as a fellow of Caius from 1793 to 1805, as dean in 1799, as a lecturer in Greek in 1801, and as steward in 1802. He was made the rector of the college living at Wheeting, Norfolk, in 1804. From 1811 to his death he was in addition the rector of Diss. In 1812 he was married to Elizabeth, the daughter of William Sayer Donne and niece of the physician Edward Charles Donne (1777–1819). Edward Charles Donne was the father of the librarian, play examiner, and author William Bodham Donne (1807–1882), who came to know Thomas Manning, Henry Crabb Robinson, and the poet Edward FitzGerald. (Some of the information provided here on William Manning has been taken from the *Lloyd-Manning Letters,* p. 46.) The gentleman whom Lamb mentions following has not been identified.

8. Unidentified. The vocalist Maria Theresa Bland (1769–1838), mentioned below, was born Romanzini and was in 1790 married to the actor George Bland, the brother of Dorothea Jordan. (See Vol. II, Letter 208, note 3.) Mrs. Bland, whom Lamb would mention in "Old China" (*Works*, II, 250), performed regularly at Drury Lane from 1789 to 1824. John Braham (see Vol. II, Letter 222, note 6) was on a tour of the provinces in 1810 with the singer Mrs. Elizabeth Billington (1768–1818).

9. Thomas Philipps (1774–1841), who was a composer as well as a vocalist. Miss B******, alluded to below, is probably another of Lamb's inventions. If not, she almost certainly was not, to the contrary of what has been stated (in, for example, Lucas [1935], II, 92), the actress and singer Fanny Burrell (b. 1795), who had become Mrs. T. Gould by 1817, of whose singing Lamb will write fondly in his letter to Mrs. William Wordsworth of February 18, 1818 (in my Vol. IV), and whose acting he will praise in "Mrs. Gould (Miss Burrell) in 'Don Giovanni in London': Olympic Theatre" (*Works*, I, 372–373). She was only fourteen or fifteen at the time of this letter. She did not make her debut until 1815, according to Lillian Arvilla Hall's *Catalogue of Dramatic Portraits in the Theatre Collection of the Harvard College Library* (Cambridge: Harvard University Press, 1930), I, 187. And she was not "discovered by Lamb"—the words are Talfourd's, quoted in *Works*, I, 538—until she performed in the extravaganza by William Thomas Moncrieff (1794–1857), *Giovanni in London; or, the Libertine Reclaimed,* which did not open in London until December 26, 1817. Lamb's quotation is a corruption of Francis Quarles's "An Elegie," lines 142 and 144.

10. *A New and Improved Grammar of the English Tongue: For the Use of*

Schools . . . by William Hazlitt . . . To Which Is Added, A New Guide to the English Tongue, in a Letter to Mr. W. F. Mylius, Author of the School Dictionary. By Edward Baldwin, Esq. (London: M. J. Godwin, 1810). (See Letter 232, note 6.) Godwin wrote and published, again under his pseudonym Edward Baldwin, Esq., in 1810, *Outlines of English Grammar: Partly Abridged from Mr. Hazlitt's New and Improved Grammar.*

11. Properly "paronomasia": a playing on words of similar sounds; a pun. The anecdote about the beggar woman, related below, Lamb would incorporate in the 1822 version of "A Complaint of the Decay of Beggars in the Metropolis" (*Works,* II, 387).

12. Louisa and (presumably) Fanny Holcroft. The Hazlitts mentioned below could be either John and Mary or William and Sarah. Among those also mentioned below are John and Susannah Rickman, Marmaduke Thompson (possibly), Randal and Elizabeth Norris, John and Eliza and Eliza Anne Fenwick, George and Maria Tuthill, William and Ann Harwood (see Letter 296, note 9, in the entry about Ann Holcroft), John D. and Jane Collier, "Nurse" Mary Grant (probably), Ralph Fell and his wife, and (probably) James Marshal. Mrs. Lum, William Dollin, and Sutton have not been identified: a Mrs. Lum of 1 Stuart Street is listed in *Holden's Annual Directory* for 1811; Dollin is again mentioned in these letters, in Letter 259 (see its source note); a Mr. Sutton appears in Lamb's "Susan Yates: First Going to Church," in *Mrs. Leicester's School* (*Works,* III, 327). The unnamed man and lady are still unnamed.

13. The complimentary close, the signature, what is here treated as a postscript, and Lamb's note exist in only some editions of these letters, and the placement of what is here treated as a postscript varies from edition to edition: in his of 1905 Lucas placed "Mary sends her love" above the salutation, showed the letter to end with "inquire after you," and added "[*Rest cut away*]"; in his of 1935 Lucas placed "Mary sends her love" in two locations—both above the salutation and following "inquire after you"—and then added "[*Rest cut away*]." The complimentary close and signature here are provided from Macdonald, I, 323.

246. *C. L. to Robinson*

[February 7, 1810]

Dr R—

My Brother whom you have met at my rooms (a plump good looking man of seven & forty) has written a book about humanity,[1] which I transmit to you herewith. Wilson the Publisher has put it in his head that you can get it Reviewed for him. I dare say it is not in the scope of your Review—but if you could put it in any likely train, he would rejoyce. For alas! our boasted Humanity partakes of Vanity. As it is, he teazes me to death with chusing to suppose that I could get it into all the Reviews at a moments notice—I! ! who have been set up as a mark for them to throw at & would willingly consign them all to Hell flames & Megaera's snaky locks.—[2]

But here's the Book—& dont shew it Mrs. Collier, for I remember she makes excellent Eel soup, and the leading points of the Book are directed against that very process—[3]

Yours truly

C Lamb

At Home to-night—Wednesday

MS: Dr. Williams's Library. Pub.: Fitzgerald, III, Supplemental Letters; Hazlitt, I, 415–416; Ainger (1888), I, 266–267; Ainger (1900), II, 197; Macdonald, I, 332–333; Ainger (1904), I, 323–324; Harper, III, 306–307; Lucas (1905), VI, 411–412; Lucas (1912), V, 433–434; Lucas (1935), II, 93. Address: Henry Robinson Esq/56 Hatton Garden/with a Treatise on Cruelty to Animals. Date, by Robinson: Feby 7 1810.

1. *A Letter to the Right Hon. William Windham, on His Opposition to Lord Erskine's Bill, for the Prevention of Cruelty to Animals,* which was published, without John Lamb's name, by Maxwell and Walter Wilson (see Vol. II, Letter 107, source note) at 17 Skinner Street, Snow Hill, London, in 1810. The volume that Charles Lamb fashioned containing his copies of that treatise and other works—among them the *Speech of the Right Hon. W. Windham, in the House of Commons, June 13, 1809, on Lord Erskine's Bill for the More Effectual Prevention of Cruelty towards Animals* (London: J. Budd, 1810)—is described in Luther S. Livingston's "A Literary Curiosity from Charles Lamb's Library: Discovery of a Book That Has Hitherto Baffled Lamb Students," *The Bookman,* 8 (January 1899), 453–458. Lamb's volume, which is briefly described in *Bibliography of the Writings of Charles and Mary Lamb: A Literary History,* comp. J. C. Thomson (Hull: J. R. Tutin, 1908), pp. 137–138, is now in the collection of The Philip H. & A. S. W. Rosenbach Foundation. (See Doris Braendel, "The Lamb Collection at the Rosenbach Foundation: A Checklist," *Wordsworth Circle,* 2 [on its cover mistakenly marked "Volume III"] [Summer 1971], 88–90, items 93, 97, 100, 106, and 116.) Robinson's "Review," mentioned below, was the *London Review,* which Robinson had cofounded with the dramatist Richard Cumberland (1732–1811) in February 1809. It had ceased, apparently without Lamb's knowledge, after four quarterly numbers in two volumes—February to May and August to November—in November 1809. (See *H. C. R. on Books and Writers,* I, 13.) I know of no review of John Lamb's treatise.

2. *Paradise Lost,* X, 559–560. Megaera ("the denier") is, with her sister Furies, or Eumenides, depicted with snakes in her hair.

3. Here is the passage directed against that process, quoted from Lucas (1935), II, 94:

> If an eel had the wisdom of Solomon, he could not help himself in the ill-usage that befalls him; but if he had, and were told, that it was necessary for our subsistence that he should be eaten, that he must be skinned first, and then broiled; if ignorant of man's usual practice, he would conclude that the cook would so far use her reason as to cut off his head first, which is not fit for food, as then he might be skinned and broiled without harm; for however the other parts of his body might be convulsed during the culinary operations, there could be no feeling of consciousness therein, the communication with the brain being cut off; but if the woman were immediately to stick a fork into his eye, skin him alive, coil him up in a skewer, head and all, so that in the extremest agony he could not move, and forthwith broil him to death: then were the same Almighty Power that formed man from the dust, and breathed into his nostrils the breath of life, to call the eel into

a new existence, with a knowledge of the treatment he had undergone, and he found that the instinctive disposition which man has in common with other carnivorous animals, which inclines him to cruelty, was not the sole cause of his torments; but that men did not attend to consider whether the sufferings of such insignificant creatures could be lessened: that eels were not the only sufferers; that lobsters and other shell fish were put into cold water and boiled to death by slow degrees in many parts of the sea coast; that these, and many other such wanton atrocities, were the consequence of carelessness occasioned by the pride of mankind despising their low estate, and of the general opinion that there is no punishable sin in the ill-treatment of animals designed for our use; that, therefore, the woman did not bestow so much thought on him as to cut his head off first, and that she would have laughed at any considerate person who should have desired such a thing; with what fearful indignation might he inveigh against the unfeeling metaphysician that, like a cruel spirit alarmed at the appearance of a dawning of mercy upon animals, could not rest satisfied with opposing the Cruelty Prevention Bill by the plea of possible inconvenience to mankind, highly magnified and emblazoned, but had set forth to the vulgar and unthinking of all ranks, in the jargon of proud learning, that man's obligations of morality towards the creatures subjected to his use are imperfect obligations!

The passage is also given in *The Bookman,* 8 (January 1899), 454–455.

247.   *C. L. to John Mathew Gutch*

[February 9, 1810]

Dear G————

I did not see your Brother who brought the Withers, but I understood he said you were daily expecting to come to Town. This has prevented my writing. The Books have pleased me excessively. I should think you could not have made a better selection. I never saw Philarete before. Judge of my pleasure. I could not forbear scribbling certain Critiques in *Pencil* on the blank leaves. Shall I send them? or—may I expect to see you in Town? Some of them are remarks on the Character of Wither & of his writings. Do you mean to have any thing of that kind? What I have writ on Philarete is poor, but I think some of the rest not so bad. At all Events shall I send them? I have noted typographical & sometimes **Editorial** slips—in commas &c I am afraid **too late to correct**—. Perhaps I have exceeded my commission in scrawling over the Copies, but my Delight therein must excuse me, & Pencil marks will rub out: Where is the **Life?**— Write for I am quite in the dark.

Yours with many Thanks
C Lamb

Perhaps I could digest the few Critiques prefixed to the Satires, Huntings &c into a short Abstract of *W's character & works* at the end of the life. But may be you dont want any thing & have said all you wish in the Life.[1]

MS: By permission of the Harvard College Library, Cambridge, Mass. Pub.: Fitzgerald, III, 106; Hazlitt, I, 408–409; Ainger (1888), I, 259; Ainger (1900), II, 186–187; Macdonald, I, 323–324; Ainger (1904), I, 316; Harper, III, 308–309; Lucas (1905), VI, 413–414; Lucas (1912), V, 436; Lucas (1935), II, 99–100. Address: Mr. J. M. Gutch/Small Street/Bristol. Postmark: February 9, 1810. About Gutch see Vol. I, Introduction, pp. xxxvi–xxxvii.

1. "There are now before me," wrote Swinburne in "Charles Lamb and George Wither" (*The Complete Works of Algernon Charles Swinburne,* ed. Sir Edmund Gosse and Thomas James Wise [London: Heinemann; New York: Wells, 1925–1927], IV, 248), "the two volumes of selections from the lyrical and satirical poems of George Wither, rather meanly printed, in small octavo proof-sheets, interleaved with quarto sheets of rough thin paper, which are made precious by the manuscript commentary of Lamb. The second fly-leaf of the first volume bears the inscription, 'Jas Pulham Esqr. from Charles Lamb.' A proof impression of the well-known profile sketch of Lamb by Pulham has been inserted between this and the preceding fly-leaf. The same place is occupied in the second volume by the original pencil drawing, to which is attached an engraving of it 'Scratched on Copper by his Friend Brook Pulham'; and on the fly-leaf following is a second inscription, 'James Pulham Esq. from his friend Chas Lamb.' On the reverse of the leaf inscribed with these names in the first volume begins the commentary afterwards republished, with slight alterations and transpositions, as an essay 'on the poetical works of George Wither.' " The two volumes about which Swinburne wrote are those that make up the edition of the selection of Wither's poems Gutch had printed (probably on the presses he used to print *Felix Farley's Bristol Journal*), had one of his brothers bring to Lamb (see the last sentence in this note), and in which Lamb had scribbled his "certain Critiques" (a page and three-quarters of them, on paper watermarked 1807, are in the Berg Collection, New York Public Library) and taken the pleasure he expresses in this letter. Thus "encouraged to proceed in his selection by his warm-hearted friend and schoolfellow, Charles Lamb," remarked Gutch on the development of the edition in the Appendix to his *Robin Hood Garlands and Ballads, with the Tale of the Lytell Geste* (London: John Russell Smith and Joseph Lilly, 1850), I, 321, Gutch, upon Lamb's return of the volumes, took them for another opinion to another friend— the physician and classical scholar John Nott (1751–1825) of the Hot Wells, Bristol. In them Nott commented on Wither and on Lamb's critiques. Gutch remarked that he sent the volumes back to Lamb when Lamb, perhaps in 1815, certainly by 1818, requested them for the purpose of preparing "On the Poetical Works of George Wither" (*Works,* I, 181–184). Seeing Nott's commentary prompted Lamb to comment on Nott, sarcastically, in the volumes, and to add there to his original critiques of Wither. By 1825, presumably, Lamb had presented the volumes, which Gutch had apparently presented to him, to James Brook Pulham (d. 1860). Pulham, who had been appointed to the treasurer's department of the East India House in 1807 and was retired in 1835, in 1825 did the caricature in profile of Lamb that Swinburne noticed and that is, in one of its states, reproduced in Volume V of this edition of Lamb letters. Gutch in the meantime had proceeded with Nott in the preparation of an expanded edition of Wither's poems. The result, in which Nott incorporated as his own many of Lamb's critiques that are in the copy of the two-volume edition formerly in

Lamb's possession, is listed under Wither's name in the *British Museum General Catalogue of Printed Books,* CCLIX, 787: "Juvenilia; a Collection of Poems. 2 vol. (Vol. 3–4: Fair Virtue.—Selections from Abuses Stript and Whipt.—Selections from Britain's Remembrancer.—Selections from a collection of emblems.—Selections from Hallelujah.) [Edited by J. M. Gutch and John Nott.] 4 vol. [Bristol, 1820.] *Vols. 3 and 4, bound in one, are without any general title-pages; and all before sig. C 3 of vol. 4 is apparently wanting. The Juvenilia is a reprint of the edition of 1622, and the other portions are reprints of various editions.*" Lucas, who saw that copy of the four-volume edition, noted that there is this inscription on one of its flyleaves: "This selection of the Poems of Wither was printed by Gutch, of Bristol, about twenty years since, and was edited by Dr. Nott. The work remained unfinished, and was sold for waste-paper; a few copies only were preserved. 1839" (*Works,* I, 456). The copy of the two-volume edition formerly in Lamb's possession, the copy that had passed among Gutch and Lamb and Nott and that Lamb had presented to Pulham, passed into Swinburne's library at The Pines, Putney. It moved Swinburne, who idolized Lamb, to write "Charles Lamb and George Wither" in order to give "a fuller account than has yet been given of Lamb's remarks on Wither and his editors or critics" (*The Complete Works of . . . Swinburne,* IV, 247–248); to publish the essay in *Nineteenth Century,* 17 (January 1885), 66–91; and to republish it, in 1886, as part of his *Miscellanies* (pp. 157–200). In the present letter Lamb mentions Wither's *Faire Virtve, the Mistress of Phil'Arete* (1622), the satires—*Abuses Stript and Whipt* (1613) and *Wither's Motto: Nec Habeo, Nec Careo, Nec Curo* (1621)—and *The Shepherd's Hunting* (1615). Lamb asks about the life of Wither that Gutch wrote and printed but neither included with the poems nor published and that Lamb probably never saw. The following passage about it is in a letter from Gutch to one Edward Farr of March 2, 1857, a passage Farr quoted in his letter to *The Athenaeum,* No. 1590 (April 17, 1858), 500: "When I quitted Bristol I left in the warehouse the sheets of all that I had printed, but on my inspection of the parcels I found that many sheets had been either purloined or eaten by mice,—so that if I had not preserved for my own private library sheets of all, I could not have made a perfect copy. This I have done, and it is the only one in existence." Farr, who thought Gutch to be deceased—the *DNB* and the obituary in the *Gentleman's Magazine,* 211 (December 1861), 682–686, show the date of Gutch's death as September 20, 1861—was inquiring after the whereabouts of Gutch's biography of and communications pertaining to Wither. A *Catalogue of the . . . Library of John Mathew Gutch . . . Which Will Be Sold by Auction . . . on . . . 16th of March, 1858, and Eight Following Days* (London[: Sotheby & Wilkinson], 1858) is shown to be in the British Museum. In *The Athenaeum,* No. 1588 (April 3, 1858), 436, and in the *Gentleman's Magazine,* 211 (December 1861), 685–686, are listings of some of the items for sale and sold. Gutch's printed sheets forming the biography of Wither are not mentioned. I have not been able to identify Gutch's brother who brought to Lamb the two volumes of Wither's poems, but Gutch's brothers are identified in the *Gentleman's Magazine,* 190 and 211 (November 1851 and December 1861), 549–550 and 684: Robert (1777–1851), a Christ's Hospitaler, a Cantabrigian, the author of published occasional sermons and of a tract, from 1801 to perhaps 1809 the curate of Epsom, Surrey, and from 1809 to his death the rector of Segrave, Leicestershire (pp. 549–550); Richard, who "died a young man, after having been a *détenu* in France, and escaping from Verdun"; Charles, who "died when a boy"; and George, the youngest, who in 1861 lived in Paddington, London, and was "one of the District Surveyors of the county of Middlesex" (p. 684).

248. *C. L. to George Dawe*

Monday [February 26? 1810]

Dear Sir,

I may seem not a little inappetent of a treat by neglecting this night's opportunity of hearing Mr. Fuseli. But the truth is, I am invited to meet John Thelwal of democratic fame, which may be my only opportinity of seeing the illustrious Ex-demagogue; and for Mr. F. I have, by your indulgence, 3 nights more to come. I hope you will not have come out of your way to join me & that this Letter may be useless: but if you read it, I hope you will admit of its plea. "Song" (and I suppose *Painting too*) Milton says "charms the sense, Eloquence the Soul."[1] And John is eloquent.

Yours

C Lamb

(turn over)

in case you should come, which you left in great doubt, or else I should not have taken the liberty of altering my engagement, I hope you will make use of my old woman[2] to get you Tea; I have given orders to that effect—

MS: Mr. W. Hugh Peal, Leesburg, Va. Unpublished. Address, on a scrap of paper pasted to the letter: Mr. Dawe. My dating of the letter is derived from this information: Henry Fuseli, according to John Knowles's *The Life and Writings of Henry Fuseli* (3 vols.; London: Henry Colburn and Richard Bentley, 1831), I, 304, resumed a course of lectures on painting at the Royal Academy on Monday, February 26, 1810; John Thelwall (see my Vol. I, Letter 21, note 8) had by that time taken the large house, at 57 Lincoln's Inn Fields, in which he gave lodging to those whose speech impediments he was trying to correct and entertained the public with talks on elocution and literature and readings from poems and plays; Lamb—according to the description of Thelwall in Talfourd's *Literary Sketches and Letters: Being the Final Memorials of Charles Lamb, Never before Published* (see Letter 242, note 1), p. 253—sometimes attended those entertainments.

1. *Paradise Lost,* II, 556.
2. Mary, presumably.

249. *C. L. to Charles Lloyd, the elder*

E. I. Ho.
10 Mar. 1810

[. . .]

"Parade of dress"[1] strikes the ear as too modern; though in reality the modernest English is not more removed from Greek than the ancientest, yet the imagination is unwilling to receive a word in a Translation of Homer which has not the sanction of years.

[. . .]

"Whelming tide."[2] A bad Epithet. We may speak of Vessels sunk beneath the whelming tide, but hardly of vessels sailing over it. It is a property of the sea to overwhelm, but ships riding over it do not naturally remind one of that property.

[. . .]

Patriotic[3] strikes my ears also as too modern. Besides that in English few words of more than three syllables chime well into a verse.

[. . .]

[. . .][4] modern and novel phraseology. I mean the phrase of novels. The word sentiment was scarcely Anglicised before the time of Sterne.

[. . .]

Sentiments[5]—I would root this word out of a translation of Homer. It came in with Sterne, and was a child he had by Affectation.

[. . .]

I doubt if Homer had any such an idea as we have when we talk of *striving to excel in virtue.*[6] I am afraid the phrase is more correspondent to the Telemachus of Fenelon than of Homer. Orestes' revengeful slaughter of Ægisthus is the model to which Nestor directs Telemachus, something different from what we mean by virtue.

[. . .]

Exit[7] is a sad tombstone-word. It is thrice bad: bad as being Latin; as being a word of stage-direction; and as being inscribed on half the tombstones in the Kingdom.

[. . .]

"Envy will pine, &c.
Benevolence survey it with delight."[8]

I should suspect these personifications are the Translator's. They sound *post*-Homeric.

[. . .]

Uncle[9]—rather a hazardous word; would you call Pallas his niece? I cannot conceive of such relationships as Uncles and Nieces and Cousins (at least the names of them) among the Gods.

My Dear Sir,—

The above are all the faults I, who profess myself to be a mere English Reader, could find after a scrupulous perusal twice over of your neat little Book. I assure you it gave me great pleasure in the perusal, much more in this shape than in the Manuscript, and I should be very sorry you should give up the finishing of it on so poor pretence as your *Age*,[10] which is not so much by ten years as Dryden's when he wrote his fables, which are his best works allowed, and not more than Milton's when he had scarce entered upon his original Epic Poem. You have done nearly a third; persevere and let us see the whole. I am sure I should prize it for its Homeric plainness and truth above the confederate jumble of Pope, Broome and Fenton[11] which goes under Pope's name, and is far inferior to his **Iliad**. I have picked out what I think blemishes, but they are but a score of words (I am a mere word pecker) in six times as many pages. The rest all gave me pleasure, and most of all the Book in which Ulysses and Nausicaa meet.[12] You have infused a kind of biblical patriarchal manner into it, it reads like some story of Jacob and Rachel, or some of those primitive manners. I am ashamed to carp at words, but I did it in obedience to your desires, and the plain reason why I did not acknowledge your kind present *sooner* was that I had no criticisms of value to make. I shall certainly beg the opinion of my friend[13] who read the two first Books on this enlarged Performance. But he is so very much engaged that I cannot at present get at him, and besides him I have no acquaintance that takes much interest in Poetry, Greek or English. But I hope and adjure you to go on and do not make excuses of Age till you have completed the Odyssey, and done a great part of Horace besides. Then you will be entitled to hang up your Harp.

I am, dear Sir, with Love to all your family,

Your hble. Serv.,

C. Lamb

MS: unrecovered. Text: *Lamb and the Lloyds,* pp. 214–219, here reconstructed. Also pub.: Ainger (1900), II, 185–186; Ainger (1904), I, 315–316; Harper, III, 307–308; Lucas (1935), II, 95–97. Here Lamb's criticisms and evaluation are of the senior Charles Lloyd's *A Translation of the First Seven Books of the Odyssey of Homer.* (See Letter 238, note 1, and Letter 239.) The bracketed ellipses in my reconstruction of this letter replace passages of Lamb's criticisms that Lucas believed too slight, it would seem, to be published in *Lamb and the Lloyds.* The other texts of this letter were derived from that text.

1. In Lloyd's translation of Book I, a portion of lines 199–200—"Should he return, their fears would soon express / How much swift feet excell'd parade of dress"—for "*εἰ κεῖνόν γ' Ἰθάκηνδε ἰδοίατο νοστήσαντα, / πάντες κ' ἀρησαίατ' ἐλαφρότεροι πόδας εἶναι / ἢ ἀφνειότεροι χρυσοῖό τε ἐσθῆτός τε,*" in Homer's Book I, lines 163–165.

2. In Lloyd's Book I, line 200, for *οἴνοπα πόντον,* in Homer's Book I, line 183.

3. In Lloyd's Book II, line 44, for *ἐσθλός* in Homer's Book II, line 33.

4. The phrase "express his sentiments," in Lloyd's Book II, line 107, for *προσέειπε* in Homer's Book II, line 84. The use of "sentiment(s)" (from the Latin *sentire*) to mean "attitude" or "opinion" dates from 1639. Observed in the *DNB* is that the humorist and sentimentalist Laurence Sterne (1713–1768) first used the epithet "sentimental" in a letter of 1740.

5. In Lloyd's Book II, line 161—"Those sentiments, as tho' by heaven imprest"—for "*. . . κείνη τοῦτον ἔχῃ νόον, ὅν τινά οἱ νῦν / ἐν στήθεσσι τιθεῖσι θεοί. μέγα μὲν κλέος αὐτῇ,*" in Homer's Book II, lines 124–125.

6. In Lloyd's Book III, line 254—"Be brave, and strive in virtue to excel"—for "*ἄλκιμος ἔσσ', ἵνα τίς σε καὶ ὀψιγόνων εὖ εἴπῃ,*" in Homer's Book III, line 200. Lamb writes generally of Lloyd's Book III, lines 245–262:

> . . . Atrides' fate,
> As this ye know, 'tis needless to relate,
> How he return'd, and by a treach'rous wife,
> And base Ægisthus' treason lost his life;
> But vengeance soon pursued these wicked deeds,
> And by Orestes' hands the traitor bleeds;
> Ægisthus guileful he deprived of breath,
> And thus revenged his noble father's death:
> And thou, my friend, of whom I augur well,
> Be brave, and strive in virtue to excel,   [254]
> That thy good deeds may live in future days,
> And be reported with deserved praise.
> To him Telemachus again replied:
> O Nestor! son of Neleus, Græcia's pride!
> Orestes justly made Ægisthus bleed,
> And all the Greeks applaud the filial deed;
> His memory will live in future song:
> Oh, that to me such courage did belong!

About François de Salignac de la Mothe Fénelon see my Vol. I, Letter 96, note 3; about his *Télémaque* see Vol. II, Letter 222, note 4.

7. In Lloyd's Book V, line 364, for *θανάτῳ* in Homer's Book V, line 312.

8. In Lloyd's Book VI, lines 241–242—"Envy will pine at such a happy sight, / Benevolence surveys it with delight"—for "*. . . πόλλ' ἄλγεα δυσμενέεσσι, / χάρματα δ' εὐμενέτῃσι. μάλιστα δέ τ' ἔκλυον αὐτοί,*" in Homer's Book VI, lines 184–185.

9. In Lloyd's Book VI, line 423, for *πατροκασίγνητον* in Homer's Book VI, line 330.

10. Sixty-one. Dryden was sixty-eight when he published *Fables, Ancient and Modern* (1700), referred to below; Milton was perhaps forty-nine when he turned seriously to the composition of *Paradise Lost.*

11. The translator and divine William Broome (1689–1745) and the poet Elijah Fenton (1683–1730), to both of whom Pope denied proper credit for their work on his translation of the *Odyssey*.

12. Their meeting is described in Lloyd's Book VI, lines 167–257. The story of the meeting and union of Jacob and Rachel, mentioned below, is told in Genesis 29:9–30.

13. Probably John Stoddart. (See Letter 239, note 1.) Concerning the penultimate sentence in Lamb's paragraph see Letter 238, note 1; Letter 237, note 7; and Letter 268 and its notes.

250.   *M. A. L. to Sarah Stoddart Hazlitt*

[Friday, March 30, 1810]

My dear Sarah

I have taken a large sheet of paper as if I were going to write a long letter, but that is by no means my intention, for I only have time to write three lines to notify, what I ought to have done the moment I received your welcome letter. Namely that I shall be very much joyed to see you.[1] Every morning lately I have been expecting to see you drop in, even before your letter came, and I have been setting my wits to work to think how to make you as comfortable as the nature of our inhospitable habits will admit. I must work while you are here, and I have been striving very hard to get through with something before you come that I may be quite in the way of it, and not teize you with complaints all day that I do not know what to do.

I am very sorry to hear of your mischance.[2] Mrs Rickman has just buried her youngest child. I am glad I am an old maid, for you see there is nothing but misfortunes in the marriage state.

Charles was drunk last night, and drunk the night before, which night before was at Godwins, where we went, at a short summons from Mrs G. to play a solitary rubber, which was interrupted by the entrance of Mr & little Mrs Liston[3] and after them came Henry Robinson who is now domesticated at Mrs Godwin's fireside & likely to become a formidable rival to Tommy Turner. We finished there at twelve Oclock, Charles and Liston brimfull of Gin & water & snuff, A[f]ter which Henry Robinson spent a long evening by our fireside at home and there was much gin & water drunk, albeit only one of the party partook of it. And H. R professed himself highly indebted to Charles for the useful information he gave him on sundry matters of taste and imagination, even after Charles could not speak plain for tipsyness. But still he swallowed the flattery and the spirits as savourily as Robinson did his cold water.

Last night was to be a night of temperance, but it was not. There was a certain son of one of Martin's employers One young Mr Blake[4] to do whom honor, Mrs Burney brought forth, first rum, then a single bottle of champaine, long kept kept in her secret hoard—then two bottles of her best current wine which she keeps for Mrs Rickman came out & Charles partook liberally of all these beverages, while Mr Young Blake & Mr Ireton talked of high matters such as the merits of the Whip Club & the merits of red & white champaine. Do I spell that last word right? Rickman was not there so Ireton had it all his own way.

The alternating Wednesdays[5] will chop off one day in the week from your jolly days and I do not know how we shall make it up to you but I will contrive the best I can. Mr Phillips comes again pretty regularly, to the great joy of Mrs Reynolds. Once more she hears the well-loved sounds of "How do you do Mrs Reynolds? How does Miss Chambers do?"

I have spun out my three lines amazingly. Now for family news. Your brothers little twins are not dead, but Mrs John Hazlitt & her baby may be for anything I know to the contrary for I have not been there for a prodigious long time. Mrs Holcroft still goes about from Nicholson[6] to Tuthil & from Tuthil to Godwin, & from Godwin to Tuthil & from Tuthil to Nicholson to consult on the publication or no publication of the life of the good man her husband. It is called the Life Everlasting. How does that same Life go on in your parts?

Good bye, God bless you, I shall be glad to see you when you come this way.

Yours most affectionately

M Lamb

I am going in great haste to see Mrs Clarkson[7] for I must get back to dinner, which I have hardly time to do. I wish that dear good amiable woman would go out of town. I thought she was clean gone & yesterday there was a consultation of Physicians held at her house to see if they could keep her among them here a few weeks longer.

MS: Berg Collection, New York Public Library. Pub.: Lucas (1905), VI, 426–428; Lucas (1912), V, 449–451; Lucas (1935), II, 97–99. Address: Mrs. Hazlitt/ at Mr Hazlitt's/Winterslow/near/Salisbury. Postmark: March 30, 1810.

1. Sarah Hazlitt was with the Lambs in probably April 1810. A letter of 1810 to her from Hazlitt at Salisbury, directed to Lamb at the East India House, is published, with the incorrect date of April 1809 and other inaccuracies (see *Hazlitt*, pp. 170 and 491), in *Lamb and Hazlitt*, pp. 105–108.

2. Sarah Hazlitt had miscarried on March 6. The details of a record of her miscarriages and the births and deaths of her and Hazlitt's children, a record kept apparently by her and now in the British Museum (Add. MS. 38,898), are given in *Hazlitt*, p. 170: a son (William), born on January 15, died on July 5, 1809; miscarriages on March 6 and September 6, 1810; William, born on September 26, 1811 (see Letter 264, note 1); a miscarriage on October 15, 1813; and John, born on September 28, 1815, died while ill with the measles on June 19, 1816. Susannah (Mrs. John) Rickman, mentioned following, and her husband had buried their infant Martha at St. Margaret's Church, Westminster, on March 14, 1810. Mrs. Gertrude Alison Anderson located that date in the registers of St. Margaret's and made it public in "On the Dating of Lamb's Letters," *London Mercury*, 18 (August 1928), 393.

3. The comedian John Liston (1776?–1846), whose spurious biography Lamb would concoct in "Biographical Memoir of Mr. Liston" (*Works*, I, 248–254), and the comedienne the former Sarah Tyrer (1780?–1854), to whom Liston had been married in 1806 or 1807. After serving as a master in 1799 at St. Martin's grammar school, Leicester Square, and touring with the actor Stephen, or George Stephen, Kemble (1758–1822) in the north of England, Liston was engaged in 1805 to play comic parts at the Haymarket. He performed there almost yearly until 1830. He performed, additionally, at Covent Garden from 1806 to 1822 and at Drury Lane in 1823. In perhaps 1831 he was engaged at the Olympic, from which he retired in 1837, the highest-paid comic actor of his day. His wife played first in Dublin. From 1801 to 1805 she was at Drury Lane and the Haymarket, where she made famous the character of Queen Dollalolla in *Tom Thumb*, by the burlesque writer Kane O'Hara (1714?–1782). Mrs. Liston made her first appearance at Covent Garden in 1806 and her last, on that or any other stage, in 1822. The Listons' daughter Emma became the wife of the composer George Herbert Buonaparte Rodwell (1800–1852), who would study under Vincent Novello, one of Lamb's correspondents in later years. Robinson was not living with the Godwins, as Mary's remarks below suggest. He was, however, so he wrote in his reminiscences for 1810, becoming "more acquainted with Godwin . . . , was with him frequently, though his acquaintance was of the least agreeable kind. He made me feel my inferiority unpleasantly, and also in another way disagreeably by demands on my purse for small sums, and trying to make use of me with others. I now and then saw interesting persons at his house; indeed, I saw none but remarkable persons there" (*H. C. R. on Books and Writers*, I, 14). Thomas Turner of London and Binfield, Berkshire, was an attorney who had been Godwin's friend since 1803. In 1812 Turner was married to Cornelia (b. 1795), the daughter of Lafayette's aide-de-camp Jean-Baptiste Chastel de Boinville (d. 1813) and of the former Harriet Collins. It was Mrs. Boinville and Mrs. Turner who in 1814 moved Shelley to write "Lines [or "Stanza"] Written at Bracknell" and "Stanzas: April 1814."

4. He (whose first name is not known), whom Martin Burney came to know presumably while pursuing his legal career, was perhaps a son of the senior partner in the law firm of Blake and White, London. That firm is listed in *Kent's Directory* for 1810 and in *Holden's Annual Directory* for 1811. The latter directory lists four other attorneys named Blake, but only one partnership—Mary's language implies a partnership—with that name in its title. (See Letter 243, note 2.) Ireton, mentioned below, is almost certainly the musical writer William Ayrton (1777–1858). He and his wife were neighbors of the James Burneys in Little James Street, Pimlico (see *H. C. R. on Books and Writers*, I, 16), were friends of

Robinson and the Rickmans, and were to become correspondents of the Lambs. Probably it was Ayrton to whom Lamb would allude in "my friend A.'s piano," in "A Chapter on Ears" (*Works,* II, 38). Ayrton, the younger son of the distinguished musician Edmund Ayrton (1734–1808), became the musical director of the King's Theatre for the 1817 and 1821 seasons. (See Letter 326, note 1.) He contributed to, and from 1823 to 1833 edited, the periodical *The Harmonicon.* He published his *Sacred Minstrelsy* during the period 1834 to 1835 and his collection of instrumental and vocal music called the *Musical Library* during the period 1834 to 1836. His wife, Marianne, to whom he had been married in 1803, was the daughter of the composer Dr. Samuel Arnold (1740–1802) and the sister of the dramatist Samuel James Arnold (1774–1852). The Whip Club, whose name had been changed in 1809 to The Four-in-hand Club, was an organization of amateur coach and carriage drivers. Its regalia and examples of its exercises are described in John Ashton's *The Dawn of the XIXth Century in England* (5th ed.; London: T. Fisher Unwin, 1906), pp. 189–194.

5. The evenings in which the Lambs at this time entertained. Phillips, of whom Mary writes below, is Edward Phillips. Mrs. Reynolds had been Miss Elizabeth Chambers.

6. See Letter 232, note 1, about him and about what became *Memoirs of the Late Thomas Holcroft.*

· 7. Dorothy Wordsworth's letter to Catherine Clarkson of April 12–13, 1810, shows that Mrs. Clarkson was staying at Hatcham House, New Cross, London, the home of her uncle Joseph Hardcastle (1753–1819), a Methodist, philanthropist, and cotton importer. Miss Wordsworth's next published letter to Mrs. Clarkson, of May 11, 1810, is addressed to her at the home of her brother-in-law, John Clarkson (initially identified in Vol. II, Letter 187, note 1), at Purfleet, Grays, Essex. See *Wordsworths' Letters,* II, 395 and 407; the information given above about Hardcastle is drawn from I, 487.

251. *C. L. to Basil Montagu*

Mr. Hazlitt's, Winterslow, near Sarum

[Thursday,] 12th July, 1810

Dear [Montague,—]

I have turned and twisted the MSS.[1] in my head, and can make nothing of them. I knew when I took them that I could not; but I do not like to do an act of ungracious necessity at once; so I am ever committing myself by half-engagements and total failures. I cannot make any body understand why I can't do such things. It is a defect in my occiput. I cannot put other people's thoughts together. I forget every paragraph, as fast as I read it; and my head has received such a shock by an all-night journey on the top of the coach, that I shall have enough to do to nurse it into its natural pace before I go home. I must devote myself to imbecility. I must be gloriously useless while I stay here. How is Mrs. [M.]? Will she pardon my inefficiency? The city of Salisbury is full of weeping and wailing. The Bank has stopt payment;

XV. John Milton. From the Lenox Portrait, an oil painting possibly by Sir Peter Lely (1618–1680), owned by Charles Lamb from 1821 to 1833. Courtesy of the Collection of The New York Public Library, Astor, Lenox and Tilden Foundations. See Letter 291, note 5.

XVI. Facsimile of the first page of a letter from Charles Lamb to Samuel Taylor Coleridge, June 7, 1809 (Letter 236). By permission of The Huntington Library, San Marino, California.

and every body in the town kept money at it, or has got some of its notes. Some have lost all they had in the world. It is the next thing to seeing a city with the plague within its walls. The Wilton people are all undone. All the manufacturers there kept cash at the Salisbury bank; and I do suppose it to be the unhappiest county in England, this where I am making holiday.

We purpose setting out for Oxford Tuesday fortnight, and coming thereby home.[2] But no more night-travelling. My head is sore (understand it of the inside,) with that deduction from my natural rest, which I suffered coming down. Neither Mary nor I can spare a morsel of our rest. It is incumbent on us to be misers of it. Travelling is not good for us—we travel so seldom. If the Sun be Hell, it is not for the fire, but for the sempiternal motion of that miserable Body of Light. How much more dignified leisure hath a muscle,[3] glued to his unpassable rocky limit, two inch square. He hears the tide roll over him backwards and forwards twice a day, (as the d——d Salisbury Long Coach goes and returns in eight and forty hours,) but knows better than to take an outside night-place a top on't. He is the Owl[4] of the Sea. Minerva's fish. The fish of Wisdom!

Our kindest remembrances to Mrs. [M].

Yours truly,
C. Lamb

MS: unrecovered. Text: "C" (the initial of "Barry Cornwall," a pseudonym of Bryan Waller Procter), "Recollections of Charles Lamb," *The Athenaeum*, No. 378 (January 24, 1835), 73. Also pub.: Talfourd (1837), I, 318–320; Purnell, II, 102–104; Fitzgerald, III, 23–25; Hazlitt, I, 410–411; Ainger (1888), I, 260–261; Ainger (1900), II, 187–189; Macdonald, I, 324–325; Ainger (1904), I, 317–318; Harper, III, 309–311; Lucas (1905), VI, 415; Lucas (1912), V, 437–438; Lucas (1935), II, 100–101. The locutions within square brackets, locutions taken from Talfourd's text, are used in place of the two-em dashes in Procter's text. Procter's text seems not only to be closer than the texts of others to what the original must have been, but seems also to have been derived, as was probably Talfourd's alone among the others, from the original. See my Vol. II, Letter 132, note 2, for the identifications of Montagu; his third (and present) wife, Anna; and her daughter, Anne, later the wife of Procter. "Lamb," it is noted in Lucas (1935), II, 102, "probably addressed to him [Montagu] many other letters, also to his third wife. . . . But the correspondence was destroyed by Mrs. Procter." It is not known precisely when the Lambs had left home for Winterslow. According to this and the next letter, the Lambs intended to leave Winterslow for Oxford and Blenheim Palace, Oxfordshire, on Tuesday, July 24, and were back home by Monday, August 6. They would in all likelihood have been away from the Temple for about a month.
1. Manuscripts, explained Procter, somewhat, in *The Athenaeum*, No. 378

(January 24, 1835), 73, that Lamb "was requested to reconstruct . . . on the subject of the punishment of Death."

2. This sentence, particularly, indicates it was of this visit that Hazlitt wrote in the second part of "On the Conversation of Authors" (*Hazlitt's Works*, XII, 42): "L—— once came down into the country to see us. He was 'like the most capricious poet Ovid among the Goths.' The country people thought him an oddity, and did not understand his jokes. It would be strange if they had; for he did not make any, while he staid. But when we crossed the country to Oxford, then he spoke a little. He and the old colleges were hail-fellow well met; and in the quadrangles, he 'walked gowned.'" (Hazlitt's quotations are, in order, from *As You Like It*, III, iii, 7–8; and Lamb's sonnet "Written at Cambridge," line 8 [*Works*, V, 55].)

3. For "mussel."

4. The attribute and favorite bird of Minerva (the Roman deity identified with the Greek Athena, or Pallas Athene), the goddess of wisdom.

252. *C. L. to William Hazlitt*
Thursday [August 9, 1810]

Dear H.,

Epistemon[1] is not well. Our pleasant excursion has ended sadly for one of us. You will guess I mean my sister. She got home very well (I was very ill on the journey) and continued so till Monday night, when her complaint came on, and she is now absent from home.

I am glad to hear you are all well. I think I shall be mad if I take any more journeys with two experiences against it. I find all well here. Kind remembrances to Sarah—have just got her letter.

H. Robinson has been to Blenheim. He says you will be sorry to hear that we should have asked for the Titian Gallery there. One of his friends knew of it, and asked to see it. It is never shown but to those who inquire for it.

The pictures are all Titians,[2] Jupiter and Ledas, Mars and Venuses, &c., all naked pictures, which may be a reason they don't show it to females. But he says they are very fine; and perhaps it is shown separately to put another fee into the shower's pocket. Well, I shall never see it.

I have lost all wish for sights. God bless you. I shall be glad to see you in London.

Yours truly,
C. Lamb

MS: unrecovered. Text: Lucas (1935), II, 102. Also pub.: Talfourd (1848), I, 167–168; Sala, I, 436–437; Purnell, I, 436–437; Fitzgerald, II, 264; Hazlitt, I,

413–414; Ainger (1888), I, 261; Ainger (1900), II, 189–190; Macdonald, I, 325–326; Ainger (1904), I, 318; Harper, III, 311–312; Lucas (1905), VI, 416; Lucas (1912), V, 438–439. Address, from Macdonald: Mr Hazlitt, Winterslow, near Salisbury. The original of this letter is listed, shown to be dated August 9, 1810, and in part quoted in Harry B. Smith's *A Sentimental Library: Comprising Books Formerly Owned by Famous Writers, Presentation Copies, Manuscripts, and Drawings* (privately printed, 1914), p. 134.

    1. Possibly from the *Odyssey*, XVI, 374—ἐπιστήμων—meaning "skillful," "knowing," "wise."

    2. Which Hazlitt saw later and described in "Pictures at Oxford and Blenheim," in his *Sketches of the Principal Picture-galleries in England. With a Criticism on "Marriage a-la-Mode"* (1824). In *Hazlitt's Works,* the relevant section is at X, 69–75.

253.   *C. L. to Mrs. Thomas Clarkson*

Mondy 18th [17th] Sept 1810

Dear Mrs. Clarkson,

    I did not write till I could have the satisfaction of sending you word that my Sister was better. She is in fact quite restored, and will be with me in little more than a Week.—

    I received Mr C's Letter & transmitted it to Hazlitt—.¹ My kind Love to him, & to Miss W. Tell her I hope that while she stays in London, she will make our Chambers her Lodging. If she can put up with half a Bed, I am sure she will be a most welcome visitor to Mary and to me.— The Montagu's set out for the North this day. What fine things they are going to see, for the first time! which I have seen, but in all human probability shall never see again!—the mountains often come back to me in my dreams, or rather I miss them at those times, for I have been repeatedly haunted with the *same dream,* which is that I am in Cumberland, that I have been there some weeks, & am at the end of my Holydays, but in all that time I have not seen Skiddaw &c—the Hills are all vanished, & I shall go home without seeing them. The trouble of this dream denotes the weight they must have had on my mind, while I was there, which was almost oppressive, & perhaps is caused by the great difficulty I have in recalling any thing like a distinct form of any one of those great masses to my memory. Bless me I have scarce left room to say Good B'ye.—

C Lamb

    MS: Lockwood Library, State University of New York at Buffalo. Pub.: Macdonald, I, 327–328; Harper, III, 312–313; Lucas (1935), II, 103. Address: Mrs. Clarkson/Bury/Suffolk. Postmark: September 18, 1810.

1. A letter regarding, perhaps, a portrait of Clarkson that Hazlitt would complete in the summer of 1811. (See *Hazlitt*, p. 182.) Dorothy Wordsworth, referred to in the next sentence as Miss W., had been away from Allan Bank (see
my Vol. II, Letter 227, note 1) visiting friends since about the beginning of July
and would not return to it until October 25. Robinson brought her from the
Clarksons to the Lambs in September. (See *H. C. R. on Books and Writers*, I, 16.)
Lamb writes of her stay in London in the next letter. The Montagus were setting
out for the North, for Allan Bank and its environs, in order to visit the Wordsworths and to enter Algernon, Montagu's eldest son by the late Laura Rush
Montagu (identified in my Vol. II, Letter 132, note 2), in the Reverend Mr.
John Dawes's school at Ambleside with Derwent and David Hartley Coleridge.
On October 18 Basil and Anna Montagu left for London with Coleridge, who
had been living at Greta Hall, Keswick, since May. As part of an effort to over-
come his addiction to opium, Coleridge had accepted their invitation to go and
live with them, at 55 Frith Street, Soho, and to consult their friend Dr. Anthony
Carlisle with a view toward accepting medical assistance from him. Before the
Montagus and Coleridge left Allan Bank, Wordsworth, who was certain that the
Montagus would find Coleridge exasperating, privately tried to dissuade Montagu
from taking Coleridge in. Wordsworth argued, according to Coleridge later (see
Coleridge's Letters, III, esp. 376, 382, 399, and 403–408; see also *H. C. R. on
Books and Writers*, I, 74–81), that Coleridge had become one who powders his
hair, a nuisance, a liar, a debtor to the pubs, a drunkard—and that Wordsworth
had given up hope for him. Either in advance of their setting out for or during the
eight days it took the Montagus and Coleridge to reach London, Montagu decided
it would be better after all to have Coleridge in lodgings near them rather than with
them in their home. On October 28 Montagu acted on his decision, tactlessly acted
on it by telling Coleridge what Wordsworth had said about him. Coleridge, in
dejection, moved from the Montagus' to Hudson's Hotel, Covent Garden. The
breach, for some time threatening to occur and then, rudely, having occurred between Wordsworth and Coleridge, would be patched in May 1812. But the old
intimacy was lost. Within a few days after he had moved, Coleridge had to bear
other shocks. He heard, from one who has not been identified, that Dr. Carlisle,
to whom Coleridge had confided the details of his opium habit, had betrayed that
confidence by divulging those details to some woman who had made them a subject for gossip. That ended for Coleridge the possibility of his receiving any
guidance or treatment toward a cure from Carlisle. Coleridge also heard that an
intimate of the Montagus had gone against him and that the Montagus were
liable to go more against him than they already had gone. The person who
brought Coleridge that information was John James Morgan (d. 1820). Morgan,
the friend of Southey since their school days together in Bristol in the 1780s and
of Coleridge since 1795, the friend who would run himself so ruinously into debt
in a few years that he would have to flee London—would at one point have to flee
England and at another, during his last year, when palsy disabled him, have to
depend on money from Lamb and Southey and others to survive—was a lawyer
turned businessman upon inheriting at least a share and perhaps ultimately all of
his family's cheese business, at 104 Bishopsgate Street Within, and marrying into
the tobacco business of Matthew Brent, at 103 Bishopsgate Street Within. (See
E. K. Chambers, *Samuel Taylor Coleridge: A Biographical Study* [Oxford:
Clarendon Press, 1938], pp. 260 and 291–292; *Coleridge's Letters*, III, 35, 442, and
443; and *Southey's Correspondence*, IV, 361–362.) Morgan urged Coleridge to
come with him. On November 3 Coleridge joined him and his wife, the former
Mary Brent, and her sister, Charlotte Brent, at their home, 7 Portland Place,
Hammersmith, London. By December 21 he had left them for Brown's Coffee
House, Mitre Court, Fleet Street, but he returned to them shortly. On about
February 9, 1811, he went into rooms at 34 Southampton Buildings, Chancery

Lane. In the evening of March 14, having decided he was not well enough to be living alone (see *Coleridge's Letters,* III, 308), he took the Hammersmith stage back to the Morgans'.

254. *C. L. to William Wordsworth*

E. I. Ho—
Friday 19 Oct 1810

Dr. W.

I forwarded the Letter which you sent to me without opening it to your Sister at Binfield.[1] She has returned it to me, and begs me to tell you that she intends returning from B. on Monday or Tuesday next when Priscilla leaves it, and that it was her earnest wish to spend another week with us in London, but she awaits another Letter from home to determine her. I can only say that she appeared so much pleased with London, and that she is so little likely to see it again for a long time, that if you can spare her, it will be almost a pity not. But doubtless she will have heard again from you, before I can get a reply to this Letter & what she next hears she says will be decisive. If wanted, she will set out immediately from London. Mary has been very ill which you have heard I suppose from the Montagues. She is very weak and low spirited now.— I was much pleased with your continuation of the Essay on Epitaphs.[2] It is the only sensible thing which has been written on that subject & it goes to the Bottom. In particular I was pleased with your **Translation** of that Turgid Epitaph into the plain feeling under it. It is perfectly a **Test.**— But what is the reason we have so few good Epitaphs after all?—

A very striking instance of your position might be found in the Church yard of Ditton upon Thames if you know such a place. Ditton upon Thames has been blessed by the residence of a Poet, who for Love or Money, I do not well know which, has dignified every grave stone for the last few years with bran new verses, all different, and all ingenious, with the Author's name at the Bottom of each.[3] This sweet Swan of Thames has artfully diversified his strains & his rhymes, that the same thought never occurs twice. More justly perhaps, as no thought ever occurs at all, there was a physical impossibility that the same thought should recur. It is long since I saw and read these inscriptions, but I remember the impression was of a smug **usher** at his

desk in the intervals of instruction levelling his pen.— Of Death as it
consists of **dust** and worms and mourners and uncertainty he had
never thought, but the **word** death he had often seen separate, & con-
junct with other words, till he had learned to skill of all its attributes
as glibly as Unitarian Belsham[4] will discuss you the attributes of the
word God in a Pulpit, and will talk of infinity with a tongue that
dangles from a scull that never reached in thought and thorough
imagination **two** inches, or further than from his hand to his mouth or
from the vestry to the Sounding Board[. But the epi]taphs[5] were trim
and sprag & patent & pleased the Survivors of Thames Ditton above
the old mumpsimus of **Afflictions Sore.** .—

    To do justice though, it must be owned that even the excellent
Feeling which dictated this **Dirge** when new, must have suffered
something in passing thro' so many thousand applications, many of
them no doubt quite misplaced, as I have seen in Islington Church
Y'd (I think) an Epitaph to an Infant who died Ætatis 4 months
with this seasonable inscription appended Honor thy Fathr & thy
Mothr. That thy days may be long in the Land &c— —. Sinc[e]rely
wishing your children better, [. . .] Colerg. Montagues, South[ey]
&c—

                                                              I rem[ain,

                                                                  . . .]

Friday 19 Oct 1810

    MS: The University of Texas Library, Austin, Texas. Pub.: Talfourd (1848), I,
180–182; Sala, I, 253–254; Purnell, I, 253–254; Fitzgerald, II, 88–89; Hazlitt, I,
414–415; Ainger (1888), I, 262–263; Ainger (1900), II, 191–193; Macdonald, I,
328–329; Ainger (1904), I, 319–320; Harper, III, 313–315; Lucas (1905), VI,
417–418; Lucas (1912), V, 439–440; Lucas (1935), II, 103–105. Address: Mr
Wordsworth/Grasmere/near/Kendal/Westmorland. Postmark: October 19, 1810.
    1. In Berkshire, where Dorothy Wordsworth was visiting her maternal uncle the
Reverend Dr. William Cookson (1754–1820), canon of Windsor and rector of
Binfield; his wife, the former Dorothy Cowper, or Couper (b. 1754), of Penrith;
and their sons and daughters. Also visiting at the Cooksons' home were Christopher
Wordsworth and his wife, the former Priscilla Lloyd (mentioned below), and their
sons—John (1805–1839), Charles (1806–1892), and Christopher (1807–1885).
"I enjoyed London very much," Dorothy Wordsworth wrote Catherine Clarkson
from Binfield on Monday, October 15, "walked all the mornings with Henry
Robinson, went to the British Museum on Friday and Covent Garden in the
evening. Miss Lamb was with me and I left her perfectly well on Saturday
morning. . . . Unless I have worse news from home I shall stay till Priscilla
goes—which will be about the 27th and I shall stay another week in London
too!" (*Wordsworths' Letters*, II, 437 and 438). But the "worse news from home,"
a letter from her brother William notifying Dorothy Wordsworth that his daughter

Catharine (1808–1812) was seriously ill, arrived at Binfield on Thursday, October 18. Dorothy reached London the next afternoon, rested at the Lambs' until Monday evening, October 22, and then left on a mail coach for home. "Henry Robinson was kinder to me than I can express," she wrote Mrs. Clarkson from there on the thirtieth. "I shall remember him with affection and gratitude as long as I live. The kindness, too, of Charles Lamb and his sister were unbounded. I never was a hundredth part so comfortable in London and I should have stayed at least a fortnight if all had gone on well at home. John Monkhouse [see Letter 256, note 2] and the Lambs attended me to the Mail" (*Wordsworths' Letters*, II, 439).

2. The whole work is an essay in three parts published under the general title "Upon Epitaphs" in *Wordsworth's Prose Works*, II, 27–75. The first part was first published in *The Friend*, No. 25 (February 22, 1810), 403–416. (That part is in *Wordsworth's Prose Works*, II, 27–40, and in *The Friend*, ed. Barbara Rooke, II, 336–346.) The second and third parts, though intended for supplemental numbers of *The Friend*, numbers Coleridge never prepared (see *The Friend*, ed. Barbara Rooke, I, lxxvi–lxxvii), were first published, as "The Country Church-yard, and Critical Examination of Ancient Epitaphs" and "Celebrated Epitaphs Considered," in *Wordsworth's Prose Works*, II, 41–59 and 60–75. The part that pleased Lamb, the second part, Wordsworth thus must have sent in manuscript to Lamb, perhaps because Wordsworth had incorporated in its first sentence the question Lamb had incorporated in the eleventh chapter of *Rosamund Gray* (*Works*, I, 26) and, according to Talfourd's 1837 edition of Lamb letters, Lamb when a boy had asked of Mary. (See, for example, *The Letters of Charles Lamb, with a Sketch of His Life* [2 vols.; Boston: Dana Estes, n.d.], I, 76.) The first sentence of "The Country Church-yard, and Critical Examination of Ancient Epitaphs" reads so: "When a Stranger has walked round a Country Church-yard and glanced his eye over so many brief chronicles, as the tomb-stones usually contain, of faithful wives, tender husbands, dutiful children, and good men of all classes; he will be tempted to exclaim in the language of one of the characters of a modern Tale, in a similar situation, 'Where are all the *bad* people buried?' " (*Wordsworth's Prose Works*, II, 41). The passage incorporating what Lamb below calls the "Turgid Epitaph" and Wordsworth's "Translation" of it is this:

Let us return to an instance of common life. I quote it with reluctance, not so much for its absurdity as that the expression in one place will strike at first sight as little less than impious; and it is indeed, though unintentionally so, most irreverent. But I know no other example that will so forcibly illustrate the important truth I wish to establish. The following epitaph is to be found in a church-yard in Westmoreland; which the present Writer has reason to think of with interest as it contains the remains of some of his ancestors and kindred. The date is 1673.

Under this Stone, Reader, inter'd doth lye,
  Beauty and Virtue's true epitomy.
At her appearance the noone-son
  Blush'd and shrunk in 'cause quite outdon.
In her concentered did all graces dwell:
  God pluck'd my rose that he might take a smel.
I'll say no more: but weeping wish I may
  Soone with thy dear chaste ashes com to lay.
                                    Sic efflevit Maritus.

Can anything go beyond this in extravagance? yet, if the fundamental thoughts be translated into a natural style, they will be found reasonable and affecting—'The woman who lies here interred, was in my eyes a perfect image of beauty and virtue; she was to me a brighter object than the sun in heaven: God took her, who was my delight, from this earth to bring her nearer to Himself. Nothing further is worthy to be said than that weeping I wish soon to lie by thy dear chaste ashes. Thus did the husband pour out his tears.' [*Wordsworth's Prose Works,* II, 51–52]

In November 1835 Wordsworth, at the request of Edward Moxon, composed as an epitaph for Lamb the lines that in December 1835 became the first thirty-eight lines of "Written after the Death of Charles Lamb" (*Wordsworth's Poetical Works* [1940–1949], IV, 272–276). Although even the section comprising those first thirty-eight lines is much too long to have been cut on Lamb's gravestone, a fact Wordsworth recognized, its lines 30–31 and 38, slightly modified, are inscribed on a memorial tablet to Lamb in Edmonton Church:

> Still, at the centre of his being, lodged
> A soul by resignation sanctified:
>   . . . . .
> O, he was good, if e'er a good Man lived!

3. Either the poet and all his productions are Lamb's fancies or the poet and all his productions have altogether vanished. Mr. Derek Brown, the district librarian of the District Central Library, Esher, Surrey, could not answer my questions about Lamb's passage from his many resources. He forwarded the questions to Mr. T. S. Mercer, the secretary of the Ditton Historical Research Society, Thames Ditton, Surrey, who searched in vain among the flat tombstones in the old Thames Ditton Churchyard for a signed epitaph. So had Eric Parker, who included Lamb's passage on the Thames Ditton Churchyard poet in *Highways and Byways in Surrey* (2d ed.; London: Macmillan, 1950), pp. 252–253. If this poet ever existed, Parker concluded, this poet, as he may have once lingered beyond the grave in his inscriptions, "has come to his end by rain and hobnails."

4. Thomas Belsham (1750–1829), who after serving as the minister to the Independent congregation at Worcester in 1778 and as a professor of divinity from 1781 to 1789 at the dissenting academy at Daventry, Northamptonshire, adopted Unitarianism while at Hackney College, London, from 1789 to 1796. He succeeded Joseph Priestley as the morning preacher at the Gravel Pit Chapel, Hackney, in 1794, and became the minister at the Essex Street Chapel, London, in 1805. Among his works are *Elements of the Philosophy of the Human Mind* (1801), *A Summary View of the Evidence and Practical Importance of the Christian Revelation* (1807), and *Epistles of St. Paul Translated* (1822).

5. A piece, with Lamb's signature and three or four words on the verso, has been cut from the paper. The adjective "sprag," used below, means smart, lively, clever; "patent" here means open, evident, plain; "mumpsimus" designates one who is excessively, obstinately, stupidly conservative, who is stuck fast in obsolete ways. See Vol. I, Letter 14, note 2, for the epitaph beginning "Afflictions sore long time I bore."

255.   *M. A. L. and C. L. to Dorothy Wordsworth*
Novr 13. 1810

My dear friend

My brother's letter,[1] which I did not see, I am sure has distressed you sadly. I was then so ill as to alarm him exceedingly, and he thought me quite incapable of any kind of business. It is a great mortification to me to be such an useless creature, and I feel myself greatly indebted to you for the very kind manner in which you take this ungracious matter: but I will say no more on this unpleasant subject. I am at present under the care of Dr Tuthill. I think I have derived great benefit from his medicines. He has also made a water drinker of me, which, contrary to my expectations, seems to agree with me very well.

I very much regret that you were so untimely snatched away, the lively recollection you seem to retain of London scenes will I hope induce you to return, in happier times, for I must still hope for better days.

We have had many pleasant hours with Coleridge,[2] if I had not known how ill he is I should have had no idea of it, for he has been very chearful. But yet I have no good news to send you of him, for two days ago, when I saw him last he had not begun his course of medicine & regimen under Carlisle. I have had a very chearful letter from Mrs Clarkson. she complained a little of your friend Tom, but she says she means to devote the winter to the task of new molding him, I am afraid she will find it no easy task.

Mrs Montague was very sorry to find you gone. I have not seen much of her for I have kept very much at home since her return. I mean to stay at home and keep early hours all this winter.

I have a new maid[3] coming this evening, Betty, that you left here, went from me last week, and I took a girl lately from the country, who was fetched away in a few days by her sister who took it into her head that the Temple was an improper place for a girl to live in. I wish the one that is coming may suit me. She is seven & twenty with a very plain person therefore I may hope she will be in little danger here.

Henry Robinson, and many other friends that you made here, enquire continually after you. The spanish lady[4] is gone and now poor Robinson is left quite forlorn.

The sheets remind me so much of you that I wish for you every showy shop I pass by. I hope we had many pleasant fireside hours together, but I almost fear the stupid dispirited state I was in made me seem a very flat companion; but I know I listened with great pleasure to many interesting conversations. I thank you for what you have done for Phillips,[5] his fate will be decided in about a week. He has lately breakfasted with Sir Joseph Banks, who received him with great civility but made him no promise of support. Sir Joseph told him a new candidate had started up who it was expected would be favoured by the Councel. I am afraid Phillips stands a very poor chance.

I am doing nothing, I wish I was, for if I were once more busily employed at work, I should be more satisfied with myself. I should not feel so helpless & so useless.

I hope you will write soon, your letters give me great pleasure, you have made me so well acquainted with all your houshold, that I must hope for frequent accounts how you are all going on. Remember us affectionately to your brother & sister. I hope the little Katherine[6] continues mending. God bless you all & every one.

Your affectionate friend
M Lamb

Mary has left a little space for me to fill up with nonsense, as the Geographers used to cram monsters in the voids of their maps & call it Terra Incognita. She has told you how she has taken to water, like a hungry otter. I too limp after her in lame imitation,[7] but it goes against me a little *at first*. I have been **aquavorous** now for full four days and it seems a moon. I am full of cramps & rheumatisms, and cold internally so that fire wo'nt warm me, yet I bear all for virtues sake. Must I then leave you, Gin, Rum, Brandy, Aqua Vitæ—pleasant jolly fellows—. Damn Temperance & them that first invented it, some **Ante Noahite.** Coleridge has powdered his head, and looks like Bacchus, Bacchus ever sleek and young.[8] He is going to turn sober, but his Clock has not struck yet, meantime he pours down goblet after goblet, the 2d to see where the 1st is gone, the 3d to see no harm happens to the second, a fourth to say there's another coming, and a 5th to say he's not sure he's the last. William Henshaw is dead. He died yesterday aged 56. It was but a twelvemonth or so back that his Father an ancient **Gunsmith** & my Godfather sounded me as to my willingness to be guardian to this William in case of his (the old man's death). William had three times broke in business, twice in England, once in t'other Hemisphere. He returned from America a sot & hath liquidated all debts. What a hopeful ward I am rid of. Ætatis 56.——— I must have taken care of his morals, seen that he did not form imprudent connections, given my consent before he could have married &c.— From all which the stroke of death hath relieved me. Mrs. Reynolds is the name of the Lady to whom I will remember you tomorrow. **Farewell.**— Wish me strength to continue. I've been eating jugg'd Hare. The toast & water makes me quite sick.

C. Lamb

MS: University of Texas Library. Pub.: Talfourd (1837), I, 320–321; Sala, I, 324; Purnell, I, 324; Fitzgerald, II, 158; Hazlitt, I, 412–413; Ainger (1888), I, 262; Ainger (1900), II, 190–191; Macdonald, II, 21; Ainger (1904), I, 319; Harper, III, 315–317; Lucas (1905), VI, 419–421; Lucas (1912), V, 441–444; Lucas (1935), II, 106–108. Address: Miss Wordsworth/Grasmere/near Kendal/ Westmorland. Postmark: November 13, 1810. Mary begins the letter.

1. Dorothy Wordsworth wrote of that (unrecovered) letter in her letter of November 6 to Henry Robinson:

I am much afraid that Miss Lamb is very poorly.—I have had a letter from Charles, written in miserably bad spirits. I had thoughtlessly (and you cannot imagine how bitterly I reproach myself for it) I had thoughtlessly requested her to execute some commissions for me; and her Brother writes to beg that I will hold her excused from every office of that sort at present, she being utterly unable to support herself under any fatigue either of body or mind—Why had not I the sense to perceive this truth in its full extent? I have caused them great pain by forcing them to a refusal, and myself many inward pangs. I feel as if I *ought* to have perceived that everything out of the common course of her own daily life caused excitement and agitation equally injurious to her—Charles speaks of the necessity of absolute quiet and at the same time of being obliged sometimes to have company that they would be better without. Surely in such a case as theirs it would be right to select whom they will admit, admit those only when they are likely to be bettered by society; and to exclude *all* others! They [have not] one true Friend who would not take it the more kindly of them to be so treated. Pray, as you most likely see *Charles* at least from time to time, tell me how they are going on. [See note 7, below.] There is nobody in the world out of our own house for whom I am more deeply interested. [*Wordsworths' Letters*, II, 443–444]

2. Robinson reported Coleridge and himself at the Lambs' on November 14 and 15 and December 20. (See *H. C. R.'s Diary*, I, 195 and 197.) Mentioned below is, presumably, the Thomas Clarksons' son, Thomas. See my Vol. II, Letter 187, note 1.

3. She (see Mary's fourth paragraph in and Lamb's portion of the next letter), Betty, and the others to whom Mary refers in this paragraph have not been identified.

4. A Madame Lavaggi, the wife of the treasurer of the kingdom of Galicia, Spain, both of whom Robinson had met in Spain in 1808. Shortly before the battle of Corunna, in January 1809, Robinson had arranged for passage to England for the Lavaggis and their papers and accounts of state. Madame Lavaggi insisted on being put ashore just before their ship sailed and elected not to come to England until 1810. She arrived in London in October 1810, on perhaps the day before Dorothy Wordsworth left for home. (See *H. C. R.'s Diary*, I, 179–180, 182–186, and 194.) Where Madame Lavaggi went after she left London I cannot say.

5. Edward Phillips had applied for a position with the Royal Society—formally, The Royal Society of London for Improving Natural Knowledge, the oldest scientific society in Great Britain. Its council would pass Phillips over, probably in favor of one of its own members, the (unidentified) "rich merchant who lately failed"—so described in Letter 257, fourth paragraph. What Miss Wordsworth had done for Phillips is not known. Sir Joseph Banks, mentioned below, was the incumbent president of the Royal Society. He is initially identified in Vol. II, Letter 222, note 11.

6. Catharine Wordsworth. Lamb's portion of this letter begins below Mary's signature.

7. In *Richard II*, II, i, 23, the adjective is "base" rather than "lame." Robin-

son on December 23 and 25 wrote the following to Miss Wordsworth, in answer
to her letter of November 6 to him (quoted in part in note 1, above):

> . . . I postponed answering your acceptable and obliging letter till I could
> speak to you concerning our common friends the Lambs.
>
> Mary, I am glad to say, is just now very comfortable; But I hear she has
> been in a feeble & tottering condition. She has put herself under Dr Tuthill
> who has prescribed water to her. Charles, in consequence, resolved to ac-
> comodote . . . himself to her, And since Lord Mayor's day [November 9]
> has abstained from all other liquor as w[ell] as from smoaking. We shall all
> rejoice indeed if this experiment succeeds.
>
> Who knows but this promising resolution may have been strengthened by
> the presence of Coleridge? . . .
>
> I have kept back my letter that I may inclose it under a frank to Mr
> Southey. Coleridge spent an afternoon with us on Sunday [December 23]. He
> was delightful. C. Lamb was unwell & could not join us. His change of habit,
> tho' it on the whole improves his health, yet when he is ill or low spirited
> leaves him without a remedy or relief. M. Lamb desired me to say she is
> very much better. [*H. C. R.'s Correspondence with the Wordsworth Circle,*
> I, 63 and 65]

8. It is "Bacchus ever fair and ever young" in line 48 of John Dryden's
"Alexander's Feast: Or, the Power of Music; an Ode in Honor of St. Cecilia's
Day." William Henshaw and his father have not been identified beyond what
Lamb writes of them below.

256.   *M. A. L. and C. L. to Dorothy Wordsworth*

[Friday, November 23, 1810]

[M]y dear Friend,

Miss Monkhouse[1] left town yesterday, but I think I am able to
answer all your enquiries. I saw her on sunday evening at Mrs
Montagu's. She looked very well & said her health was greatly improved. She promised to call on me before she left town but the
weather having been very bad I suppose has prevented her. She
received the letter which came through my brother's hands and I
have learned from Mrs Montagu that all your commissions are
executed. It was Carlisle that she consulted, and she is to continue
taking his prescriptions in the country. Mr Monkhouse[2] & Mr Addison drank tea with us one evening last week. Miss Monkhouse is a
very pleasing girl, She reminds me, a little, of Miss Hutchinson. I
have not seen Henry Robinson for some days past, but I remember
he told me he had received a letter from you, and he talked of
spanish papers which he should send to Mr Southey.[3] I wonder he
does not write, for I have always understood him to be a very regular
correspondent, and he seemed very proud of your letter. I am toler-

ably well, but I still affect the invalid—take medicines, and keep at home as much as I possibly can. Water-drinking, though I confess it to be a flat thing, is become very easy to me. Charles perseveres in it most manfully.

Coleridge is just in the same state as when I wrote last, I have not seen him since Sunday, he was then at Mr Morgan's but talked of taking a lodging.

Phillips feels a certainty that he shall lose his election, for the new candidate is himself a Fellow of the Royal Society, and [it] is thought Sir Joseph Banks will favour him. It will now be soon decided.

My new maid is now sick in bed. Am I not unlucky? she would have suited me very well if she had been healthy, but I must send her away if she is not better tomorrow.

Charles promised to add a few lines, I will therefore leave him plenty of room, for he may perhaps think of something to entertain you. I am sure I cannot.

I hope you will not return to Grasmere till all fear of the Scarlet Fever is over,[4] I rejoice to hear so good an account of the children, & hope you will write often, when I write next I will endeavour to get a frank. This I cannot do but when the parliament is sitting, and as you seemed anxious about Miss Monkhouse I would not defer sending this, though otherwise it is not worth paying one penny for.

> God bless you all
> yours affectionately
> M Lamb

We[5] are in a pickle. Mary from her affectation of physiognomy has hired a stupid big country wench who looked honest as she thought, and has been doing her work some days but without eating—eats no butter nor meat, but prefers cheese with her tea for breakfast— & now it comes out that she was ill when she came with lifting her mother about (who is now with God) when she was dying, and with riding up from Norfolk 4 days & nights in the Waggon. She got advice yesterday & took something which has made her bring up a quart of blood, [a]nd she now lies a dead weight upon our humanity in her [b]ed incapable of getting up, refusing to go into

an hospital, having no body in town but a poor asthmatic dying
Uncle whose son lately married a drab who fills his house, and
there is no where she can go, and she seems to have made up he[r]
mind to take her flight to heaven from **our bed.**— O God! O God!—
for the little wheelbarrow which trundled the Hunchback[6] from
door to door to try the various charities of different professions of
Mankind!—

Here's her Uncle just crawled up, he is far liker Death than **He.**
O the Parish, the Parish, the hospital, the infirmary, the charnel
house, these are places meet for such guests, not our quiet mansion
where nothing but affluent plenty & literary ease should abound——
Howard's House,[7] Howard's House, or where the Parylitic descended
thro' the sky-light (what a God's Gift) to get at our Savior—. In this
perplexity such topics as Spanish papers & Monkhouses sink into comparative insignificance. What shall we do?— If she died, it were
something, gladly would I pay the coffin-maker & the bellman &
searchers[8]—O Christ——.

C L

MS: University of Texas Library. Pub.: Sala, I, 254–255; Purnell, I, 254–255;
Fitzgerald, II, 89–90; Hazlitt, I, 417; Ainger (1888), I, 264; Ainger (1900), II,
193–194; Macdonald, I, 330; Ainger (1904), I, 321; Harper, III, 317–318;
Lucas (1905), VI, 422–424; Lucas (1912), V, 444–446; Lucas (1935), II, 109–
111. Address: Miss Wordsworth/Grasmere/near Kendal/Westmoreland. Postmark:
November 23, 1810. Mary begins the letter, which has a small piece missing from
its upper left corner.
    1. Mary Monkhouse (1787–1858), the sister of John and Thomas Monkhouse
(see note 2, below, and Vol. II, Letter 164, note 3), was to become, in 1812, the
wife of Mary Wordsworth's brother Thomas Hutchinson. Miss Monkhouse had been
in town receiving treatment for consumption by Anthony Carlisle and a Dr.
Ainsley. (See *Wordsworths' Letters*, II, 439 and 457.) By December 30, 1810, she
was at the farm Thomas Hutchinson had taken in 1808 at Hindwell, Radnorshire,
Wales. Thomas Hutchinson is identified in my Vol. I, Letter 44, note 6, but
partly by the statement to the effect that he had become in 1888—an error for
"1788 or 1789"—the owner of a farm at Sockburn, or Sockburn-on-Tees, Durham.
It appears, rather, that upon the death either of Thomas' grandfather Henry
Hutchinson (1706–1788) or Thomas' granduncle the elder Thomas Hutchinson
(1718–1789), Thomas had inherited the farmhouse and its furniture and the farm
stock, but rented the land from his uncle George Hutchinson (1730–1804), of
Stockton-on-Tees, Durham. See *Wordsworths' Letters*, I, 31, note 3, and 142 and
its note 1; but see also Mary Moorman's *William Wordsworth: A Biography.
The Early Years: 1770–1803* (1957; rpt. Oxford: Oxford University Press paper-
back, 1968), p. 436.
    2. John Monkhouse (1782–1866), the brother of Thomas and Mary, had stayed
with her while she was in London. John was at this time a farmer in partnership
with Thomas Hutchinson at Hindwell. By October 1814 (see *Wordsworths' Letters*,

III, 162) John had become a farmer in partnership with another at Stow, or Stowe, near Hay, Breconshire, Wales. His late wife, to whom he had been married in 1806, was Isabella (1784–1807), a daughter of Henry Addison (1754–1793)—he had been an attorney at Penrith—and of the former Jane Hindson (1754–1837). The Addison whom Mary Lamb mentions following is one of John Monkhouse's brothers-in-law—either Richard (b. 1785), of 28 Bernard Street, Russell Square, London, a law partner of Dorothy Wordsworth's brother Richard (see my Vol. II, Letter 133, note 4); or Henry, of Wales, whom Dorothy Wordsworth may have alluded to in her letter to Margaret, Lady Beaumont, of February 28, 1810, and did name in her letter to Richard Wordsworth of March 23, 1810. (See *Wordsworths' Letters,* II, 390 and 395.) The Miss Hutchinson to whom Mary Lamb refers is probably Mary Wordsworth's sister Sara (see my Vol. I, Letter 44, note 6), later the Lambs' correspondent. Sara had in mid-March 1810 left the William Wordsworths' home for her brother Thomas', at Hindwell.

3. Possibly in 1809 but probably in 1810 Robinson had introduced Southey to Don Manuel Abella, a secretary at the Spanish embassy in London. Don Manuel subsequently provided Southey, occasionally through Robinson, with documents and information for some of the historical articles Southey wrote during the period 1809 to 1813 for the *Edinburgh Annual Register* and incorporated in his *History of the Peninsular War* (3 vols.; 1823–1832). See *H. C. R. on Books and Writers,* I, 11; *New Southey Letters,* I, esp. 544; and *Southey's Correspondence,* III, 304, and IV, 78–79 and 80. For the request of Dorothy Wordsworth of Robinson, which she made on behalf of William Wordsworth in her letter of November 6, 1810, to "procure any Spanish, Portuguese or French papers for Mr Southey," and for the (consenting) answer of Robinson, which he gave in his letter of December 23 and 25, 1810, see *Wordsworths' Letters,* II, 444, and *H. C. R.'s Correspondence with the Wordsworth Circle,* I, 63.

4. In order to avoid the scarlet fever that was in the two houses next to Allan Bank, the Wordsworths who were at home and the maid Sarah Youdell had left on October 26 for Hackett, a cottage above Colwith, between Elterwater and Little Langdale. They had returned to Allan Bank from Hackett, the home of Miss Youdell's parents—John, a quarryman, and Betty—on October 29. For the same reason, Dorothy, Mary, William, this time all of the children—John, Dorothy, Thomas, Catharine, and William (1810–1883)—and the maid Fanny had left Allan Bank on November 8 or 9 for Elleray, a cottage on the outskirts of Windermere. They returned to Allan Bank from Elleray, the home of John Wilson, later the "Christopher North" of *Blackwood's Edinburgh Magazine,* on December 18. See *Wordsworths' Letters,* II, esp. 441, 447, 448–449, and 455.

5. From Lamb. The members of the maid's family mentioned below have not been identified.

6. In "The Story of the Hunchback," one of the tales of *The Book of One Thousand Nights and One Night;* a wheelbarrow does not figure in the versions I read. Lamb's "he is far liker Death than He," in the first sentence of the next paragraph, is a variation of Coleridge's "And she is [was] far liker Death than he"—two early substitutions Coleridge had considered for the present line 193 of "The Rime of the Ancient Mariner." See *Coleridge's Poetical Works* (1912), I, 194.

7. Perhaps 23 Great Ormonde Street, Queen Square, where the philanthropist and prison reformer John Howard (1726?–1790) had lived from 1777 to his death, but probably Coldbath Fields Prison, whose erection he had recommended. Lamb alluded in unflattering terms presumably to Howard in "The Old Benchers of the Inner Temple" and openly expressed his dislike of him in a footnote to "Christ's Hospital Five and Thirty Years Ago" (*Works,* II, 88–89 and 17; see II, 369 and 319). In a portion of that footnote—"This fancy of dungeons for children [in Christ's Hospital and possibly elsewhere] was a sprout of Howard's brain; for

which . . . methinks, I could willingly spit upon his statue"—may be an allusion
to the story that in order easily to receive a visitor, Howard had once locked his
son in an outhouse. Although the story was later judged apocryphal, the son,
John (1765?–1799), did while a boy become insane. For the account of the
"Parylitic" (below) see Mark 2:3–12.
    8. The bellman, or town crier, would then proclaim the death, and searchers, in
order officially to report its cause, would necessarily view the body.

257.   *C. L. to William Hazlitt*

[East India House]
Wednesdy. 28 Nov 1810

Dear Hazzlit,—

    I sent you on Saturday a Cobbet[1] containing your reply to Edinb.
Rev. which I thought you would be glad to receive as an example of
attention on the part of Mr. Cobbet to insert it so—speedily; did you
get it?— We have received your Pig and return you thanks, it will be
drest in due form with appropriate sauce this day.—

    Mary has been very ill indeed since you saw her, that is, as ill as
she can be to remain at home. But she is a good deal better now,
owing to a very careful regimen, she drinks nothing but water and
never goes out, she does not even go to the Captain's.[2] Her indisposi-
tion has been ever since that night you left Town, the night Miss W.
came; her coming, and that damn'd infernal bitch Mrs. Godwin
coming & staying so late that night, so overset her that she lay broad
awake all that night, and it was by a miracle that she escaped a very
bad illness which I thoroughly expected.—

    I have made up my mind that she shall never have any one in the
house again with her, and that no one shall sleep with her not even
for a night, for it is a very serious thing to be always living with a kind
of fever upon her, & therefore I am sure you will take it in good part
if I say that if Mrs. Hazlit comes to town at any time, however glad
we shall be to see her in the daytime, I cannot ask her to spend a
night under our roof. Some decision we must come to, for the harass-
ing fever that we have both been in, owing to Miss Wordsw*t*—coming,
is not to be borne, & I had rather be dead than so alive. However at
present owing to a regimen & medicines which Tuthill has given her,
who very kindly volunteer'd the care of her, she is a great deal quieter,

though too much harrassed by Company, who cannot or will not see how late hours & society teaze her.—

Poor Phillips had the cup dash'd out of his lips as it were. He had every prospect of the situation, when about ten days since **one** of the Council of the R. Society started for the Place himself, being a rich merchant who lately failed, and he will certainly be elected on Friday next.[3] P. is very sore & miserable about it.—

Coleridge is in Town, or at least at Hammersmith. He is writing or going to write in the Courier against Cobbet & in favor of Paper Money.—.

No news.— remember me kindly to Sara, I write from the **office**——

Yours ever

C Lamb

I just open'd it to say the Pig upon proof hath turned out as good as I predicted. My fauces yet retain the sweet porcine odor.—[4] I find you have recd the Cobbet, I think your Paper complete——

Mrs. Reynolds, who is a sage woman, approves of the Pig.—

MS: The Philip H. & A. S. W. Rosenbach Foundation, Philadelphia. Pub.: Sala, I, 437–439; Purnell, I, 437–439; Fitzgerald, II, 264–266; Hazlitt, I, 418–419; Ainger (1888), I, 265–266; Ainger (1900), II, 195–197; Macdonald, I, 331–332; Ainger (1904), I, 322–323; Harper, III, 318–320; Lucas (1905), VI, 424–425; Lucas (1912), V, 447–448; Lucas (1935), II, 111–113. Address: Mr Hazlitt/Winterslow/near/Salisbury/Wilts. Postmark: November 28, 1810.

1. *Cobbett's Weekly Political Register* (see Letter 318, note 2) for November 24, 1810, where is published, under the heading "Mr. Malthus and the Edinburgh Reviewers," Hazlitt's letter containing the "Queries Relating to the Essay on Population." The letter (in *Hazlitt's Works*, VII, 357–361, 408–410, and 411) is dated November 21, 1810, is signed "The Author of a Reply to the Essay on Population," and is in response to a criticism in the *Edinburgh Review,* 16 (August 1810), 464–476, of Hazlitt's *A Reply to the Essay on Population, by the Rev. T. R. Malthus. In a Series of Letters. To Which Are Added, Extracts from the Essay; with Notes* (1807).

2. To the home, that is, of James and Sarah Burney. Miss W., referred to below, is Dorothy Wordsworth.

3. See Letter 255, note 5. Coleridge (see Lamb's next paragraph and Letter 253, note 1) had written the following to John Rickman in a letter of November 14, 1810: "The Report of the [Parliamentary] Bullion Committee was sent down to me at Keswick & either was lost on the road or missed me—and it is now out of print & not to be bought—I am at present writing on this Subject in opposition to these Scholars of the Edinburgh Review, and cannot go on without it—Now I hope, you may have it in your power to lend it me or to procure me the loan of it . . . and at the same time if you should happen to have the last 15 or 20 Numbers of Cobbett, & will entrust them to me . . . , I shall have all I want—" (*Coleridge's Letters,* III, 299). Coleridge's comments on the bullion matter that

appear in both *The Courier* and *Essays on His Own Times: Forming a Second Series of The Friend,* ed. Sara Coleridge (London: William Pickering, 1850), III, 751, 753–757, 861–866, and 869–876, are in the communications of May 7 and 9, 1811, and the essays, titled "Bullion Commerce" and "Bank-notes and Gold," of August 2 and 13, 1811.

4. Lamb's developed appreciation of roast pig is "A Dissertation upon Roast Pig" (*Works,* II, 120–126).

258.   *C. L. to William Godwin*

Monday eveng. [November or December 1810?]

Dear Godwin,

I have found it for several reasons indispensable to my comfort & to my sister's to have no visitors in the forenoon. If I cannot accomplish this, I am determined to leave town. I am extremely sorry to be obliged to do any thing in the slightest degree that may seem offensive to you or to Mrs. Godwin; but when a general rule is fixed upon, you know how odious in a case of this sort it is to make exceptions: I assure you I have given up more than one friendship, in stickling—for this point. It would be unfair to those from whom I have parted, with regret, to make exceptions which I would not do for them. Let me request you **not** to be offended, and to request Mrs. G. not to be offended, if I beg both your compliances with this wish. Your friendship is as dear to me as that of any person on earth, & if it were not for the necessity of keeping tranquillity at home, I would not seem so unreasonable—

If you were to see the agitation that my sister is in between the fear of offending you & Mrs. G.—and the difficulty of maintaining a system which she feels we must do to live without wretchedness, you would excuse this seeming strange request: which I send with a trembling anxiety as to its reception with you, whom I would never offend. I rely on your goodness

C Lamb

MS: Lord Abinger, Bures, Suffolk; transcribed from the microfilm of the Abinger Collection in the William R. Perkins Library, Duke University, Durham, N.C. Pub.: Hazlitt, I, 416–417; Macdonald, I, 256–257; Harper, III, 320–321; Lucas (1905), VI, 425–426; Lucas (1912), V, 448–449; Lucas (1935), II, 113. The general content of the letter suggests the date assigned to it.

259. *C. L. to Coleridge*

[Late December 1810?]

Dear Col.

we are gone out & shall return about three.———— What a fine morning————. I expect Wm. Dollin to dinner.— If he comes before we return, he need not be in your way—. Give him a book, and go you on with your writing.— He is as silent as an old glove—

C L

MS: Victoria University Library, Toronto. Pub.: Kathleen Coburn, "A Note from Lamb to Coleridge," *CLSB,* N.S. Nos. 10–11 (April–July 1975), 34 and, in facsimile, 35. Watermark: 1799. Regarding the time when Lamb may have written his note, Professor Coburn, in her note cited above, wrote that the watermark date "and the biographical facts together suggest . . . March 1800 when Coleridge was staying at 36 Chapel Street Pentonville with Lamb and was trying to extricate himself from newspaper commitments to finish his translation of *Wallenstein.*" Lamb may, however, have written his note at the time assigned to it here. For then Mary had improved, then too the Lambs were having Coleridge in, and Coleridge, who was usually writing, may then have been writing for *The Courier.* (See Letter 255, notes 2 and 7, and Letter 257, fifth paragraph.) The only other mention of William Dollin in Lamb's letters occurs in Letter 245, near the reference to note 12, a letter of 1810. I cannot say if Mary Dollin, mentioned in Vol. I, Letter 45, at the reference to note 2, was related to William, or if William was the person whose name seems to be spelled "Dollan" in Godwin's diary entry for October 8, 1800, whom Godwin had joined that evening for supper at the Lambs'. I thank Winifred F. Courtney for providing me with that information from Godwin's (unpublished) diary.

260. *M. A. L. to Mary Matilda Betham*

Wednesday [March 6, 1811]

alas Wednesday shines no [more][1] to me now.

My dear Matilda,

Coleridge has given me a very chearful promise that he will wait on Lady Jerningham[2] any day you will be pleased to appoint; he offered to write to you, but as I found it was to be done *Tommorrow,* and as I am pretty well acquainted with his to-morrows, I thought good to let you know his determination *to-day.* He is in town at present but as he is often going to Hammersmith for a night or two you had better perhaps send the invitation through me, and I will manage it for you as well as I can. You had better let him have four or five days previous notice, and you had better send the invitation as soon as you can, for he seems tolerably well just now. I mention all these betters [becau]se I wish to do the *best* I can for [you, perc]eiving, as I do, that it is a thing [you have s]et your heart upon. He dined [one d]ay in company with Catilana³ (Is that the way you spell her Italian name, I am reading Sallust and had like to have written her **Catiline.**) How I should have liked, and how you would have liked, to have seen Coleridge and Catilana together.

You have been very good of late to let me come & see you so seldom, and you are a little goodish to come so seldom here, because you stay away from a kind motive,⁴ but if you stay away always, as I begin to fear you mean to do, I would not give one pin for your good intentions. In plain words, Come and see me very soon for though I be not so *sensitive* as *some people,* I begin to feel strange qualms for having driven you from me.

Yours affectionately

M Lamb

Miss Duncan played famously in the new comedy⁵ which went off as famously.—— By the way she put in a spiteful piece of wit I verily believe of her own head, & methought she stared me full in the face. The words were "As silent as an author in company." Her hair & herself looked remarkably well.

MS: Mr. Roger W. Barrett, Chicago. Pub.: Lucas (1905), VI, 428–429; Lucas (1912), V, 451–452; Lucas (1935), II, 115. Address: Miss Betham/49 Upper Marybone Stree[t]. Postmark: March 6, 1811. Mary should have spelled the (London) street name in the address "Marylebone."

1. The lower left corner of the first leaf has been torn away. ("Wednesday"— the Lambs used frequently to entertain on Wednesday evenings—and Mary's comment about the day are located at the bottom of the verso of the first leaf on the original.) The locutions that disappeared with that corner—the word "more" and those in brackets below—are taken from Lucas (1935), II, 115.

2. Frances, Lady Jerningham (d. 1825), formerly the Honourable Frances Dillon, the eldest daughter of Henry Dillon, eleventh Viscount Dillon (1705–1787), and of the former Lady Charlotte Lee, was the widow of Sir William Jerningham, sixth baronet (1736–1809). She was a sister-in-law of the poet and dramatist Edward Jerningham (1727–1812), who in 1808 had attended Coleridge's lectures on the "Principles of Poetry" (see Vol. II, Letter 222, note 10) and introduced himself to their author. Lady Jerningham had requested Mary Matilda Betham, her friend since 1794, to see if Coleridge would accept an invitation to dinner. He would, and dined at the home of Lady Jerningham on Sunday, March 10. He and his hostess wrote of the evening to separate correspondents. (See *Coleridge's Letters,* III, 311, and *The Jerningham Letters [1780–1843],* ed. Egerton

Castle [2 vols.; London: Richard Bently, 1896], II, 7.) Hammersmith, the London borough mentioned below, was the home of the John James Morgans and Charlotte Brent.

3. The soprano Angelica Catalani (1780–1849), who had made her debut in Venice in 1795, had first appeared in London at the King's Theatre in 1806 (and had also in 1806 become the wife of one Captain Valabrègue) and was to reign as prima donna in England until 1813. She then accepted the management of the Paris opera, failed as a manager because of the wastefulness and unsound counsel of her husband, and subsequently resumed her singing career. She toured the Continent, with great success, until 1828 and in that year retired from the stage. In 1830 she opened a charity singing school for girls in Florence. She died of cholera in Paris. Coleridge seems not to have left a record of his dining with her. Mentioned below is the Roman historian Sallust, born Gaius Sallustius Crispus (86–34 B.C.). His *De conjuratione Catilinæ,* or *Bellum Catilinarium,* appears often in translation as *The Catiline Conspiracy.*

4. Probably that of not wishing to interfere in the slightest with Mary's recovery of health. But the news, which the Lambs would receive while entertaining Coleridge and Hazlitt in the evening of the date of this letter, of George Burnett's death in a Marylebone workhouse and the effect the news would have that evening on Coleridge in the presence of Mary combined gradually to overset her. Possibly on Thursday, March 7, she wrote Dorothy and William Wordsworth (neither Mary's letter nor Dorothy's response or William's has been recovered) of her awareness of a difficulty between Wordsworth and Coleridge. According to the report Coleridge was given of what Mary had written, she had pressed Wordsworth immediately to come to town. For in her estimation Coleridge's mind, from its various shocks, had become "seriously unhinged." On Friday, March 8, Mary called on the Godwins and alarmed them by her perturbed conversation, though on the same Friday, Lamb, as if nothing were wrong, wrote John Morgan to expect him and Mary for a meal in the Morgan household on Sunday. (See the next letter.) So ill was Mary by five o'clock in the morning of Saturday, March 9, however, that within the next two hours Lamb had to take her to an asylum in the country. Later that Saturday Lamb notified Morgan (if by a letter it has not been recovered) of what had happened to Mary and, presumably, did not go to Morgan's house on Sunday. Morgan, also on Saturday, told Coleridge of the sad event. Coleridge mentioned it, Burnett's death, and his own consequent illness in a letter of March 12 to Robinson. In a letter of March 14 to Mary Matilda Betham, Coleridge wrote of the sequence of all the events in detail. Mary Lamb returned home between May 6 and 11. See *Wordsworths' Letters,* II, 489; *Coleridge's Letters,* III, 306–310; and *H. C. R. on Books and Writers,* I, 78, 24–25, and 32.

5. Which is published with the title *Ourselves, a Comedy, in Five Acts. As Performed . . . at the Theatre-Royal, Lyceum* (London: J. Barker, 1811). Its author—the author as well of such works as *He Deceives Himself. A Domestic Tale* (1799) and *The School for Friends, a Comedy, in Five Acts* (1805)—was Marianne Chambers (fl. 1799–1811). *Ourselves* was performed by members of the Drury Lane company at the Lyceum from March 1 to 19, 1811, with Maria Rebecca Duncan, later Maria Rebecca Duncan Davison (see Vol. II, Letter 208, note 3), in the role of Miss Beaufort. Her lines (II, i, 20–21) from which Mary misquotes below read, "Lud, you look as dull as a domino at a masquerade, or a poor author in company."

261.   *C. L. to John James Morgan*

Friday night 8 Mar 1811

There—do'nt read any further, because the Letter[1] is not intended for you but for Coleridge, who perhaps might not have opened it directed to him suo nomine. It is to invite C. to Lady Jerningham's on Sunday. Her address is to be found within. We come to Hammersmith notwithstanding on Sunday, and hope Mrs. M. will not think of getting us Green Peas or any such expensive luxuries. A plate of plain Turtle, another of Turbot, with good roast Beef in the rear, &, as alderman Curtis[2] says, whoever ca'nt make a dinner of that ought to be damn'd.

C Lamb

MS: Bodleian Library, Oxford (MS. Autogr. b. 3, page 43). Pub.: Harper, III, 322; Lucas (1905), VI, 429–430; Lucas (1912), V, 452–453; Lucas (1935), II, 116.

1. A letter, which has not been recovered, that accompanied or was a part of this letter. The Latin, below, translates as "in his own name." See the preceding letter, notes 2 and 4, about Lady Jerningham's invitation to Coleridge and the Lambs' plans to visit the Morgans.

2. Sir William Curtis (1752–1829) was the alderman of the Tower ward from 1785 to 1821, a sheriff of London in 1789, a member of Parliament for London from 1790 to 1818 and in 1820, and the lord mayor of London from 1795 to 1796. "He was a man of great importance as head of the tory party in the city, though he was a pitiably bad speaker, very badly educated, and the constant butt of all the whig wits. . . . No man of his time was ever the subject of so much ridicule, of which Peter Pindar's 'The Fat Knight and the Petition' is a good example" (*DNB*; about Peter Pindar see my Vol. I, Letter 49, note 3). The sources of the statements Lamb attributes to Curtis here and near the end of a letter to Bernard Barton postmarked May 15, 1824 (in Vol. V), are probably reports in the newspapers or magazines about him or of his speeches and sayings.

262.   *C. L. to Godwin*

Temple
28th or 29th March 1811

Dear Godwin,

I send the Poem,[1] at length finish'd. If it will do, your part remains, which is, to furnish the needful. I think some parts are happy, but it will probably on the whole appear a different thing from the Prose Original. I shall be sorry if it disappoints you.— I wait your decision with **manly fortitude.**

Yours Ever

C L

MS: Lord Abinger. Unpublished.

1. Unrecovered. The poem may have been *Beauty and the Beast: Or a Rough Outside with a Gentle Heart. A Poetical Version of an Ancient Tale Illustrated with a Series of Elegant Engravings. And Beauty's Song at Her Spinning Wheel, Set to Music by Mr Whitaker,* which the Godwins published at the Juvenile Library, perhaps in 1811. It is not known who did the illustrations. The music was probably by the songwriter and music publisher John Whitaker (1776–1847). Godwin, in a letter now in the Wordsworth Library, Grasmere, had asked Wordsworth if he would versify the ancient tale of *La Belle et la bête.* On March 9, 1811, the day after receiving the letter, Wordsworth declined its request (see *Wordsworths' Letters,* II, 467–469), but suggested that Godwin apply to the man of letters William Taylor (1765–1836). Some have assumed, from Lamb's having previously written works appealing to children for the Godwins, that Godwin turned to Lamb rather than to Taylor and that Lamb agreed to and did write *Beauty and the Beast.* Lucas, for reasons that still obtain, could not accept the assumption: "There is no proof that Charles Lamb wrote this little book"; moreover, its verses "exhibit an easier mastery of the mock-heroic couplet than he elsewhere gives indication of possessing, and they lack any traces of his peculiar humour, such as are to be found in *Prince Dorus*" (*Works,* III, 498 and 499). Probably the poem Lamb sent with his present note is *Prince Dorus: Or, Flattery Put out of Countenance. A Poetical Version of an Ancient Tale, Illustrated with a Series of Elegant Engravings,* which the Godwins published at the Juvenile Library in 1811. The engravings used for the illustrations were supposedly (see *Works,* III, 498) cut from drawings done by the artist Mary Ann Flaxman (1768–1833), a half-sister of the sculptor and draftsman John Flaxman (1755–1826). Lucas pointed out in *Works,* III, 498, that the version of the ancient tale from which the author of *Prince Dorus* could have worked is that titled "The Prince That Had a Long Nose" in *Adventures of Musul; or, the Three Gifts* (London: Vernor & Hood and E. Newbery, 1800). It is generally assumed, from internal and strong external evidence, that the author of *Prince Dorus* was Lamb. The external evidence is in two places in Robinson's diary and in Robinson's reminiscences (written during the period 1845–1853; the passage in those reminiscences is quoted last, below):

May 15th [1811]. . . . A very pleasant call on Charles and Mary Lamb. Read his version of the story of Prince Dorus—the long-nosed king. Gossiped about writing. Urged him to try his hand at a metrical *Umarbeitung* ["remodeling"] of *Reynard the Fox.* He believed, he said, in the excellence, but he was sure it would not succeed now. The sense for humour, he maintained, is utterly extinct.

Nov. 2nd [1824]. . . . I also read Lamb's *Prince Dorus* to the party [at Flaxman's]. It pleased quite as much as it deserved. [*H. C. R. on Books and Writers,* I, 33 and 314]

1811. *C. Lamb* wrote this year for children a version of the nursery tale of *Prince Dorus.* I mention this because it is not in his collected works [*Works* (1818)], & like 2 vols. of *Poems* [*Poetry*] *for Children,* likely to be lost. I this year tried to persuade him to make a new version of the old tale of

Reynard the Fox. He said he was sure it wd. not succeed. 'Sense for humour,' said L. 'is extinct. No satire but personal satire will succeed.' [*Blake, Coleridge, Wordsworth, Lamb, etc., Being Selections from the Remains of Henry Crabb Robinson*, ed. Edith J. Morley (Manchester: The University Press; London and New York: Longmans, Green, 1922), p. 44]
Beauty and the Beast and *Prince Dorus* are in *Works,* III, 453–471 and 432–450.

263.   *C. L. to Mary Matilda Betham*

Friday [September 27? 1811]

Dear Miss Betham,

I am very sorry, but I was preengaged for this evening, when Eliza communicated the contents of your Letter. She herself also is gone to Walworth to pass some days with Miss Hays. G-d forbid I should

> pass my days
> with Miss H——s

but that is neither here nor there. We will both atone for this accident by calling upon you as early as possible.

I am setting out to engage Mr Dyer[1] to your Party, but what the issue of my adventure will be, cannot be known, till the wafer has closed up this note for ever.

Yours truly

C Lamb

MS: Princeton University Library, Princeton, N.J.; from the Lamb material presented to the library by Charles Scribner. Pub.: Hazlitt, II, 396; Lucas (1912), V, 405; Lucas (1935), II, 117. The date is indicated by the next two letters and by two of Mrs. John Fenwick's letters of 1811 to Mary Hays: on Sunday evening, September 15 (misdated September 16), Mrs. Fenwick remarked on Miss Hays's invitation to Eliza Anne—John and Eliza Fenwick's daughter—to visit Miss Hays at Wandsworth (not Walworth, as Lamb here writes), London; on Thursday evening, September 26 (misdated September 28), Mrs. Fenwick mentioned that Eliza Anne was spending that evening with the Lambs. See *The Fate of the Fenwicks,* pp. 44 and 46. For identifications of the Fenwicks and Mary Hays see my Vol. II, Letter 108, note 1; and Vol. I, Letter 58, note 1.
  1. George Dyer.

264. *M. A. L. to Sarah Stoddart Hazlitt, and C. L. to William Hazlitt*

Temple
[Wednesday,] 2 Oct 1811

My dear Sarah

I have been a long time anxiously expecting the happy news[1] that I have just received, I address you because as the letter has been lying some days at the India House I hope you are able to sit up and read my congratulations on the little live boy you have been so many years wishing for. As we old women say "May he live to be a great comfort to you." I never knew an event of the kind that gave me so much pleasure as the Little-long-looked-for-come-at-last's arrival, and I rejoiced to hear his honour had begun to suck, the word was not distincly written and I was a long time making out the welcome fact. I hope to hear from you soon for I am desirous to know if your nursing labours are attended with any difficulties. I wish you a happy *getting up,* and a merry christening.

Charles sends his love, perhaps though he will write a scrap to Hazlitt at the end. he is now looking over me, he is always in my way for he has had a months holydays at home, but I am happy to say they end on monday—when mine begin for I am going to pass a week at Richmond with Mrs Burney. She has been dying but she went to the Isle of Wight & recovered once more, and she is finishing her recovery at Richmond.[2] When there I intend to read Novels & play at Piquet all day long.—

Yours truly,
M Lamb

Dear Hazlitt,

I cannot help accompanying my sisters congratulations to Sarah with some of my own to you on this happy occasion of a man child being born—

Delighted Fancy already sees him some future **rich alderman** or opulent merchant; painting perhaps a little in his leisure hours **for amusement** like the late H. Bunbury Esq.—[3]

Pray, are the Winterslow Estates entailed; I am afraid lest the young dog when he grows up should cut down the woods, and leave no groves for widows to take their lonesome solace in. The Wem Estate of course can only devolve on him, in case of your brother leaving no male issue.

Well, my blessing & heavens be upon him & make him like his father, with something a better temper and a smoother head of hair, and then all the men & women must love him

Martin & the Card-boys[4] join in congratulations. Love to Sarah. Sorry we are not within Caudle-shot.—

C Lamb

If the Widow be assistant on this notable occasion, give our due respects & kind remembrances to her—

MS: Lockwood Library, State University of New York at Buffalo. Pub.: Sala, I, 439–440; Purnell, I, 439–440; Fitzgerald, II, 266–267; Hazlitt, I, 420; Ainger (1888), I, 267; Ainger (1900), II, 198; Macdonald, I, 333; Ainger (1904), I, 324; Harper, III, 322–323; Lucas (1905), VI, 430–431; Lucas (1912), V, 453–454; Lucas (1935), II, 117–118. Address: Mrs. Hazlitt/Winterslow/near Sarum/Wilts. Postmark: October 2, 1811.

1. That Sarah Hazlitt had, on September 26, 1811, given birth to William (d. 1893). He would be called to the bar at the Middle Temple in 1844 and become a registrar in the court of bankruptcy, a position he held for more than thirty years and from which he was retired in 1891. He would also become a contributor to the *Morning Chronicle,* a translator (principally of writings in French), and the author of works on bankruptcy law. In 1833 he would be married to Catherine Reynell (1804–1860). Their son was William Carew Hazlitt (1834–1913), the author, bibliographer, and editor whose works on the Lambs are cited in the present volumes.

2. Sarah (Mrs. James) Burney did not die until 1832. In the second paragraph in the next letter Lamb gives his explanation of Mary's going to Mrs. Burney. Lamb's portion of this letter begins with "Dear Hazlitt," below.

3. William Henry Bunbury (1750–1811), an artist and a caricaturist of inherited means and social prominence, to which he had added by having been made a colonel in the West Suffolk Militia and an equerry to Frederick Augustus, Duke of York and Albany (1763–1827). I have not been able to determine the later disposition of what Lamb in his next paragraph calls the "Winterslow Estates"—Middleton Cottage, another residence, perhaps a third, and a malt house and a garden, all in Winterslow or Salisbury (see Ralph M. Wardle, *Hazlitt* [Lincoln: University of Nebraska Press, 1971], p. 104)—the real estate Sarah Stoddart Hazlitt owned at the time of her marriage, possibly owned altogether by the terms of the will of the elder John Stoddart, her father. The "Wem Estate"—the house into which John and William Hazlitt's father, the Reverend Mr. William Hazlitt, had brought his family in 1787 and left in 1813—was owned by the Unitarian congregation of Wem, Shropshire. See my Vol. II, Letter 167, note 8, about the children of John and Mary Hazlitt.

4. Martin Burney, that is, and the (other) cards players. The widow, to whom Lamb refers in his postscript, is, presumably, the elder Mrs. John Stoddart, Sarah's mother.

265. *C. L. to Morgan*

[Saturday, October 12, 1811]

Dear M.,

The dark November fogs are come, Night travelling with flambeaux is expensive; without, dangerous. Add to this, that the migrative Actress has not yet taken her flight, and in all birdish probability sets out tomorrow. Our dinner at Hammersmith must cool for another day. Where is the Lecturer, quasi lecturus?¹ he has not been heard of at his own abode this fortnight. By his hostess's anxious enquiries I must suspect he has out-stay'd the stay-maker's patience. Meantime where are my Books?

Written in confusion from my Inn² in the Temple, surrounded by mother, daughter, brother and dog of the Fenwick breed, who have been incommoding me night and day for a week. Mary has been staying at Capt. Burney's 3 or 4 days for quiet; I am in a [pure (?)] West Indian fever.

Can you understand these dark sayings?— Kind remembrance to Mr. M. and Miss B.³ How is thy nose? do styptics flourish?

Thine, without the advantage of solitude

C. Lamb

I suppose you understand by the foregoing that we come to Hammersmith the Sunday after; not tomorrow.

MS: unrecovered. Text: Lucas (1935), II, 119. The date is established not by the (premature) coming of the November fogs, mentioned in the opening sentence of the letter, but, rather, by what follows in the letter and by two of Mrs. John Fenwick's letters of 1811 to Mary Hays: from the Lambs' on Saturday evening, October 12, Mrs. Fenwick wrote that Eliza Anne had suddenly been notified to make ready to sail shortly with her acting company for Barbados, the West Indies; on Wednesday, October 16 (misdated October 13), Mrs. Fenwick wrote that her daughter had gone. See *The Fate of the Fenwicks*, pp. 48–50.

1. Meaning, conjecturally (for the Latin is corrupt), "[the one] almost become a lecturer." Lamb refers to Coleridge, who, having talked himself into some temporary trouble with the Morgans and Charlotte Brent by the night of October 8, asked Morgan on the night of October 12 to send his books and "other *paucities*" (*Coleridge's Letters*, III, 338) to him at 6 Southampton Buildings, Chancery Lane. How long Coleridge had been staying there, when he was not staying in Hammersmith, or who was his hostess, or "stay-maker," when she was not Mrs. Morgan, I cannot say. Coleridge was arranging for and preparing the series of seventeen lectures on Shakespeare and Milton he would give under the auspicies of the London Philosophical Society in Scot's Corporation Hall, Crane Court, Fleet Street, on Monday and Thursday evenings beginning on Monday,

November 18, 1811, and ending on Monday, January 27, 1812. See John Payne Collier, *Seven Lectures on Shakespeare and Milton. By the Late S. T. Coleridge. A List of All the MS. Emendations in Mr. Collier's Folio, 1632; and an Introductory Preface* (1856; rpt. New York: Burt Franklin, 1968), pp. i–lix and 1–149; *Coleridge's Shakespearean Criticism*, II, 21–183; *Coleridge on Shakespeare: The Text of the Lectures of 1811–12*, ed. R. A. Foakes (Charlottesville, Va.: The University Press of Virginia, 1971); and *Coleridge's Letters*, III, esp. 347 and 353.

    2. The Lambs' apartment seemingly become an inn by the presence of Mrs. Fenwick, Eliza Anne, Orlando, and their dog. Orlando, Eliza Anne's brother, is initially identified in Vol. II, Letter 108, note 1.

    3. The remembrance is to Mary (Mrs. John James) Morgan—despite the "Mr."—and to Charlotte Brent.

266.   *C. L. to Mary Matilda Betham*

[November 17, 1811]

Dear Miss B.—

I send you three Tickets which will serve the first course of C.'s Lectures, six in number, the first begins tomorrow. Excuse the cover being not *or fa*,[1] is not that french? I have no writing paper.

Yours truly,

C. Lamb

    N. B. It is my present, not C's id. est he gave 'em me, I you.

MS: unrecovered. Text: *A House of Letters*, p. 137. Also pub.: Hazlitt, II, 396; Lucas (1912), V, 405; Lucas (1935), II, 120.

    1. Possibly meaning "correct," "proper," or "as it should be," from *au fait* ("expert" or "to the point"); possibly meaning "where it should be," from *où [il] fait*. In Lucas (1935), II, 120, Lamb's expression is given as *oo fa*. In his concluding paragraph Lamb explains that the present of the three tickets is his present, not Coleridge's: that is, Coleridge gave the tickets to Lamb, and Lamb gives them to Miss Betham.

267.   *C. L. to Mrs. John James Morgan*

[March 18, 1812]

    take Soap Lees and Whiting *no other impediments* the proportion of 6 pennorth of the former to a cake of the latter, mix them together & lay it on pretty thick on the marble & let it lie for three weeks—

This will restore your Great grandfathers old monument provided it be of marble, & bleach it as white as his bones—

Probatum est[1]

C L

MS: Quoted by permission of The Carl H. Pforzheimer Library, New York. Unpublished. Address: Mrs. Morgan/7. Portland Place/Hammersmith. Postmark: March 18, 1812. The "7." may be a postal endorsement.
    1. "It has been proved."

268. *C. L. to Charles Lloyd, the elder*

India House
Tuesday, 8 Sep., 1812

Dear Sir,—

I return you thanks for your little Book.[1] I am no great Latinist, but you appear to me to have very happily caught the Horatian manner. Some of them I had seen before. What gave me most satisfaction has been the 14th Epistle (its easy and Gentlemanlike beginning, particularly), and perhaps next to that, the Epistle to Augustus, which reads well even after Pope's delightful Imitation of it. What I think the least finish'd is the 18th Epistle. It is a metre which never gave me much pleasure. I like your *eight* syllable verses very much. They suit the Epistolary style quite as well as the *ten*. I am only sorry not to find the Satires in the same volume. I hope we may expect them. I proceed to find some few oversights, if you will indulge me, or what seem so to me, for I have neglected my Latin (and quite lost my Greek) since I left construing it at School. I will take them as I find them mark'd in order.

[. . .]

I do not quite like rendering *ligna,*[2] *boards*. I take the passage to allude to the religious character of their groves, and that Horace means to say, If you are one who think virtue to be mere words, and account no more of a grove (that is, of a consecrated place) than of so much timber.— As I should say, if you look upon a Church as only so much brick and mortar, *i.e.* divested of its sacred character. I don't know if I am right—but *boards* sound awkward to me: *timber* I think should be the word. Timber is a word we apply to wood dead or alive. Boards only to the dead wood.

[. . .]

Our wills to resign[3] is literally the rendering of *testamenta resignare*—and would it not also as aptly apply to *voluntates deponere?* The resignation of the will in an hour of sickness gives one a Christian idea. At all events, resign should have been written re-sign, which would have precluded the Ambiguity.

[. · .]

"Of the old dove thou keep'st the nest."[4] Turning to the original, I find it "vetuli notique columbi. *Tu* nidum servas, *ego,*" &c., which I have always translated a pair of old and well acquainted Doves, one of us (*you*) keep to your nest, the other (I) praise the Country. I have always taken columbi to be plural and to refer to *Tu et ego.* Referring to Creech, I find he translates it as I would.

[. · .]

I don't know whether *libertine*[5] in our unhappy perversion of the meaning would be any great compliment to the memory of a parent. In English it always means a person of loose morals, though by transposing the order of the words you have perhaps obviated the objection. A *libertine father* would have shock'd the ear. The transposition leads us to the Latin meaning, by making us pause a little. I believe this is a foolish objection.

[. · .]

You have two or three times translated "solennis" by "solemn." Has not the English word acquired a gravity and religion, which the Latin did not intend? [. . .] "Solemnly unsound"—does "solemnia insanire" mean anything more than to be mad with leave of custom—to be orderly or warrantably mad?[6] [. . .] "To spend the morning solemnly at home." Does "solenne fuit" mean anything more than that it was customary or habitual with them to stay at home? Our *solemn* is applied only *directly* to forms of religious or grave occasions, as a solemn hymn or funeral; and *indirectly* or ironically to grave stupid people—as a solemn coxcomb—which latter I am afraid you will think me for being so verbose on a trifling objection.

[. · .]

It[7] should have been rendered by the word *sock,* which refers to Comedy. The Cothurnus or Buskin was the high-rais'd shoe of the *tragic* actor.

[. · .]

Let me only add that I hope you will continue an employment which must have been so delightful to you. That it may have the power of stealing you occasionally from some sad thoughts is my fervent wish and hope.[8] Pray, Dear Sir, give my kindest remembrances

to Mrs. Lloyd, and to Plumstead—I am afraid I can add no more
who are likely to remember me. Charles and I sometimes correspond.
He is a letter in my debt. [. . .]

MS: unrecovered. Text: *Lamb and the Lloyds,* pp. 223–224 and 227–231,
here reconstructed. Also pub.: Harper, III, 323–327; Lucas (1935), II, 121–123.
    1. The senior Charles Lloyd's *The Epistles of Horace; Translated into English
Verse,* which was printed, privately in Birmingham by Orton and Hawkes Smith,
in 1812. The epistles in Lloyd's volume available to Lamb before their appearance
in that volume (see the third sentence in this letter and the postscript to Letter
237), all translations of the first book of Horace's *Epistles,* are Epistle i: "To
Mæcenas"; Epistle ii: "To Lollius"; Epistle iii: "To Julius Florus"; Epistle iv:
"To Albius Tibullus"; Epistle vii: "To Mæcenas"; and Epistle x: "To Aristius
Fuscus." For those are, separately, in that order, also in the *Gentleman's Magazine,* 79 (March 1809), 255–256; 80 (January 1810), 63–64; 80 (March 1810),
253–254; 81 (July 1811), 62; 80 (August 1810), 159–160; and 80 (April 1810),
358–359. The first twenty-eight lines of Lloyd's translation of Horace's Book I,
Epistle xiv: "To My Steward," which most satisfied Lamb, read so:

      Steward of my woods and self-restoring farm,
      (Despised by thee) which formerly was warm
      With five bright fires—a place of some renown,
      Which sent five Senators to Varias' town;
      Let us contend, who is the most inclined,
      I to pluck up the thorns which choak the mind,
      Or thou the thorns which my estate molest;
      And whether Horace or his farm thrive best.
      Lamia has lost his brother, and my grief
      For him who mourns, despairing of relief,
      Detains me here, tho' there my heart and soul
      Bear me impatient of undue controul.
      I call the country, thou the town-man blest;
      He hates his own, who others' lots likes best:
      The place is blamed unjustly, for we find
      That change of place, can never change the mind;
      At Rome by others hurried here and there,
      Thou for the country didst prefer thy prayer;
      My steward now, thy fickle heart resorts
      Again to Rome, its bagnios, and its sports;
      While I, consistent with myself pursue
      One steady plan, and this thou know'st is true;
      And when by hateful business forced to move
      To Rome, I leave with grief the farm I love:
      Our inclinations differ—hence we see
      That I and thou must ever disagree;
      For what thou call'st a wild deserted waste,
      Exactly suits my own and others taste.

"To Augustus"—Pope's imitation of it was published in 1737—is the first
epistle of Horace's second book. The eighteenth epistle, of Horace's first book, is
"To Lollius." Its meter is established in the opening two lines of the original—
"Si bene te novi, metues, liberrime Lolli, / scurrantis speciem praebere, professus
amicum"—and in the opening two lines of Lloyd's translation: "If rightly I know
thee, thou wilt not offend, / My Lollius, by flattery the ears of a friend." (The
Latin is quoted from *Horace: Satires and Epistles,* ed. Edward P. Morris [1939;

rpt. Norman, Okla.: University of Oklahoma Press, 1968], p. 113.) Lloyd probably disappointed the hope Lamb expresses regarding Horace's *Satires,* for Lloyd seems never to have had printed or sent to Lamb a translation of that work. All except the last of the bracketed ellipses in my reconstruction of this letter replace what may have been passages of Lamb's criticisms not published in *Lamb and the Lloyds.* The other texts of this letter were derived from that text.

2. In Horace's Book I, Epistle vi: "To Numicius," a portion of lines 31–32— ". . . Virtutem verba putas et / lucum ligna . . ."—which Lloyd had translated as "Think'st thou that virtue is composed of words, / As some men think a grove composed of boards?" (I, vi, 45–46).

3. In Lloyd's translation of Book I, Epistle vii: "To Maecenas," a portion of lines 11–14—

> Now fathers and mothers are pale for their boys,
> And the forum's engagements, its bustle and noise,
> And officious attention, together combine
> To bring fevers, which cause us our wills to resign

—from

> dum pueris omnis pater et matercula pallet,
> officiosaque sedulitas et opella forensis
> adducit febris et testamenta resignat. [I, vii, 7–9]

Lamb's *"voluntates deponere"* (below) is not in the epistle.

4. In Lloyd's translation of Book I, Epistle x: "To Aristius Fuscus," a portion of lines 1–14—

> We who a country life enjoy,
> Whom rural pleasures never cloy,
> Wish health and peace may always crown
> Our Fuscus, who prefers the town;
> For tho' in this we disagree,
> We feel like twins a sympathy
> In other things;—what one refuses,
> The other does, and so he chooses;
> Of the old dove thou keep'st the nest,   [9]
> While I (and think myself more blest)
> Extol the scenes which nature yields,
> Rivers which flow thro' verdant fields,
> The moss clad rocks, the shady groves,
> Which tranquil meditation loves

—from

> Vrbis amatorem Fuscum salvere iubemus
> ruris amatores. Hac in re scilicet una
> multum dissimiles, at cetera paene gemelli,
> fraternis animis (quicquid negat alter, et alter)
> adnuimus pariter vetuli notique columbi.   [5]
> Tu nidum servas; ego laudo ruris amoeni
> rivos et musco circumlita saxa nemusque.
> Quid quaeris? Vivo et regno, simul ista reliqui,
> quae vos ad caelum effertis rumore secundo,
> utque sacerdotis fugitivus liba recuso;
> pane egeo iam mellitis potiore placentis. [I, x, 1–11]

The translator and scholar Thomas Creech (1659–1700), to whose *The Odes, Satyrs, and Epistles of Horace* (first published in 1684) Lamb below refers, had converted the passage this way:

> All Health I Lover of the Country send
> To *Fuscus,* the gay City's greatest Friend;
> Brothers in all things else, what one approves,

Or flies, the other likewise hates or loves,
We Nod together like old acquainted Doves.   [5]
And now we disagree in this alone,
Our Humours differ here; you love the Town,
And I the pleasant Plains, and purling Flood,
The Groves, and mossy Banks, and shady Wood.
In short, I live, I reign, since I'm retir'd
From that which you as much as Heav'n admir'd.

[6th ed. (1737), p. 289: I, x, 1–11]

5. In Lloyd's translation of Book I, Epistle xx: "To His Book," line 35—"from a father libertine descended"—from *libertino natum patre* (I, xx, 20).

6. Lamb preceding criticized Lloyd's translation of Book I, Epistle i: "To Maecenas," line 130—"Thou think'st me then quite solemnly unsound"—from *Insanire putas sollemnia me* (I, i, 101). Lamb following criticizes a part of Lloyd's translation of Book II, Epistle i: "To Augustus," lines 149–150—"'Twas long a custom sanctioned at Rome, / To spend the morning solemnly at home"—from "Romae dulce diu fuit et sollemne recluse / mane domo vigilare . . ." (II, i, 102–103).

7. The Latin *socco*, in Book II, Epistle i: "To Augustus," line 174, which Lloyd had translated as "buskins" (II, i, 254).

8. The senior Mr. and Mrs. Charles Lloyd had lost three of their children in quick succession in 1811: Thomas, who had died on September 12; Caroline (b. 1789?), their fourth daughter, who had died on October 15; and Robert, who had died on October 26. (About Thomas and Robert see Vol. I, Letter 41, note 1, and Letter 34, note 7.) Plumstead Lloyd, mentioned below, is identified in Vol. II, Letter 104, note 4. The following statement, pertaining to Lamb's final two sentences, is in Lucas (1905), VI, 432: "A letter from Lamb to Charles Lloyd, Junior, belonging to this period, is now no more, in common with all but two of his letters, the remainder of which were destroyed by Lloyd's son, Charles Grosvenor Lloyd. Writing to Daniel Stuart on October 13, 1812, Wordsworth says, 'Lamb writes to Lloyd that C.'s play . . . is accepted.'" (See my Vol. I, Letter 10, near the end of note 4, about Charles Grosvenor Lloyd; Letter 55, note 4, about Daniel Stuart; Letter 25, note 4, about Coleridge's play—*Remorse. A Tragedy, in Five Acts;* and *Wordsworths' Letters*, III, 48, for the context of Wordsworth's remark.) "The remainder of the [present] letter," noted Lucas in *Lamb and the Lloyds*, p. 231, "is torn away."

269. *C. L. to John Dyer Collier*

Sunday Morn! [October 4? 1812]

Dear Sir,

Mrs. Collier has been kind enough to say that you would endeavor to procure a Reporter's situation for W. Hazlitt. I went to consult with him upon it last night, and he acceded very eagerly to the proposal, and requests me to say how very much obliged he feels to your kindness, and how glad he should be for its success. He is indeed at his wits end for a livelihood, and, I should think, especially qualified for such an employment, from his singular facility in retaining all conversations at which he has been ever present.— I think you may recommend him with confidence.[1] I am sure I shall feel *myself* obliged to you for your exertions, having a great regard for him.

Yours truly
C Lamb

MS: The Folger Shakespeare Library, Washington, D.C. Pub.: Hazlitt, I, 425; Macdonald, I, 334; Harper, III, 327–328; Lucas (1905), VI, 432; Lucas (1912), V, 455; Lucas (1935), II, 124. Address: J. Collier Esqr/56 Hatton Garden. See note 1 for the dating, and Vol. II, Letter 224, source note, about the Colliers.

1. Soon after the birth of his son William, on September 26, 1811, Hazlitt had left his family in Winterslow and come to London hoping to raise money he sorely needed by obtaining subscriptions to a series of lectures he proposed to give on philosophy. By December 26 he had completed his arrangements for them. Between January 14 and April 28, 1812, he delivered eleven or twelve lectures at the Russell Institution, a subscription library in Great Coram Street, Russell Square. Robinson, who attended perhaps all those lectures except one, reported them to have been on Thomas Hobbes, John Locke, disinterestedness and self-love, David Hartley, Claude Adrien Helvétius and selfishness, free will and necessity, John Horne Tooke, and, in part at least, the utility of metaphysics. (See *H. C. R. on Books and Writers,* I, 57–58, 60, 62, 63, 64, 65, 68, and 69–70, and *Hazlitt,* pp. 183–190.) Hazlitt thereafter remained in London, borrowing or trying to borrow money from friends, trying also to finish a portrait (later destroyed) he had started in 1811 of Henry Robinson's brother Thomas (1770–1860)—Thomas was a tanner in Bury St. Edmunds—and trying to find employment. On September 28, 1812, Henry Robinson spoke with Dr. John Stoddart about securing Hazlitt a post on the *Times.* On September 30 Robinson met Stoddart in the company of Mary Lamb and learned that John Walter of the *Times* had promised to do something for Hazlitt and that James Perry of the *Morning Chronicle,* whom Hazlitt personally had approached, had conditionally promised to engage him. On October 4, probably (on September 20 or 27, possibly), Lamb wrote this letter recommending Hazlitt to John Dyer Collier, Perry's foreign editor. On October 10 Robinson received a letter from Catherine Clarkson informing him that Perry had hired Hazlitt. Hazlitt shortly rented the house at 19 York Street, Westminster, owned by Jeremy Bentham (1748–1832) and recently vacated by Bentham's colleague in the promulgation of utilitarianism James Mill (1773–1836)—a house once the home of Milton and Andrew Marvell—and began, at four guineas a week, six years in journalism as a parliamentary reporter for the *Morning Chronicle.* See *H. C. R. on Books and Writers,* I, 104, 110, and 116; *Hazlitt,* pp. 181–183 and 191–192; and John Payne Collier's *An Old Man's Diary, Forty Years Ago* (4 parts in 2 vols.; London: printed by Thomas Richards, 1871–1872), II, iv, 86.

270. *M. A. L. to Mrs. John Dyer Collier*

[Autumn 1812?]

Dear Mrs. C.,

   This note will be given to you by a young friend of mine, whom I wish you would employ: she has commenced business as a mantua-maker, and, if you and my girls would try her, I think she could fit you all three, and it will be doing her an essential service. She is, I think, very deserving, and if you procure work for her among your friends and acquaintances, so much the better. My best love to you and my girls. We are both well.

Yours affectionately,
Mary Lamb

MS: unrecovered. Text: Lucas (1935), II, 124–125. Also pub.: Lucas (1905), VI, 433; Lucas (1912), V, 456. John Payne Collier included and explained Mary's note to his mother, the former Jane Payne, in *An Old Man's Diary* (fully cited in the last sentence in note 1 to the preceding letter in the present edition), II, iii, 80: "Southey and Coleridge, as is well known, married two sisters of the name of Fricker: I never saw either of them, but a third sister settled as a mantua-maker in London, and for some years she worked for my mother and her daughters. She was an intelligent woman, but by no means above her business, though she was fond of talking of her two poet-married relations. She was introduced to my mother by the following [the present] note from Mary Lamb, who always spoke of my sisters as *her* girls." That third sister was Martha Fricker. She is distinguished from Eliza, the other sister who was not and appears never to have been married, by the fact that it was Martha who settled in London, in the autumn of 1812 or early in the winter of 1812–1813. Coleridge wrote of her in 1814 as "the Angel of the Race, self-nibbling Martha!" In 1816 he wrote of her as the only one of the "Brood" he had "any regard for, & who deserved it—whom the fine Ladies at Keswick [Edith Fricker Southey and Sara Fricker Coleridge] had left as a laborious Mantua-maker in London after having tantalized her with a year's intercourse with Sirs, Lords, and Dukes at Keswick, with a broken constitution because a broken Heart" (*Coleridge's Letters*, III, 518, and IV, 673; see III, 431 and 435). John Payne Collier's sisters have not been identified.

271. *C. L. to an unidentified addressee*

Saturday [autumn 1812?]

An accident prevents the pleasure we expected in seeing you on Monday; pray, come on *Wednesday* Eveng. instead

C Lamb

MS: Mr. W. Hugh Peal. Unpublished. This and the next letter appear to belong to the same general period as Letters 269, 270, and 273.

272.   *C. L. to Mrs. John Dyer Collier*

Sunday aftern*n* [autumn 1812?]

Dr. Mrs. C.—

We should have been with you tonight, but my sister has had an accident which disables her from walking. A stone fell on her foot, while she was removing a grate, and the bruise has kept her at home since Friday. She could not come out without inflaming it. I would come by myself, but also am not very well. We hope to come & see you soon.

Yours

C Lamb

MS: **Mr. W.** Hugh Peal. Unpublished. Address: Mrs. Collier/Hatton Garden.

273.   *C. L. to Mr. or Mrs. John Dyer Collier*

Temple

12 Jan 1813

C Lamb & Sister's respects, entreat Mrs. Collier to excuse them this Evening, they neither of them being well. Assure Mrs. C. that nothing but having been a good deal fatigued should have prevented them

MS: **Dr. D. G.** Wilson, Bushey, Watford, Hertfordshire. Unpublished.

274.   *C. L. to Miss F. Manning*

E. I. H.

4 June 1813

C Lamb's respects to Miss M—is sorry that her Letter has arrived too late to send by the present fleet. He will keep it till an opportunity recurs of sending it by *Batavia;* for no regular ships go to China any more this year. In the mean, by the China fleet just arriv'd & one or two more Bengal ships, he hopes to have tidings of her brother.—[1]

MS: Mr. W. Hugh Peal. Pub.: *Lamb and His Hertfordshire,* p. 93. Address: Miss F. Manning/Newnham/near/Cambridge. Postmark: June 4 [1813]. Thomas Manning's sister and probably the brother who is named in the letter quoted in the note below are mentioned in Letter 245, at the reference to note 7.

1. The last published letter from Manning to Lamb is dated October 11, 1810.

Dear Lamb

Just going to leave Calcutta for God knows where!

very Strange in mind—cannot write.

Give one of these boxes of India Ink to ⟨Your⟩ Mary & the other to my brother Edward when you see him.

I'll write to you before I am out of the bounds of civilization

Thomas Manning

[*Manning-Lamb Letters,* p. 114, and a facsimile between pp. 114 and 115] Manning had come from Canton to Calcutta early in 1810 and left it for Bengal and Tibet in September 1811, determined to see the forbidden city of Lhasa. He traveled as a doctor, with only one Chinese servant and without any assistance from the Calcutta government. He reached Lhasa in December, became the first Englishman to enter it, and during the next four months had several interviews with the (seven-year-old) Dalai Lama. Manning, alone, departed in April 1812, compelled by Peking officialdom to return to India. He arrived in Calcutta in June and, a few months later, made his way back to Canton, there remaining until 1816. The next letter from Lamb to Manning that is known is dated December 25, 1815 (Letter 310). The next published letter from Manning to Lamb is postmarked May 30, 1819, almost two years after Manning had returned from Peking and Canton to England. See the *Manning-Lamb Letters,* pp. 118–126, and my Vol. I, Letter 53, source note.

275.   *C. L. to Montagu*

30 Mar 1814

Dr. Montagu,

The Bearer of this I have known all his life. I knew him at *Christs Hospital,* and thro' life he has borne himself irreproachably; always as steady as Old Time. But Nature has fought against him. His fits and he were born together. I remember he had them when quite a child, and he has them now to a terrible degree. I suppose with such obstacles even your kindness could *professionally* avail him nothing.[1] But as I saw Sir S. Romillys name & the Chancellors to his pitiable Paper, I thought you would perhaps not be averse to set your name to a £1 or a 10/6—next to mine— —having such examples at your own Bar before you. this is a case which ⟨cannot be⟩ can need no ⟨colour⟩ painting forth.

Yours ever

[. . .]

MS: Massachusetts Historical Society, Boston, Mass. Pub.: David Bonnell Green, "Three New Letters of Charles Lamb," *Huntington Library Quarterly,* 27 (November 1963), 83–84. Address: B. Montagu Esqr/Lincolns Inn.
1. Lamb gives "White" as the surname of this man, apparently an epileptic, and writes at length of him in a letter to Montagu of June 20, 1815 (Letter 297). David Bonnell Green presented that letter and wrote thus of its subject in "A New Letter of Charles Lamb to Basil Montagu," *Huntington Library Quarterly,* 31 (February 1968), 199: "Of all the boys named White who were contemporary with Lamb at the school, the one most likely to be the man Lamb refers to is Thomas White, who was there from 1783 to 1790 and was later bound to his father, a scrivener of the Middle Temple. There is, it appears, no evidence in the admission papers [in Christ's Hospital] that Thomas White—or any of the other boys—suffered from fits, but these may have developed subsequent to admission." Lamb had seen on White's "pitiable Paper" (below) the name of Montagu's friend the law reformer Sir Samuel Romilly (1757–1818). Romilly was, more particularly, the chancellor of the county palatine of Durham from 1805 to 1815; a member of Parliament from 1806 to 1807, from 1808 to 1812, and in 1818; and the author, among other works, of *Thoughts on the Probable Influence of the Late Revolution in France upon Great Britain* (1790) and *Observations on Criminal Law of England* (1810). Lamb had also seen on White's paper the name of Lord Chancellor John Scott, first Earl of Eldon. (See Letter 243, note 2.) Lamb's signature has been cut from this letter.

276.   *C. L. to William Hazlitt or Leigh Hunt*

[Spring 1814?]

Dr **H—**

I understand you have got (or had) a snivelling methodistical adulteration of my Essay on Drunkenness. . I wish very much to see it, to see how far Mr Basil Montagu's Philanthropical Scoundrels have gone to make me a **Sneak.** There certainly was no crying "Peccavi"[1] in the 1st. Draught.—

Yours, though I seldom see you.

Ch Lamb

MS: Princeton University Library. Pub.: Lucas (1935), II, 144. The subject of Lamb's note may be Lamb's manuscript of "Confessions of a Drunkard" (*Works,* I, 133–139; see I, 430–434) after the manuscript had been editorially altered for publication but before it was published—anonymously, as "The Confessions of a Drunkard: To the Editor of *The Philanthropist*"—in *The Philanthropist: Or Repository for Hints and Suggestions Calculated to Promote the Comfort and Happiness of Man,* 3 (January 1813), 48–54. (That citation is taken from "Bibliographical List [1794–1834] of the Published Writings of Charles and Mary Lamb," in *The Works in Prose and Verse of Charles and Mary Lamb,* ed. Thomas Hutchinson [London: Henry Frowde: Oxford University Press, 1908], I, xxviii; see *H. C. R. on Books and Writers,* I, 128.) *The Philanthropist,* which was issued from 1811 to 1816 and in 1819 and extends to seven volumes, was founded by the Quaker, scientist, and philanthropist William Allen (1770–1843) and jointly edited by him and the utilitarian philosopher James Mill. Among those who wrote for *The Philanthropist* were Mill and Montagu. Among those who could have submitted for Lamb or influenced Lamb to submit the manuscript of "Confessions of a Drunkard" to the editors of *The Philanthropist* were Montagu and Hazlitt. That point was made by Thomas Hutchinson (the discoverer of Lamb's essay in the magazine, the editor of the Lambs' works, not the brother of Mary Wordsworth) in "Lamb and the Utilitarians: The 'Confessions of a Drunkard,' " *The Athenaeum*, No. 3903 (August 16, 1902), 225: "perhaps by Basil Montagu or William Hazlitt—who, as occupant from 1811 [properly 1812: see Letter 269, note 1] onwards of the house . . . which stood in [Jeremy] Bentham's garden at Westminster, must have had frequent opportunities of meeting James Mill—the manuscript of the 'Confessions' would be put into the hands of the joint-editors of the *Philanthropist*." Hazlitt, also, could have obtained the manuscript from Mill or Montagu after Mill and Allen had as editors altered it for publication. The foregoing argument, then, proceeding from the assumption that the subject of Lamb's note may be Lamb's manuscript after it had been edited for publication in *The Philanthropist*, would lead to the conclusion that Lamb in his note is addressing Hazlitt and that Lamb wrote his note in, say, December 1812 or early January 1813. But the subject of Lamb's note may be Lamb's manuscript after Mill and Allen had edited and published it and after Montagu had acquired and re-edited it for its second appearance, as an anonymous essay in a collection of essays against strong drink that Montagu compiled and called *Some Enquiries into the Effects of Fermented Liquors. By a Water Drinker* (London: J. Johnson, 1814), pp. 201–215. Montagu could have asked Hazlitt or Leigh Hunt to read the essays forming *Some Enquiries into the Effects of Fermented Liquors* before Montagu published it, for an evaluation or with the hope for an early and a favorable review, by Hazlitt in the *Morning Chronicle, The Champion,* or *The Examiner*— Hazlitt in the late spring of 1814 was contributing to all three—or by Hunt in *The Examiner.* That argument would lead to the conclusion that Lamb in his note is addressing Hazlitt or Hunt and that Lamb wrote his note in probably the spring of 1814. Possibly relevant to such a case is the notice in Jeremiah Stanton Finch's "Charles Lamb's 'Companionship . . . in Almost Solitude,' " *Princeton University Library Chronicle,* 6 (1945), 197, that the original of Lamb's note was removed, presumably by Charles Scribner or an official responsible for the Scribner collection in the Princeton University Library, from a copy now in the Scribner collection of the 1814 edition of Montagu's *Some Enquiries into the Effects of Fermented Liquors.* Another argument is John M. Turnbull's, in "The Originally Intended Destination of Lamb's 'Confessions of a Drunkard,' " *Notes and Queries,* 194 (August 6, 1949), 341–342. Turnbull's argument proceeds from a conviction that the subject of Lamb's note is the "1813 text of the Essay," to the possibility that Lamb's essay may have been "residual *Reflector* copy"—copy, that is, intended for *The Reflector* of John and Leigh Hunt before that serial ceased on March 23, 1812—and to the conclusion that Lamb in his note would be addressing Leigh Hunt and would have written his note "between publication of the January [1813] issue of the *Philanthropist* and Hunt's commitment, on the 3rd February, 1813, to his two years' imprisonment for libel on the Prince Regent, say some time in January. Why," Turnbull added, "Lamb should have bothered him [Hunt] at such a juncture in so peremptory a tone is no more inexplicable than the same treatment in 1814, while he was still in gaol, might have been" (p. 342). The allusion in that last sentence is to Lucas (1935), II, 144, where Lamb's note is headed "To Leigh Hunt (?)" and shown to be not dated but assigned the date of 1814, and where Lucas stated but did not explain the following: "This letter of Lamb's, which I take to be written to Hunt rather than Hazlitt, refers to the second appearance of the *Confessions* in Basil Montagu's collection of arguments in favour of abstinence, *Some Enquiries into the Effects of Fermented Liquors,* 1814." James Henry Leigh Hunt had seen Lamb at Christ's Hospital between 1791 and 1799, when Hunt was a student at the institution and Lamb occasionally returned to it. "Lamb's visits to the school, after he left it," wrote Hunt in about 1849 or 1850, "I remember well, with his fine intelligent face. Little did I think I should have the pleasure of sitting with it in after-times as an old friend, and seeing it careworn and still finer" (*Hunt's Autobiography*, I, 83). Hunt had certainly met Lamb by January 17, 1812, when Robinson reported having joined Hunt and Lamb that evening in Barron Field's rooms, at 4 Hare Court, Inner Temple. (See *H. C. R. on Books and Writers*, I, 59, and Letter 296, note 1.) Hunt had probably met Lamb by July 27, 1811, the approximate date of issue of the second number of *The Reflector*, which is the first number containing contributions by Lamb. The two men could have met long before then, as is pointed out in *Hunt's "Reflector*," pp. 61–65—through Lamb's brother, who had subscribed to Hunt's *Juvenilia* (1801) and thus may have known its author; through Barron Field, who had subscribed to *Juvenilia*, known Hunt by 1804 and Lamb by perhaps 1809, written for the first number (December 1810 or January 1811) of *The Reflector*, and whose brother Francis John Field (see Letter 296, note 1) had worked with Lamb at the East India House since 1806; through Robinson, who may have known Hunt since 1808; or through George Dyer, who had known Hunt by 1808 and written for the first number of *The Reflector*. No one seems to have left a record of the first meeting of Lamb and Hunt. The most Lamb left on or bearing on the subject is in his public letter of 1823, the "Letter of Elia to Robert Southey" (*Works*, I, 232): "Accident introduced me to the acquaintance of Mr. L. H.—and the experience of his many friendly qualities confirmed a friendship between us. . . . I was admitted to his household for some years, and do most solemnly aver that I believe him to be in his domestic relations as correct as any man. . . . He is . . . one of the most cordial-minded men I ever knew, and matchless as a fire-side companion." By 1813 Hunt had contributed to various periodicals and published *Juvenilia; or, a Collection of Poems. Written between the Ages of Twelve and Sixteen . . .* (1801); *Classical Tales, Serious and Lively. With Critical Essays on the Merits and Reputation of the Authors* (5 vols.; 1806–1807); *Critical Essays on the Performers of the London Theatres, Including General Observations on the Practice and Genius of the Stage* (1807), which consists for the most part of selections from the theatrical writings Hunt had written for *The News*, a paper his brother John (1775–1848) had started in 1805; *An Attempt to Shew the Folly and Danger of Methodism. In a Series of Essays . . .* (1809); *Reformist's Reply to an Article in the "Edinburgh Review"* (1810); and "The Feast of the Poets," a notorious satirical poem that had appeared in *The Reflector* of March 23, 1812, and would, in 1814, reappear as *The Feast of the Poets, with Notes, and Other Pieces in Verse*. Hunt had edited his and his brother John's *The Examiner* (a weekly) from its beginning on January 3, 1808, would edit it into 1821—and through the period 1813 to 1815, when John was in Coldbath Fields Prison and Leigh in Horsemonger Lane Jail for having ridiculed George, Prince of Wales, Prince Regent, afterward George IV, in *The Examiner* of March 12, 1812—and had edited also their *The Reflector* (a quarterly) from its beginning on about January 1, 1811, to its end on March 23, 1812. In 1809 Leigh Hunt had been married to Marianne Kent (1787?–1857), the eldest daughter of Thomas and Ann Kent and from 1803 the stepdaughter of Rowland Hunter. (See Vol. II, Letter 193, note 1.) In 1810 Marianne Hunt had given birth to Thornton Leigh Hunt (d. 1873), who became a journalist, the author of the novel *The Foster Brother* (1845), and the editor of *The Autobiography of Leigh Hunt* (2d ed.; 1859, though dated 1860), *The Poetical Works of Leigh Hunt* (1860), and *The Correspondence of Leigh Hunt* (2 vols.; 1862). Lamb in 1814 called him "Serious infant" and "my favourite child" in the second and last lines of "To T. L. H.: *A Child*" (*Works*, V, 35–36), in March 1816 will call him "our old grave friend" (Letter 312).

    1. "I have sinned."

PART VIII

Letters 277–297
4 Inner Temple Lane, Inner Temple
August 9, 1814——June 20, 1815

277. *C. L. to William Wordsworth*

Dear Wordsworth,

I cannot tell you how pleased I was at the receit of the great Armful of Poetry[1] which you have sent me, and to get it before the rest of the world too! I have gone quite through with it, and was thinking to have accomplishd that pleasure a second time before I wrote to thank you, but M. Burney came in the night (while we were out) and made holy theft of it, but we expect restitution in a day or two. It is the noblest conversational poem I ever read. A day in heaven. The part (or rather main body) which has left the sweetest odour on my memory (a bad term for the remains of an impression so recent) is the Tales of the Church yard.[2] The only girl among seven brethren born out of due time and not duly taken away again—the deaf man and the blind man—the Jacobite and the Hanoverian whom antipathies reconcile—the **Scarron-**entry of the rusticating parson upon his solitude—these were all new to me too. My having known the story of Margaret (at the beginning) a very old acquaintance even as long back as I saw you first at Stowey, did not make her reappearance less fresh—. I dont know what to pick out of this Best of Books upon the best subjects for partial naming—

that gorgeous Sunset is famous,[3] I think it must have been the identical one we saw on Salisbury plain five years ago, that drew Phillips from the card table where he had sat from rise of that luminary to its unequall'd set, but neither he nor I had gifted eyes to see those symbols of common things glorified such as the prophets saw them, in that sunset—the wheel—the potters clay—the washpot—the winepress—the almond tree rod—the baskets of figs—the fourfold visaged foor—the throne & him that sat thereon

One ⟨image⟩ feeling I was particularly struck with as what I recognised so very lately at Harrow Church on entering in it after a hot & secular day's pleasure, the instantaneous coolness and calming almost transforming properties of a country church just entered—a certain fragrance which it has—either from its holiness, or being kept shut all the week, or the air that is let in being pure country—exactly what you have reduced into words but I am feeling I cannot.[4] The reading your lines about it fixed me for a time, a monument in Harrow Church, (do you know it?) with its fine long Spire white as washd marble, to be seen by vantage of its high scite as far as Salisbury spire itself almost——

I shall select a day or two very shortly when I am coolest in brain to have a steady second reading, which I feel will lead to many more, for it will be a stock book with me while **eyes** or spectacles shall be lent me.

There is a deal of noble matter about mountain scenery, yet not so much as to overpower & discountenance a poor **Londoner** or South-country man entirely,[5] though Mary seems to have felt it occasionally a little too powerfully, for it was her remark during reading it that by your system it was doubtful whether a Liver in Towns had a Soul to be Saved. She almost trembled for that invisible part of us in her.

Save for a late excursion to Harrow & a day or two on the banks of the Thames this Summer, rural images were fast fading from my mind, and by the wise provision of the Regent all that was countryfy'd in the Parks is all but obliterated.[6] The very colour of green is vanishd, the whole surface of **Hyde Park** is dry crumbling sand (Arabia **Arenosa**) not a vestige or hint of grass ever having grown there, booths & drinking places go all round it for a mile & half I am confident—I might saw two miles in circuit—the stench of liquors, **bad** tobacco, **dirty people & provisions,** conquers the air & we are stifled & suffocated in **Hyde Park.**

Order after Order has been issued by L*d* Sidmouth[7] in the name of the Regent (acting in behalf of his Royal father) for the dispersion of the Varlets, but in vain. The vis unita of all the Publicans in London Westmr. Marybone & miles round is too powerful a force to put down. The Regent has rais'd a phantom which he cannot lay. There they'll stay probably for ever. The whole beauty of the Place is gone— that lake-look of the Serpentine[8]—it has got foolish ships upon it—but something whispers to have confidence in nature & its revival——

> at the coming of the *milder day*
> These monuments shall all be over grown——

Meantime I confess to have smokd one delicious **Pipe** in one of the cleanliest & goodliest of the booths—a tent rather ("O call it not a booth!")⁹—erected by the public Spirit of Watson who keeps the Adam & Eve at Pancras (the Ale houses have all emigrated with their train of bottles, mugs, cork-screws, waiters, into Hyde Park—whole **Ale** houses with all their **Ale!**)— in company with some of the guards that had been in France & a fine French girl (habited like a Princess of Banditto) which one of ⟨these [?] English⟩ the dogs had transported from the Garonne to the Serpentine—the unusual scene, in H. Park, by Candlelight in open air, good tobacco, bottled stout, made it **look like** an interval in a campaign, a repose after battle, I almost fancied scars smarting & was ready to club a story with my comrades of some of my lying deeds.—

After all, the fireworks were splendent—the Rockets in clusters, in trees & all shapes, spreading about like young stars in the making, floundering about in Space (like unbroke horses) till some of Newton's calculations should fix them, but then they went out——. Any one who could see em & the still finer showers of gloomy rain fire that fell sulkily & angrily from 'em, & could go to bed without dreaming of the Last Day, must be as hardend an Atheist as ✱✱✱✱✱✱¹⁰

Again let me thank you for your present & assure you that fireworks & triumphs have not distracted me from receiving a calm & noble enjoyment from it (which I trust I shall often) & I sincerely congratulate you on its appearance——

with kindest remembrances to you & household we remain—

Yours sincerey
C Lamb & sister¹¹

MS: University of Texas Library. Pub.: Talfourd (1837), I, 326–329; Talfourd (1848), I, 202–206; Sala, I, 264–268; Purnell, I, 264–268; Fitzgerald, II, 99–103; Hazlitt, I, 426–429; Ainger (1888), I, 271–274; Ainger (1900), II, 203–208; Macdonald, I, 339–343; Ainger (1904), I, 328–331; Harper, III, 328–333; Lucas (1905), VI, 434–436; Lucas (1912), V, 457–459; Lucas (1935), II, 126–129. Address: W. Wordsworth Esq/Rydal Mount/near Ambleside/or else at Grasmere/near Kendal/Westmorland. In late May or June 1811 the Wordsworths had moved from Allan Bank, Grasmere, into a smaller but more comfortable house, formerly the parsonage, in Grasmere. After William and Mary's daughter Catharine died, on June 4, 1812, perhaps from an aneurysm in a cerebral artery, and after their son Thomas died, on December 1, 1812, apparently from pneumonia ensuing upon the measles, the Wordsworths had found they could not endure in a house with a view of the churchyard holding the graves of the two children. In January 1813 Wordsworth had leased Rydal Mount, a house, once the farmhouse of Keens farm, two miles southeast of Grasmere down the Ambleside road. On probably May 12, 1813 (see Mark L. Reed's *Wordsworth: The Chronology of the Middle Years, 1800–1815* [Cambridge, Mass.: Harvard University Press, 1975], p. 529), Wordsworth and his family had moved into Rydal Mount, which was to become his and Mary's and Dorothy's permanent home.

1. *The Excursion, Being a Portion of The Recluse, a Poem,* a copy of which Wordsworth had sent to Lamb before Longman's published the poem, in late July or early August 1814. (See *Wordsworths' Letters,* III, 151.) Martin Burney, as Lamb will explain in his letter to Wordsworth of September 19 (Letter 280, second paragraph), had borrowed Lamb's copy of the poem for Hazlitt, who used it to write "Character of Mr. Wordsworth's New Poem, *The Excursion*" (*Hazlitt's Works,* XIX, 9–25) for *The Examiner* of August 21 and 28 and October 2, 1814. When Lamb had his copy back, he acted upon the request of Wordsworth and the suggestion of Southey and used it to write "Review of *The Excursion; a Poem.* By William Wordsworth" (*Works,* I, 160–172) for the *Quarterly Review,* 23 (October 1814), 100–111. See Letters 280, 281, 286, and 287.

2. In the sixth and seventh books of *The Excursion,* the tales the Pastor tells in "The Churchyard among the Mountains." Lamb, following, notices as new to him those tales told in VII, 632–714, from which he quoted in his reveiw of the poem (*Works,* I, 169–170); VII, 395–515; and VI, 392–521. If by "Scarron-entry" Lamb means "scarry-entry"—an entry into or over terrain precipitous or rocky— the passage in this letter that Lamb's compound virtually begins would seem to refer to the tale the Pastor tells of the Priest who had come with his wife and three children from afar into a mountain cottage, the parsonage:

> . . . All unembowered
> And naked stood that lowly Parsonage
>
> · · · · ·
>
> Rough and forbidding were the choicest roads
> By which our northern wilds could then be crossed;
> And into most of these secluded vales
> Was no access for wain, heavy or light.
> So, at his dwelling-place the Priest arrived
> With store of household goods, in panniers slung
> On sturdy horses graced with jingling bells,
> And on the back of more ignoble beast
>
> · · · · ·
>
> And far remote the chapel stood,—remote,
> And, from his Dwelling, unapproachable,
> Save through a gap high in the hills, an opening
> Shadeless and shelterless, by driving showers
> Frequented, and beset with howling winds.

[*The Excursion,* VII, 54–55, 59–66, and 140–144]

If by "Scarron-entry" Lamb means "Charon-entry"—from Charon, the ferryman who transported the shades of the dead across the river Styx and thus lived partly between two worlds—the passage in this letter that Lamb's compound virtually begins would seem to refer generally to the entry, in the fifth book of *The Excursion,* of the Pastor into the poem itself and so "upon" his solitude. "Nothing can be conceived finer than the manner of introducing these tales," wrote Lamb, in his review, of Wordsworth's manner and the Pastor. "With heaven above his head, and the mouldering turf at his feet [see *The Excursion,* V, esp. 342–345 and 653]— standing betwixt life and death—he seems to maintain that spiritual relation which he bore to his living flock, in its undiminished strength, even with their ashes; and to be in his proper cure, or diocese, among the dead" (*Works,* I, 168). The story of Margaret, with which Lamb had become acquainted when he and Wordsworth were together at Coleridge's cottage, at Nether Stowey, in July 1797 (see Vol. I, Letter 28), the story from which Lamb quoted in his review of *The Excursion* (*Works*, I, 166–167), is narrated by the Wanderer in *The Excursion*, I, 497–916. Her story appears originally in "The Ruined Cottage," a poem Wordsworth had started in about 1795, retitled "The Pedlar" by October 1800, and published—expanded and revised, with the Pedlar called the Wanderer—as the first book of *The Excursion*. See *Wordsworth's Poetical Works* (1940–1949), V, 365–369 and 376–415.

3. Not a sunset but another heavenly splendor—Lamb will correct himself in his letter to Wordsworth of September 19 (Letter 280, fourth paragraph)—as it is described in the Solitary's account, in *The Excursion*, II, 827–874, of the Pensioner caught abroad in a mountain storm and then found:

> So was he lifted gently from the ground,
> And with their freight homeward the shepherds moved
> Through the dull mist, I following—when a step,
> A single step, that freed me from the skirts
> Of the blind vapour, opened to my view
> Glory beyond all glory ever seen
> By waking sense or by the dreaming soul!
> The appearance, instantaneously disclosed,
> Was of a mighty city—boldly say
> A wilderness of building, sinking far
> And self-withdrawn into a boundless depth,
> Far sinking into splendour—without end!
> Fabric it seemed of diamond and of gold,
> With alabaster domes, and silver spires,
> And blazing terrace upon terrace, high
> Uplifted; here, serene pavilions bright,
> In avenues disposed; there, towers begirt
> With battlements that on their restless fronts
> Bore stars—illumination of all gems!
> By earthly nature had the effect been wrought
> Upon the dark materials of the storm
> Now pacified; on them, and on the coves
> And mountain-steeps and summits, whereunto
> The vapours had receded, taking there
> Their station under a cerulean sky.
> Oh, 'twas an unimaginable sight!
> Clouds, mists, streams, watery rocks and emerald turf,
> Clouds of all tincture, rocks and sapphire sky,
> Confused, commingled, mutually inflamed,
> Molten together, and composing thus,
> Each lost in each, that marvellous array
> Of temple, palace, citadel, and huge
> Fantastic pomp of structure without name,
> In fleecy folds voluminous, enwrapped.
> Right in the midst, where interspace appeared
> Of open court, an object like a throne
> Under a shining canopy of state
> Stood fixed; and fixed resemblances were seen
> To implements of ordinary use,
> But vast in size, in substance glorified;
> Such as by Hebrew Prophets were beheld
> In vision—forms uncouth of mightiest power
> For admiration and mysterious awe.

This little Vale, a dwelling-place of Man,
Lay low beneath my feet; 'twas visible—
I saw not, but I felt that it was there.
That which I *saw* was the revealed abode
Of Spirits in beatitude. . . .

The description reminds Lamb of a sunset he and Edward Phillips had witnessed
from the Hazlitts' in October 1809 (see Letters 235, 242, and 243) and prompts
Lamb to recall (below) Ezekiel 1:15–16 and 10:9–13, Isaiah 29:16 and
Jeremiah 18:6, Psalms 60:8 and 108:9, Revelation 14:19–20, Jeremiah 1:11,
Jeremiah 24, Ezekiel 1:5–25, Ezekiel 1:26–28 and Revelation esp. 4. Lamb's
"fourfold visaged foor" is an error for "fourfold-visaged four."

4. The words of Wordsworth, in *The Excursion*, V, 138–170, are these:

As chanced, the portals of the sacred Pile
Stood open; and we entered. On my frame,
At such transition from the fervid air,
A grateful coolness fell, that seemed to strike
The heart, in concert with that temperate awe
And natural reverence which the place inspired.
Not raised in nice proportions was the pile,
But large and massy; for duration built;
With pillars crowded, and the roof upheld
By naked rafters intricately crossed,
Like leafless underboughs, in some thick wood,
All withered by the depth of shade above.
Admonitory texts inscribed the walls,
Each, in its ornamental scroll, enclosed;
Each also crowned with wingèd heads—a pair
Of rudely-painted Cherubim. The floor
Of nave and aisle, in unpretending guise,
Was occupied by oaken benches ranged
In seemly rows; the chancel only showed
Some vain distinctions, marks of earthly state
By immemorial privilege allowed;
Though with the Encincture's special sanctity
But ill according. An heraldic shield,
Varying its tincture with the changeful light,
Imbued the altar-window; fixed aloft
A faded hatchment hung, and one by time
Yet undiscoloured. A capacious pew
Of sculptured oak stood here, with drapery lined;
And marble monuments were here displayed
Thronging the walls; and on the floor beneath
Sepulchral stones appeared, with emblems graven
And foot-worn epitaphs, and some with small
And shining effigies of brass inlaid.

The Lambs had been in the vicinity of Harrow in the summer of 1805 (see Vol.
II, Letter 182, near the reference to note 1) and in Harrow in the summer (as
Lamb remarks below) of 1814.

5. The "prevailing charm of the poem"—I quote from Lamb's review of it—
"is, perhaps, that, conversational as it is in its plan, the dialogue throughout is
carried on in the very heart of the most romantic scenery which the poet's native
hills could supply; and which, by the perpetual references made to it either in
the way of illustration or for variety and pleasurable description's sake, is brought
before us as we read. We breathe in the fresh air, as we do while reading Walton's
Complete Angler; only the country about us is as much bolder than Walton's, as

the thoughts and speculations, which form the matter of the poem, exceed the trifling pastime and low-pitched conversation of his humble fishermen" (*Works,* I, 162).

6. The *Annual Register* for 1814, "Chronicle," pp. 67–69, reports that despite "a constant succession of spectacles of jubilation" following the signing of the Treaty of Paris of May 30, 1814, the councils of the prince regent (see Letter 276, near the end of its source note) had declared August 1 as a day for a national jubilee in celebration primarily of the peace restored between Britain and France. Hyde Park ("in which," the *Annual Register* also reports, "there was a grand fair"), Green Park, The Mall of St. James's Park, and Constitution Hill were opened altogether to the people. "Arabia Arenosa," in Lamb's next sentence, translates as "Sandy Arabia"; "saw" is a mistake for "say."

7. Henry Addington, first Viscount Sidmouth (see Vol. II, Letter 122, note 4), the home secretary from 1812 to 1821. The Latin in Lamb's next sentence translates, "united strength."

8. In Hyde Park. B. in "Letters of Charles Lamb," *Notes and Queries,* 184 (April 24, 1943), 248, explained that Lamb refers following to "the Naumachia, or mock sea-battle, on the Serpentine—part of the Peace celebrations of 1814." Lamb quotes from "Hart-leap Well," lines 175–176, a poem of which he had spoken to Robinson on January 8, 1811, as "one of Wordsworth's most exquisite pieces" (*H. C. R. on Books and Writers,* I, 18).

9. Unidentified, as is the given name of Watson, mentioned below as keeping The Adam and Eve inn on the Hampstead Road, St. Pancras, London. The Garonne, mentioned farther below, is a river (and an irrigation canal) in southwest France.

10. Godwin, probably.

11. See Vol. II, Letter 126, note 8.

278. *C. L. to Coleridge*

[East India House]
13 Aug 1814

Dear Resuscitate,

there comes to you by the vehicle from Lad Lane this day a volume of German, what it is I cannot justly say, the characters of those northern nations having been always singularly harsh and unpleasant to me.[1] It is a contribution of Dr. Southey towards your wants and you would have had it sooner but for an odd accident. I wrote for it three days ago and the Dr. as he thought sent it me—a book of like exterior he did send—but being disclosed how far unlike—it was the "Well bred Scholar" a book with which it seems the Dr. laudably fills up those hours which he can steal from his medical avocations. Chesterfield, Blair, Beattie, portions from the Life of Savage, make up a prettyish system of morality and the Belle Lettres, which Mr. Mylne a Schoolmaster has properly brought together and calls the Collection

by the denomination above mentioned. The Dr. had no sooner discovered his Error than he dispatched man and horse to rectify the
mistake, and with a pretty kind of ingenuous modesty in his note
seemeth to deny any knowlege of the "Well bred Scholar"——false
modesty surely and a blush misplaced, for what more pleasing than
the consideration of professional austerity thus relaxing, thus improving—but so when a child I remember blushing, being caught on
my knees to my maker, or doing otherwise some pious and praise-
worthy action—*now* I rather love such things to be seen—

Henry Crabb Robinson is out upon his circuit, and his books are inac-
cessible without his leave & key—he is attending the midland Circuit—
a short term but to him as to many young Lawyers a long vacation
sufficiently dreary—. I thought I could do no better than transmit to
him not extracts but your very letter itself, than which I think I never
read any thing more moving, more pathetic, or more conducive to the
purpose of persuasion—the Crab is a sour Crab if it does not sweeten
him—I think it would draw another third volume of Dodsley[2] out of
me—. but you say you dont want any English books? perhaps after
all that's as well, ones romantic credulity is for ever misleading into
misplaced acts of fool✳✳✳——. Crab might have answered by this
time—his juices take a long time suppling—but they'll run at last, I
know they will, pure golden pippin—. His address is at T. Robinson's,
Bury, or if on Circuit, to be forwarded immediately—such my peremptory superscription—. a fearful rumour has since reachd me that the
Crab is on the eve of setting out for France[3]—if he is in England your
letter will reach him, and I flatter myself a touch of the persuasive of
my own which accompanies it will not be thrown away—if it be, he is
a **Sloe,** and no true hearted Crab, and theres an end. For that life of
the German Conjurer which you speak of, **Colerus de vita Doctoris
Vix-intelligibilis,**[4] I perfectly remember the last evening we spent
with Mrs. Morgan and Miss Brent in London Street (by that token we
had raw rabbits for Supper, and Miss Brent prevaild upon me to take
a glass of brandy and water after supper, which is not my habit), I
perfectly remember reading portions of that life in their parlour, and I
think it must be among their Packages. It was the very last evening
we were at that house. What is gone of that frank hearted circle,
Morgan, and his gos-lettuces?[5]—he eat walnuts better than any man
I ever knew—. Friendships in these parts stagnate—. one piece of news

I know will give you pleasure—Rickman is made a Clerk to the House of Commons, £2000 a year, with greater expectatns.—but that is not the news—but it is, that poor card-playing Phillips, that has felt himself for so many years the outcast of **Fortune,** which feeling pervaded his very intellect till it made the destiny it feared, withering his hopes in the great and little games of life—by favor of the single star that ever shone upon him since his birth, has strangely stept into Rickmans Secretaryship—sword, bag, **House** & all—from a hopeless £100 a year eaten up aforehand with desperate debts, to a clear £400 or £500— it almost reconciles me to the belief of a moral government of the **World**—. the man stares & gapes and seems to be always wondering at what has befaln him—he tries to be eager at Cribbage, but alas! the source of that Interest is dried up for ever, he no longer plays for his next days meal, or to determine whether he shall have a half dinner or a whole dinner, whether he shall buy a pair of black silk stockings or wax his old ones a week or two longer, the poor man's relish of a **Trump,** the Four Honors,[6] is gone—and I do not know whether if we could get at the bottom of things whether poor star-doomed Phillips with his hair staring with despair was not a happier being than the sleek well combed oily-**pated** Secretary that has succeeded. The gift is however clogged with one stipulation, that the Secretary do remain a Single Man. Here I smell Rickman. Thus at once are gone all Phillipps' matrimonial dreams. Those verses which he wrote himself, and those which a superior Pen[7] (with modesty let me speak as I name no names) endited for him to **Elisa, Amelia** &c—for Phillips was always a wivehunting, probably from the circumstance of his having formed an extreme rash connection in early life which paved the way to all his after misfortunes, but there is an obstinacy in human nature which such [acc]ident only serve to **whet on to try again.** Pleasure thus at two entrances quite shut out, I hardly know how to determine of Phillippss result of happiness. He appears satisfyd, but never those bursts of gaiety, those moment-rules from the Cave of Despondency,[8] that used to make his face shine & shew the lines that care had marked in it. I would bet an even wager he marries secretly, the Speaker finds it out, and he is reverted to his old Liberty & a hundred pounds a year—. these are but speculations—I can think of no other news—

I am going to eat Turbot, Turtle, Venison, marrow pudd,[9]—cold punch, claret, madeira, at our annual feast at 1/2 past 4 this day.

Mary has ordered the bolt to my bedroom door inside to be taken off, & a practicable latch to be put on, that I may'nt bar myself in and be suffocated by my neckloth, so we have taken all precautions, three watchmen are engaged to carry the body up stairs, **Pray for me—** They[10] **keep bothering me** (I'm at office) and my ideas are confus'd. Let me know if I can be of any service as to books——God forbid the Architectonicon should be sacrificed to a foolish scruple of some Book-proprietor, as if books did not bel[ong] with the highest propriety to those that understand 'em best.

C Lamb

MS: Huntington Library. Pub.: Talfourd (1837), I, 329–332; Sala, I, 156–158; Purnell, I, 156–158; Fitzgerald, II, 10–12; Hazlitt, I, 429–431; Ainger (1888), I, 269–271; Ainger (1900), II, 200–203; Macdonald, I, 336–339; Ainger (1904), I, 326–327; Harper, I, facsimile, and III, 333–337; Lucas (1905), VI, 438–439, and VII, 972–973; Lucas (1912), V, 461–463; Lucas (1935), II, 130–133. Addresses, by Lamb: ⟨S. T. Coleridge Esq/J. Wade Esq/2 Queen Square/Bristol⟩; by Coleridge: J. J. Morgan, Esqre/Mrs Smith's/Ashley/Box/ near Bath. Endorsements, in another hand: "Mr. Lamb"; in still another hand: "Found in the Pocket of a Bristol Stage." Postmarks: August 13, 1814; Bristol, August 16, 1814. See note 5 below. Coleridge had visited his family at Keswick after concluding his lectures of 1811–1812 on Shakespeare and Milton (see Letter 265, note 1) and returned to London in April 1812. In London he had managed a reconciliation of sorts with Wordsworth and thus stilled the powers that had kept them apart since October 1810. (See Letter 253, note 1.) Coleridge had lectured on drama in Willis's Rooms, King Street, St. James's Square, in May and June 1812 and on belles lettres at the Surrey Institution, Blackfriars Road, from November 1812 into January 1813. (See *Coleridge's Shakespearean Criticism,* II, 193–197 and 199–203.) On January 23, 1813, he had seen, at Drury Lane, the first performance of his *Remorse. A Tragedy, in Five Acts.* (See my Vol. I, Letter 25, note 4; see also Letter 279, note 1.) He had left London for Bristol in October 1813. In Bristol he had stayed with Josiah Wade, a linen draper and an editor of the *Mercantile Gazette* whom Coleridge had known since 1794, and had lectured on Shakespeare and on education at The White Lion, Broad Street, Bristol, in October and November. Also in November he had lectured, perhaps on Milton and on education, in Mangeon's Room, in the hotel in Clifton, and passed a few days in London. In January 1814 he may have commenced a course of lectures on Shakespeare and Milton at The White Lion, Bristol. In April he had given a course at that place on Milton, on "poetic taste," and on *Don Quixote.* (See *Coleridge's Letters,* III, esp. 443, 449–450, 459, 464, 466–467, and 474–475; and *Coleridge's Shakespearean Criticism,* II, 205–238.) In July he had begun the series of essays—"On the Principles of Genial Criticism concerning the Fine Arts . . ."—that would, in August and September, appear in John Mathew Gutch's *Felix Farley's Bristol Journal.* (See *Coleridge's Letters,* III, esp. 520; and Coleridge's *Biographia Literaria, with His Aesthetical Essays,* ed. J. Shawcross [1907; rpt. London: Oxford University Press, 1965], II, 219–246 and 304–305.) Coleridge would move in September 1814 from Josiah Wade's into the cottage near Bath owned by a Mrs. E. Smith, a grocer, and live there until about December 5, 1814. That cottage, which John and Mary Morgan and Charlotte Brent had by then vacated or shortly were to vacate for lodgings in

Paul Street, Portland Square, London, had sheltered the Morgans and Miss Brent since December 1813, when financial reverses had temporarily compelled their removal from London. The period 1812 to 1814 had been bad for Coleridge, with illnesses, worries about money and his increasing dependence on drugs, and wishes for death and thoughts of dying all elements of his despondency. Lamb's probable awareness of Coleridge's distresses and the probable fact that until recently Lamb had not for a long time heard from Coleridge could account for the salutation of this letter. Coleridge's letter to which Lamb is responding has not been recovered.

1. The volume of German has not been identified, but it was almost certainly one Coleridge intended to use for a projected translation and analysis of the first part (1808) of *Faust* and perhaps of other writings of Goethe. Henry Robinson had learned the publisher John Murray (1778–1843) wished to bring out such a work. Robinson had thought Coleridge the man to prepare it and had asked Lamb to write Coleridge to write to Murray. Lamb did write to Coleridge (his letter has not been recovered), and, on August 23, Coleridge did write to Murray. Murray offered Coleridge one hundred pounds; on August 31 Coleridge proposed to Murray a reasonable counteroffer. Murray did not answer, and nothing came of the plan. (See *Coleridge's Letters*, III, 521–525, 526, 528–529, 536; and IV, 562.) Dr. Southey, mentioned in the following sentence, is Robert's brother Henry Herbert Southey (see my Vol. I, Letter 29, note 2), who, with financial assistance from Robert and their uncle the Reverend Mr. Herbert Hill (see Vol. I, Letter 2, note 8), had earned his M.D. at the University of Edinburgh in 1806, begun his practice in Durham, and moved to London in 1812. He would become physician in ordinary to George IV and to Adelaide, queen of William IV. Among Dr. Southey's publications are *Observations on Pulmonary Consumption* (1814) and the biography of Dr. Robert Gooch (1784–1830) in *Lives of the British Physicians* (1830), a book compiled and partly written by Dr. William MacMichael (1784–1839). The book Dr. Southey had first sent to Lamb, in error for the German volume, is William Milns's *The Well-bred Scholar; or, Practical Essays on the Best Method of Improving the Taste and Assisting the Exertions of Youth in Their Literary Pursuits* (1794). Mentioned below are the statesman and writer Philip Dormer Stanhope, fourth Earl of Chesterfield (1694–1773), and the poets Robert Blair (1699–1746) and James Beattie (1735–1803). About Samuel Johnson's *Life of Savage* see my Vol. II, Letter 110, note 1.

2. Probably Robert Dodsley's *A Collection of Poems, by Several Hands* (3 vols.; 1748). The asterisks, below, may be a substitution for the suffix "ery." The locution "suppling" is, presumably, an error for "supplying." About Thomas Robinson, Henry Crabb Robinson's brother, see Letter 269, note 1.

3. Henry Robinson arrived in Rouen on August 26, went to Paris on August 29, left Paris for Amiens and Calais and Boulogne on October 8, and was back in London by October 14. See *H. C. R.'s Diary*, I, 282 and 292, and *H. C. R. on Books and Writers*, I, 150.

4. "Colerus on the life of Doctor Scarcely-intelligible," a reference to the biography of Baruch, or Benedict de, Spinoza (1632–1677) by Johannes Colerus (1647–1707), a Lutheran minister of Amsterdam. The work was first published, in Dutch, in 1705. It was translated and published in English and French in 1706. The French translation—*Vie de Benedict de Spinosa*—the German rationalist theologian Heinrich Eberhard Gottlob Paulus (1761–1851) included in the second volume of his edition of Spinoza's *Opera quœ supersunt omnia* (2 vols.; 1802–1803). It is noted in *Coleridge's Letters*, IV, 635, that Henry Robinson's copy of Paulus' edition, which is now in the library of Manchester College at Oxford, contains Coleridge's annotations. See note 10 to the present letter. No. 19 London Street, Fitzroy Square (see below), was the address of Mary Morgan and Charlotte Brent from perhaps September to near the end of

November 1813. During at least most of that period John Morgan had been away in Ireland in order to be out of the reach of his creditors.

5. Properly cos, or cos lettuce, a variety of lettuce, including romaine, introduced from the island of Cos, or Stanko, or Stanchio, in the Aegean. "I am hesitating," Coleridge wrote Morgan on August 16, 1814, "whether I should send a letter of C. Lamb's to you—but hang it! I will—& will pay the Postage— it recalled old times—but I don't understand the *Gos-lettuces*—" (*Coleridge's Letters*, VI, 1030). About John Rickman and Edward Phillips, discussed below, see my Vol. I, Letter 86, note 4; and Vol. II, Letter 198, note 1.

6. In whist (not cribbage), the ace, king, queen, and knave of trumps.

7. Lamb's, one gathers, though the verses have vanished. The women in Phillips' life, two of whom Lamb names or invents names for below, have not been identified. It seems Phillips was never married.

8. Called the Slough of Despond in John Bunyan's *The Pilgrim's Progress.*

9. For "pudding." Lamb here is writing of the meal shortly to be served at the annual feast of the East India House clerks. William Foster explained in *The East India House: Its History and Associations* (London: John Lane, Bodley Head, 1924), pp. 91–92, that the presentation by the East India House to its staff of such a feast dates from at least 1716, when it is first mentioned in the minutes of the institution, to April 8, 1816, when the directors of the institution abandoned it in favor of an annual contribution of six hundred pounds to a fund, then begun, for the dependent survivors of deceased members of the home establishment.

10. Approximately a line and one-half have been canceled preceding. "Architectonicon," in Lamb's last sentence, is an epithet for Coleridge derived from Coleridge's conceived but never constructed "Christianity the one true Philosophy —or 5 Treatises on the Logos, or communicative Intelligence, Natural, Human, and Divine": its prefatory essay was to have contained "fragments of *Auto-biography*," from which Coleridge may have developed his *Biographia-literaria; or Biographical Sketches of My Literary Life and Opinions* (1817); the second treatise was to have been "Logos architectonicus, or an attempt to apply the constructive, or mathematical, Process to Metaphysics & Natural Theology"; the fourth treatise was to have been "on Spinoza, and Spinozism with a Life of B. Spinoza—this entitled, Logos Agonistes" (*Coleridge's Letters*, III, 533). The notion, in Lamb's last sentence also, that books belong "with the highest propriety to those that understand 'em best" reappears, revised in expression and imagined as Coleridge's, in "The Two Races of Men" (*Works*, II, 25).

279.   *C. L. to Coleridge*

[26th August,] 1814

Let thy hungry soul rejoice, there is Corn in Egypt.[1] Whatsoever thou hast been told [to the contrary] by designing friends, who perhaps enquired carelessly, or did not enquire at all, in hope of saving their money, there is a stock of "Remorse" on hand enough as Pople conjectures for seven years consumption, judging from the experience of the last two years. Methinks it makes for the benefit of sound Literature that the best books, do not always go off the best. Enquire in seven years time for the Rokebys, the Laras, the Jacquelinas,[2] and where shall they be found—fluttering fragmentally in some thread-paper—whereas thy Wallenstein & thy Remorse are safe on Longmans or Pople's shelves, as in some Bodly—there they shall remain—no need of a chain to hold them fast—perhaps for ages—tall copies—and people sh'ant run about hunting for them as in old Ezra['s] shrievalty they did for a Bible, almost without effect, till the great great grand-neice (by the mothers side) of Jeremiah or Ezekiel (which was it) remembered something of a book, with odd reading in it that used to lye in a green closet in her Aunt Judiths bed chamber.

[Thy caterer Price[3] was at Hamburgh when last Pople heard of him, laying up for thee, like some miserly old father for his generous-hearted son to squander.]

Mr C Aders whose books do also pant after that free circulation which thy custody is sure to give them, is to be heard of at his kinsman Mess[rs.] Jameson & Aders No 7 Lawrence Pountney Lane, London——according to the information which Crabius left me with his parting breath. Crabius is gone to Paris. I prophesy he & the Parisians will part with mutual contempt. His head has a twist Allemag[ne],[4] like thine, Dear Mystic.

I have been reading Mme d Stael on Germany. An impudent, clever woman. But if Faust be no better than in her abstract of it, I counsel thee to let it alone. How canst thou translate the language of cat-monkeys? qua—wa—peep—peep—peep whee—whee—sipt—sipt—sipt mal—wu—waaa—fie on such fantasies.[5] But I will not forget to look for Proclus. It is a [kind of] book which when one meets with it one shuts the lid faster than one opens it: Yet I have some bastard kind of recollection that some where, some time ago upon—some stall or other I saw it. It was either that or Plotinus[6] or [Saint] Augustines City of God. So little do some folks value, what to others *sc* to you well used had been the pledge of immortality. Bishop Bruno I never touched upon. Stuffing too good for the brains of such a hare as thou describest—. May it burst his pericran as the gobbets of fat & Turpentine (a nasty thought of the Seer) di[d] that old dragon of the Pochrougha. May he go mad in trying to understand his author. May he lend the third Vol of him before he has quite translated the second to a friend who shall lose it, & so spoil the publication, and may his friend find it and return it, just as thou or some such less dilatory

Spirit shall have announced the whole for the press; Lastly may he be hunted by the Reviewers & the devil jug him. .

So I think I have ansd all thy questions except about Morgans cos lettuce. The first [personal] peculiarity I ever observed in him (all worthy souls are subject to em) was a particular kind of rabbit like delight in munching salads with oil without vinegar—after dinner—a steady contemplative browsing on them—didst never take note of it.?— Canst think of any other queries in [the solution of] which I can give thee satisfaction? Do you want any books, that I can————procure— for you? Old Jemy Bowyer[7] is dead at last. Trollope has got his living worth a 1000£ a year [net]. See thou sluggard thou heretic sluggard what mightest thou not have arrived at.— Lay by thy animosity against Jemy in his grave—. Do not en*tail* it on thy *Poster*ity

Ch Lamb

My Love to the whole Morganus System whereof thou art not the smallest luminary.

MS: unrecovered; a copy: Wordsworth Collection, Cornell University Library, Ithaca, N.Y. Pub.: Talfourd (1837), I, 332–335; Sala, I, 159–161; Purnell, I, 159–161; Fitzgerald, II, 13–15; Hazlitt, I, 431–433; Ainger (1888), I, 274–276; Ainger (1900), II, 208–211; Macdonald, I, 343–345; Ainger (1904), I, 331– 333; Harper, IV, 9–11; Lucas (1905), VI, 440–442; Lucas (1912), V, 464–466; Lucas (1935), II, 134–135. The bracketed portion of the date and the bracketed locutions within the body of the letter are taken from Lucas (1935). What I have treated as a postscript—it seems to be one and was probably written near the top of the first page on the original letter—appears as the opening sentence on the copy and does not appear in the previously published texts of the letter.

1. Genesis 42:1 and 2, here in reference to existing copies of Coleridge's *Remorse. A Tragedy, in Five Acts.* W. Pople, the bookseller of 67 Chancery Lane who had printed the prospectus for Coleridge's lectures of 1811–1812 on Shakespeare and Milton (the prospectus is given in *Coleridge's Shakespearean Criticism,* II, 23–24), had published, in 1813, the first three editions of *Remorse.*

2. Sir Walter Scott's *Rokeby* (1813), Lord Byron's "Lara," and Samuel Rogers' "Jacqueline" (the last two form a volume published in 1814). About Coleridge's translations from Schiller's *Wallenstein,* mentioned below, see Vol. I, Letter 62, note 1. By "Bodly" Lamb means the Bodleian Library, Oxford, which was founded by the diplomatist and scholar Sir Thomas Bodley (1545–1613) and opened in 1602. Its books were chained to their shelves until 1761, when the process of removing the chains was begun. See, for example, Burnett Hillman Streeter, *The Chained Library: A Survey of Four Centuries in the Evolution of the English Library* (London: Macmillan, 1931), pp. 206–207. Lamb's story, fanciful as it is, of the search for and recovery of a Bible in the time of the fifth-century B.C. scribe and priest Ezra may derive from the legend, told in 2 Esdras 14:37–48 esp., of Ezra and his recovery of Holy Scripture:

> So I took the five men, as he [the Lord] commanded me, and we pro- ceeded to the field, and remained there. And on the next day, behold, a voice called me, saying, "Ezra, open your mouth and drink what I give you

to drink." Then I opened my mouth, and behold, a full cup was offered to me; it was full of something like water, but its color was like fire. And I took it and drank; and when I had drunk it, my heart poured forth understanding, and wisdom increased in my breast, for my spirit retained its memory; and my mouth was opened, and was no longer closed. And the Most High gave understanding to the five men, and by turns they wrote what was dictated, in characters which they did not know. They sat forty days, and wrote during the daytime, and ate their bread at night. As for me, I spoke in the daytime and was not silent at night. So during the forty days ninety-four books were written. And when the forty days were ended, the Most High spoke to me, saying, "Make public the twenty-four books [of the Hebrew canon] that you wrote first and let the worthy and the unworthy read them; but keep the seventy [esoteric, apocalyptic books] that were written last, in order to give them to the wise among your people. For in them is the spring of understanding, the fountain of wisdom, and the river of knowledge." And I did so. [*The Apocrypha of the Old Testament* . . . , ed. Bruce M. Metzger (New York: Oxford University Press, 1965), pp. 57–58]

3. Unidentified. Charles Aders, referred to in the next paragraph, a wealthy German businessman and an art collector who would become a friend of the Lambs, was the partner of (the otherwise unidentified) Jameson by 1807 and, according to the London directories, was established with him in London by 1812 as Jameson & Aders, Merchants and Insurance Brokers, 11 Great Distaff Lane. The firm was at 7 Laurence Pountney Lane in 1814–1815 and at 25 Laurence Pountney Lane from 1816. Robinson, who appears to have known Jameson by 1807 and to have first met Aders in Altona, Germany, in 1807 (see *H. C. R.'s Diary*, I, 152), had probably been responsible for bringing them together with Coleridge at a dinner party on January 17, 1812 (see *H. C. R. on Books and Writers*, I, 58), and thus for the occasion from which developed the friendship between Coleridge and Aders. It was probably Robinson who would introduce the Lambs and Aders. Their names are first associated in the entry in Robinson's diary of January 24, 1819 (*H. C. R. on Books and Writers*, I, 228), where Robinson recorded that he took the Lambs to see Aders' collection of paintings—early Flemish and German most notably, of which Lamb would write, in 1831, in "To C. Aders, Esq. *On His Collection of Paintings by the Old German Masters*" (*Works*, V, 85). On July 6, 1820, Aders was married to Elizabeth, or Eliza, Smith (b. 1787?—she is miscalled "Emma" in the *DNB* entry for her father and in *Bryan's Dictionary of Painters and Engravers* [rev. ed.; 1964]), a water colorist and miniature painter, the daughter of the portrait painter and mezzotint engraver John Raphael Smith (1752–1812). She had exhibited, as had her brother, John Rubens Smith (b. 1775), at the Royal Academy between 1799 and 1808. She would exhibit, in Berlin in 1830, "un tableau de la *Vierge*, d'après Van Eyck," one of her copies after superior artists for which, as for her charm, she became admired. In her the poet Samuel Rogers may have once had some romantic interest, and for her Coleridge, in 1826, composed "The Two Founts: Stanzas Addressed to a Lady on Her Recovery with Unblemished Looks, from a Severe Attack of Pain." A pen drawing that the German artist Jacob Götzenberger (1800–1860) had contributed to her album moved Lamb, in 1827, to write "Angel Help" and moved Mary to write "Another Version of the Same." (See *Works*, V, 48–49 and 109, where Mary's poem is considered as Lamb's and titled "Nonsense Verses"; and James T. Wills's "New Lamb Material in the Aders Album: Jacob Götzenberger and Two Versions of 'Angel Help,' " *Harvard Library Bulletin*, 22 [October 1974], 406–413.) From about 1820 to 1832 the Aderses entertained wonderfully in their home, almost as much an art gallery as a home, at 11 Euston Square. Among their guests, in addition to Coleridge and

the Lambs and Robinson, were William Blake, Thomas Campbell, John Flaxman (see Vol. I, Letter 2, note 13), Carlyle's close friend the Scottish divine Edward Irving (1792–1834), Walter Savage Landor, Sir Thomas Lawrence (see Vol. II, Letter 200, note 3), Blake's intimate the painter John Linnell (1792–1882), Basil Montagu, Samuel Rogers, and Dorothy and Mary and William Wordsworth. The Aderses had also a home on the Rhine, in the resort of Godesberg, Germany, where they welcomed Coleridge and William Wordsworth and Wordsworth's daughter Dorothy in the summer of 1828. In 1832 the Aderses arranged for their collection of paintings to be displayed publicly at the Suffolk Street Gallery, Pall Mall. In August 1835 most, apparently, of the paintings were sold at public auction or reserved for private sale. Aders' business losses, signified by the fact of the auction, became in perhaps 1836 disastrous. In April 1839 the remainder, it appears, of the collection was sold. Aders seems to have been ruined, and no more seems to have been recorded about him. Mrs. Aders is mentioned in Robinson's diary in 1842—from June 10 to 21 regarding a portrait, possibly two portraits, she had by that latter date completed of Wordsworth, and on October 1 regarding her presents to Robinson of editions of the *Descriptive Catalogue* and *Poems* of Blake. She is mentioned in the diary finally on February 1, 1849, in connection with news of the death of David Hartley Coleridge. (See *H. C. R. on Books and Writers,* II, 618, 625, and 687–688.) No more seems to have been recorded about her. The fullest account of the Aderses is M. K. Joseph's *Charles Aders: A Biographical Note, Together with Some Unpublished Letters Addressed to Him by S. T. Coleridge and Others, and Now in the Grey Collection, Auckland City Library* (Auckland, N.Z.: Auckland University College, Bulletin No. 43, English Series No. 6, 1953).

4. "[Toward] Germany." In his next paragraph Lamb writes of reading *De l'Allemagne* (1813; English tr., 1813), by the French novelist and miscellaneous writer Anne Louise Germaine Necker, Baronne de Staël-Holstein (1766–1817). Southey had introduced Coleridge to her in October 1813, when she was in London.

5. Cf. *The Merry Wives of Windsor,* V, v, 93: "Fie on sinful fantasy!" Proclus, or Proculus (410–485), mentioned below, was a Neoplatonist, a grammarian, and an elucidator of Plato. It is noted in *Coleridge's Letters,* III, 279, that the British Museum holds Coleridge's annotated copy of a two-volume 1792 edition of *Philosophical and Mathematical Commentaries of Proclus, . . . and a Translation . . . of Proclus's Theological Elements,* by the Platonist Thomas Taylor (1758–1835).

6. An identification of the Roman scholar Plotinus, almost surely by Lucas rather than by Lamb, follows in the Lucas editions. Plotinus (204–270), because of his *Enneades* (first published Latin translation, of a Greek text, 1492; republished in 1580), is generally considered to have been the most important of the Neoplatonists. St. Augustine's *City of God* (*De civitate Dei*) originally appeared in portions during the period 413 to 426. The abbreviation *sc,* below, is for *scilicet,* which translates as "to wit" or "namely." Lamb has appropriated "well used had been the pledge of immortality" from *Paradise Lost,* IV, 200–201. The Bruno referred to is not the bishop of whom Southey had written (see Vol. I, Letter 44, note 3), but, rather, the Italian philosopher of Nola—Giordano, christened Fillippo, Bruno (ca. 1548–1600)—one of Coleridge's favorites. From perhaps 1809 Coleridge had been thinking of writing, possibly by the time of this letter had begun to write, a biography of him. But Coleridge was prevented from doing so when a Mr. Hare refused to lend Coleridge a unique collection of some works of Bruno that Coleridge had seen Hare purchase at a book sale. (See *Coleridge's Letters,* III, esp. 127 and 279; and IV, esp. 592, 656, 687, and 926.) The passage in the Apocrypha to which Lamb refers is Bel and the Dragon 27. The seer is Daniel.

7. The Reverend Mr. James Boyer (see Vol. I, Introduction, pp. xxxii–xxxiii), the late upper-grammar master of Christ's Hospital. He had died on July 28, 1814, leaving the former Catherine Till (d. 1828), to whom he had been married in 1781 and by whom he had had seven children. His death is noticed, but without details, in the *Gentleman's Magazine*, 84 (August 1814), 194. Good accounts of him are Meadows White's "Irreverendus: Some Thoughts on James Boyer" and (the unsigned) "James Boyer: Continued," in the *CLSB* of September 1966 and April 1967. (It is stated in the latter article that Boyer took his B.A. degree, in 1756, and his M.A. degree, in 1759, from Balliol College, Oxford. *Alumni Oxonienses* shows he received only the B.A.) Boyer's living, of Colne Engaine, Essex, passed to the Reverend Dr. Arthur William Trollope (1768–1827), mentioned in Lamb's following sentence, the headmaster of Christ's Hospital from 1799 to 1826. Lamb's forms of "entail" and "Posterity" hold allusions to Boyer's practice of whipping students.

280. *C. L. to William Wordsworth*
[Monday, September 19, 1814]

My dear W—

I have scarce time or quiet to explain my present situation, how unquiet and distracted it is.— Owing to the absence of some of my compeers, and to the deficient state of payments at E. I. H. owing to bad peace speculations in the Calico market—(I write this to W. W. Esq. Collector of Stamp duties for the conjoint northern counties, not to W. W. Poet)[1] I go back & have for this many days past to evening work, generally at the rate of nine hours a day. The nature of my work too, puzzling & hurrying, has so shaken my spirits, that my sleep is nothing but a succession of dreams of business I cannot do, of assistants that give me no assistance, of terrible responsibilities. I reclaimd your book which Hazlit has uncivilly kept, only 2 days ago and have made shift to read it again with shatterd brain. It does not lose—rather some parts have come out with a prominence I did not perceive before— but such was my aching head yesterday (Sunday), that the book was like a Mountn. Landscape to one that should walk on the edge of a precipice. I perceived beauty dizzily. Now what I would say is, that I see no prospect of a quiet half day or hour even till this week and the next are past. I then hope to get 4 weeks absence, & if *then* is time enough to begin I will most gladly do what you require, tho' I feel my inability, for my brain is always desultory & snatches off hints from things, but can seldom follow a **"work"** methodically. But that shall be no excuse. What I beg you to do is to let me know from Southey, if that will be time enough for the "Quarterly." **i.e.** suppose it done in 3 weeks from this date (19 Sept.) : if not it is my bounden duty to express my regret, and decline it. Mary thanks you and feels highly grateful for your Patent of Nobility,[2] and acknowleges the author of Excursion as the legitimate Fountain of Honor. We both agree, that to our feeling Ellen is best as she is. To us there would have been something repugnant in her challenging her **Penance** as a **Dowry!** the fact is explicable, but how few to whom it could have been rendered explicit!

The unlucky reason of the detention of Excursion was, Hazlit & we having a misunderstanding.[3] He blowed us up about 6 months ago, since which the union hath snapt, but M. Burney borrowd it for him & after reiteratd messages I only got it on friday. His remarks had some vigor in them, particularly something about an old ruin being *too modern for your Primeval Nature, and about a lichen,* but I forget the Passage, but the whole wore a slovenly air of dispatch and disrespect. That objection which M Burney had imbibed from him about Voltaire, I explained to M B (or tried) exactly on your principle of its being a characteristic speech. That it was no settled comparative estimate of voltaire with any of his own tribe of buffoons—no injustice, even if *you* spoke it, for I dared say you never could relish Candide. I know I tried to get thro' it about a twelvemonth since & could'nt for the **Dullness.** Now I think I have a wider range in buffoonery than you. Too much toleration perhaps.

I finish this after a raw illbakd dinner fast gobbled up to set me off to Office again after Working there till near four. O Christ! how I wish I were a rich man, even tho' I were squeezed camel-fashion at getting thro' that **Needles eye** that is spoken of in the **written word.**[4] Apropos, are you a **Xtian?** or is it the Pedlar & the Priest that are?—

I find I miscalld that celestial splendor of the mist going off, a *sunset.* That only shews my inaccuracy of head.

Do pray indulge me by writing an answer to the point of time mentiond above, or *let Southey.* I am asham'd to go bargaining in this way, but indeed I have no time I can reckon on till the 1st. week in **Octor.** God send I may not be disappointed in that!

Coleridge swore in [a] letter to me he would review Excn. in the Quarterly.[5] Therefore, tho' *that* shall not stop me, yet if I can do anything, *when* done, I must know of him if he has anything ready, or I shall fill the world with loud exclaims.

I keep writing on knowing the Postage is no more for much writing, else so faggd & disjointed I am with damnd India house work, I scarce know what I do. My left arm reposes on "Excursion." I feel what it would be in quiet. It is now a sealed Book.—

O happy Paris,[6] seat of idleness & pleasure! from some return'd English I hear, that not such a thing as a Counting house is to be seen in her streets, scarce a desk—. Earthquaks swallow up this mercantile city & its **gripple** merchants, as Drayton hath it, "born to be the curse of this brave isle." I invoke this not on account of any parsimonious habits the mercantile interest may have, but to confess truth because I am not fit for an Office—

Farewell, in haste, from a head that is ill to methodize, a stomach to digest & all **out of Tune.**[7] Better harmonies await you—

C Lamb

MS: University of Texas Library. Pub.: Talfourd (1848), I, 195 and 206–210; Sala, I, 256–258 and 273; Purnell, I, 256–258 and 273; Fitzgerald, II, 91–93 and 108; Hazlitt, I, 433–436, and II, 6; Ainger (1888), I, 276–278 and 286; Ainger (1900), II, 211–214 and 224–225; Macdonald, I, 345–347 and 355–356; Ainger (1904), I, 333–335 and 343; Harper, IV, 12–15; Lucas (1905), VI, 443–444; Lucas (1912), V, 466–468; Luacs (1935), II, 136–138. Address: W. Wordsworth Esq/Rydal Mount/near Grasmere near Kendal/Westmorland. In his first paragraph Lamb dates the evening in which he is writing and explains why he cannot begin until his vacation begins his reveiw of Wordsworth's *The Excursion*. See Letter 277, note 1, and the next letter.

1. By the gift of William Lowther, first Earl of Lonsdale of the second creation (see Vol. II, Letter 133, near the end of note 4), Wordsworth had in March 1813 succeeded a Mr. Wilkin as distributor of stamps for the county of Westmorland and parts of the county of Cumberland. Wordsworth would retain the position—its area being extended in 1820 and 1823—until August 1842, then would manage to have it transferred to his son William.

2. If Lamb took "Patent of Nobility" from Coleridge's "On Donne's Poem 'To a Flea,'" line 4, he had to have seen the poem in manuscript: Coleridge wrote it in 1811, but it was not published until 1912, in *Coleridge's Poetical Works* (1912), II, 980–981. "Fountain of Honor" (below) is from Francis Bacon's "Essay of a King." For the story of Ellen, of her bearing a child out of wedlock, the child's death, her suffering and death, see *The Excursion*, VI, 778–1052.

3. Its cause has not been discovered. Here is the particularly vigorous passage in Hazlitt's "Character of Mr. Wordsworth's New Poem, *The Excursion*" (see Letter 277, note 1) to which Lamb refers below: "Such is the severe simplicity of Mr. Wordsworth's taste, that we doubt whether he would not reject a druidical temple, or time-hallowed ruin, as too modern and artificial for his purpose. He only familiarises himself or his readers with a stone, covered with lichens, which has slept in the same spot of ground from the creation of the world, or with the

rocky fissure between two mountains caused by thunder, or with a cavern scooped out by the sea. His mind is, as it were, coeval with the primary forms of things, holds immediately from nature; and his imagination 'owes no allegiance' but 'to the elements' " (*Hazlitt's Works,* XIX, 10). Directed against Wordsworth's estimates of Voltaire and *Candide* in *The Excursion,* II, 479–486—

> . . . How poor,
> Beyond all poverty how destitute,
> Must that Man [a deceased cottager] have been left, who, hither driven,
> Flying or seeking, could yet bring with him
> No dearer relique, and no better stay,
> Than this dull product of a scoffer's pen,
> Impure conceits discharging from a heart
> Hardened by impious pride! . . .

—is this passage in Hazlitt's "Character of Mr. Wordsworth's New Poem, *The Excursion*":

> From the chemists and metaphysicians our author turns to the laughing sage of France, Voltaire. . . . We cannot, however, agree with Mr. Wordsworth that *Candide* is *dull.* It is, if our author pleases, 'the production of a scoffer's pen,' or it is any thing, but dull. . . . It may not be proper in a grave, discreet, orthodox, promising young divine, who studies his opinions in the contraction or distension of his patron's brow, to allow any merit to a work like *Candide;* but we conceive that it would have been more in character, that is more manly in Mr. Wordsworth, nor do we think it would have hurt the cause he espouses, if he had blotted out the epithet, after it had peevishly escaped him. Whatsoever savours of a little, narrow, inquisitorial spirit, does not sit well on a poet and a man of genius. The prejudices of a philosopher are not natural. There is a frankness and sincerity of opinion, which is a paramount obligation in all questions of intellect, though it may not govern the decisions of the Spiritual Courts, who may be safely left to take care of their own interests. There is a plain directness and simplicity of understanding, which is the only security against the evils of levity on the one hand, or of hypocrisy on the other. A speculative bigot is a solecism in the intellectual world. We can assure Mr. W. that we should not have bestowed so much serious consideration on a single voluntary perversion of language, but that our respect for his character makes us jealous of his smallest faults. [*Hazlitt's Works,* XIX, 14–15]

"Now, you rascally Lake Poet," said Lamb to Wordsworth at the dinner party become famous that the historical painter Benjamin Robert Haydon (1786–1846) gave on December 28, 1817, "you call Voltaire a dull fellow"—and all there agreed that now and then Voltaire seemed to them so. (The entry in *Haydon's Diary* [II, esp. 173] about the evening, in part quoted here, is quoted at length in my Vol. IV, Letter 336, notes.) In "Detached Thoughts on Books and Reading" Lamb stated he "should not care to be caught in the serious avenues of some cathedral alone, and reading *Candide*" (*Works,* II, 176).

4. In Matthew 19:24 (and *Richard II,* V, v, 16–17). Mentioned near the end of Lamb's paragraph are the Pedlar, or Wanderer, and the Priest, or Pastor, of *The Excursion.* Mentioned in Lamb's next paragraph is the description in *The Excursion* praised in the second paragraph in Letter 277 and quoted in its note 3.

5. The letter has not been recovered. Coleridge did not review *The Excursion,* though in his *Biographia-literaria,* chs. xxi and xxii, he expressed himself on the review it received in the *Edinburgh Review* (see Letter 287, note 2) and on the poem itself.

6. Where the Thomas Clarksons now were, a fact Wordsworth had evidently related in his (unrecovered) letter to Lamb. The quotation below, from Michael Drayton's "Upon the Noble Lady Astons Departure for Spaine," lines 38–39—

"gripple" means "griping," "niggardly," "usurious"—Lamb incorporated into "The Good Clerk, a Character; with Some Account of 'The Complete English Tradesman' " (*Works,* I, 129).

7. Wordsworth's "The World Is Too Much with Us," line 8.

281. *C. L. to Robert Southey*

20 Octobr 1814

Dear S.

I have this day deposited with Mr. G. Bedfd.[1] the Essay you suggested to me. I am afraid it is wretchedly inadequate. Who can cram into a strait coop of a review any serious idea of such a vast & magnifict. poem as Excursn—?

I am myself, too, peculiarly unfit from constitutional causes & want of time. However, it is gone.—

I have 9 or 10 days of my holy days left, but the rains are come.

Kind remembs. to Mrs. S. & sisters.—

Yours truly

C L

MS: The Philip H. & A. S. W. Rosenbach Foundation. Pub.: Macdonald, I, 335–336; Harper, IV, 15–16; Lucas (1935), II, 139. Address: R. Southey Esq/ Keswick/near/Penrith/Cumberland. Postmark: October 20, 1814.

1. Grosvenor Charles Bedford (1773–1839), an acquaintance of Coleridge and Rickman; a friend of William Gifford (1756–1826), who from 1809 to 1824 was the editor of the *Quarterly Review* (about Gifford and Lamb see Letter 287, source note); and the intimate of Southey since 1788–1792, when Bedford and Southey were students at Westminster School. Bedford's earliest public writings are in *The Flagellant,* a Westminster School weekly issued in March and April 1792 for which Bedford and Southey were largely responsible. (See *New Southey Letters,* I, 2–3.) Bedford's poem "The Rhedycinian Barbers" is in the *Monthly Magazine* of May 1797 and in the first (1799) volume of Southey's *Annual Anthology.* Bedford had translated and privately printed the Greek poet Musaeus' *The Loves of Hero and Leander* (1797), published (anonymously, as a pamphlet) *A Letter to the Right Hon. William Pitt on His Political Experiments* (1804), assisted Southey with his *Specimens of the Later English Poets, with Preliminary Notices* (see my Vol. II, Letter 211, note 1), and edited the documents and written the memoir of the antiquary Barré Charles Roberts (1789–1810) privately printed as *The Letters and Miscellaneous Papers by Barré Charles Roberts, Student of Christ Church, Oxford; with a Memoir of His Life* (1814). Bedford would review Southey's *Roderick, the Last of the Goths* (1814) for the *Quarterly Review* of April 1815 and help Southey with his quasi-novel, *The Doctor, &c.* (1834–1847). Bedford earned his living at the Exchequer, which he had entered, as a clerk, in 1792 and was to leave, as the chief clerk in the auditor's office, in 1834. A biographical sketch of him, from which most of the information in this note is drawn, is in *New Southey Letters,* II, 481–482.

282. *M. A. L. to Barbara Betham*

Novr 2 1814

It is very long since I have met with such an agreeable surprize as the sight of your letter, my kind young friend afforded me. Such a nice letter as it is too. And what a pretty hand you write. I congratulate you on this attainment with great pleasure, because I have so often felt the disadvantage of my own wretched hand-writing.

You wish for London news—I rely upon your sister Ann, for gratifying you in this respect, yet I have been endeavouring to recollect who you might have seen here, and what may have happened to them since, and this effort has only brought the image of little Barbara Betham, unconnected with any other person, so strongly before my eyes, that I seem as if I had no other subject to write upon. Now I think I see you with your feet propped upon the fender, your two hands spread out upon your knees—an attitude you always chose when we were in familiar confidential conversation together—telling me long stories of your own home, where now you say you are "Moping on with the same thing every day" and which then presented nothing but pleasant recollections to your mind. How well I remember your quiet steady face bent over your book.— One day conscience-struck at having wasted so much of your precious time in reading, and feeling yourself as you prettily said "Quite useless to me" you went to my drawers and hunted out some unhemmed pockethandkerchiefs, and by no means could I prevail upon you to resume your story-books till you had hemmed them all. I remember too your teaching my little maid[1] to read—your sitting with her a whole evening to console her for the death of her sister, and that she in her turn endeavoured to ⟨console⟩ become a comforter to you, the next evening, when you wept at the sight of Mrs Holcroft from whose school you had recently eloped because you were not partial to sitting in the stocks. Those tears, and a few you once dropped when my brother teased you about your supposed fondness for an apple dumpling were the only interruptions to the calm contentedness of your unclouded brow. We still remain the same as you left us, neither taller, nor wiser, or perceptibly older, but three years must have made a great alteration in you. How very much, dear Barbara, I should like to see you!

We still live in Temple Lane, but I am now sitting in a room you never saw. Soon after you left us we we[re] distressed by the cries of a cat which seemed to proceed from the garrets adjoining to ours, and only separated from ours by a locked door on the farther side of my brother's bedroom, which you know was the little room at the top of the kitchen stairs. We had the lock forced and let poor puss out from behind a pannel of the wainscot, and she lived with us from that time, for we were in gratitude bound to keep her as she had introduce[d] us to four untenanted, unowned rooms, and by degrees we have taken possession of these unclaimed apartments—First putting up lines to dry our clothes—then moving my brothers bed into one of these, more commodious than his own room—and last winter my brother being unable to pursue a work[2] he had begun, owing to the kind interruptions of friends who were more at leisure than himself, I persuaded him that he might write at his ease in one of these rooms, as he could not ere hear the door knock, or hear himself denied to be at home, which was sure to make him call out and convict the poor maid in a fib. Here I said he might be almost really not at home. So I put in an old grate & made him a fire in the largest of these garrets, and carried in one table, and one chair, an[d] bid him write away, and consider himself as much alone as if he we[re] in a n[e]w lodging in the midst of Salisbury plain, or any other wide unfrequented place where he could expect few visitors to break in upon his solitude. I left him quite delig[h]ted with his new acquisiti[on,] but in a few hours he came down again with a sadly dismal face. He could do nothing he said with those bare white-washed walls before h[is] eyes. He could not write in that dull unfurnished prison.

The next day before he came home from his office, I had gatherrd up various bits of old carpetting to cover the floor, and to a little brea[k] the blank look of the bare walls I hung up a few old prints that used [to] ornament the kitchen, and after dinner, with great boast of what an improvement I had made, I took Charles once more into his new study. A week of busy labours followed, in which I think you would not have disliked to have been our assistant: My brother & I almost covered the walls with prints, for which purpose he cut out every print from every book in his old library, coming in every now and then to ask my leave to strip a fresh poor author, which he might not do you know without my permission as I am elder sister. There was such pasting—such consultation where their portraits and where [th]e series of pictures from Ovid,[3] Milton & Shakespear would show to most advantage and in what obscure corner authors of humbler note might be allowed to tell their stories. All the books gave up their stores but one, a translation from Ariosto, a delicious set of four & twenty prints, & for which I had marked out a conspicuous place, when lo! we found, at the moment the scissars were going to work, that a part of the poem was printed at the back of every picture. What a cruel disappointment!—— To conclude this long story about nothing, the poor despised garret is now called the print room and is become our most favorite sitting room.[4]

Your Sister Ann will tell you that your friend Louisa is going [to] France. Miss Skepper is out of town. Mrs Reynolds desire[s] to be remembered to you, and so does my neighbour Mrs Norris who was your doctress when you were unwell, her three little children are grown three big children. The Lions still live in Exeter Change. Returning home through the Strand I often hear them roar about twelve o clock at night. I never hear them without thinking of you, because you seemed so pleased with the sight of them, & said your young companions would stare when you told them you had seen a Lion.

And now my dear Barbara fare well, I have not written such a long letter a long time but I am very sorry I had nothing amusing to write about. wishing you may pass happily through the rest of your school days, and every future day of your life I remain

your affectionate friend
M Lamb

My brother sends his love to you with the kind remembrance your letter shewed you have of us as I was. He joins with me in respects to your good father & mother and to your brother John who if I do not mistake the name is your tall young brother who was in search of a fair lady with a large fortune. Ask him if he has found her yet. you say you are not so tall as Louisa—you must be, you cannot so degenerate from the rest of your family. Now you have begun I shall hope to have the pleasure of hearing from [you] again. I shall always receive a letter from you with very great delight.

MS: The Historical Society of Pennsylvania, Philadelphia. Pub.: Harper, IV, 16–21; Lucas (1905), VI, 446–448; Lucas (1912), V, 470–473; Lucas (1935), II, 140–143. Address: Miss Barbara Betham. About Mary Matilda Betham's sister and occasional charge Barbara—who at the time of this letter was fourteen and residing with her family in Stonham Aspall, Suffolk, and who (as Mary Lamb indicates in the penultimate sentence in her second paragraph) had last visited the Lambs in 1811—see Vol. II, Letter 222, note 13. See there also about Barbara's sister Anne (who is named in the second and fifth paragraphs of this letter), her brother John and sister Louisa and their parents (who are mentioned in the postscript), and the tallness characteristic of the family (which is alluded to in the second paragraph and the postscript). Noticed in *A House of Letters*, p. 149, is the present residence (given above) of Barbara; noticed in *Six Life Studies of Famous Women*, pp. 260 and 240, are her age and an instance of Mary Matilda's having taken her to dine with the Lambs.

1. Perhaps Jane. (See Letter 233, note 4.) The sister mentioned immediately below has not been identified. None of the maids referred to in the fifth paragraph in Letter 255 would seem to be the maid referred to here. Mrs. Holcroft, of whose school I have found no record, is Louisa, the widow of Thomas Holcroft and since 1812 the wife of James Kenney. (See Letter 235, in the paragraph below the reference to note 3, and Vol. II, Letter 133, note 7.) Robinson remembered her as "an ingratiating little woman, who could make herself liked by those who did not think her prudent." On April 4, 1812, he remarked on his taking tea with her and her new husband at the Lambs'. See *H. C. R. on Books and Writers*, I, 11 and 68.

2. Unidentified. Probably it was a work never finished or, if finished, never published.

3. "This Ovid, denuded of pictures, was presented by Mary Lamb to [Mary] Matilda Betham, and is in the author's [M. Betham-Edwards'] possession" (*Six Life Studies of Famous Women*, p. 266, note).

4. Robinson had called on June 29, 1814:

[Found] Lamb as delighted as a child with a garret he had appropriated and adorned with all the copperplate engravings he could collect, having rifled every book he possessed for the purpose.

It was quite delightful to observe his innocent delight. Schiller says all great men have a childlikeness in their nature. [*H. C. R. on Books and Writers*, I, 145]

Louisa, whom Mary mentions in her next paragraph, is Miss Louisa Holcroft (b. 1806), later Mrs. John Badams, a daughter of the late Thomas Holcroft and the present Mrs. James Kenney. (See Vol. II, Letter 198, note 6.) It is noted in Lucas (1935), II, 143, that Louisa was "about to go to France with her mother and stepfather, James Kenney." Miss Skepper is Anne Benson Skepper, later Mrs. Bryan Waller Procter, the stepdaughter of Basil Montagu. (See my Vol. II, Letter 132, note 2.) About Elizabeth Reynolds and Elizabeth Norris see Vol. I, Introduction, pp. xxviii–xxix. Randal and Elizabeth Norris' children were Richard (d. 1836), who was deaf and mentally retarded; Jane (1799?–1891); and Elizabeth (1808?–1894). By August 1823 the sisters would open or assume the management of a girls' boarding school—then or later in Goddard House—in the Hertfordshire village of Widford, where their mother and brother would reside after the death, in 1827, of Randal Norris. After the death, in 1843, of the senior Elizabeth Norris, the sisters—according to a conversation Lucas had with Mrs. Elizabeth Coe, once their pupil, a daughter of Thomas Hunt and his wife of Widford—inherited money from a maternal uncle, closed Goddard House School, settled in separate residences, and were married. Jane was married to Arthur, and Elizabeth, to Charles, sons of George Tween of Blakesware and farmers of Widford. (See *At the Shrine of St. Charles*, pp. 14–36; *The Life of Lamb*, II, 175; and *Lamb and His Hertfordshire*, esp. pp. 247–248.) About Exeter Change see my Vol. I, Letter 102, note 9.

283. *C. L. to John Scott?*

4 Inner Temple Lane
Monday 28 Nov 1814

Sir,

I beg leave to offer you the accompanying Essay[1] (originally written for Mr Hunt's "Reflector," but not published, owing to the stopping of that work). Should it suit you to pay for occasional trifles of this sort, at your common rate, I should perhaps trouble you sometimes. If not, I will send for the M. S. next week, & you will have the goodness to leave it out for that purpose. I am, Sir, with respect

Your Hble Ser
C Lamb

MS: Mr. W. Hugh Peal. Pub.: Lucas (1935), II, 143. The journalist John Scott (1784–1821), the son of Alexander Scott, an upholsterer in Aberdeen, was once Byron's schoolfellow at the grammar school in New Aberdeen and, from 1796 to 1799, a student at Marischal College, Aberdeen University. He had come to London, without his degree, in 1799; worked as a clerk in the War Office; been drawn into journalism before 1803 by his interest in literature and politics; and been married, in perhaps 1806, to Caroline, the daughter of the London print seller Paul Colnaghi, or Colnago (1751–1833). From 1813 to 1814 Scott had been the editor, printer, and publisher of *Drakard's Paper* (listed also as *Drakard's Newspaper* and *Drakard's News*), a weekly Scott had established in January 1813, presumably with financial support from his acquaintance the newspaper proprietor and publisher John Drakard (1775?–1854). In January 1814 Scott had changed the name of the paper to *The Champion.* It remained in his hands until July 1817 and passed, in 1818, into those of John Thelwall. (See Vol. I, Letter 21, note 8.) Between 1814 and 1820 Scott traveled and wrote such works as *A Visit to Paris in 1814* (1815); *Paris Revisited in 1815 by Way of Brussels, Including a Walk over the Field of Battle at Waterloo* (1816); *The House of Mourning* (1817), a poem on the loss of the Scotts' son Paul (1807–1816); and *Sketches of Manners, Scenery, etc. in the French Provinces, Switzerland, and Italy* (1821). In 1820 Scott became the first editor of the *London Magazine* and wrote for its fifth, eleventh, and twelfth numbers "Lord Byron: His French Critics: the Newspapers; and the Magazines," "Blackwood's Magazine," and "The Mohock Magazine" (*London Magazine,* 1 and 2 [May, November, and December 1820], 492–497, 509–521, and 666–685). He wrote for the thirteenth number "The Mohocks" (*London Magazine,* 3 [January 1821], 76–77). In those articles he placed the blame for extravagant opinions expressed in *Blackwood's Edinburgh Magazine* on John Gibson Lockhart (1794–1854), a contributor to *Blackwood's* since 1817, the author of *Peter's Letters to His Kinsfolk* (1819), a son-in-law of Sir Walter Scott and afterward his biographer. By those articles John Scott provoked a duel with Lockhart's intimate the conveyancer Jonathan Henry Christie (1792?–1876) fought on a moonlit field between Chalk Farm and Primrose Hill, London, on February 16, 1821. Scott, whose second was

Peter George Patmore (see Vol. II, Letter 228, note 1), suffered a bullet wound from which he died on February 27. Lamb and Byron subscribed to the fund raised for Scott's widow and two infant children. T. Rowland Hughes's "John Scott: Editor, Author and Critic," *London Mercury*, 21 (April 1930), 518–528, supplements the biography of Scott in the *DNB*.

1. Presumably, "On the Melancholy of Tailors" (*Works*, I, 172–175 and 449–451), which Lamb signed "Burton, *Junior*" (see Letter 286, at the reference to note 1), and is in *The Champion* of December 4, 1814. Lamb may have, as has been generally supposed, contributed other pieces to *The Champion* while it was under Scott's conduct. Although no others have been positively identified as Lamb's, John M. Turnbull, in "Notes and Observations: A Retort to *Elia*," *Review of English Studies*, 3 (January 1927), 68–70, proposed that this response, so finely indignant, in *The Champion* of December 11, 1814, to Lamb's playful indictment of tailors is a hoax and Lamb its perpetrator:

ON THE MELANCHOLY OF TAILORS
For The Champion

Sir,—I often read your weekly miscellany, and am much entertained with its contents. But, on looking into that of last Sunday, I experienced feelings of a very unpleasant description. Your learned and witty correspondent, or assistant, "Burton, Junior," has endeavoured to make himself and his readers merry at the expence of a numerous, and, to say the least in their behalf, a *useful* set of men,—the "Tailors." He first asserts that they are, one and all,—boys, journeymen, and masters,—tinctured with melancholy; and then he pretends to assign some of the causes of this unhappy state of mind, but with an evident intention of exposing them to the derision of the thoughtless and the dissipated.

This ingenious gentleman "intends no harm to any individual"; or at least such would be his declaration, I have no doubt, if taxed with the mischief likely to result from this effusion of his pen: but he ought to recollect, that it is impossible to calculate the extent of evil which satire, like his, pointed with wit, may produce to a company of persons, at whom it is indiscriminately and anonymously directed.

With respect to his accusation,—for in such a light I consider his assertion, that tailors are all melancholy,—if it can be shown that many are as sprightly in their dispositions and conduct as any other set of men who have their insides and outsides to provide for by their industry, it will be pronounced a palpable falsehood, and the gentleman will take shame to himself for having published it.

On this then, sir, I have the best of all possible proof. I have a proof of it in my own family, and in my own person. My three sons are tailors, I am a tailor, my father, grandfather, and great grandfather were tailors: and yet, sir, so far are we, or were they, from being melancholy, that we have been always celebrated as the life of the neighbourhood, and the spirit of every company: and as for myself, and my boys more particularly—our foreheads are never wrinkled with care, nor our lips lowered with sullenness. We rise early in the morning, sit close to our business during the day, and live temperately, as physicians, I believe, recommend all persons whose employments are sedentary to do; and feel ourselves in the evening contented, cheerful, and happy:—and this I have good reason to believe is not a blessing peculiar to us; others in the same trade are, I have no doubt, equally fortunate.

Had I not been able to refute the statement of the gentleman, that we are a melancholy class of mortals, still I should not have agreed with him in his allegation of the causes of this gloomy state of mind which he says prevails among us. He seems to think that tailors do not eat so much roast beef and plumb-pudding as other men, and that they confine themselves chiefly to a vegetable diet, and especially to cabbage. This is either an illiberal sneer,— or if meant as a serious attack on the vegetable, I can refute him though he has taken the pains to quote Burton, senior, and to extract his reference to Galen [the medical writer Claudius Galen, or Galenus, or Gallien (ca. 130–200)—see *Works*, I, 175], on the pernicious qualities of a wholesome plant. My family being of German extraction, are remarkably fond of cabbage, yet we feel none of those ill effects which he asserts it produces. So far from feeling dull and stupid after it, we are all life and jollity, sing a pleasant song, and go comfortably to bed.

No sir, if tailors are dull and melancholy, there is another cause to be assigned for it,—*the losses they sustain by giving credit*. This immediately affects the masters; but, as it prevents their giving to the journeymen large wages, it affects them also, and this is the only thing connected with the trade that ever makes me uncomfortable.

I remain, sir,
An admirer of your principles, so far
as I know them,
J. D.

Two of Turnbull's several observations about the response are, first, the misspelling (in the fifth paragraph) "plumb-pudding," a misspelling that occurs with comments in the first paragraph in Lamb's letter to Joseph Hume dated December 29, 1807 (Vol. II, Letter 218); second, the signature, "J. D.": Lamb had the critic John Dennis (1657–1734) figure in "On the Melancholy of Tailors," and Lamb would, in 1825, assume the identity "J——s D——n" in "The Superannuated Man" and sign that essay "J. D." (*Works*, I, 175, and II, 428 and 425). B., in "Letters of Charles Lamb," *Notes and Queries*, 184 (April 24, 1943), 248, proposed that the following (unsigned) communication about Manning in *The Champion* of December 18, 1814, could "hardly have been from anyone but Lamb":

The obstacles opposed to the introduction of foreigners and foreign literature into China are most forcibly exemplified in the case of Mr. Manning, who has made considerable progress in the Chinese language and customs. This gentleman had for many years been endeavouring, but in vain, to make his way from Canton to the interior of China; but the Chinese, with their vigilant and instinctive jealousy, kept so strict an eye upon him, that he found the attempt to be utterly impracticable; he therefore proceeded by sea to Cochin China, but with no better success; the people of that country being tinctured with the same species of political jealousy and caution with their neighbours. Determined, however, to persevere in his object, he proceeded to Calcutta, and thence to the northern frontier of Bengal; here he was fortunate enough to penetrate into Bootan, where he met with and by some means engaged himself to the commander of the Chinese forces as his body physician, accompanied him as far as Lassa in Tibet, and was just on the eve of departure thence, and on the point of realising his hopes, by proceeding along the upper regions of Tartary to the capital of China, when an order was received from Pekin, to recall the general, and to send back immediately to Bengal the European physician whom he had been guilty of retaining about his person.

Regarding "five essay-letters [in *The Champion*] which can with confidence be ascribed to Lamb, though solely on internal evidence," see "Charles Lamb and 'The Champion': An Address by Dr. Josephine Bauer . . . ," in the *CLSB* of January 1955. Regarding John and Leigh Hunt's *The Reflector*, mentioned below, see Letter 276, source note.

284. *C. L. to John Scott*

Saturday [December 3? 1814]

Sir,

Your explanation is perfectly pleasant to me, and I accede to your proposal most willingly. As I began with the beginning of this month, I will if you please call upon you for *your part of the engagement* (supposing I shall have performed mine) on the 1st of March next, & thence forward if it suit you quarterly—. You will occasionally wink at **Briskets** & **Veiny Pieces**—[1]

Your hbl Ser
C Lamb

MS: unrecovered; a facsimile: George Birkbeck Hill, *Talks about Autographs* (Boston and New York: Houghton, Mifflin, 1896), facing p. 24. Also pub.: Harper, III, 328; Lucas (1905), VI, 433–434; Lucas (1912), V, 456; Lucas (1935), II, 125–126. Address, from Hill, p. 24: J. Scott, Esq.,/3 Maida Place, Edgware road. Postmark, from Hill, p. 24: 1814. The remarks in this letter referring to a March payment and quarterly payments thenceforward for the writings of Lamb to be published in *The Champion* suggest he wrote the letter in December, on the Saturday between the date of the preceding letter (Monday, November 28) and the appearance (in *The Champion* of Sunday, December 4) of "On the Melancholy of Tailors."

1. Possibly an allusion to the peculiar diet of tailors considered in "On the Melancholy of Tailors" (*Works*, I, 175), though the diet is constituted almost solely of cabbage.

285. *C. L. to John Scott?*

Monday evg. 12 Dec 1814

Sir,

I am sorry to seem to go off my agreement, but very particular circumstances have happened to hinder my fulfillment of it at present.[1] If any single Essays ever occur to me in future, you shall have the refusal of them. Meantime I beg you to consider the thing as at an end.—

Yours,
with thanks & acknowlg*ts*
C Lamb

MS: Mrs. Donald F. Hyde, Somerville, N.J. Pub.: Harper, IV, 21; Lucas (1905), VI, 449; Lucas (1912), V, 473; Lucas (1935), II, 144.

1. Those hindering "very particular circumstances" were, with little doubt, associated with the confinement or the illness leading to the confinement of Mary. On December 11 Robinson reported her as not ill but as having "undergone great fatigue" (*H. C. R. on Books and Writers*, I, 156) from writing "On Needlework" for the *New British Lady's Magazine and Monthly Mirror of Literature and Fashion*, 1 (April 1, 1815), 257–260. (Her article, which is in *Works*, I, 176–180, she signed "Sempronia," a name Lamb would use in 1826 in "That You Must Love Me, and Love My Dog" [*Works*, II, 267].) Mary was taken to an asylum between December 12 and 19, 1814. On December 20 Robinson entered this in his diary: "Late Lamb called on me to sit with him while he smoked his pipe. I had called on him last night at Anthony Robinson's suggestion, and he seemed absolutely grateful for the visit. He wanted society, being alone; but I abstained from inquiring after his sister, and trust he will appreciate the motive" (*H. C. R. on Books and Writers*, I, 157). See Letter 290, note 1, about her return home. About Anthony Robinson see Vol. II, Letter 208, note 2.

286. *C. L. to William Wordsworth*

[December 28, 1814]

Dear W.

your experience about tailors seems to be in point blank opposition to **Burton**,[1] as much as the author of the Excursion does toto cœlo differ in his notion of a country life from the picture which W. H. has exhibited of the same. But with a little explanation you and B. may be reconciled. It is evident that he confined his observations to the genuine native London tailor. What freaks Tailor-nature may take in the country is not for him to give account of. And certainly some of the freaks recorded do give an idea of the persons in question being beside themselves, rather than in harmony with the common moderate self enjoymt. of the rest [of] mankind. A flying tailor I venture to say is no more in rerum naturâ than a flying horse or a Gryphon. His wheeling his airy flight[2] from the precipice you mention had a parallel in the melancholy Jew who toppled from the monument. Were his limbs ever found? Then, the man who cures diseases by words, is evidently an inspired tailor. Burton never affirmed that the act of sewing disqualified the practiser of it from being a fit organ for supernatural revelation. He never enters into such subjects. Tis the common uninspired tailor which he speaks of. Again the person who makes his smiles to be *heard*, is evidently a man under possession; a demoniac taylor. A greater hell[3] than his own must have a hand in this. I am not certain that the cause which you advocate has much reason for triumph. You seem to me to substitute light headedness for light heartedness by a trick, or not to know the difference. I confess, a grinning tailor would shock me.—**Enough of tailors.**—

The " 'scapes" of the great god Pan[4] who appeared among your mountains some dozen years since, and his narrow chance of being submerged by the swains, afforded me much pleasure. I can conceive the water nymphs pulling for him. He would have been another **Hylas. W. Hylas.** In a mad letter which Capel Loft wrote to M. M. Phillips (now Sr. Richd.) I remember his noticing a metaphysical article by **Pan**, signed H. and adding "I take your correspondent to be the same with **Hylas.**" **Hylas** has[5] put forth a pastoral just before. How near the unfounded conjecture of the certainly inspired Loft (unfounded as we thought it) was to being realized! I can conceive him being "good to all that wander in that perilous flood."— One J. Scott (I know no more) is editr. of Champn. Where is Coleridge?—

That Review you speak of,[6] I am only sorry It did not appear last month. The circumstances of haste & peculiar bad spirits under which it was written, would have excused its slightness & inadequacy, the full load of which I shall suffer from its lying by so long as it will seem to have done from its postponement. I write with great difficulty & can scarce command my own resolution to sit at writing an hour together. I am a poor creature, but I am leaving off Gin. I hope you will see good will in the thing. I had a difficulty to perform not to mak[e i]t all Panegyreck; I have attempted to personate a mere **stranger** to you; perhaps with too much strangeness. But you must bear that in mind when you read it, & not think that I am in mind **distant from you or your Poem; but that both are close to me among the nearest of persons & things.** I do but act the stranger in the Review. **Then,** I was puzzled about extracts & determined upon not giving one that had been in the Examiner,[7] for Extracts repeated give an idea that there is a meagre allowce. of good things. By this way, I deprived myself of Sr. W. **Irthing** & the reflections that conclude his story, which are the flower of the Poem. H. had given the reflections before me. *Then* it is the **first** Review I ever did & I did not know how long I might make it. But it must speak for itself, if Giffard & his crew do not put words

in its mouth, which I expect.— farewell. Love to all—. Mary keeps
very bad.

C Lamb

MS: The University of Texas Library. Pub.: Talfourd (1848), I, 211–214;
Sala, I, 259–261; Purnell, I, 259–261; Fitzgerald, II, 94–96; Hazlitt, I, 436–438;
Ainger (1888), I, 278–280; Ainger (1900), II, 214–217; Macdonald, I, 348–350;
Ainger (1904), I, 335–337; Harper, IV, 21–24; Lucas (1905), VI, 449–451;
Lucas (1912), V, 473–475; Lucas (1935), II, 145–147. Address: W. Wordsworth
Esq/Rydale Mount/Grasmere/near Kendal/Westmorland. Postmark: December
28, 1814.

1. Lamb, that is, as Burton, *Junior,* in "On the Melancholy of Tailors." (See
Letter 283, note 1.) The letter to which Lamb is replying, evidently one in which
Wordsworth had described the tailors in his experience, has not been recovered.
The Latin, below, translates as "in all ways imaginable." The passage in which
the Latin occurs refers to Hazlitt's sometimes savage comments on country life in
the installment of "Character of Mr. Wordsworth's New Poem, *The Excursion*"
(see Letter 277, note 1) in *The Examiner* of October 2, 1814: "All country
people hate each other. They have so little comfort that they envy their neighbours
the smallest pleasure or advantage, and nearly grudge themselves the necessaries of
life. From not being accustomed to enjoyment, they become hardened and averse
to it—stupid for want of thought—selfish for want of society. There is nothing
good to be had in the country, or, if there is, they will not let you have it. They
had rather injure themselves than oblige any one else." Other such comments are
these: "The benefits of knowledge are never so well understood as from seeing the
effects of ignorance, in their naked, undisguised state, upon the common country
people. Their selfishness and insensibility are perhaps less owing to the hardships
and privations, which make them, like people out at sea in a boat, ready to
devour one another, than to their having no idea of anything beyond themselves
and their immediate sphere of action. They have no knowledge of, and consequently can take no interest in, any thing which is not an object of their senses,
and of their daily pursuits. They hate all strangers, and have generally a nick-
name for the inhabitants of the next village" (*Hazlitt's Works,* XIX, 21–22).

2. Cf. Thomas Gray, "Elegy Written in a Country Churchyard," line 7. Mentioned below is the Jew Lyon Levi (b. 1760?), a diamond merchant so melancholy over his commercial speculations that he had leaped to his death on
January 18, 1810, from The Monument, designed by Sir Christopher Wren
(1632–1723) and erected on Fish Street Hill to commemorate the fire of London
of 1666. A few lines are given to Levi in the *Gentleman's Magazine,* 80 (January
1810), 79.

3. If a pun—on "hell" as it means the receptacle into which tailors discard
their shreds (and printers their refuse type)—it is violated by the use of "hand"
that follows. The pun is well made in Lamb's *Satan in Search of a Wife; with the
Whole Process of His Courtship and Marriage, and Who Danced at the Wedding
by an Eye Witness,* Part the First, stanza xxiii (*Works,* V, 114).

4. "The great god Pan" is in Plutarch's "Why the Oracles Cease to Give
Answers," in *Opera moralia* (translated by several hands as *Plutarch's Morals*
during the period 1684 to 1694 and revised by W. W. Goodwin during the period
1874 to 1878). In Wordsworth's "Composed by the Side of Grasmere Lake"
(composed in 1807, but not published until 1819), line 12, Pan is "Great Pan";
in *The Excursion,* IV, 887, he is "The simple shepherd's awe-inspiring God!"
Lamb is writing of Hazlitt's escapades among the country women and their pro-

tectors at Keswick in 1803, escapades that Wordsworth, apparently nettled by Hazlitt's "Character of Mr. Wordsworth's New Poem, *The Excursion*," had related to Lamb. On June 15, 1815, Wordsworth, stung then by Hazlitt's sneering allusions to him in "Comus," in *The Examiner* of June 11, 1815 (*Hazlitt's Works*, V, 233), told the story to Robinson, who recorded it: "It appears that Hazlitt, when at Keswick, narrowly escaped being ducked by the populace, and probably sent to prison for some gross attacks on women. ⟨He even whipped one woman, *more puerorum* ['in the way of boys'], for not yielding to his wishes.⟩ The populace were incensed against him and pursued him, but he escaped to Wordsworth, who took him into his house at midnight, gave him clothes and money (from three to five pounds). Since that time," Robinson added, "Wordsworth, though he never refused to meet Hazlitt when by accident they came together, did not choose that with his knowledge he should be invited. In consequence, Lamb never asked Hazlitt while Wordsworth was in town, which probably provoked Hazlitt, and which Lamb himself disapproved of. But Lamb, who needs very little indulgence for himself, is very indulgent towards others, and rather reproaches Wordsworth for being inveterate against Hazlitt" (*H. C. R. on Books and Writers*, I, 169–170, where the angle brackets signify and enclose a passage written in the original in shorthand or in a composite of shorthand and longhand). In apparently 1824 Wordsworth told the story to Benjamin Robert Haydon, who recorded a part of it: "He [Wordsworth] was relating to me with great horror Hazlitt's licentious conduct to the girls of the Lake, & that no woman could walk after dark, for 'his Satyr & *beastly* appetites.' Some girl called him a black-faced rascal, when Hazlitt enraged pushed her down, '& because, Sir,' said Wordsworth, 'she refused to gratify his abominable & devilish propensities,' he lifted up her petticoats & *smote* her on *the bottom*" (*Haydon's Diary*, II, 470; for more on the affair see *Hazlitt*, pp. 134–139). Named first below is the Hylas of Greek legend, the favorite of Hercules taken from him by having been taken captive by the nymphs of the spring where Hylas had sought water, so attracted were they to his beauty. The letter from the barrister and miscellaneous writer the elder Capell, or Capel, Lofft (1751–1824) to "M[onthly] M[agazine]," or Sir Richard, Phillips (see Vol. I, Letter 29, note 2; and Letter 232, note 7) is in the *Monthly Magazine*, 27 (March 1, 1809), 132–133. On page 132 is Lofft's expression Lamb misquotes— "I am glad to find the metaphysical subject revived by W. H. I hope and think he is the same with Hylaus." Lofft was expressing himself on a letter bearing the caption "Proposal for the Basis of a New System of Metaphysical Philosophy" and the signature "W. H.," in the *Monthly Magazine*, 27 (February 1, 1809), 15–19. Geoffrey Carnall in "A Hazlitt Contribution," in the *TLS* of June 19, 1953, p. 397, shows the letter to have indeed been written by Hazlitt. Neither (the presumably pseudonymous) "Hylaus," or "Hylas," nor the pastoral that Lamb ascribes to him has been identified.

5. For "had." Below, Lamb quotes from Milton's "Lycidas," lines 184–185. John Scott, after whom Wordsworth had evidently inquired, shortly presented Wordsworth with a copy of *A Visit to Paris in 1814*. Wordsworth thanked him for it in a letter of May 14, 1815. Haydon, who had known Scott since probably 1813 and was to meet Wordsworth, in London, in May 1815, would introduce the two men at his home on June 12, 1815, moments after Haydon had made the cast for his life mask of Wordsworth. (See Letter 283, source note; *Wordsworths' Letters*, III, 237 and facing p. 250; and *Haydon's Diary*, I, 450.) Coleridge, after whom Lamb inquires, had on about December 5, 1814, left Mrs. Smith's cottage at Ashley, Box, near Bath (see Letter 278, source note), for Calne, Wiltshire, where he would generally remain until perhaps March 23, 1816. He planned at first to reside with a Mr. Page, a surgeon of Calne; had by mid-March 1815 moved in with the John Morgans and Charlotte Brent, new residents themselves of the

town; and looked to them all for help in his struggles to regain his health and
restrict his ingestion of laudanum.

6. Lamb's "Review of *The Excursion;* a Poem. By William Wordsworth." (See
Letter 277, note 1.) William Gifford did, as Lamb expected Gifford would to a
degree, deform it before he published it, in the (delayed) October issue of his
Quarterly Review. The outrage Lamb felt when he saw how grotesquely Gifford
had deformed the review is manifest in the next letter. "The Enclosed is from
Lamb," wrote Wordsworth to Southey in January 1815 of that letter, "pray return
it by a speedy opportunity. I should be infinitely obliged to you if you could
procure from Gifford, from the Printer, or from anybody his original MS which
has been so cruelly garbled and disfigured. I am so vexed on his account and for
the apprehended loss of the original Composition, that I have not the slightest
feeling for any injury done to myself, by Gifford's treatment of it. I cannot say
how happy I should be if a piece of prose that so exquisite a Writer as Lamb
thinks the prettiest he ever wrote [see the next letter, first paragraph] could be
recovered. I know that you will sympathize with me; and I am confident you will
do all that can be done" (*Wordsworths' Letters*, III, 186). Southey wrote to
Grosvenor Charles Bedford on January 14, 1815, partly, perhaps, in obedience to
Wordsworth's request: "I beseech you, try if you can recover the MSS. of Lamb's
'Review,' which has been made the thing it is by Gifford's merciless mutilations.
. . . If there be a logical arrangement, he is sure to dislocate it by pulling out
the middle joint of every articulated paragraph. If there be a felicitous phrase, he
is sure to gouge the sentence. To own the truth, I am too angry to write to him
just now, and shall therefore make my reply through you" (*Selections from the
Letters of Robert Southey*, ed. John Wood Warter [London: Longman *et al.*,
1856], II, 393). Lamb's manuscript has never been recovered. Lucas was informed
by John Murray—the publisher Sir John Murray (1851–1928), one assumes, the
grandson of the publisher John Murray (1778–1843), the latter the founder of
the *Quarterly Review* and the employer of Gifford as its first editor—that the
manuscript "no longer exists" (*Works*, I, 448).

7. In, that is, Hazlitt's "Character of Mr. Wordsworth's New Poem, *The
Excursion*." The story of Sir Alfred Irthing (not "Sr. W. Irthing," as Lamb
designates him below), whose descendants in the region of Grasmere and whose
largely ruined estate are noticed in *Wordsworth's Poetical Works* (1940–1949),
V, 468, is in *The Excursion*, VII, 923–975. The reflections flowing from the story
form VII, 976–1057. Hazlitt quoted VII, 976–1007 (*Hazlitt's Works*, XIX, 24–
25), in the installment of his review in *The Examiner* of October 2, 1814. Although Lamb is correct in stating that his own review of the poem is the first
review he ever did, he had attempted, in November 1803, to review the first two
volumes of Godwin's *The Life of Geoffrey Chaucer*. See my Vol. II, Letters
152–155.

287. *C. L. to William Wordsworth*

[January 7, 1815]

Dear Wordsworth,

I told you my Review was a very imperfect one. But what you will
see in the Quarterly is a spurious one which Mr Baviad Gifford has
palm'd upon it for mine. I never felt more vexd in my life than when

I read it. I cannot give you an idea of what he has done to it out of spite at me because he once sufferd me to be called a lunatic in his **Thing.** The *language* he has altered throughout. Whatever inadequateness it had to its subject, it was in point of composition the prettiest piece of prose I ever writ, & so my sister (to whom alone I read the MS) said. That charm if it had any is all gone: more than a third of the substance is cut away & that not all from one place, but *passim,* so as to make utter nonsense. Every warm expression is changed for a nasty cold one. I have not the cursed alteration by me, I shall never look at it again, but for a specimen I remember—I had said the Poet of the Excursn. "walks thro common forests as thro' some Dodona or enchanted wood & every casual bird that flits upon the boughs, like that miraculous one in Tasso, but in language more piercing than any articulate sounds, reveals to him far higher lovelays." It is now (besides half a dozen alterations in the same half dozen lines) "but in language more *intelligent* reveals to him"—that is one I remember—.[1] But that would have been little, putting his damnd Shoemaker phraseology (for he was a shoemaker) in stead of mine which has been tinctured with better authors than his ignorance can comprehend—for I reckon myself a dab at **Prose**—verse I leave to my betters—God help them, if they are to be so reviewd by friend & foe as you have been this quarter. I have read "It wont do."—[2] But worse than altering words, he has kept a few members only of the part I had done best which was to explain all I could of your "Scheme of harmonies" as I had ventured to call it between the external universe & what within us answers to it. To do this I had accumulated a good many short passages, rising in length to the end, weaving in the Extracts as if they came in as a part of the text, naturally, not obtruding them as **specimens.** Of this part a little is left, but so as without conjuration no man could tell what I was driving it.[3] A proof of it you may see (tho' not judge of the whole of the injustice) by these words—I had spoken something about "natural methodism"—& after follows "and therefore the tale of Margaret shd. have been postponed" (I forget my words, or **his words**): **now** the reasons for postponing it are as deducible from what goes before, as they are from the 104th psalm—. The passage whence I deduced it, has vanished, but clapping a **colon** before a **therefore** is always reason enough for Mr Baviad Gifford to allow to a reviewer that is not himself. I assure you my complaints are **founded**. I know how **sore** a word alterd makes one, but indeed of this Review the whole complexion is **gone**. I regret only that I did not keep a copy. I am sure you would have been pleased with it, because I have been feeding my fancy for some months with the notion of pleasing you. Its imperfection or inadequateness in size & method I knew, but for the *writing-part* of it, I was fully satisfied. I hoped it would make more than atonement. Ten or twelve distinct passages come to my mind which are **gone,** and what is left is of course the worse for their having been there, the eyes are pulld out & the bleeding sockets are left. I read it **at Arch's shop**[4] with my face burning with vexation secretly, with just such a feeling as if it had been a **review** written against **myself,** making false quotations from me—. But I am ashamd to say so much about a short piece. How are *you* served! and the labors of years turn'd into contempt by scoundrels—

But I could not but protest against your taking that thing as mine. Every *pretty* expression, (I know there were many) every warm expression, there was nothing **else,** is vulgarized & **frozen**—but if they catch me in their **camps** again let them spitchcock me. They had a right to do it, as no name appears to it, and Mr Shoemaker Gifferd I suppose never **wa[i]ved** a right he had since he commenced author. God confound him & **all caitiffs**

C L

MS: University of Texas Library. Pub.: Talfourd (1848), I, 215–219; Sala, I, 261–264; Purnell, I, 261–264; Fitzgerald, II, 96–99; Hazlitt, I, 439–441; Ainger (1888), I, 280–282; Ainger (1900), II, 217–220; Macdonald, I, 350–352; Ainger (1904), I, 337–339; Harper, IV, 24–27; Lucas (1905), VI, 452–453; Lucas (1912), V, 476–478; Lucas (1935), II, 148–149. Address: W. Wordsworth Esq/ Rydale Mount/Grasmere/near Kendal/Westmorland. Postmark: January 7, 1815. In writing here in outrage over the license Gifford had taken with Lamb's manuscript of "Review of *The Excursion;* a Poem. By William Wordsworth," Lamb writes of one of what would amount to five offenses committed against him between 1811 and 1823 by the "Thing," or the *Quarterly Review,* and, directly or indirectly, by its first editor, William Gifford—who had in 1772 been an apprentice to a shoemaker; had in 1782 earned a bachelor's degree in arts at Exeter College, Oxford; had become known by his satires *The Baviad* (1794) and *The Mœviad* (1795), modeled after the satires of the Roman poet Persius, or Aulus Persius Flaccus (34–62), and directed against those late-eighteenth-century poetasters customarily designated the Della Cruscans and against the corruptions of contemporary dramatists. During the period 1797 to 1798 Gifford had edited and written for the *Anti-Jacobin, or Weekly Examiner.* (See Letter 281, note 1; Letter 277, note 1; and Vol. I, Letter 44, note 9.) Lamb had probably been suspicious of Gifford since his association with the *Anti-Jacobin.* (See, for example, Letter 236, near the reference to note 6.) But his character did not forcibly emerge for Lamb until Gifford cruelly abused Lamb in the *Quarterly Review,* 6 (December 1811), 485. There, in evaluating the edition by William Henry Weber (1783–1818) of *The Dramatic Works of John Ford* (1811), Gifford stated that Weber had "polluted his pages with the blasphemies of a poor maniac" by having quoted the praises of Ford and his *The Broken Heart* (1633) from Lamb's *Specimens of English Dramatic Poets, Who Lived about the Time of Shakspeare: With Notes* (*Works,* IV, 218), praises recurring in Lamb's "Characters of Dramatic Writers, Contemporary with Shakspeare" (*Works,* I, 49–50). Gifford added of Lamb that for "this unfortunate creature, every feeling mind will find an apology in his calamitous situation." In a letter (which has not been recovered) to Gifford or John Murray, the founder of the *Quarterly Review,* Southey protested and expressed his sorrow over the publication of Gifford's statements. In a letter to Southey of February 13, 1812, Gifford claimed grief, shock, and innocence of malice upon learning what he had done. "I call God to witness," reads a portion of Gifford's excuse, "that in the whole course of my life I never heard one syllable of Mr. Lamb or his family. I knew not that he ever had a sister, or that he had parents living [Lamb had not parents living], or that he or any person connected with him had ever manifested the slightest tendency to insanity. In a word, I declare to you *in the most solemn manner* that all I ever knew or ever heard of Mr. Lamb was merely his name. Had I been aware of one of the circumstances which you mention, I would have lost my right arm sooner than have written what I have. . . . I considered Lamb as a thoughtless scribbler, who, in circumstances of ease, amused himself by writing upon any subject. Why I thought so I cannot tell, but it was the opinion I formed to myself, for I now regret to say I never made any inquiry upon the subject; nor by any accident in the whole course of my life did I hear him mentioned beyond the name" (*Southey's Correspondence,* V, 151; see *New Southey Letters,* II, 28, and Samuel Smiles's *A Publisher and His Friends: Memoir and Correspondence of the Late John Murray, with an Account of the Origin and Progress of the House, 1768–1843* [London: John Murray; New York: Scribner's, 1891], I, 200–201). Southey accepted Gifford's excuse as sincere. Its sincerity was questioned by the reviewer— Coleridge's biographer James Dykes Campbell (1838–1895), according to Lucas in *Works,* I, 447, and IV, 610—of the edition by the scholar and man of letters Sir Israel Gollancz (1863–1930) of *Charles Lamb's Specimens of English Dramatic Poets . . . Including the Extracts from the Garrick Plays* (1893):

> Had Gifford merely called Lamb a "fool" or a "madman," the epithet would have been mere "common form" as addressed by the *Quarterly* of those days to a wretch who was a friend of other wretches such as Hunt and Hazlitt; but he went far beyond such common form and used language of the utmost precision. Weber, wrote Gifford, "has polluted his pages with the blasphemies of a poor maniac, who it seems once published some detached scenes from the 'Broken Heart.' For this unfortunate creature every feeling mind will find an apology in his calamitous situation." This passage has no meaning at all if it is not to be taken as a positive statement that Lamb suffered from chronic mental derangement; yet Gifford when challenged confessed that when he wrote it he had known absolutely nothing of Lamb, except his name! It seems to have struck neither Gifford nor Southey that this was no excuse at all, and something a good deal worse than no excuse—that even as an explanation it was not such as an honourable man would have cared to offer. Gifford added a strongly-worded expression of his feeling of remorse on learning that his blows had fallen with cruel effect on a sore place. Both feeling and expression may have been sincere, for, under the circumstances, only a fiend would be incapable of remorse. But the excuse or explanation is open to much suspicion, owing to the fact (revealed in the Murray 'Memoirs'

[Smiles's *A Publisher and His Friends,* I, 200]) that Lamb's friend Barron **Field** [see **Letter 296,** note 1] had been Gifford's collaborator in the preparation of the article in which the offending passage occurs. Field was well acquainted with Lamb's personal and family history, and while the article was in progress the collaborators could hardly have avoided some exchange of ideas on a subject which stirred one of them so deeply. . . . This is, of course, pure assumption, but it is vastly more reasonable and much more likely to be in substantial accordance with the facts than Gifford's statement that when he called Lamb a poor maniac, whose calamitous situation offered a sufficient apology for his blasphemies, he was imaginatively describing a man of whom he knew absolutely nothing, except that he was "a thoughtless scribbler." . . . The apology, whether truthful or the opposite, reveals deep-seated corruption of principle if not of character. [*The Athenaeum,* No. 3487 (August 25, 1894), 267]

The second of the offenses forming the subject of the present note is the subject of the present letter. An account of the third is given in Letter 320, near the reference to note 9. The fourth is in the review, believed to be by Dr. Robert Gooch, of Dr. John Reid's *Essays on Hypochondriasis and Other Nervous Affections* (see Letter 278, note 1, and Vol. I, Letter 58, note 2) in the *Quarterly Review,* 27 (April 1822), 120–121. The reviewer quoted from and asserted that Lamb's "Confessions of a Drunkard" (see Letter 276, source note) is a "fearful picture of the consequences of intemperance, and which we have reason to know is a true tale." The reviewer was answered in a note, probably the product of Lamb and the editors of the *London Magazine,* to "Confessions of a Drunkard" when it was republished in the *London Magazine,* 6 (August 1822), 99 and 117–121:

We have been induced, in the first instance, to re-print a Thing, which he [Elia] put forth in a friend's [Basil Montagu's] volume some years since, entitled the Confessions of a Drunkard, seeing that Messieurs the Quarterly Reviewers have chosen to embellish their last dry pages with fruitful quotations therefrom; adding, from their peculiar brains, the gratuitous affirmation, that they have reason to believe that the describer (in his delineations of a drunkard forsooth!) partly sate for his own picture. . . . We deny not that a portion of his own experiences may have passed into the picture, (as who, that is not a washy fellow, but must at some times have felt the after-operation of a too generous cup?)—but then how heightened! how exaggerated!—how little within the sense of the Review, where a part, in their slanderous usage, must be understood to stand for the whole!—but it is useless to expostulate with this Quarterly slime, brood of Nilus, watery heads with hearts of jelly, spawned under the sign of Aquarius, incapable of Bacchus, and therefore cold, washy, spiteful, bloodless.——Elia shall string them up one day, and show their colours—or rather how colourless and vapid the whole fry—when he putteth forth his long promised, but unaccountably hitherto delayed, Confessions of a Water-drinker. [*Works,* I, 432]

The fifth of the offenses is in Southey's review, headed "Progress of Infidelity" in the *Quarterly Review,* 28 (January 1823), 493–536, of *Histoire de la théophilantropie, depuis sa naissance jusqu'à son extinction,* a work by the constitutional bishop of Blois and French revolutionist Henri Baptiste Grégoire (1750–1831) that had taken its place in an expanded edition of Grégoire's *Histoire des sectes religieuses, depuis le commencement du siècle dernier jusqu'à l'époque actuelle* (first published, in two volumes, in 1810):

Unbelievers have not always been honest enough thus to express their real feelings; but this we know concerning them, that when they have renounced their birthright of hope, they have not been able to divest themselves of fear. From the nature of the human mind this might be presumed, and in fact it is so. They may deaden the heart and stupify the conscience, but they cannot destroy the imaginative faculty. There is a remarkable proof of this in Elia's Essays, a book which wants only a sounder religious feeling, to be as delightful as it is original. In that [Elia essay] upon 'Witches and other Night Fears,' he says, 'it is not book, or picture, or the stories of foolish servants, which create these terrors in children. They can at most but give them a direction. Dear little T[hornton] H[unt], who of all children has been brought up with the most scrupulous exclusion of every taint of superstition, who was never allowed to hear of goblin or apparition, or scarcely to be told of bad men, or to hear or read of any distressing story, finds all this world of fear, from which he has been so rigidly excluded *ab extra,* in his own "thick-coming fancies"; and from his little midnight pillow this nurse-child of optimism will start at shapes, unborrowed of tradition, in sweats to which the reveries of the cell-damned murderer are tranquillity' [*Works,* II, 68].—This poor child, instead of being trained up in the way in which he should go, had been bred in the ways of modern philosophy; he had systematically been prevented from knowing any thing of that Saviour who said, 'Suffer little children to come unto me, and forbid them not; for of such is the kingdom of heaven'; care had been taken that he should not pray to God, nor lie down at night in reliance upon his good Providence! [Pp. 524–525]

Southey had written in kindness the passage somewhat critical of *Elia. Essays Which Have Appeared under That Signature in the London Magazine* (1823). He had revised the passage—substituted "sounder" for "saner"—and had meant to revise it further, in proof. But Gifford neglected to send the proof sheets to him. (See *New Southey Letters,* II, 245 and 252–253; *Works,* I, 478; and Kenneth Curry's *Southey* [London and Boston: Routledge & Kegan Paul, 1975], pp. 66– 67.) Lamb thought Southey might have spared him and *Elia* and Leigh Hunt and his son Thornton. Yet because Lamb's love and respect for Southey still held, Lamb intended not to retort—expressed himself so in a letter to Bernard Barton of July 10, 1823 (in my Vol. IV). But soon afterward Lamb did retort, in "Letter of Elia to Robert Southey," published in the *London Magazine,* 8 (October 1823), 400–407, republished in *Works,* I, 226–236. Southey and Lamb consequently exchanged marvelously gracious private letters (in Vol. V, Lamb's letter to Southey of November 21, 1823, and its notes), and the air was cleared forever. Lamb avowed in his private letter that he had not in his public letter been striking against Southey so much as against the *Quarterly Review.* Against its editor Lamb had struck four years earlier, Lamb as the patron saint of shoe-makers, in "Sonnet: St. Crispin to Mr. Gifford"—

> All unadvised, and in an evil hour,
>> Lured by aspiring thoughts, my son, you daft
>> The lowly labours of the Gentle Craft
> For learned toils, which blood and spirits sour.
> All things, dear pledge, are not in all men's power;
>> The wiser sort of shrub affects the ground;
>> And sweet content of mind is oftener found
> In cobbler's parlour, than in critic's bower.
> The sorest work is what doth cross the grain;
>> And better to this hour you had been plying
>> The obsequious awl with well-waxed finger flying,
> Than ceaseless thus to till a thankless vein;
>> Still teazing Muses, which are still denying;
> Making a stretching-leather of your brain. [*Works,* V, 104]

1. The published passage reads so: "To a mind constituted like that of Mr. Wordsworth, the stream, the torrent, and the stirring leaf—seem not merely to suggest associations of deity, but to be a kind of speaking communication with it. He walks through every forest, as through some Dodona; and every bird that flits among the leaves, like that miraculous one in Tasso, but in language more

intelligent, reveals to him far higher love-lays" (*Works,* I, 163). The description
of the bird is provided, in a note, from Edward Fairfax's translation (see my Vol.
I, Letter 21, note 7, and Letter 24, note 4) of Tasso's *Gerusalemme Liberata,*
Book xvi, stanza 13:

> With partie coloured plumes and purple bill,
> A woondrous bird among the rest there flew,
> That in plaine speech sung love laies loud and shrill,
> Her leden was like humaine language trew,
> So much she talkt, and with such wit and skill,
> That strange it seemed how much good she knew.

[Quoted from *Works,* I, 163]
("Leden" means "language"—that of a bird, that of birds universally; in *Works,*
I, 448, Lucas explained that in preparing Lamb's review of *The Excursion* for
republication he had "collated the extracts with the first edition of the *Excursion*
and . . . also corrected the Tasso.") The acknowledgment Lamb makes below—
"I reckon myself a dab at *Prose*—verse I leave to my betters"—he would, in effect,
make again, in "Witches, and Other Night-fears" (*Works,* II, 69–70).

2. "This will never do" opens the review of *The Excursion* in the *Edinburgh
Review,* 24 (November 1814), 1–30. The reviewer was the Scottish advocate and
critic Francis Jeffrey, later Lord Jeffrey (1773–1850), who, in 1802, had helped
to found the *Edinburgh Review.* He edited it from 1803 to 1829, when he resigned to become dean of the Faculty of Advocates. "Scheme of harmonies"
(below) is not in Lamb's published review.

3. For "at." Lamb's next two sentences pertain to the observation that follows
the extracts from *The Excursion,* IV, 165–185 and 1058–1077, in Lamb's published review: "This is high poetry; though (as we have ventured to lay the basis
of the author's sentiments in a sort of liberal Quakerism) from some parts of it,
others may, with more plausibility, object to the appearance of a kind of Natural
Methodism: we could have wished therefore that the tale of Margaret [*The
Excursion,* I, 497–916] had been postponed, till the reader had been strengthened
by some previous acquaintance with the author's theory, and not placed in the
front of the poem, with a kind of ominous aspect, beautifully tender as it is"
(*Works,* I, 166). For a discussion of Lamb's published review see John I. Ades,
"Lamb on Wordsworth's *Excursion,*" *Re: Arts and Letters,* 3 (1969), 1–9.

4. Perhaps that of the booksellers and publishers John and Arthur Arch. See
Vol. I, Letter 40, note 3.

288.   *C. L. to William Sargus*

Inner Temple Lane, London
23 Feb 1815

Mr Sargus,

This is to give you notice that I have parted with the cottage to Mr
Grig Junr to whom you will pay rent from Michaelmas last. The rent
that was due at Michaelmas, I do not wish you to pay me. I forgive it
you, as you may have been at some expences in repairs.—

Yours
Ch. Lamb

MS: The Charles Lamb Society, London. Pub.: Harper, IV, 27–28; Lucas (1905), VI, 454; Lucas (1912), V, 478; Lucas (1935), II, 150. Address: Mr. Wm. Sargus/Cottage/Westmill Green/Herts. Subscriptions, in an unidentified hand: "read to W*m* [or 'M*r*'] Sargus 27. April 1815 by me—"; in the hand of (the unidentified) William Enever: "Rad to Wm Sagus [or 'Sargus'] By me Wm Enever April 27." William Sargus (1773?–1853), whose surname is also listed as "Saggus," "Saggas," and "Saggers" in the Westmill parish registers, the County Record Office, Hertford (see the *CLSB* of November 1950), was the tenant of Button Snap at the time of this letter. Button Snap is the property at Cherry Green, Westmill, Hertfordshire, consisting of a thatched cottage of four rooms, a barn, and approximately three-quarters of an acre of ground of which Lamb would, in 1821, write in "My First Play" as having devolved to him through the "testamentary beneficence" of his godfather Francis Fielde (d. 1809). Fielde was the gentlemanly oilman of the house at the corner of Featherstone Buildings, Holborn, to which Richard Brinsley Sheridan had in 1772 supposedly brought his fiancée Elizabeth Ann Linley (see Vol. II, Letter 228, note 1); of 62 High Holborn by 1793; and of New Cavendish Street, Cavendish Square, from 1804 to 1809—the "grandiloquent, yet courteous" oilman identified and characterized in "My First Play," and further identified by Lucas in his notes to the essay (*Works*, II, 97–98 and 372–373) and by Phyllis G. Mann in "Francis Fielde," in the *CLSB* of November 1949. The benefaction, the property, never the Lambs' home, was, wrote Lamb in his essay, "the only landed property which I could ever call my own—situate near the road-way village of pleasant Puckeridge, in Hertfordshire. When I journeyed down to take possession, and planted foot on my own ground, the stately habits of the donor descended upon me, and I strode (shall I confess the vanity?) with larger paces over my allotment of three quarters of an acre, with its commodious mansion in the midst, with the feeling of an English freeholder that all betwixt sky and centre was my own. The estate has passed into more prudent hands, and nothing but an agrarian can restore it" (*Works*, II, 98). The estate, whose deeds date from 1708, had passed from a family named Ives to a yeoman of Braughing, Hertfordshire, named Francis Merchant. He left it to his nephews George Merchant and Thomas Wyman, yeomen of Braughing, who in March 1779 sold it for twenty pounds each to Francis Fielde. He left it to his second wife, Sarah, by a will made in March 1804 and proved in November 1809. Sarah Fielde, evidently complying with a prior request of her late husband, conveyed the property to Lamb by indentures of lease and release dated August 20 and 21, 1812. By an indenture of feoffment dated February 15, 1815 (its concluding portion, showing the signature of Hazlitt as witness, is reproduced with the present letter in facsimile in the *CLSB* of September 1948), Lamb conveyed the property for fifty pounds to Thomas Greg (not "Grig," as Lamb spells it), the younger (1794?–1839), of Broad Street Buildings, London. The younger Thomas Greg left it in 1839 to his nephew Robert Philips Greg of Coles Park, Westmill, who in 1884 conveyed it to his nephew Thomas Tylston Greg of 15 Clifford's Inn, London. He willed it in August 1919 to his wife, Mary Hope Greg of Coles, Buntingford, Hertfordshire, who on September 2, 1927, presented it to the Royal Society of Arts. On September 3, 1949, the Charles Lamb Society, by an endowment of four hundred pounds from its members, purchased the property from the Royal Society of Arts. Mrs. Charles Tickle is the tenant of Button Snap today. (Much of the foregoing has been drawn from *Lamb and His Hertfordshire*, p. 49; Phyllis G. Mann's "Button Snap: What Did Godfather Fielde Pay for It?" in the *CLSB* of January 1955; and Thomas Greg's "Charles Lamb as a Landed Proprietor," *The Athenaeum*, No. 3819 [January 5, 1901], 18, which is partly quoted in *Works*, II, 373–375.) Button Snap, a name not on the deeds, was assumed by Thomas Greg the author of *The Athenaeum* article to be Lamb's nomination. Button Snap was considered by Archibald Jackson, an area historian whom Reginald L. Hine cited in *Lamb and His Hertfordshire,* to be possibly a derivation of Burton—a surname on Westmill deeds of 1623, 1663, and 1726—and was interpreted by Hine, with the support of Jackson, to be most likely a local corruption of Bury-tons Knapp, after the knap, or knoll, on which the cottage stands, "close to the traces of an ancient moat surrounding the old Bury [or manor or manor house] of the de Tany family at Westmill Green" (*Lamb and His Hertfordshire,* p. 45). Hine implicitly acknowledged there that Button Snap could be Lamb's play on the surname Button, which is common in Hertfordshire. For Hine recognized what Lucas had heard—"of an old man who claimed to be related to a cousin of Charles Lamb named Eliza Button, and who was the possessor of two scrap-books in each of which Lamb had written an acrostic, one being on the name Button. All efforts to trace the old man have failed." Lucas thought, however, "that the odd title of Lamb's cottage . . . may have some family connection" (*The Life of Lamb,* I, 325). One of those two scrapbooks is in The Henry E. Huntington Library, San Marino, California, and contains Lamb's acrostic to Ellen Button, once the owner of the scrapbook. George L. Barnett published that acrostic in "Charles Lamb and the Button Family: An Unpublished Poem and Letter," *Huntington Library Quarterly,* 19 (February 1956), 191–195 (my source for most of what follows in this note), and there presented an undated letter (in my Vol. VI), possibly of 1830 to George Dyer, in which Lamb conveys his and Mary's love to "Ellen & mother." Peter A. Brier republished the acrostic in "An Unpublished Poem by Charles Lamb: 'Acrostic to E. B.,'" *English Language Notes,* 10 (September 1972), 29–30. Lamb wrote the acrostic—"Ellen, friend of tuneful Dyer," its first line reads—in or after 1828, the date with which the paper in the scrapbook is watermarked, and probably after October 19, 1832, as the preceding entry in the scrapbook suggests, a poem of that date by Mary Matilda Betham. The other of those scrapbooks is in The University of Texas Library, Austin, Texas, and contains Lamb's acrostic to Emma Button, once the owner of that scrapbook and perhaps later become the owner of the name in the inscription inside its front cover—"Mrs. Staunton, Albion Lodge, Peckham." Major S. Butterworth published that acrostic in "A Lamb Letter," *Academy and Literature,* 67 (July 23, 1904), 72, and there presented the letter (in my Vol. V) of July 5, 1825, to the editor, author, and Edinburgh bookseller John Aitken (1793–1833). Lucas republished the acrostic, erroneously as part of the letter to Aitken, in his editions of the Lamb letters—see, for example, Lucas (1935), III, 11. Lamb wrote the acrostic—"EMMA, eldest of your name," reads its first line—probably after December 3, 1829, as a preceding entry of that date in the scrapbook suggests. (Neither acrostic is in *Works.*) A poem signed "Sarah Button" succeeds Lamb's entry to Emma. If the claim of the old man of whom Lucas had heard is altogether accurate, then Eliza, Ellen, Emma, and Sarah were members of a family related to Lamb's after whom Lamb may have named Button Snap.

289.   *C. L. to Joseph Hume*

[March 1815?]

Bis dat qui dat cito

I hate the pedantry of expressing that in another language, which we have sufficient terms for in our own. So, in plain English I very much wish you to give your vote tomorrow at Clerkenwell instead of

Saturday. It would clear up the brows of my favourite candidate and stagger the hands of the other party. It commences at 9. How easy as you come from Kensington (apropos, how is your excellent family) to town down Bloomsbury, through Leather Lane, avoiding Lay-stall St for the disagreeableness of the name;[1] why, it brings you in 4 minutes and a half to the spot renowned on northern milestones "where Hicks's Hall formerly stood." There will be good cheer ready for every independent Freeholder; where you seé a green flag hang out, go boldly in; call for ham or beef or what you please and a mug of Meux's Best. How much more gentlemanlike to come in the front of the battle openly avowing ones sentiments, than to lag in on the last day when the Adversary is dejected, spiritless, laid low. Have the first cut at them—. By Saturday you'll cut into the mutton. I'd go myself tomorrow cheerfully, but I am no freeholder (Fuimus Troes—fuit Ilium,[2] but I sold it for £50)—if they'd accept a copyholder, we clerks are naturally *copy*holders

By the way, get Mrs Hume or the agreeable Amelia or Caroline to stick a bit of Green in your hat. Nothing daunts the adversary more than to wear the colours of your Party. Stick it in Cockade-like. It has a sort of martial and no disagreeable effect——

Go my dear Freeholder, and if any chance calls you out of this transatory scene earlier than expected, the Coroner shall sit lightly on your corpse.— He shall not too anxiously enquire into the circumstance of blood found upon your razor.— That might happen to any gentleman in shaving—nor into your having been heard to express a contempt of life, and scolding Louisa for something which Julia did and other little trifling incoherencies.——

Yours Sincerely,
C. Lamb

MS: unrecovered; a copy: Lord Abinger. Pub.: Hazlitt, I, 423–424; Ainger (1888), I, 268–269; Ainger (1900), II, 199–200; Macdonald, I, 334–335; Ainger (1904), I, 325–326; Harper, IV, 28–29; Lucas (1905), VI, 455; Lucas (1912), V, 479–480; Lucas (1935), II, 151. In *Godwin* (II, 221) and in the editions of Hazlitt, Ainger, Macdonald, and Harper the addressee of the letter is shown to be Godwin, probably because the original or, more likely, this copy of the original letter was among Godwin's effects. The references in the letter to Kensington, where Hume and his family lived, and to his wife and their daughters Amelia, Caroline, Louisa, and Julia show the addressee to be Hume. (See Vol. II, Letter 185, note 7.) The allusion to the sale of Button Snap, in the last sentence in the first paragraph in this letter, indicates the composition date to be after, in all likelihood shortly after, the date of that sale. Because of Mrs. Gertrude Alison Anderson's discovery of this unpublished remark in Robinson's diary entry for March 16, 1811—"C. Lamb stepped in to announce Dr. Tuthill's defeat as candidate for the post of physician to St. Luke's Hospital" (Lucas [1935], II, 150; see my Vol. I, Introduction, p. lxxxviii, and Vol. II, Letter 208, note 1)—Lucas supposed this letter to be about Hume's coming to Clerkenwell to support another attempt, evidently again unsuccessful, of George Leman Tuthill to gain election to the medical staff of St. Luke's. The Latin heading the body of the letter translates, "He gives doubly who gives quickly."

1. A name given to that (Clerkenwell) street for its former feature of a dung-hill, or laystall. The expression quoted, below, was an idiom originating in 1782, when Hicks's Hall, the Middlesex sessions house built in 1612 in St. John Street, West Smithfield, by the textiles dealer and money lender Baptist Hicks, or Hickes, first Viscount Campden (1551–1629), was razed and a new sessions house, on Clerkenwell Green, was opened. The milestones on the Great North Road were thenceforth inscribed as being so many miles "from where Hicks's Hall formerly stood."

2. "Trojans are we no more—Troy is no more" (*Aeneid*, II, 325). The term "copyholder" (see below), in addition to designating one who holds copy, designates under British law one who holds an estate in copyhold—one whose ownership of an estate is shown by a copy of the manorial court roll establishing title.

290.   *C. L. to Mrs. Joseph Hume?*

[March 1815?]

Dear Mrs. H.,

Sally who brings this with herself back has given every possible satisfaction in doing her work, etc., but the fact is the poor girl is oppressed with a ladylike melancholy, and cannot bear to be so much alone, as she necessarily must be in our kitchen, which to say the truth is damn'd solitary, where she can see nothing and converse with nothing and not even look out of window. The consequence is she has been caught shedding tears all day long, and her own comfort has made it indispensable to send her home. Your cheerful noisy children-crowded house has made her feel the change so much the more.

Our late servant always complained of the *want of children,* which she had been used to in her last place. One man's meat is another man's poison, as they say. However, we are eternally obliged to you, as much as if Sally could have staid. We have got an old woman coming, who is too stupid to know when she is alone and when she is not.

Yours truly,
C. Lamb, for self and sister[1]

Have you heard from . . . . . .

MS: unrecovered. Text: Lucas (1935), II, 152. Also pub.: Lucas (1912), V, 480–481. The preceding letter and the salutation of and last sentence in the first paragraph in this letter suggest its addressee. The date assigned to the preceding letter has alone prompted the date assigned to this one. None of the servants Lamb mentions nor the person about whom he asks in his postscript has been identified.

1. Mary had returned home from her confinement (see Letter 285, note 1) by February 19, 1815. "At two dined with the Lambs at Anthony Robinson's," Henry Robinson then recorded. "I had not before seen Miss Lamb since her last illness. She looked pale and thin, but in no respect *alarmingly*. Charles Lamb was very agreeable" (*H. C. R. on Books and Writers*, I, 162).

291. *C. L. to William Wordsworth*

[Sunday, April 16, 1815]

The conclusion of this epistle getting gloomy I have chosen this part to desire *our* kindest **Loves** to Mrs Wordsworth and to **Dorothea.** Will none of you ever be in London again?[1]

Dear Wordswth.

You have made me very proud with your successive book-presents.— I have been carefully through the two volumes to see that nothing was omitted which used to be there. I think I miss nothing but a Character in Antithet. manner which I do not know why you left out; the moral to the boys building the giant, the omission whereof leaves it in my mind less complete; and one admirable line gone (or something come in stead of it) the stonechat & the glancing sand-piper, which was a line quite alive.—— I demand these at your hand.— I am glad that you have not sacrificed a verse to those scoundrels.[2] I would not have had you offer up the poorest rag that lingered upon the stript shoulders of little Alice fell, to have atoned all their malice. I would not have given em a red cloak to save their souls.— I am afraid lest that substitution of a **shell** (a flat falsification of the history) for the household implement as it stood at first, was a kind of **tub** thrown out to the beast, or rather thrown out for him. The tub was a good honest tub in its place, & nothing could fairly be said against it. You say you made the alteration for the "friendly reader" but the malicious will take it to himself. Damn em; if you give 'em an inch, &c—. The preface is noble and such as you should write. I wish I could set my name to it—**Imprimatur**—but you have set it there yourself, and I thank you.[3] I had rather be a door-keeper in your margin, than have their proudest text swelling with my eulogies—. The poems in the volumes which are new to me are so much in the old tone that I hardly received them as novelties. of those, of which I had no previous knowledge, the four yew trees and the mysterious company which you have assembled there, most struck me—Death the Skeleton & Time the Shadow—.[4] It is a sight not for every youthful poet to dream of— it is one of the last results he must have gone thinking-on for years for.—— Laodamia is a very original poem, I mean original with reference to your own manner. You have nothing like it. I should have seen it in a strange place, and greatly admired it, but not sus- pected its derivation.— Let me in this place, for I have writ you several letters without naming it, mention that my brother who is a picture collector, has picked up an undoubtable picture of Milton.[5] He gave a few shillings for it, and could get no history with it, but that some old lady had had it for a great many years. Its age is ascertain- able from the state of the canvas, and you need only see it to be sure that it is the original of the heads in the Tonson Editions, with which we are all so well familiar.— Since I saw you I have had a treat in the reading way which comes not every day. The Latin Poems of V. Bourne[6] which were quite new to me. What a heart that man had, all laid out upon town scenes, a proper counterpoise to *some people's* rural extravaganzas. Why I mention him is that your Power of Music reminded me of his poem of the balad singer in the Seven Dials. Do you remember his epigram on the old woman who taught Newton the A. B. C. which after all he say[s] he hesitates not to call Newton's **Principia**——. I was lately fatiguing myself with going thro' a volume of fine words by *Ld. Thurlow,*[7] excellent words, and if the heart could live by words alone, It could desire no better regale—but what an aching vacuum of matter—I dont stick at the madness of it, for that is only a consequence of shutting his eyes and thinking he is in the age of the old Elsabeth poets—. from thence I turned to V. Bourne—what a sweet unpretending pretty-mannered *matter-ful* creature—sucking from every flower, making a flower of every thing—his diction all latin and his thoughts all English—. Bless him, Latin was'nt good enough for him, why wasnt he content with the language which Gay & Prior wrote in——.

I am almost sorry that you printed Extracts from those first Poems,[8] or that you did not print them at length. They do not read to me as they do all together. Besides they have diminished the value of the original (which I possess) as a curiousity. I have hitherto kept them distinct in my mind as referring to a particular period of your life. All the rest of your poems are so much of a piece, they might have been written in the same week—these decidedly speak of an earlier period. They tell more of what you had been reading.

We were glad to see the poems by a female friend. .[9] The one of the wind is masterly, but not new to us. Being only three, perhaps you might have clapt a *D.* at the corner and let it have past as a print[e]rs mark to the uninitiated, as a delightful hint to the better-instructed. As it is, **Expect a formal criticism on the Poems of your female friend** and she must expect it—

I should have written before, but I am cruelly engaged and like to be, on Friday I was at office from 10 in the morning (two hours dinner except) to 11 at night, last night till 9. My business and office business in general has increased so. I dont mean I am there every night, but I must expect a great deal of it. I never leave till 4—and do not keep a holyday now once in ten times, where I used to keep all red letter days, and some fine days besides which I used to dub **Natures** holydays.[10] I have had my day. I had formerly little to do. So of the little that is left of life I may reckon two thirds as dead, for **Time** that a man may call his own is his **Life,** and hard work & thinking about it taints even the leisure hours, stains Sunday with workday contemplations—this is **Sunday,** and the headache I have is part late hours at work the 2 preceding nights & part later hours over a consoling pipe afterwds. But I find stupid acquiescence coming over me. I bend to the yoke, & it is almost with me & my household as with the man & his consort—[11]

> To them each evening had its glittering star
> And every Sabbath day its golden sun——

to such straits am I driven for the Life of life, **Time**——. O that from that superfluity of Holyday leisure my youth wasted, "**Age might but take some hours youth wanted not.**"— N. B. I have left off spirituous liquors for 4 or more months, with a moral certainty of its lasting. Farewell, dear Wordsworth———

MS: University of Texas Library. Pub.: Talfourd (1837), II, 16–17; Talfourd (1848), I, 188–194; Sala, I, 269 (paginated in error as 296)–273; Purnell, I, 269–273; Fitzgerald, II, 104–108; Hazlitt, II, 3–6; Ainger (1888), I, 283–286; Ainger (1900), II, 220–224; Macdonald, I, 352–355; Ainger (1904), I, 340–343; Harper, IV, 29–34; Lucas (1905), VI, 456–458; Lucas (1912), V, 481–484; Lucas (1935), II, 153–155. Address: Wm Wordsworth Esqr/Rydal Mount/near Kendal/Westmorland. Postmark: April 17, 1815. Lamb tells he is writing on Sunday (April 16) near his conclusion.

1. Wordsworth and his wife would be in London from May 6 to June 19 (see Letter 298, note 2), coming principally so that Wordsworth could extend to William Lowther, Lord Lonsdale, the courtesy of personally explaining that the reason for his declining Lord Lonsdale's recent offer of the customs collectorship at Whitehaven, Cumberland, an office more lucrative than Wordsworth's present stamp distributorship, was, it appears, his and his family's unwillingness to leave the beauty and quiet of Rydal Mount for Whitehaven. While the Wordsworths were in London Sara Hutchinson joined them, they all saw the Lambs, and Wordsworth was introduced to Benjamin Robert Haydon and Leigh Hunt. (See Letter 280, note 1, and *Wordsworths' Letters*, III, 231–239.) Lamb begins his letter proper by expressing his pride at having received *Poems by William Wordsworth: Including Lyrical Ballads, and the Miscellaneous Pieces of the Author. With Additional Poems, a New Preface, and a Supplementary Essay* (2 vols.; 1815) and by expressing his perplexity at two omissions and a substitution in the volumes: the omission of "A Character, in the Antithetical Manner," later re-titled "A Character"; the omission of the original lines 19–24 in "Rural Architecture"—

> —Some little I've seen of blind boisterous works
> By Christian disturbers more savage than Turks,
> Spirits busy to do and undo:
> At remembrance whereof my blood sometimes will flag;
> Then, light-hearted Boys, to the top of the crag;
> And I'll build up a giant with you

—and the substitution of "The stone-chat, and the Landlark, restless Bird / Piping along the margin of the lake" (lines 27–28) for "The stone-chat, or the glancing sand-piper" (line 27) in "Lines Left upon a Seat in a Yew-tree, Which Stands Near the Lake of Esthwaite, on a Desolate Part of the Shore, Commanding a Beautiful Prospect." Wordsworth would restore all in later editions of his poems.

2. Wordsworth's detractors generally, with little doubt Francis Jeffrey particularly. (See Letter 287, note 2.) Alice Fell, mentioned below, is in "Alice Fell; or, Poverty." Perhaps the cloak to which Lamb refers—Alice's wretched one is not given a color—is Martha Ray's scarlet one, in "The Thorn." In the 1807 version of "The Blind Highland Boy: A Tale Told by the Fire-side, after Returning to the Vale of Grasmere," Wordsworth (faithful to the tale of the Grasmere parish clerk George Mackereth, the "eye-witness" in Wordsworth's note to the poem) has the Boy set off on his voyage in "—A Household Tub, like one of those / Which women use to wash their clothes" (lines 113–114). In the 1815 version, Wordsworth (trustful of the opinion of Coleridge, the "Friend" in Wordsworth's note to the poem) has the Boy set off in "The Shell of a green Turtle, thin / And hollow;—you might sit therein, / It was so wide and deep" (lines 118–120). Despite Lamb's objections here to the alteration and Barron Field's objections in a letter to Wordsworth of 1828 (see *Wordsworths' Letters*, IV, 308), Wordsworth would not return his lines of 1807 to the poem. See also *Wordsworth's Poetical Works* (1940–1949), III, 91, 92, and 447–448.

3. In the Preface to the Edition of 1815 Wordsworth acknowledged Lamb as one of his "most esteemed Friends" and, by quoting from Lamb's "On the Genius and Character of Hogarth; with Some Remarks on a Passage in the Writings of

the Late Mr. Barry" (*Works*, I, 73), indicated his acceptance of Lamb's understanding of the imagination as "that power which . . . 'draws all things to one;
which makes things animate or inanimate, beings with their attributes, subjects
with their accessories, take one colour and serve to one effect'" (*Wordsworth's
Poetical Works* [1940–1949], II, 439). Lamb in his essay (in *Works*, I, the part
at 79–86) quoted from and remarked on "Account of a Series of Pictures in the
Great Room of the Society of Arts, Manufactures, and Commerce, at the Adelphi,"
by the painter, professor of painting, and Royal Academician James Barry
(1741–1806).

4. Lamb writes especially of lines 13–33—quotes from lines 27–28—in "Yew-
trees," a poem Wordsworth first published in 1815:

> . . . But worthier still of note
> Are those fraternal Four of Borrowdale,
> Joined in one solemn and capacious grove;
> Huge trunks! and each particular trunk a growth
> Of intertwisted fibres serpentine
> Up-coiling, and inveterately convolved;
> Nor uninformed with Phantasy, and looks
> That threaten the profane;—a pillared shade,
> Upon whose grassless floor of red-brown hue,
> By sheddings from the pining umbrage tinged
> Perennially—beneath whose sable roof
> Of boughs, as if for festal purpose decked
> With unrejoicing berries—ghostly Shapes
> May meet at noontide; Fear and trembling Hope,
> Silence and Foresight; Death the Skeleton [27]
> And Time the Shadow;—there to celebrate,
> As in a natural temple scattered o'er
> With altars undisturbed of mossy stone,
> United worship; or in mute repose
> To lie, and listen to the mountain flood
> Murmuring from Glaramara's inmost caves.

"Laodamia," referred to below, Wordsworth first published also in 1815.

5. John Lamb's picture is known today as the Lenox Portrait of John Milton
and hangs near a portrait of Oliver Cromwell done by the portrait painter Sir
Peter Lely (1618–1680) in the president's office of The New York Public
Library. Similarities in size and style of the two paintings have caused the conjecture that Lely did both. Lely was strongly influenced by Sir Anthony Van
Dyck, or Vandyke (1599–1641); the Lenox Portrait shows an influence of Van
Dyck, as Charles Lamb observes in the second paragraph in the next letter. The
Lenox Portrait, in oils, is one in a class of portraits of Milton that includes the
heads the publishers Jacob (1656?–1736), Jacob (d. 1767), and Richard (d.
1772) Tonson reproduced in their editions of Milton's works. The prototype of the
class is the crayon drawing formerly known as the Richardson, the Tonson, the
Baker, or Bayfordbury Portrait, chiefly after its successive owners—the portrait
painter and author the elder Jonathan Richardson (1665–1745), the Tonsons,
and Richard Tonson's nephew William Baker of Bayfordbury, Hertfordshire. That
portrait is now known as the Princeton Portrait, is in the Princeton University
Library, and may be the drawing from life by the engraver and portrait painter
the elder William Faithorne (1616–1691) from which Faithorne worked in preparing the drawing for his line engraving of Milton at age sixty-two used for the
frontispiece in the 1670 edition of Milton's *History of Britain . . . to the Norman
Conquest*. The Princeton Portrait may also be either a variant by Faithorne of the
same drawing Faithorne prepared for his engraving or a modified drawing by
another artist of the Faithorne engraving. John Lamb at his death in 1821 left

his picture of Milton to Charles. It would seem from his letter to Wordsworth dated "End of May nearly [1833]" (in Vol. VI) that Lamb had intended to leave the picture to Wordsworth with the stipulation that Wordsworth bequeath it to Christ's College, Cambridge, but that Lamb instead gave it as a wedding present to Emma Isola and Edward Moxon in advance of their wedding day, July 30, 1833. Upon Moxon's death, in 1858, the picture was sold with Moxon's library and other pictures and disappeared. It reappeared on March 5, 1881, when the antiquarian bookseller Bernard Quaritch (1819–1899) purchased it for £355 at Hodgson's auction room, London. Robert Lenox Kennedy (1822?–1887), president of the board of trustees of the Lenox Library, New York, purchased it for £400 from Quaritch and, in the autumn of 1881, presented it to the Lenox Library, which afterward merged with the Astor and Tilden libraries to form the foundation of The New York Public Library. (See Gerald D. McDonald's "Charles Lamb as a Collector: Memorabilia in The New York Public Library," *Bulletin of The New York Public Library,* 38 [September 1934], esp. 710–712; and John Rupert Martin's *The Portrait of John Milton at Princeton and Its Place in Milton Iconography* [Princeton, N.J.: Princeton University Library, 1961], esp. pp. 5, 11, 24, and 27.) The Lenox Portrait is reproduced as Plate XV in the present volume. The person from whom John Lamb purchased the picture has not been identified, nor has the old lady, mentioned below, once its owner.

6. In *Poemata, Latine partim reddita, partim scripta* (1734), by Vincent Bourne (1695–1747), selections from which Lamb's favorite Cowper, who had studied under Bourne's mastership at Westminster School, had translated. (See, for example, *The Poetical Works of William Cowper. With Life, Critical Dissertation, and Explanatory Notes,* ed. George Gilfillan [Edinburgh: James Nichol; London: James Nisbet; Dublin: W. Robertson, 1854], II, 295–318.) Lamb would translate selections from *Poemata,* nine in 1830, in *Album Verses, with a Few Others,* and commend and quote from *Poemata,* in 1822 and 1831, in "A Complaint of the Decay of Beggars in the Metropolis" and "The Latin Poems of Vincent Bourne" (*Works,* V, 61–67; II, 117–118; and I, 337–339). Lamb below in this paragraph mentions or refers to "Power of Music," which Wordsworth first published in 1807 and included in *Poems by William Wordsworth* (1815); Bourne's "Cantatrices," which Lamb would translate under the title "The Ballad Singers," in *Album Verses,* and commend and quote in "The Latin Poems of Vincent Bourne"; the district in London surrounding an intersection of seven streets where until 1773 stood a column supporting a clock with seven dials; and Bourne's "Perveniri ad summum nisi ex Principiis non potest," which Lamb would translate under the title "Newton's Principia," in *Album Verses.* Near the end of this paragraph Lamb writes of Bourne in effect as he was to write of him in "A Complaint of the Decay of Beggars in the Metropolis" and "The Latin Poems of Vincent Bourne"—as the "most classical, and at the same time, most English, of the Latinists" and as " 'so Latin,' and yet 'so English' all the while" (*Works,* II, 117, and I, 337). In that latter essay Lamb was to repeat the reference he makes in the conclusion of this paragraph to John Gay's language, asserting in the essay that Gay's *Trivia, or the Art of Walking the Streets of London* (1716) "alone, in verse, comes up to the life and humour" of Bourne's "Cantatrices." Lamb was not to repeat in that latter essay, "The Latin Poems of Vincent Bourne," the reference he makes in the conclusion of this paragraph to Matthew Prior's language.

7. Underscored twice. The minor poet Edward Thurlow (from 1814 Edward Hovell-Thurlow), second Baron Thurlow (1781–1829), had in 1810 privately printed his edition of Sir Philip Sidney's *Defence of Poesie,* to which he had prefixed his own sonnets. He had in 1812 published his sonnets in *Verses on Several Occasions* and in 1813 enlarged and republished that volume, as *Poems on Several Occasions.* The volume on which Lamb had been lately fatiguing himself was probably the one of 1813, though possibly one of the three Lord Thurlow had

published in 1814—*Ariadne: A Poem in Three Parts* or *Carmen Britannicum* or *The Doge's Daughter: A Poem, with Several Translations from Anacreon and Horace.* Lamb would in 1823 publish "Nugæ Criticæ. By the Author of Elia. No. 1. Defence of the Sonnets of Sir Philip Sidney"—later called "Some Sonnets of Sir Philip Sidney" (*Works,* II, 213–220)—to which he would then append this note:

> A profusion of verbal dainties, with a disproportionate lack of matter and circumstance, is I think one reason of the coldness with which the public has received the poetry of a nobleman now living; which, upon the score of exquisite diction alone, is entitled to something better than neglect. I will venture to copy one of his Sonnets in this place, which for quiet sweetness, and unaffected morality, has scarcely its parallel in our language.

TO A BIRD THAT HAUNTED THE WATERS
OF LACKEN IN THE WINTER
By Lord Thurlow

O melancholy Bird, a winter's day,
Thou standest by the margin of the pool,
And, taught by God, dost thy whole being school
To Patience, which all evil can allay.
God has appointed thee the Fish thy prey;
And given thyself a lesson to the Fool
Unthrifty, to submit to moral rule,
And his unthinking course by thee to weigh.
There need not schools, nor the Professor's chair,
Though these be good, true wisdom to impart.
He who has not enough, for these, to spare
Of time, or gold, may yet amend his heart,
And teach his soul, by brooks, and rivers fair:
Nature is always wise in every part. [*Works,* II, 438–439]

That sonnet Lamb "read beautifully" to De Quincey, recommended as "indisp[ens]able" to Bernard Barton (in a letter postmarked December 5, 1828, in my Vol. V), and copied into one of his own commonplace books and into an extract book he fashioned for Emma Isola. See *De Quincey's Writings,* III, 81, and *The Life of Lamb,* II, 296 and 205. About De Quincey and Lamb see Letter 323, note 2.

8. Extracts from *An Evening Walk* (1793), *Descriptive Sketches* (1793), and "The Female Vagrant" all appear under "Juvenile Pieces" in *Poems by William Wordsworth* (1815). What follows in Lamb's paragraph leaves not much doubt that Lamb is referring to one of the first two works. In the Preface to the Edition of 1815 Wordsworth stated that the extracts "seem to have a title to be placed here as they were the productions of youth, and represent implicitly some of the features of a youthful mind, at a time when images of nature supplied to it the place of thought, sentiment, and almost of action. . . . I will own," Wordsworth also stated, "that I was much at a loss what to select of these descriptions, and perhaps it would have been better either to have reprinted the whole, or suppressed what I have given" (*Wordsworth's Poetical Works* [1940–1949], II, 434). Wordsworth would revise and republish *An Evening Walk* and *Descriptive Sketches* in the 1820 edition and subsequent editions of his poems. "The Female Vagrant," which he had originally published in the *Lyrical Ballads* of 1798 and would revise and republish in the 1820 to 1836 editions of his poems, is itself an extract. Wordsworth had taken it from his "Adventures on Salisbury Plain," the poem that he had developed from his "Salisbury Plain," or "A Night on Salisbury Plain," the poem that Lamb had read in 1796 (see my Vol. I, Letter 2, note 7 and near the reference to note 14), and the poem that Wordsworth was to develop into

"Guilt and Sorrow; or Incidents upon Salisbury Plain" and publish, in 1842, in *Poems, Chiefly of Early and Late Years; Including The Borderers, a Tragedy.* (See *The Salisbury Plain Poems of William Wordsworth* . . . , ed. Stephen Gill [Ithaca: Cornell University Press, 1975], for a superb presentation and discussion of those poems.) A canceled line and one-half come directly after the dash in the penultimate sentence in Lamb's paragraph.

9. Dorothy Wordsworth's "Address to a Child, during a Boisterous Winter Evening. By a Female Friend of the Author," to which Lamb refers as the "one of the wind"; "The Mother's Return. By the Same"; and "The Cottager to Her Infant. By a Female Friend." On their inclusion in *Poems by William Wordsworth* (1815) Wordsworth remarked near the end of the Preface to the Edition of 1815: "Three short pieces (now first published) are the work of a Female Friend; and the Reader, to whom they may be acceptable, is indebted to me for his pleasure; if any one regard them with dislike, or be disposed to condemn them, let the censure fall upon him, who, trusting in his own sense of their merit and their fitness for the place which they occupy, *extorted* them from the Authoress" (*Wordsworth's Poetical Works* [1940–1949], II, 444). Lamb's "*D.*," below, is underscored twice.

10. Lamb would lose some of his holidays by a resolution of the court of directors of the East India Company of May 14, 1817 (see Letter 328, source note), and would deprecate his loss in letters—in Letter 328, for example, near the reference to note 9—and in "Oxford in the Vacation" (*Works,* II, 8).

11. The wedded, childless, sequestered couple Wordsworth described in *The Excursion,* V, 670–837. The passage indented below is an adaptation of its lines 836–837—"For you each evening hath its shining star, / And every sabbath-day its golden sun." The passage within quotation marks is an adaptation of Wordsworth's "The Small Celandine," line 24—"Age might but take the things Youth needed not!" Both poems are in *Poems by William Wordsworth* (1815).

292.   *C. L. to William Wordsworth*

[April 28, 1815]

Dear Wordswth.

The more I read of your two last volumes, The more I feel it necessary to make my acknowlegemts. for them in more than one short letter. The **Night Piece** to which you refer me I meant fully to have noticed,[1] but the fact is I come so fluttering & languid from business, tired with thoughts of it, frightened with fears of it, that when I get a few minutes to sit down to scribble (an action of the hand now seldom natural to me—I mean voluntary pen-work) I lose all presential memory of what I had intended to say, and say what I can,—talk about Vincent Bourne or any casual image instead of that which I had meditated— by the way I must look out **V. B.** for you.— So I had meant to have mentioned Yarrow visited, with that stanza "But thou who didst appear so fair"—than which I think no lovelier stanza can be found in the wide world of poetry[2]—yet the poem on the whole seems condemned to have behind it a melancholy of imperfect satisfaction, as if you had wronged the feeling with which in what preceded it you had resolved never to visit it, and as if the **Muse** had determined in the most delicate manner to make you & *scarce make you* feel it. Else, it is far superior to the other, which has but one exquisite verse in it, the last but one, or the two last—this has all fine, except perhaps that *that* of "studious ease & generous cares"[3]—has a little tinge of the *less romantic* about it. The farmer of Tilsbury vale is a charming counter part to poor Susan, with the addition of that delicacy towards aberrations from the strict path which is so fine in the **Old Thief** & the boy by his side, which always brings water into my eyes—. Perhaps it is the worse for being a repetition. Susan stood for the representative of poor **Rus in Urbe.** There was quite enough to stamp the moral of the thing never to be forgotten. Fast volumes of vapour &c.[4] The last verse of Susan was to be got rid of at all events. It threw a kind of dubiety upon Susan's moral conduct. Susan is a servant maid. I see her trundling her mop and contemplating the whirling phenomenon thro' blurred optics; but to term her a poor outcast seems as much as to say that poor Susan was no better than she should be, which I trust was not what you meant to express. Robin Goodfellow[5] supports himself without that *stick* of a moral which you have thrown away,——but how I can be brought in felo de omittendo for that Ending to the boy builders is a mystery. I ca'nt say positively now—I only know that no line oftener or readier occurs than that "Light hearted boys I will build up a giant with you." It comes naturally with a warm holyday & the freshness of the blood. It is a perfect summer Amulet that I tye round my legs to quicken their motion when I go out a **maying.— (N. B.)** I dont often go out a maying. *Must* is the **tense** with me now. Do you take the Pun?—[6] Young Romilly is divine, the reasons of his mothers grief being remediless—I never saw parental love carried up so high, towering above the other **Loves**—. Shakspeare had done something for the filial in Cordelia, & by implication for the fatherly too in Lears resentment—he left it for you to explore the depths of the maternal heart—. I get stupid, and flat & flattering—whats the use of telling you what good things you have written, or—I hope I may add—that I know them to be good—. Apropos—when I first opened upon the just mentioned poem, in a careless tone I said to Mary as if putting a riddle

"What is good for a "bootless bean"?"[7] to which with infinite presence of mind (as the jest book has it) she answered a **"shooless pea."**— It was the first joke she ever made. Joke the 2d I make—you distinguish well in your old preface between the verses of Dr. Johnson of the man in the Strand, and that from the babes of the wood. I was thinking whether taking your own glorious lines—

> And for the **love** was in her **soul**
> For the youthful **Romilly**—

which, by the love I bear my own soul, I think have no parallel in any of the best old Balads, and just altering it to

> And from the great respect she felt
> For Sir Samuel **Romilly**—

would not have explained the boundaries of prose expression & poetic feeling nearly as well. Excuse my levity on such an occasion. I never felt deeply in my life if that poem did not make me both lately and when I read it in MS.[8] No alderman ever longed after a haunch of buck venison more than I for a Spiritual taste of that white **Doe** you promise. I am sure it is superlative, or will be when *drest,* i.e. printed—. **All things read raw to me in MS.**[9]—to compare magna parvis, I cannot endure my own writings in that state. The only one which I think would not very much win upon me in print is Peter Bell. But I am not certain. You ask me about your preface. I like both that & the Supplement without an exception.[10] The account of what you mean by Imagination is very valuable to me. It will help me to like some things in poetry better, **which is a little humiliating in me to confess.** I thought I could not be instructed in that science (I mean the critical) as I once heard old obscene beastly Peter Pindar in a dispute on **Milton** say he thought that if he had reason to value himself upon one thing more than another it was in knowing what good verse was. Who lookd over your proof sheets, & left *ordebo*[11] in that line of Virgil?—

My brothers picture of Milton is very finely painted, that is, it might have been done by a hand **next to Vandyke's.** It is the genuine Milton, and an object of quiet gaze for the half hour at a time. *Yet* tho' I am confident there is no better one of him, the face does not quite answer to Milton. There is a tinge of petit (or petite, how do you spell it) querulousness about. Yet hang it, now I remember better, there is not—it is calm, melancholy, and poetical.——

I wish you would write more criticism, about Spenser &c—.[12] I think I could say something about him myself—but Lord bless me—these "**merchants & their** spicy drugs" which are so harmonious to sing of, they lime twig up my poor soul & body, till I shall forget I ever thought myself a bit of a genius! I ca'nt even put a few thoughts on paper for a newspaper. I "**engross**," when I should **pen** a paragraph.[13] Confusion blast all mercantile transactions, all traffick, exchange of commodities, intercourse between nations, all the consequent civilization & wealth & amity & link of society, & getting rid of prejudices, & knowlege of the face of the globe—& rot the very **firs** of the forest that look so romantic alive, and **die** into **desks.**— Vale—

yours dear W. and all yours'

C Lamb

Excuse this maddish letter. I am too tired to write **in formâ**—[14]
N. B. Dont read that Q. Review——. I will never look into another *One* of the copies[15] you sent had precisely the same pleasant blending of a sheet of 2d Vol. with a sheet of 1st. I think it was page **245**; but I sent it & had it rectifyd. It gave me in the first impetus of cutting the leaves just such a cold squelch as going down a plausible turning & suddenly reading "no through fare." Robinsons is entire; he is gone to **Bury** his father.—

MS: University of Texas Library. Pub.: Talfourd (1848), I, 195–202; Sala, I, 273–278; Purnell, I, 273–278; Fitzgerald, II, 108–113; Hazlitt, II, 6–10; Ainger (1888), I, 286–290; Ainger (1900), II, 225–230; Macdonald, I, 356 and 359–362; Ainger (1904), I, 343–347; Harper, IV, 34–39; Lucas (1905), VI, 460–463; Lucas (1912), V, 486–489; Lucas (1935), II, 157–160. Address: W. Wordsworth Esqr./Rydale Mount/near/Kendal/Westmoreland. Postmark: April 28, 1815.

1. Wordsworth would, while with his wife and Robinson at the Lambs' on May 9, 1815, recommend "A Night-piece" and "Yew-trees" to Robinson as among the best of the poems in *Poems by William Wordsworth* (1815) "for the imaginative power displayed in them." Robinson believed the two poems to be fine, but believed at the same time he did "not understand in what their excellence consists" (*H. C. R. on Books and Writers*, I, 166).

2. The stanza formed of lines 41–48 in "Yarrow Visited. September, 1814":

> But thou, that didst appear so fair
> To fond imagination,
> Dost rival in the light of day
> Her delicate creation: [44]
> Meek loveliness is round thee spread,
> A softness still and holy;
> The grace of forest charms decayed,
> And pastoral melancholy.

Lamb would quote its lines 41–44 in "Mackery End, in Hertfordshire" (*Works*, II, 77). Wordsworth's "other" poem, so referred to below, is "Yarrow Unvisited." Here are its last two verses, its lines 49–64:

Be Yarrow stream unseen, unknown!
It must, or we shall rue it:
We have a vision of our own;
Ah! why should we undo it?
The treasured dreams of times long past,
We'll keep them, winsome Marrow!
For when we're there, although 'tis fair,
    'Twill be another Yarrow!

If Care with freezing years should come,
And wandering seem but folly,—
Should we be loth to stir from home,
And yet be melancholy;
Should life be dull, and spirits low,
'Twill soothe us in our sorrow,
That earth hath something yet to show,
    The bonny holms of Yarrow!

3. In "Yarrow Visited," line 63. It and line 64 read, "To studious ease and generous cares / And every chaste affection!" Wordsworth altered those lines in 1820 to "To all the nestling brood of thoughts / Sustained by chaste affection" and in 1827 to "Of tender thoughts, that nestle there— / The brood of chaste affection." Lamb comments below on Adam, in "The Farmer of Tilsbury Vale"; Susan, in "The Reverie of Poor Susan"; and old Daniel and his grandson, in "The Two Thieves; or, the Last Stage of Avarice." Lamb's "the boy by his side" derives from two lines in that last poem—"And his Grandson's as busy at work by his side" (line 20) and "I love thee, and love the sweet Boy at thy side" (line 46).

4. A misquotation of "Bright volumes of vapour . . . ," in "The Reverie of Poor Susan," line 7. The 1800 version of that poem concludes with a verse, with lines 17–20, omitted from the 1815 version and subsequent versions:

Poor Outcast! return—to receive thee once more
The house of thy Father will open its door,
And thou once again, in thy plain russet gown,
May'st hear the thrush sing from a tree of its own.

5. Or Hobgoblin, or Puck, as in *A Midsummer Night's Dream*. The Latin, below, which pretends to be jargon of the law, may be rendered, "as a defendant on the charge of negligence." Perhaps Wordsworth had accused Lamb of having somehow neglected to prevent Wordsworth from omitting lines 19–24 from "Rural Architecture." See the preceding letter, note 1.

6. The same one Thomas Hood would make in "Ode to Melancholy," lines 115–116—"Like the sweet blossoms of the May, / Whose fragrance ends in must" (*Poems of Thomas Hood*, ed. Walter Jerrold [1907; rpt. London: Humphrey Milford: Oxford University Press, 1923], p. 91). Young Romilly and his mother— her grief, mentioned below, is caused by his death—are in Wordsworth's "The Force of Prayer; or, the Founding of Bolton Priory, a Tradition."

7. "What is good for a bootless bene?" is both the first and fifth lines of "The Force of Prayer." Referred to below is that section of the Preface to the *Lyrical Ballads* of 1800 (republished, with the additions and alterations of 1802 and 1805, in the second volume of *Poems by William Wordsworth* [1815]) where Wordsworth distinguished between Samuel Johnson's "superlatively contemptible" (untitled) parody of a stanza in Thomas Percy's "The Hermit of Warkworth. A Northumberland Ballad," the parody Wordsworth quoted as

I put my hat upon my head
And walked into the Strand,
And there I met another man
Whose hat was in his hand,

and one of the "most justly admired" stanzas in the (anonymous) ballad "Babes in the Wood," a variant of "The Children in the Wood" in the fourth (1794) edition of Thomas Percy's *Reliques of Ancient English Poetry,* the stanza Wordsworth quoted as

> These pretty Babes with hand in hand
> Went wandering up and down;
> But never more they saw the Man
> Approaching from the Town.

[*Wordsworth's Poetical Works* (1940–1949), II, 402 and 403] Lamb's first pair of indented lines is a misquotation of "The Force of Prayer," lines 11–12. The second pair contains the name of the Romilly identified in Letter 275, note 1.

8. That is, "I never felt deeply in my life if that poem did not make me [feel deeply,] both lately and when I read it in MS." The "white Doe" for which Lamb, below, expresses his longing is Wordsworth's *The White Doe of Rylstone; or the Fate of the Nortons. A Poem.* Longman's would publish it, in a quarto volume that includes "The Force of Prayer," in late May 1815.

9. "There is," Lamb will in 1820 write as a footnote to "Oxford in the Vacation" (*Works,* II, 311), "something to me repugnant, at any time, in written hand. The text never seems determinate. Print settles it. I had thought of the Lycidas as of a full-grown beauty—as springing up with all its parts absolute—till, in evil hour, I was shown the original written copy of it, together with the other minor poems of its author, in the Library of Trinity, kept like some treasure to be proud of. . . . How it staggered me to see the fine things in their ore! interlined, corrected! as if their words were mortal, alterable, displaceable at pleasure! as if they might have been otherwise, and just as good! as if inspirations were made up of parts, and those fluctuating, successive, indifferent! I will never go into the work-shop of any great artist again, nor desire a sight of his picture, till it is fairly off the easel; no, not if Raphael were to be alive again, and painting another Galatea." The Latin, following, translates as "great things with small." Lamb, below, refers to *Peter Bell, a Tale in Verse,* which Wordsworth had composed in 1798 and revised frequently since. Longman's would publish it in late April 1819. Lamb did not care for it, in manuscript or in print. Robinson had reported this in his diary on June 6, 1812: "With Charles Lamb. Lent him *Peter Bell.* To my surprise he finds nothing in it good. He complains of the slowness of the narrative, as if that were not the *art* of the poet. Wordsworth says he, has great thoughts, but *here* are none of them." This is what Robinson was to report on May 11, 1819: "I then went to Charles Lamb's. . . . Lamb spoke of *Peter Bell,* which he considers as one of the worst of Wordsworth's works. The lyric narrative Lamb has no taste for, he is disgusted by the introduction, which he deems puerile, and the story he thinks ill told, though he allows the idea to be good" (*H. C. R. on Books and Writers,* I, 103 and 230). With Wordsworth himself Lamb, as he is here, was to be circumspect: "Peter Bell . . . is excellent. For its matter, I mean. I cannot say that the style of it quite satisfies me. It is too lyrical. The auditors to whom it is feigned to be told, do not *arride me.* I had rather it had been told me, the reader, at once" (from a letter postmarked April 26, 1819, in my Vol. IV).

10. Lamb writes of liking both the Preface to the Edition of 1815 and the Essay, Supplementary to the Preface (to the Edition of 1815—*Poems by William Wordsworth* [1815]). The account of what Wordsworth meant by "Imagination" (and "Fancy") is in that Preface, in *Wordsworth's Poetical Works* (1940–1949), II, 435–444. It is stated in Lucas (1935), II, 162, that Lamb had met John Wolcot, otherwise Peter Pindar (mentioned below and identified in my Vol. I, Letter 49, note 3), at the home of Henry Rogers (1774–1832), a brother of the poet Samuel Rogers (1763–1855). Henry was until 1824 the principal working partner, and Samuel had been since 1793 the senior partner, in their family's bank. Samuel,

with whom Lamb would establish a correspondence and to whom he would address "To Samuel Rogers, Esq." and "To Samuel Rogers, Esq.: *On the New Edition of His 'Pleasures of Memory'* " (*Works*, V, 56 and 90), was, or was to become, the author of *An Ode to Superstition, with Some Other Poems* (1786), *The Pleasures of Memory* (1792), *An Epistle to a Friend* (1798), *The Voyage of Columbus* (1810), "Jacqueline" (see Letter 279 and its note 2), *Human Life* (1819), *Italy* (Part I, 1822; Part II, 1828; Parts I and II, revised and enlarged and illustrated, 1830), and *Poems* (1834). Henry and Samuel were children of Thomas Rogers (1736?–1793), a partner in the bank into which he took three of his sons—the bank of Welch and Rogers, later Rogers, Olding and Company, in Cornhill, London—and of the former Mary Radford (1734?–1776). Their other sons were Daniel (1761–1829), who had displeased his father by marrying a cousin and had settled into the life of a country squire at Wassall Grove, near Hagley and Stourbridge, Worcestershire, and whose death occasioned Lamb's "To Samuel Rogers, Esq." and letter to Samuel of March 22, 1829 (in Vol. V); Thomas (1761–1788), who had entered the bank as a partner with Samuel in 1784; and Paul (b. 1768), who had died in infancy. Among the senior Rogerses' daughters, Sarah (1772?–1855) was closest to Henry and Samuel. She lived for some time with Henry and was often with Samuel—edited the first part of *Italy*. She is probably the Miss Rogers to whom, as to Henry, Lamb begs to be remembered in his letter to Samuel of March 22, 1829. More information about the family is in Peter William Clayden's *The Early Life of Samuel Rogers* (London: Smith, Elder, 1887) and *Rogers and His Contemporaries* (London: Smith, Elder, 1889) and in Richard Ellis Roberts' *Samuel Rogers and His Circle* (London: Methuen, 1910).

11. For *videbo*, in the Preface to the Edition of 1815:

In the first Eclogue of Virgil, the shepherd, thinking of the time when he is to take leave of his farm, thus addresses his goats:

"Non ego vos posthac viridi projectus in antro
Dumosa *pendere* procul de rupe videbo."

[*Wordsworth's Poetical Works* (1940–1949), II, 436]

Virgil's lines (76–77), with Wordsworth's instance of italic, translate, "Nevermore shall I, reclining in some mossy cave, / See you in the far distance *hanging* from a bushy crag."

12. As Wordsworth wrote in the Essay, Supplementary to the Preface especially; he wrote about Spenser also in the Preface to the Edition of 1815. Wordsworth quoted the passage from which Lamb misquotes below—a misquotation from *Paradise Lost*, II, 639–640 (". . . whence Merchants bring / Thir spicie Drugs . . . ")—in the Preface to the Edition of 1815. See *Wordsworth's Poetical Works* (1940–1949), II, 414 esp. and 425, 439–440, and 436.

13. Pope, in his "Epistle to Dr. Arbuthnot," line 18, expressed it as "Who pens a Stanza when he should *engross*."

14. "In fine form." About the admonition against reading the *Quarterly Review*, in the next postscript, see particularly Letter 287.

15. Of *Poems by William Wordsworth* (1815), one copy being for Robinson: "I called," Robinson had recorded on April 13, 1815, "in the evening on Lamb. I was gratified by finding that Wordsworth had sent me the new edition of his poems, from which I anticipate great joy" (*H. C. R. on Books and Writers*, I, 164). Robinson's father, Henry (b. 1727), mentioned at the end, a tanner of Bury St. Edmunds, had died of apoplexy on April 22 or 23. See *H. C. R.'s Diary*, I, 307–308.

293. *M. A. L. to Mary Matilda Betham*

No 4 *Inner Temple Lane*
Thursday [May 4? 1815]

My dear Miss Betham

My brother and myself return you a thousand thanks for your kind communication. We have read your poem many times over with encreased interest and very much wish to see you to tell you how highly we have been pleased with it. May we beg one favor—I keep the manuscript in the hope that you will grant it—. It is that, either now, or when the whole poem is completed, you will read it over with us——. When I say with *us* of course I mean Charles.— I know that you have many judicious friends, but I have so often known my brother spy out errors in a manuscript, which has passed through many judicious hands, that I shall not be easy if you do not permit him to look yours carefully through with you—and also you *must* allow him to correct the press for you.

If I knew where to find you I would call upon you. Should you feel nervous at the idea of meeting Charles in the capacity of a *severe censor* give me a line and I will come to you any where and convince you in five minutes that he is even timid, stammers and can scarcely speak for modesty and fear of giving pain when he finds himself placed in that kind of office. Shall I appoint a time to see you here when he is from home? I will send him out any time you will name—indeed I am always naturally alone till four o clock. If you are nervous about coming remember I am equally so about the liberty I have taken and shall be till till we meet & laugh off our mutual fears.

Yours most affectionately
M Lamb

I should have written earlier but every day I hoped on the morrow to be able to set out on a pilgrimage to hunt you out somewhere and the toothache has hitherto prevented me.

I cannot find Mr Dyer at home so I have no loving message to communicate

MS: Huntington Library. Pub.: Harper, IV, 55–56; Lucas (1905), VI, 476–477; Lucas (1912), V, 503–504; Lucas (1935), II, 162–163. Watermark: 1813.

The concluding postscript to the next letter has prompted the dating of this letter. Mary Lamb writes of a manuscript copy of the work Mary Matilda Betham was to complete and publish, with notes and two appendixes, as *The Lay of Marie: A Poem* (London: Rowland Hunter, 1816). Charles Lamb did assist her with it— Letters 302–306 show him involved in supervising it through the press. Southey, in a letter dated May 30, 1814, in M. Betham-Edwards' "Letters of Coleridge, Southey, and Lamb to [Mary] Matilda Betham," *Fraser's Magazine,* 18 (July 1878), 82, had counseled her to examine and transcribe, if possible and with George Dyer's help if necessary, the manuscript *lais* of Marie de France (fl. ca. 1175–1190) and to insert the transcriptions in *The Lay of Marie* for the "antiquarian value" they would insure to it. Miss Betham partly heeded Southey's counsel by forming one appendix of "Extracts from a Dissertation [in the thirteenth volume of *Archaeologia*] on the Life and Writings of Marie, an Anglo-Norman Poetess of the Thirteenth Century. By Monsieur La Rue" and one appendix of an abstract of Marie's twelve *lais* and versions of two.

294. *C. L. to Southey*

London
6 [5] May 1815

Dear Southey,

I have received from Longman a copy of Roderick[1] with the Authors Compts, for which I much thank you. I dont know where I shall put all the noble presents I have lately received in that way, the Excursion, Wordswths. two last vol*s*, & now Roderick, have come pouring in upon me like some irruption from Helicon. The storey of the brave Maccabee was already, you may be sure, familiar to me in all its parts. I have since the receit of your present read it quite through again, and with no diminished pleasure. I dont know whether I ought to say that it has given me more pleasure than any of your long poems. Kehama is doubtless more powerful, but I dont feel that firm footing in it that I do in Roderick, my imagination goes sinking and floundering in the vast spaces of unopened-before systems & faiths, I am put out of the pale of my old sympathies, my moral sense in[2] almost outraged, I cant believe or with horror am made to believe such **desperate chances** against omnipotence, such disturbances of faith to the centre—. The more potent the more painful the spell—. Jove and his brotherhood of gods tottering with the giant assailings I can bear, for the soul's hopes are not struck at in such contests, but your Oriental Almighties are too much types of the intangible prototype to be meddled with without shuddering—. One never connects what are call'd **The attributes** with Jupiter—. I mention only what diminishes my delight at the wonderworkings of Kehama, not what impeaches its power which I confess with trembling—

but Roderick is a comfortable poem—. It reminds me of the delight I took in the first reading of the Joan of Arc—.³ It is maturer & better than *that,* though not better to me now than that was then. It suits me better than Madoc. I am at home in Spain & Xtendom. I have a timid imagination I am afraid. I do not willingly admit of strange beliefs or out of the way creeds or places. I never read books of travels, at least not farther than Paris, or Rome.⁴ I can just endure Moors because of their connection as foes with Xtians, but Abyssinians, Ethiops, Esquumaux, Dervises & all that tribe I hate. I believe I fear them in some manner. A Mahometan turban on the stage, tho' enveloping some well known face (Mr. Cooke or Mr Maddox whom I see another day good Christn. & English waiters, innkeepers &c) does not give me pleasure unalloyed. I am a Christian, Englishman, Londoner, *Templar*—God help me when I come to put off these snug relations & to get abroad into the world to come—. I shall be like the *crow on the sand* as Wordswth. has it⁵—but I wont think on it—no need I hope yet—

The parts I have been most pleased with both on 1st & 2d readings, perhaps are, Florinda's palliation of Rodericks crime confessed to him in his disguise—the retreat of Palayos family *1st* discovered—his being made King⁶—"For acclamation one form must serve, *more solemn for the breach of old observances*"——. Rodericks vow is extremely fine—and his blessing on the vow of Alphonso—

> towards the troop he spread his arms
> As if the expanded soul diffused itself
> And carried to all spirits *with the act*
> Its effluent inspiration—

It struck me forcibly that the feeling of these last lines might have been suggested to you by the Cartoon of Paul at Athens.⁷ Certain it is that a better motto or guide to that famous attitude can no where be found. I shall adopt it as explanatory of that violent but dignified motion——

I must read again Landor's Julian. I have not read it sometime. I think he must have failed in Roderick for I remember nothing of him nor of any distinct character as a character—only fine sounding passages—. I remembr thinking also he had chose a point of time **after the event** as it were, for Roderick survives to no use—but my memory is weak & I will not wrong a fine Poem by trusting to it—

The notes to your poem I have not read again,—but it will be a take-downable book on my shelf, and they will serve sometimes at breakfast or times too light for the text to be duly appreciated. Tho' some of em',—one of the serpent Penance[8]—is serious enough now I think on't—

Of Coleridge I hear nothing, nor of the Morgans. I hope to have him like a reappearing star standing up before me some time when least expected in London, as has been the case whylear—[9]

I am *doing* nothing (as the phrase is) but reading Presents, & walk away what of the day hours I can get from hard occupation—. Pray accept once more my hearty thanks & expression of pleasure for your remembrce of me. My sister desires her kind respects to Mrs S. and to all at Keswick

Yours truly
C Lamb

The next Present I look for is the White Doe.[10]

Have you seen Mat. Betham's Lay of Marie. I think it very delicately pretty as to sentiment &c.

MS: Huntington Library. Pub.: Talfourd (1837), II, 12–16; Sala, I, 202–205; Purnell, I, 202–205; Fitzgerald, II, 54–57; Hazlitt, I, 444–446; Ainger (1888), I, 290–292; Ainger (1900), II, 230–234; Macdonald, I, 356–359; Ainger (1904), I, 347–349; Harper, IV, 40–43; Lucas (1905), VI, 465–467; Lucas (1912), V, 490–492; Lucas (1935), II, 163–165. Address: R Southey Esqr/Keswick/near/Penrith/Cumberland. Postmarks: May 5 and 7, 1815.

1. *Roderick, the Last of the Goths*, which Longman's had published in 1814 and republished, in second and third editions, in 1815. Southey's poem, like Walter Savage Landor's tragedy, *Count Julian* (1812), recounts the story, part history and part legend, of Roderick, the last king of the Visigoths. King Roderick, whose reign extended from 710 to 711, had violated Florinda, daughter of the Spanish Goth Julian, the imperial count, or governor, of Ceuta, Morocco. In 711 the Moors, at the invitation of the revengeful Julian, marched on Spain and drove Roderick from his throne. Roderick, in hiding, committed himself as a penitent for his crime against Florinda to God and the salvation of Spain. In a priest's habit and as Father Maccabee he penetrated the camp of the Moors and persuaded his cousin and their captive the Asturian Pelayo the Goth (d. 737) to flee his captors and take the leadership of the growing number of Christians ready to fight the invaders. Pelayo fled with Florinda, who had been also their captive, and joined the Christian band. He was himself joined by the Cantabrian Duke Alphonso (d. 757?), later Pelayo's son-in-law Alphonso I of Spain, its ruler from 739 to 757. Pelayo was acclaimed king, led with Roderick the Christians to victory

over the Moors at Covadonga, and reigned from 718 to 737 and thus became the founder of the Spanish monarchy. Roderick had heard while still disguised as a priest the confession of Florinda, her admission of love for Roderick, and had fought so valorously in the battle that he was recognized and was greatly responsible for its issue. At its end he disappeared. The Moors had slain Julian, treacherously, and Florinda had died by his side. It is said that generations after Roderick's disappearance a tomb was discovered in a hermitage near Vizeu, or Viseu, Portugal, inscribed with Roderick's name. About Helicon, which Lamb names at the end of his next sentence, see Vol. I, Letter 6, note 1. *The Curse of Kehama,* in which Southey exhibited the wonderworkings of Hindu mythology and to which Lamb refers below, Longman's had published in 1810.

2. An error for "is."

3. Southey's *Joan of Arc, an Epic Poem.* See Vol. I, Letter 1, note 2, and Letters 3, 4, and 34. About Southey's *Madoc* (mentioned below), which is set in Wales and among the Aztecs in the country they call Aztlan, see Vol. I, Letter 11, note 3.

4. Lamb had read James Bruce's *Travels to Discover the Source of the Nile* . . . , "with infinite delight" (Vol. II, Letter 188, at the reference to note 5; notices of Bruce and his Abyssinian explorations are in Lamb's "Amicus Redivivus" and "Newspapers Thirty-five Years Ago" [*Works,* II, 211 and 220]). Yet even in the last summer of his life Lamb, when requesting the loan of some books from the antiquary and critic Charles Wentworth Dilke (1789–1864), specified "no natural history or useful learning, such as Pyramids, Catacombs, Giraffes, Adventures in Southern Africa, &c. &c." (from the letter, whose original has not been recovered, in Lucas [1935], III, 411, and my Vol. VI). The actor Cooke referred to below could be George Frederick Cooke (see Vol. II, Letter 105, note 1) or Thomas Potter Cooke (1786–1864). The latter had made his London debut in 1804, served as a stage manager of the Surrey Theatre in 1809, was to be most successful at the Lyceum in 1820, and to retire in 1860. The actor referred to as "Maddox" could be Walter Maddocks—who had appeared at Drury Lane and the Haymarket between 1789 and at least the season of 1799–1800—but probably could not be George Mattocks (d. 1804). Although Mattocks had performed from 1757, he seems to have been known mainly as a manager of the Liverpool theater and as the husband of Isabella Mattocks (1746–1826), an actress Lamb had mentioned, disparagingly, in "[The New Acting]" (*Works,* I, 152).

5. In "The Farmer of Tilsbury Vale," line 48: "As lonely he stood as a crow on the sands."

6. In Book X: "Roderick and Florinda"; Book XVI: "Covadonga"; and Book XVIII: "The Acclamation." The quotation following is from Book XVIII, lines 97–99. Roderick's vow is in Book IV: "The Monastery of St. Felix," lines 13–25. Roderick's blessing on Alphonso's vow, a blessing that embraces the troop of which Alphonso is a part, is in Book XII: "The Vow," lines 208–224. Lamb's indented lines are from its lines 212–215.

7. Raphael's "St. Paul Preaching at Athens," which in Lamb's time was displayed at Hampton Court Palace, Middlesex, and at The British Institution, London. The work was transferred to the Victoria and Albert Museum in 1865. See John Shearman's *Raphael's Cartoons in the Collection of Her Majesty the Queen and the Tapestries for the Sistine Chapel* (London: Phaidon Press, 1972), pp. 138–163, Plate I, and Plate 39.

8. In *The Poetical Works of Robert Southey, with a Memoir* [by Henry T. Tuckerman] (10 vols. in 5; Boston: Houghton, Mifflin [1860?]), IX, 410–413: "Chap. 254.—*Of the penance which was appointed King Don Rodrigo.*" About Coleridge, mentioned with the John Morgans in the next paragraph, see note 5 to Letter 286, Lamb's portion of Letter 300, and the second paragraph in Letter 301.

9. Or "whilere": erewhile.

10. *The White Doe of Rylstone.* See Letter 292, note 8.

295. *C. L. to William Wordsworth*
[?Whit Tuesday, May ?16, 1815]

Dr W.

We are just returned from our expedition which has proved very pleasant. **Thursday** is our club night—the evening I told you I expected W. H.[1]—so we must defer our meeting till you can name another open evening. I almost fear I can scarce reckon upon any particular one, I am so busy; but I hope to see you somehow soon. I dont know whether you would not have form'd a correcter estimate of Miss O Neil[2] from Isabella than from Juliet. Shakspear bothers them all sadly.—

You[r]s truly
C L

MS: Folger Shakespeare Library. Pub.: Lucas (1935), II, 163. Address: W. Wordsworth Esq/24 Edward Street/Cavendish Square. Postmark: May 1[6?], 1815. What remains of the postmark indicates it to have been May 10, 16, or 18, 1815. The first two sentences in this letter and the first paragraph in the next, where Mary writes of the expedition (into Bedfordshire and Hertfordshire) and of its having begun on Whitsun Eve (Saturday, May 13, in 1815), rule out May 10 as the date of this letter and almost surely set it at May 16.

1. William Hazlitt, whose company Lamb knew Wordsworth did not care for. See Letter 286, note 4.

2. The actress Eliza O'Neill, later Eliza, Lady Becher (1791–1872). She was the daughter of an undistinguished (and otherwise unidentified) Irish actor named O'Neill who had become a stage manager of the Drogheda theater and of the former Miss Featherstone, and was from December 1819 the wife of William Wrixon Becher, or Wrixon-Becher (1780–1850), of Ballygiblin Castle, County Cork. He was a wealthy Irishman, a member of Parliament from 1818 to 1826, created a baronet in 1831. (Those details about him are drawn from the *DNB* entry for his wife; *Shelley and His Circle*, VI, 897; and Gerrit Parmele Judd's *Members of Parliament, 1734–1832* [1955; rpt. Hamden, Conn.: Archon Books, 1972].) She first performed in Ireland—in Drogheda, Belfast, and Dublin—made her London debut as Juliet at Covent Garden on October 6, 1814, and appeared as Isabella in Thomas Southerne's *The Fatal Marriage* at Covent Garden on November 4, 1814. Her success in London was instant, wondrous, and abiding. Some hailed her, as a tragic actress, as another Sarah Siddons; some men, it has been said, were carried from Miss O'Neill's tragic performances in a faint. She retired from the stage unexpectedly, five months before she was married. George Dawe's full-length portrait of her as Juliet, which Lamb in the second paragraph in his portion of the next letter calls "Daa's Picture of Miss O Kneel" and praises to a degree, which the author of the biography of Dawe in the *DNB* stated was most effectively "exhibited by lamplight at the artist's house," is listed in every source consulted as completed in 1816.

296. *M. A. L. and C. L. to Mrs. Morgan and Charlotte Brent*
[Monday, May 22, 1815]

My dear friends

I have just heard from your good man in Bishop[s]gate Street—I forget his name—that you are all well and happily situated in a pleasant country and among good neighbours, and that you find yourselves so comfortable you have no thoughts of returning to London, which I am very sorry to hear——not sorry to hear you are well & happy, but very sorry there is no hope of seeing you: I wish I could come to you for a few days but there is a great gulph between us which I may not pass. I am very proud of having lately performed a thirty miles journey and returned safe & well. On Whitsun Eve[1] Charles & I & Baron Field, he who became such a zealous convert to Coleridge & Wordsworth, went to Luton. We arrived there, they at the top & I in the inside of a stage-coach about eight in the evening rejoicing in the design of seeing the next morning a house[2] of Lord **Bute's** said to contain some of the finest pictures in England and in particular a most marvellous Virgin & Child by Raphael. The first news we heard was that the pictures were taken down, the house full of company and no strangers admitted. We had a good supper at our Inn and the landlady graciously permitted Charles to have a pipe but still we were inconsolable for our disappointment. The house was shut against us but we walked two miles through the most beautiful park I ever saw by the side of a river and when we left the park we followed its course five or six miles till it conducted us to a farm house[3] where a *great* aunt of mine once dwelt and where I spent some portion of every year in my younger days: the last visit I made there I had the care and sole management of my little brother Charles then an urchin of three or four years, he then under my sole guidance—whom I could controul & correct at my own pleasure now become my lord & master allowed me to go & look at the house but refused leave to enter till I got to the orchard stile and then I overcame his scruples and he let me go into the house. Three or four dogs barking at me enough to frighten me from any other farmhouse in England did not deter me from going in by myself. I found no soul of a large family I had left there. a

grandaughter of my aunt's not then born received me in a most
friendly manner, sent her husband to fetch in Charles and Field and
immediately began to call us Charles & Mary with most cousin-like
familiarity. Not only all the inhabitants I knew were gone, some to
their graves and some to their husbands, but the old house was re-
built. Yet the orchard the farm yard and the garden remained.[4]
Charles says he never saw me look so happy in his life, and he was
not much less so for in the evening he said it was the pleasantest day
he ever had in his life, When I saw him smoking his pipe with the
farmer I wished to realize a dream I have twice had lately that he was
with me and he himself a little child also, for I seemed to feel as much
loss of him as his cousin Sophy a little girl of his own age who is dead
and who he well remembers playing with——. They[5] would have made
up beds for us and were very desirous that we should stay all night but
we were going to sleep at St Albans about seven miles from thence so
my cousin *Penelope* walked with us to a neighbouring village through
which we were to pass on our way, and introduced us to some more
of our kindred settled there. I was particularly struck with the sight
of her mother who I left a very pretty young daughter in law of my
aunt's now a very old looking woman and herself a grand-mother.

I was interrupted by the entrance of Mr Wordsworth or I should
have tired you with my long gossipping story of my cousins & the remainder of our adventures at St Albans——How we clambered to the
top of the Abbey[6] & how [h]aving got to the top I was frightened out
of my wits to get down again[—]How we saw a fine house (once
Lord Bacons,) and park and many fine pictures but not of so great
celebrity as Lord Bute's & a curious old silver-tongued housekeeper &
a piping bulfinch and some famous beech trees and a marble statue of
Lord Bacon & the ruins of his old house, I would have written three
pages concerning these things but after the Wordsworths were gone
Charles and his dinner succeeded and he has promised to finish my
letter & every word I write incroaches on his share which doubtless
will be so much clear loss to you.— Mr Wordsworth said he had a
letter[7] in his pocket written to Coleridge therefore I need not tell you
he is in town with his wife & Miss Hutchinson who is so like you Miss
Bren[t] that every time I see her I quarrel with her in my mind for
not being you Miss Brent. I do not think there is any news to tell you
of any of our friends. Our friends (and they are all well you left here)

come as usual on Thursday nights. I think Coleridge knows & therefore you may know, that **Rickman** has got a better place (Clerk of the House of Commons) and Phillips the card player has succeeded him as Secretary to the Speaker—Martin has entered into Partnership & is doing pretty well.[8] The[re] has arisen a feud between Hazlitt & Captain Burney. Hazlitt was engaged to write a review of Capn B's sister's novel. The Capn ordered the review to his sister's and sent her word that she was secure of praise it being to be written by his most particular friend. When she came to read the review it was anything but praise, in short downrigh[t] abuse, of her present & former works. The Captain wrote to Hazlitt giving up his acquaintaince for ever. I know of no other quarrel——nobody is married——nobody has died——Kenn[y has] one more child[9] and a successful farce.[10] Marti[n] Burney is going to write a successful tragedy. Godwin has just pub[li]shed a new book, I wish it may be successful but I am sure it is very dull. Wordsworth has just now looked into it and found these words "All modern poetry is nothing but the old, genuine poetry, new [vam]ped, and delivered to us at second, or twentieth hand." In great wrath he took a pencil and wrote in the margin "That is false, William Godwin. Signed William Wordsworth."

Has Wordsworth told you that coming to town he lost the manuscripts of "The Waggoner" and "Peter Bell" and two hundred lines of a new poem,[11] and that he is not certain he can by any means recover a correct copy of them.

My brother has got an excellent original picture of Milton. Wordsworth has twice been to see it. He (John) picked it up, all over dirt, for five shillings. We have got many new Hogarths.

Daa'[12] has got a picture of Miss O'Kneel. Wordsworth is here. He is very much pleased with his Poems. So am I. Morgan's boots shall be sent. A curious story is appended to them. When we came home from St. Albans, going into the Garrat, we heard a strange noise, of squeaking. Upon further examination, in one of Morgan's boots a rat had pup't. Four new rats were there, scarce fledged; the rat had jumpt out. One we have put prentice to a sail-maker, an other we have sent to Dr. Bell's school[13] to read, and learn virtue, another we have put with a wholesale grocer, and the fourth is waiting for my tailor to send home his breeches, that he may go out into the world clean & decent.

Wordsworth is going to be Knighted. Miss Sar. Hutchinson is not like Miss B.¹⁴ Miss ***** is a great deal prettier &c. than Miss ———. She

is a Welch ——— woman. round faced, sentimental, not ⎫
                                                      wise ⎭

do you mark how the word not is *over* wise——. I am not [⎫] that is
                                                     sober ⎭

not over *sober*. **O la!** I wish——

Daa's Picture of Miss O Kneel is a laudable Portrait, as bright as noon day her skin her drapery her every thing, but then—to suit the story—all about her is **moon & moon-light!** I ventured to hint the incongruity. **Daa'** at first lookd disconcerted, but soon his little grey rat eyes discover'd a curtain which he drew down over th[e] windo[w . . .]¹⁵

MS: Quoted by permission of The Carl H. Pforzheimer Library. Unpublished. Address: Mrs. Morgan/Miss Brent. Watermark: 1814. The date of the letter is established in its second paragraph, where Mary remarks on Wordsworth's entrance on her and the letter to be mailed to Coleridge: Robinson, also calling on Mary on May 22, 1815, found Wordsworth there, and Wordsworth had in the morning of the same day written to Coleridge, who was living with the John Morgans and Miss Brent in Calne, Wiltshire. (See *H. C. R. on Books and Writers*, I, 167, and *Wordsworths' Letters*, III, 238–239.) Mary begins this letter, with a reference to probably an employee in Morgan's concerns in Bishopsgate Street. See Letter 253, note 1.

1. Saturday, May 13. The lawyer and miscellaneous writer Barron Field (1786–1846), whom Mary is about to mention and whom Charles had known possibly since 1809 and certainly since June 21, 1811 (see Letter 276, source note, and *H. C. R. on Books and Writers*, I, 36), was a son of Henry Field (1755–1837), the apothecary for Christ's Hospital from 1807 to 1837, and of Esther (d. 1834), a daughter of John Barron of Woolacre House, near Deptford, London. The Henry Fields were the parents as well of Francis John (d. 1857), who had worked with Lamb as a clerk in the East India House since 1806 and would be made its deputy accountant general in 1832 and be retired in 1835; of Frederick (1801–1885), who was from 1807 or 1808 to 1819 a student at Christ's Hospital and would become a student at and fellow of Trinity College, Cambridge, a divine, and a respected Biblical and patristic scholar; of Henry, whom Lamb will identify in a letter to Robinson of November 20, 1824 (in Vol. V), as "a Surgeon &c a few doors (east) west of Christ Church Passage Newgate Street [London]"; of two other sons; and of Esther and Mary (or Maria) Louisa. Barron Field was in 1809 admitted to and in 1814 called to the bar at the Inner Temple. He supported himself, according to the *DNB*, before and during a portion of that period by writing. For maybe a year thereafter he supported himself by occasionally practicing law. Then, harboring misgivings about his ability to succeed as a writer or as a barrister in London, he departed to serve as an advocate-fiscal in Ceylon. He returned to England and on August 28, 1816, departed from Gravesend with his bride, the former Jane Cairncross, or Carncross (1792?–1878), to serve as the judge of the supreme court of New South Wales and its dependencies. The Fields

arrived in Sydney on February 24, 1817, stayed in the colony until February 4, 1824, sailed for home, and reached Portsmouth on June 18. Field again tried and failed to establish himself as a barrister in London and went abroad, in 1830 to assume the post of chief justice of Gibraltar. He retired in perhaps 1841 to England, by October 1844 (see *H. C. R.'s Diary*, II, 326–327) to Meadfoot House, Torquay, Devonshire, where he died. His widow died, childless, in the London suburb of Wimbledon. Field was the drama critic for the *Times* from 1805 or 1806 to about 1810 and a contributor to John and Leigh Hunt's *The Examiner* in 1808 and possibly other years, to the *Quarterly Review* in at least 1810 and 1811, to the Hunts' *The Reflector* in 1811 and 1812, to the *London Magazine* from 1822 to 1825. He was the author of *An Analysis of Blackstone's Commentaries on the Laws of England, in a Series of Questions* (1811), which was often republished; of the pamphlets *Hints to Witnesses in Courts of Justice* (1815) and *A Vindication of the Practice of Not Allowing the Counsel for Prisoners Accused of Felony to Make Speeches for Them* (1828); of an introduction to *Memoirs of James Hardy Vaux, a Swindler and Thief, Now Transported to New South Wales for the Second Time and for Life* (1819), which was republished twice. Field was the poet of "Botany Bay Flowers" and "The Kangaroo," which form his *First Fruits of Australian Poetry* (1819), and of *Spanish Sketches* (1841). In 1825 he edited a volume of *Geographical Memoirs on New South Wales. By Various Hands* in which he included papers of his own and an enlarged version of *First Fruits of Australian Poetry*. He edited for the Shakespeare Society in 1842 Thomas Heywood's *First and Second Parts of King Edward IV Histories*, in 1844 *The True Tragedy of Richard the Third, to Which Is Appended the Latin Play of "Richardus Tertius," by Dr. Thomas Legge*—Legge (1535–1607), a Latin dramatist, was in addition a master of Caius College and a regius professor and an officer of Cambridge University—in 1846 Heywood's *The Fair-maid of the Exchange, a Comedy* and Heywood and William Rowley's *Fortune by Land and Sea, a Tragi-comedy*. Field wrote the essays on Coleridge and on Lamb in *The Annual Biography and Obituary*, 19 and 20 (1835 and 1836), 320–378 and 1–16. He wrote "Memoirs of the Life and Poetry of William Wordsworth," which Wordsworth, in a letter of January 16, 1840, dissuaded him from publishing and today is (as MS. Add. 41325-7) in the British Museum. (See *Wordsworths' Letters*, V, 996 and 997–998.) Lamb, using the signature "****," reviewed *First Fruits of Australian Poetry* in *The Examiner* for January 16, 1820—commending "The Kangaroo" in the review (in *Works*, I, 197–200) and in the letter to Bernard Barton postmarked March 25, 1829 (in my Vol. V), commending it implicitly in the letter to Field of August 16, 1820 (in Vol. IV). For Field's wife and sisters Lamb composed the acrostics and sonnet "To Mrs. F[ield]: *On Her Return from Gibraltar*," "To Esther Field," and "To M[ary] L[ouisa] F[ield]: (*Expecting to See Her Again after a Long Interval*)" (*Works*, V, 93 and 94). Lamb alluded to Field (as B. F.) in "Mackery End, in Hertfordshire" (*Works*, II, esp. 78 and 79), an essay published in 1821 that includes a recollection of the journey Mary Lamb describes in the present letter. Lamb addressed Field in "Distant Correspondents: In a Letter to B. F. Esq. at Sydney, New South Wales" (*Works*, II, 104–108), an essay published in 1822 that is an elaboration of the private letter (Letter 329) of August 31, 1817. The account of Field in *Hunt's "Reflector,"* pp. 98–107, supplements the account of him in the *DNB*.

2. The mansion situated, with its botanical garden, at Luton Hoo, near the River Lea, Bedfordshire, that the architect Robert Adam (1728–1792) had constructed in 1767 for John Stuart, third Earl of Bute (1713–1792).

3. Mackery (or Mackarel, or Mackrye) End, of the Hertfordshire farm and hamlet of the same name, located between Harpenden and Wheathampstead, where Mary had taken Charles in 1778 or 1779 to visit their maternal grandaunt Anne Gladman, née Bruton (whose death had not occurred on August 3, 1799, the

date given in Vol. I, Introduction, p. xxvii, but on August 3, 1779). She and her husband, James, were the parents of Edward (1749?–1801), James (1753?–1799), and William (1757?–1761). Edward had succeeded his father as the leaseholder of Mackery End and in 1771 had been married to Sarah Taylor (1743?–1830). Although she held the lease of the farm from her husband's death to her own, she was living at the time of this letter not on the farm but in Wheathampstead, possibly in the High Street residence of her unmarried (and never to be married) daughter Maria (1772?–1851). Edward and Sarah Gladman were the parents also of Arabella (1773?–1801), who in 1796 had become the wife of John Farr (d. 1829), a farmer, later the farmer or resident of Mimms Hall, South Mimms; Elizabeth (1774?–1835), who in 1798 had become the wife of Randall Lee Barker (d. 1846), a farmer at Kimpton; Sophia, or Sophy (1776?–1802), who had never been married, whom Mary Lamb shortly mentions; Phinalepy (probably a clerk's misspelling of Penelope) and Benjamin, twins who had died in 1777 four days after their birth; Penelope (1779?–1848), who in 1803 had become the wife of her second cousin Edward Bruton (1778–1858), at the time of this letter the farmer of Mackery End, later the farmer of Kimpton Hall, Kimpton, ultimately a resident, with his wife, of Gustard Wood, Wheathampstead; and Anne (1781?–1850), who in 1805 had become the wife of Henry Sibley (d. 1830), a farmer and maltster at Wheathampstead. It was Edward and Penelope Bruton who received the Lambs and Barron Field at Mackery End. It was Penelope whom Lamb would remember with especial fondness in "Mackery End, in Hertfordshire." Two views of the farmhouse and a map of the vicinity of the hamlet are reproduced in *Works,* II, facing p. 358 and on p. 359. Information about the Lambs' visit to the farm in 1778 or 1779 and about certain (for the most part, other) of the Lambs' Hertfordshire relatives is in my Vol. I, Introduction, pp. xxv–xxvi and xxvii–xxviii. A thorough accounting of the Hertfordshire relatives is in Henry W. Gray's "New Light on Charles Lamb: A Look at the Essayist's Hertfordshire Ancestry and Kindred," *Hertfordshire Past and Present,* No. 8 ([Hertfordshire?]: Hertfordshire Local History Council, 1968), 19–28.

4. Cf. Mary Lamb's "Louisa Manners: The Farmhouse," in *Mrs. Leicester's School* (*Works,* III, esp. 284–285).

5. Edward and Penelope Bruton. Complementing each other are the rest of Mary's paragraph, with its allusions to Wheathampstead and Sarah and Anne Gladman, and the last several lines in Lamb's "Mackery End, in Hertfordshire," with their allusions to Penelope Bruton ("this hospitable cousin"), Sarah and Maria ("mother and sister") Gladman, Mary Lamb's ("Bridget's") memory, and Barron Field:

> The fatted calf was made ready, or rather was already so, as if in anticipation of our coming; and, after an appropriate glass of native wine, never let me forget with what honest pride this hospitable cousin made us proceed to Wheathampstead, to introduce us (as some new-found rarity) to her mother and sister Gladmans, who did indeed know something more of us, at a time when she almost knew nothing.—With what corresponding kindness we were received by them also—how Bridget's memory, exalted by the occasion, warmed into a thousand half-obliterated recollections of things and persons, to my utter astonishment, and her own—and to the astoundment of B. F. who sat by, almost the only thing that was not a cousin there,—old effaced images of more than half-forgotten names and circumstances still crowding back upon her, as words written in lemon come out upon exposure to a friendly warmth,—when I forget all this, then may my country cousins forget me; and Bridget no more remember, that in the days of weakling infancy I was her tender charge—as I have been her care in foolish mahood since—in those pretty pastoral walks, long go, about Mackery End, in Hertfordshire.
> [*Works,* II, 78–79]

6. St. Albans Cathedral, the great cathedral, or abbey church, consecrated in 1115, one of the most important edifices of Norman architecture in England. The "fine house," referred to below, is Verulam House, which Francis Bacon had erected as a summer residence at a cost of ten thousand pounds. His "old house," Gorambury, about a mile away, to which he had Verulam House connected by a triple avenue of elms, chestnuts, hornbeams, Spanish ashes, and beeches, had been the home of his parents and his more permanent residence when he was out of London. Bacon's statue is in St. Michael's Church, which holds also his tomb.

7. See the source note to this letter. Mary below mentions Mary Wordsworth and Sara Hutchinson.

8. About John Rickman and Edward Phillips see Vol. I, Letter 86, note 4; and Vol. II, Letter 198, note 1. See also Letter 278, near the reference to note 5. The "Partnership" into which Martin Burney had entered would seem not to be the one possibly glanced at in Letter 250, at the reference to note 4. Mary may mean not a partnership but the law office of Sharon Turner, where Burney did work and perhaps at this time. An observation of Turner about Burney—"I always thought he would flower, though it might be late. He is a man of great honour and integrity. He never told me a lie in his life!"—is in Robinson's dairy entry for June 6, 1815. (See Letter 243, note 2, and *H. C. R. on Books and Writers*, I, 168.) Mary writes next of the feud between James Burney and Hazlitt caused by "Standard Novels and Romances," *Edinburgh Review*, 24 (February 1815), 320–338, a survey of European fiction in which Hazlitt reviewed *The Wanderer; or, Female Difficulties* (5 vols.; 1814), by Madame d'Arblay (identified in my Vol. II, Letter 141, note 7), and noticed her *Evelina, or, the History of a Young Lady's Entrance into the World* (3 vols.; 1778), *Cecilia, or Memoirs of an Heiress* (5 vols.; 1782), and *Camilla: Or, a Picture of Youth* (5 vols.; 1796). He thought her, the former Frances Burney, to be "a quick, lively, and accurate observer of persons and things"; her stories to be "teazing and tedious"; her characters to be caricatures and, with exceptions, superficial, uniform, confined, fastidious, excessively refined, and of affected and insipid sentiments. He concluded with this paragraph:

> We are sorry to be compelled to speak so disadvantageously of the work [*The Wanderer*] of an excellent and favourite writer; and the more so, as we perceive no decay of talent, but a perversion of it. There is the same admirable spirit in the dialogues, and particularly in the characters of Mrs. Ireton, Sir Jasper [properly Jaspar] Herrington, and Mr. Giles Arbe, as in her former novels. But these do not fill a hundred pages of the work; and there is nothing else good in it. In the story, which here occupies the attention of the reader almost exclusively, Madame D'Arblay never excelled. [*Hazlitt's Works*, XVI, 21, 22, and 23–24]

James Burney's letter to Hazlitt to which Mary refers is published in P. P. Howe's *The Life of William Hazlitt* (1922; rev. 1928; rpt. London: Hamish Hamilton, 1947), pp. 166–167:

May 17, 1815

> Sir,—It would be strange, if not wrong, after years of intimate acquaintance, that cause of offence should happen between us, and be so taken, and be passed over in silence, and that acquaintance still continue. Your attack on my Sister's early publications dissatisfied me, and the more in coming from a quarter I had been in the habit of believing friendly. If I had seen it before publication, I should have remonstrated against some of your remarks, because I think them unjust. Your publication of such a paper showed a total absence of regard towards me, and I must consider it as the termination of our acquaintance.

Jas. Burney

Herschel Baker, citing *Hazlitt's Works,* VIII, 157 and 209, has in *Hazlitt,* p. 211, noted that "Hazlitt did not apologize, or change his mind about Fanny's [Madame d'Arblay's] 'affectations' . . . , but he did concede, a few years later . . . , that she was the cleverest member of a family noted mainly for its large 'pretentions.' "

9. The given name of James and Louisa Mercier Holcroft Kenney's new child is not known. That which follows in this note is something of what is known or not known, stated as fact or presumed, particularly about the names, dates, parents, spouses, relationships of the children or those possibly the children of the dramatists Thomas Holcroft and James Kenney. Ann—the eldest daughter of Holcroft, by his first wife, whose given and maiden names are not known, to whom he was married in 1765, whose year of death is not known; Ann (not Sophia, or Sophy [b. 1775; *q.v.*], as I misstated in Vol. II, Letter 222, note 2) was married in 1796 to Lieutenant Colonel William Tooke Harwood. (See Vol. II, Letter 222, note 2; *Holcroft,* I, lvi, 118, 255–256, and II, 107.) Betsy (b. 1808?)—a daughter of Holcroft by the former Louisa Mercier (d. 1853), his fourth wife, to whom he was married in 1799. (See Vol. II, Letter 133, note 7, and Letter 222, note 2; *Holcroft,* I, lviii, and II, 116–117 and 248; *The Lambs,* p. 170; Lucas [1905], VII, 584; Lucas [1935], II, 331.) Charles Lamb Kenney (1821–1881)—he attended the Merchant Taylors' School, became a postal clerk and then a journalist, an author of libretti and songs and of dramatic and prose works, a translator; he served as a secretary to the gardener and architect Sir Joseph Paxton (1801–1865), who designed the building (commonly called The Crystal Palace) that housed the industrial exhibition of 1850; Charles was called to the bar at the Inner Temple in 1856 and, apparently in the same year, accepted an appointment as a secretary to the diplomatist Ferinand de Lesseps (1805–1894), who negotiated the construction of the Suez Canal; Charles was married in 1859 to Rosa Stewart. (His biography is in the *DNB*.) Ellen (b. 1808?)—a daughter of Holcroft by Louisa. (See Vol. II, Letter 222, note 2; *The Lambs,* p. 170; Lucas [1905], VII, 584; Lucas [1935], II, 331.) Fanny (d. 1844)—a daughter of Holcroft by his third wife, whose given and maiden names are not known, to whom he was married in 1778, who died in 1790. (See Vol. II, Letter 133, note 7; *Holcroft,* I, liii, lvii, 204, 255–256, and 301; the *DNB* entry for Thomas Holcroft.) Harwood—a son of Holcroft, presumably by Louisa. (See *The Lambs,* p. 169; Lucas [1905], VII, 584; Lucas [1935], II, 348.) Henry—possibly a son of Holcroft or Kenney. (Henry is mentioned in the last paragraph in Letter 321.) James Kenney, the younger— see *The Lambs,* p. 170; Lucas (1905), VII, 584; the *DNB* entry for James Kenney. Kenny—possibly a son of Kenney if not Kenney himself. (Kenny is mentioned as though a child in the last paragraph in Letter 321, in the first paragraph in the letter to Mrs. Louisa Kenney of September 11, 1822 [in Vol. IV], in the third paragraph in the letter to Mrs. Louisa Kenney of about November 1822 [in Vol. IV].) Leah—possibly a daughter of Kenney. (She is mentioned in the second paragraph in the letter to James Kenney of about September 1823 [in Vol. V].) Louisa (b. 1806)—the eldest daughter of Holcroft by Louisa; the daughter Louisa was married in 1828 or 1829 to John Badams. (See Vol. II, Letter 198, note 6; *Holcroft,* I, lviii; *Mary Shelley's Letters,* I, 254.) Maria Kenney—see the *DNB* entry for James Kenney. Rachel—possibly a daughter of Kenney. (She is mentioned in the second paragraph in the letter to James Kenney of about September 1823 [in Vol. V].) Rose—possibly a daughter of Holcroft or Kenney. (She is mentioned in the third paragraph in the letter to Mrs. Louisa Kenney of about November 1822 [in Vol. IV].) Sophia, or Sophy (b. 1775)—a daughter of Holcroft by the former Matilda (not Maria) Tipler (d. 1775?) of Nottingham, his second wife, to whom he was married in about 1772; Sophia was married shortly before 1794 to a Mr. Cole (not in 1796 to Lieutenant Colonel William Tooke Harwood), a merchant of Exeter, Devonshire, and, by 1799, of Hamburg, Germany. (See Vol. II, Letter 222, note 2; *Holcroft,* I, lvi, 157, 255–256, and II, 40, 84, 107,

and 285.) Sophia, or Sophy—a daughter of Kenney or of Holcroft by Louisa (my statement in Vol. II, Letter 222, note 2, to the contrary); this Sophia, who had a twin sister (whose given name is not known), was married to a Dr. Jefferson of Leamington, Warwickshire; was the mother of Alfred Ainger's friend W. J. Jefferson of Folkestone, Kent; and was an acquaintance of William Carew Hazlitt. (See Ainger [1888], II, 315 and 317, and Lucas [1935], II, 330, where she is referred to or designated as Kenney's daughter; *The Lambs*, pp. 169 and 170, and Lucas [1905], VII, 584, where she is identified as Holcroft's daughter by Louisa; Lucas [1935], II, 331, where she is identified as Holcroft's daughter and her twin is identified, erroneously, as Holcroft's daughter Louisa.) Teresa, or Therese, Kenney—see *The Lambs*, p. 170; Lucas (1905), VII, 584; *Mary Shelley's Letters*, I, 274. Thomas (d. 1852), the younger—a son of Holcroft by Louisa; the given and maiden names of Thomas' wife are not known. (See Vol. II, Letter 208, note 2; a biographical sketch of him is in Frederic Boase, *Modern English Biography* . . . [1892–1901 and 1908–1921; rpt. London: Frank Cass, 1965].) Villiers—a son of Holcroft, presumably by Louisa; Villiers was the brother whom the younger Thomas joined in India. (See Vol. II, Letter 208, note 2; *The Life of Lamb*, II, 25.) Virginia Kenney—see *The Lambs*, p. 170; Lucas (1905), VII, 584; the *DNB* entry for James Kenney. William (1773–1789)—a son of Holcroft by Matilda; William committed suicide from the shame he felt at having stolen from his father. (See *Holcroft*, I, lvi, 157, 255–256, and 301–304.)

10. James Kenney's "The Fortune of War," which had opened at Covent Garden on May 17, 1815, and was performed fourteen times thereafter. If Martin Burney did write "a successful tragedy" (below), it seems not to have been acted or published. (See Vol. II, Letter 202, note 5.) Godwin's book to which Mary refers is *Lives of Edward and John Philips, Nephews and Pupils of Milton: Including Various Particulars of the Literary and Political History of Their Times. To Which Are Added, I. Collections for the Life of Milton, by John Aubrey, F. R. S., Printed from the MS. Copy in the Ashmolean Museum at Oxford. II. The Life of Milton, by Edward Philips, Printed in the Year 1694.* Its page 247 contains the passage causing Wordsworth's "great wrath" and notation. The book is listed as or stated to have been published in 1809, or listed as or stated to have been published in 1809 and republished in 1815 in Ford K. Brown's *The Life of William Godwin* (London and Toronto: Dent; New York: Dutton, 1926), p. 224, where is the comment that Godwin's friend Sir James Mackintosh (see my Vol. II, Letter 108, note 2) "contributed to the *Edinburgh Review* a long and favourable criticism" of the book, but not the detail that the criticism is in the *Edinburgh Review*, 25 (October 1815), 485–501; in *The Cambridge Bibliography of English Literature;* in the narrative portion of the account of Godwin in the *DNB;* in *Godwin*, II, 177, where is the remark that the book was Godwin's "chief literary work of the year 1809"; in Elton Edward Smith and Esther Greenwell Smith's *William Godwin* (New York: Twayne, 1965), pp. [13], 135, and 160–161, where the publisher of an 1809 and an 1815 edition is given as Longman, Hurst, Rees, Orme, and Brown; in George Woodcock's *William Godwin: A Biographical Study* (London: The Porcupine Press, 1946), pp. 185, 190, and 260. Godwin's book is listed as published in 1815 in Samuel Austin Allibone's *A Critical Dictionary of English Literature and British and American Authors* . . . (1858; rpt. Detroit: Gale Research, 1965); in *The New Cambridge Bibliography of English Literature;* in the bibliographical portions of the accounts of Godwin and of Edward (1630–1696?) and John (1631–1706) Phillips (Godwin misspelled that surname) in the *DNB* and the eleventh edition of *The Encyclopædia Britannica;* in William Thomas Lowndes's *The Bibliographer's Manual of English Literature* . . . , ed. Henry G. Bohn (1864; rpt. Detroit: Gale Research, 1967); in Burton Ralph Pollin's *Education and Enlightenment in the Works of William Godwin* (New York: Las Americas, 1962), p. 282. In *Shelley and His Circle*, III, 148–149, 150–151, and

185–186 are Godwin's letters of May 10, 14, and 19, 1813, to Dr. Charles Burney (1757–1817—see my Vol. II, Letter 141, note 7), and in *Shelley and His Circle,* III, 149–150, is this declaration about them and *Lives of Edward and John Philips:*

> It is clear . . . from these letters that Godwin in 1813 is doing basic research for the book and not merely revising material for a second edition. Furthermore no copy of an 1809 edition appears in any library catalogue that we have consulted (most of which, however, do list the 1815 edition), and the 1815 edition which we have examined, in The New York Public Library, gives no indication of being a second edition. Hence, we may take it that the book first appeared in 1815 and that Godwin was working on it as early as May 1813. The myth of an 1809 edition was apparently started by Kegan Paul's comment [in *Godwin,* II, 177, provided above]. . . . But although it may be that Godwin did some work on the book in 1809 it was certainly not published in that year.

Mary's language in this letter pertaining to the subject—"Godwin has just pub-[li]shed a new book" and "Wordsworth has just now looked into it"—strengthens the probability that the book first appeared in 1815.

11. Evidently "Artegal and Elidure." The loss about which Mary Lamb writes would seem to have been temporary and of the notebook, now in the Wordsworth Library, Grasmere, formed of MS. 3 of "The Waggoner," MS. 6 of "Peter Bell, a Tale in Verse," and one of the three manuscripts known to Ernest de Selincourt of "Artegal and Elidure." (See *Wordsworth's Poetical Works* [1940–1949], II, 498, 529, and 469.) Perhaps the notebook was in "the unfortunate Portmanteau," lost upon the Wordsworths' arrival in London, about which Mary Wordsworth had written Thomas Monkhouse (see my Vol. II, Letter 164, note 3) on Sunday morning, May 7, 1815. That letter, mistakenly shown as postmarked May 8, 1816, is published in *The Letters of Mary Wordsworth, 1800–1855,* ed. Mary E. Burton (Oxford: The Clarendon Press, 1958), pp. 30–31.

12. From Lamb. About the picture by George Dawe ("Daa' ") of Eliza O'Neill see note 2 to the preceding letter.

13. That of the divine and educationalist (and pensioner of the East India Company) Dr. Andrew Bell (1753–1832), the founder of the Madras, or monitorial, system of education. Southey and his second wife—the poetess born Caroline Anne Bowles (1786–1854)—were to write and edit, respectively, the first volume and Southey's son Charles Cuthbert (see my Vol. I, Letter 19, note 13) was to write the second and third volumes of *The Life of the Rev. Andrew Bell . . . Prebendary of Westminster, and Master of Sherburn Hospital, Durham. Comprising the History of the Rise and Progress of the System of Mutual Tuition* (1844). The remark, below, that "Wordsworth is going to be Knighted" is more nonsense, possibly inspired by Wordsworth's close association with Sir George Howland Beaumont, to whom *Poems by William Wordsworth* (1815) is dedicated, and with William Lowther, Lord Lonsdale.

14. Brent. The allusions in the next sentence are to Charlotte Brent and Sara Hutchinson. What Lamb intends by the dash in the sentence following that one is not known. Sara Hutchinson, though not of Welsh ancestry, had been living off and on for five years with her brother Thomas at Hindwell, Radnorshire, Wales. See Letter 256, notes 1 and 2.

15. One-half of the last line has been cut away, probably for its signature.

297. *C. L. to Montagu*

4 Inner Temple Lan[e]
20th. June 1815

Dear Sir,

You were pleased to express an interest in what I related to you of the case of poor **White,**[1] and a desire to have the particulars of it more fully stated. He has a wife and four children to support from a precarious income of 25 shillings a week from a situation as copying clerk in the office of Mr. Blackstock in Kings Bench Walks, which he holds, as I apprehend, entirely from the charity of his employer. He has formerly filled leading situations in the offices of very respectable Solicitors, who have been obliged successively to discharge him on account of severe **fits** to which he is liable, and which have latterly increased to a most pitiable degree. I have known him from a child, and was his schoolfellow at Christs Hospital. He was all his life subject to this malady, and the perpetual anxiety about it impressed a singularly old look upon his countenance when a child. The same care-worn features have accompanied him through life. He is and always was as steady as it is possible for a h[u]man [creature to be, but][2] this cruel infirmity has always made war against him. He is the most broken down creature I ever saw. He can never tell at what time to expect these dreadful visitations, but they come upon him in the streets, or wherever he chances to be, sometimes twice or three times in a day. To serve him in his own line of profession with these terrible disadvantages against him seems quite out of the question, however ready your goodness might be to attempt it; but if anything could be done for his family,— if a presentation could be procured for one of his boys to Christs Hospital (where the father was brought up) it would be conferring a most valuable benefit, and help to lighten a part of the miserable burden which life has always proved to my poor friend.— I cannot forbear mentioning the affecting way in which he apologized to me for having a wife & family. He said that people might wonder with an infirmity like his always upon him he should chuse to involve others in his calamity, but indeed the very forlornness of his condition had made it more necessary for him than for other persons [that someone might still] feel an [i]nterest in taking care of & nursing him. I am sure [to] you no excuse will be necessary, but I thought his plea was irresistible.—

With every thanks to you for the kind concern you take in this poor mans calamity, I remain,

Dear Sir,
Yours truly
[. . .]³

B. Montagu Esqr—

MS: Koopman Collection, Brown University Library, Providence, R.I. Pub.: David Bonnell Green, "A New Letter of Charles Lamb to Basil Montagu," *Huntington Library Quarterly,* 31 (February 1968), 199–200. Address: [B.] M[ontag]u [Esq]r/[Lincolns] Inn.

1. Thomas White, of whom (it has been presumed) Lamb had written to Montagu in a letter of March 30, 1814 (Letter 275). White's wife and children, mentioned below, have not been identified. White's employer was Thomas Blackstock (d. 1833), who was from 1800 to 1833 a solicitor and a commissioner for taking affidavits in the county palatine of Lancaster, whose office in 1815 was at 4 King's Bench Walk, Inner Temple. Blackstock is noticed in *Clarke's New Law List,* ed. Samuel Hill (London: W. Clarke and Sons, 1815), p. 47, and his death recorded in the *Gentleman's Magazine,* N.S. 1 (January 1834), 116.

2. A conjectural passage, like the one within square brackets near the end of the paragraph, offered in the article cited in the source note to this letter. The words of Lamb have been lost as a result of the wearing or tearing away of portions of the lower edges of his folio sheet.

3. "This is the writing of Charles Lamb—" reads a notation below a cutout at this point in the leaf. "Some friend requested the signature & I gave [?] it to him/ B Montagu."

PART IX

Letters 298–331
4 Inner Temple Lane, Inner Temple
August 9, 1815 — October 1817?

298. *C. L. to William Wordsworth*

9th Aug 1815

Dear Wordsworth,

We acknowlege with pride the receit of both your handwritings,[1] and desire to be ever had in kindly remembrance by you both & by Dorothy. Miss Hutchinson has just transmitted us a letter containing, among other chearful matter, the annunciation of a child born. Nothing of consequence has turned up in our parts since your departure. Mary and I felt quite queer after your taking leave (you W. W.) of us in St. Giles's.[2] We wishd we had seen more of you, but felt we had scarce been sufficiently acknowleging for the share we had enjoyed of your company. We felt as if we had been not enough *expressive* of our pleasure. But our manners *both* are a little too much on this side of too-much-cordiality. We want presence of mind and presence of heart. What we feel comes too late like an after thought impromptu. But perhaps you observed nothing of that which we have been painfully conscious of and are every day in our intercourse with those we stand affected to through all the degrees of love. Robinson is on the Circuit.[3] Our Pangyrist I thought had forgotten one of the objects of his youthful admiration, but I was agreeably removed from that scruple by the laundress knocking at my door this morning almost before I was up with a present of fruit from my young friend &c———. There is something inexpressibly pleasant to me in these *presents*. Be it fruit, or fowl, or brawn, or *what not*. *Books* are a legitimate cause of acceptance. If presents be not the soul of friendship,[4] undoubtedly they are the most spiritual part of the body of that intercourse. There is too much narrowness of thinking in this point. The punctilio of acceptance methinks is too confined and straitlaced. I could be content to receive money, or clothes, or a joint of meat from a friend; why should he not send me a dinner as well as a dessert? I would taste him in the beasts of the field and thro' all creation. Therefore did the basket of fruit of the juvenile Talfourd not displease me. Not that I have any thoughts of bartering or reciprocating these things. To send him any thing in return would be to reflect suspicion of mercenariness upon what I know he meant a free will offering. Let him overcome me in bounty. In this strife a generous nature loves to be overcome. Alsager[5] (whom you term **Alsinger**—and indeed he is rather *singer* than *sager,* no reflection upon his naturals neither) is well and in harmony with himself & the world. I dont know how he and those of his constitution keep their nerves so nicely balanced as they do. Or have they any? or are they made of packthread? He is proof against weather, ingratitude, meat under done, every weapon of fate. I have just now a jagged end of a tooth pricking against my tongue, which meets it half way in a wantonness of provocation, and there they go at it, the tongue pricking itself like the viper against the file, and the tooth galling all the gum inside & out to torture, tongue & tooth, tooth & tongue, hard at [it], and I to pay the reckoning, till all my mouth is as hot as brimstone, & I'd venture the roof of my mouth that at this moment, at which I conjecture my full-happinessed friend is picking his crackers, that not one of the double rows of ivory in his privileged mouth has as much as a flaw in it, but all perform their functions, & having performed it, expect to be picked (luxurious steeds!) & rubbed down. I dont think he could be robbed, or could have his house set on fire, or ever want money. I have heard him express a similar opinion of his own impassibility. I keep acting here Heautontimorumenos.[6] M. Burney has been to Calais & has come home a travelld monsieur. He speaks nothing but the Gallic Idiom. Field is on circuit. So now I believe I have given account of most that you saw at our cabin. Have you seen a curious letter in Morn Chron by C. Ll. the Genius of Absurdity respecting Bonapartes suing out his Habeas Corpus. That man is his own **Moon.** He has no need of ascending into that gentle planet for mild influences. You wish me some of your leisure. I have a glimmering aspect, a chink-light of liberty before me which I pray God prove not fallacious. My remonstrances have stirred up others to remonstrate, and altogether there is a plan for separating certain parts of business from our department, which if it take place will produce me more time, i.e. my evenings free. It may be a means of placing me in a more conspicuous situation which will knock at my nerves another way, but I wait the issue in submission. If I can but begin my own day at 4 oClock in the afternoon, I shall think myself to have Eden days of peace & liberty to what I have had.

As you say, how a man can fill 3 volumes up with an Essay on the Drama[7] is wonderful. I am sure a very few sheets would hold all I had to say on the subject, and yet I dare say ********** as **Von Slagel** ***. Did you ever read Charron on Wisdom? or Patrick's Pilgrim? if neither, you have two great pleasures to come. I mean some day to attack Caryl on Job, six Folios. What any man can write, surely I may read.[8] If I do but get rid of auditing Warehousekeepers Accts. & get no worse-harassing task in the place of it, what a Lord of Liberty I shall be. I shall dance & skip and make mouths at the invisible event, and pick the thorns out of my pillow & throw em at rich mens night caps, & talk blank verse hoity toity, and sing a **Clerk I** was in **London** Gay, ban, ban, Ca-caliban, like the emancipated monster & go where I like up this street or down that ally——

Adieu & pray that it may be my luck: Good be to you all.

C Lamb

MS: University of Texas Library. Pub.: Talfourd (1837), II, 6–9; Talfourd (1848), II, 64–66; Sala, I, 278–281; Purnell, I, 278–281; Fitzgerald, II, 113–116; Hazlitt, I, 447–449; Ainger (1888), I, 294–297; Ainger (1900), II, 236–240; Macdonald, I, 363–365; Ainger (1904), I, 351–354; Harper, IV, 45–49; Lucas (1905), VI, 469–471; Lucas (1912), V, 495–497; Lucas (1935), II, 168–170. Address: W Wordsworth Esqr/Rydale Mount/near Kendal/Westmorland. Postmark: [August] 9, 1815.

1. The Lambs (writes Lamb) "acknowlege . . . receit" of a letter or letters now not recovered. The letter mentioned below, presumably Sara Hutchinson's, now also not recovered, announced the birth, at Hindwell on July 14, 1815, of Thomas and Mary Hutchinson's first child, Thomas (d. 1903). He would serve from 1841 to 1903 as the vicar of Kimbolton, Herefordshire, and be married in 1847 to Emma Sarah Gill (1820–1905), the daughter of a captain in the royal navy.

2. Probably the parish or church of St. Giles-in-the-Fields, Holborn. William and Mary Wordsworth and Sara Hutchinson had left London on Monday, June 19, to visit Thomas and Catherine Clarkson and her family in Bury St. Edmunds. The Wordsworths had left there on June 29 for the Christopher Wordsworths in Bocking (in Essex), Cambridge, the George Howland Beaumonts at Coleorton, and home. Sara Hutchinson had remained in Bury St. Edmunds, intending to return briefly to London, spend a day with Mary Lamb, and be back at Hindwell before Mary Hutchinson had her baby. See *Sara Hutchinson's Letters*, pp. 80–81.

3. A mistake Lamb corrects in the next letter: Robinson toured Holland and Belgium, going mainly to see the battlefield at Waterloo, from August 6 to September 2. A narrative of his experiences is in *H. C. R.'s Diary*, I, 317–322. Lamb and Wordsworth's "Pangyrist," Lamb soon makes clear, is Thomas, later Sir Thomas, Noon Talfourd (1795–1854), who was to become a barrister and a judge, the author of *Ion* (privately circulated in 1835; acted and published in 1836) and less successful tragedies, the coexecutor with the East India House employee Charles Ryle of Lamb's will, and the editor of *The Letters of Charles Lamb, with a Sketch of His Life* and *Final Memorials of Charles Lamb; Consisting Chiefly of His Letters Not before Published, with Sketches of Some of His Companions.* (See my Vol. I, Introduction, pp. lxii–lxvii.) He was born in Reading, Berkshire,

to Edward Talfourd, a well-to-do brewer, and his wife, a daughter of Thomas Noon, the minister of the Independent, or Congregational, chapel at Reading. Thomas Noon Talfourd received his early education in private schools, from 1808 to 1810 in the grammar school established by the Nonconformists in 1807 at Mill Hill, Middlesex, and from 1810 to 1812 in the grammar school at Reading under the headmastership of the educator and author Dr. Richard Valpy (1754–1836). Henry Peter Brougham, later Baron Brougham and Vaux (1778–1868) and lord chancellor of England, perhaps influenced Talfourd in his decision to enter the legal profession. He took rooms in the Inner Temple and in 1813 began to read law in the office, contiguous to the Lambs' apartment, of the barrister, special pleader, and writer of law manuals the elder Joseph Chitty (1776–1841). Talfourd made the acquaintance of Barron Field, who encouraged in him an enthusiasm for Wordsworth's poetry. Field introduced Talfourd, toward the end of 1814, to Lamb's *John Woodvil* and some of Lamb's poems and essays. In the course of his walks Talfourd searched the bookstalls and libraries for a copy of Lamb's *Rosamund Gray,* found one in a circulating library near Holborn, and became so captivated by its freshness, beauty, and morality that his "curiosity to see its author rose almost to the height of pain" (*The Letters of Charles Lamb, with a Sketch of His Life* [Boston: Dana Estes, n.d.], I, 256—one of the American editions of the work abbreviated in this edition of Lamb letters as "Talfourd [1837]"). Talfourd's curiosity was gratified in the beginning of 1815, when William Evans (d. 1826) invited Lamb and Talfourd to dinner. Lamb and William Evans (not the William Evans identified in my Vol. I, Letter 3, note 29, and mentioned outside the parentheses in Letter 243, note 4) knew each other through their association with the East India Company—Evans had joined it as a baggage agent in 1804 and become an assistant baggage-warehouse keeper in 1808 and baggage-warehouse keeper in 1812. Talfourd and Evans knew each other through their association with *The Pamphleteer*—Talfourd was one of its contributors, Evans was one of its proprietors, and the editor and printer Abraham John Valpy (see my Vol. I, Letter 5, note 5), a son of the Reading schoolmaster under whom Talfourd had studied, was its printer. Although his duties for Chitty prevented Talfourd from attending the dinner, he did go at ten that evening to Evans' Weymouth Street address, met Lamb as Lamb was preparing to leave, and chatted with him for a half-hour there, while they strolled back to the Inner Temple, and until two in the morning in the Lambs' apartment. They did not see one another again until there appeared Talfourd's "An Attempt to Estimate the Poetical Talent of the Present Age, Including a Sketch of the History of Poetry, and Characters of Southey, Crabbe, Scott, Moore, Lord Byron, Campbell, Lamb, Coleridge, and, Wordsworth," in *The Pamphleteer,* 5 (May 1815), 413–471. Then Lamb, excited by the praise Talfourd had given him and by the company in which Talfourd had placed him, "came almost breathless into the office," Talfourd recalled, "and proposed to give me what I should have chosen as the greatest of all possible honors and delights—an introduction to Wordsworth, who I learned, with a palpitating heart, was actually at the next door. I hurried out with my kind conductor, and a minute after was presented by Lamb to the person whom in all the world I venerated most, with this preface:—'Wordsworth, give me leave to introduce to you my only admirer' " (*The Letters of Charles Lamb* [the edition fully cited earlier in this note], I, 259). Talfourd thereafter became a regular member of the Lambs' circle of friends. He left Chitty's office and tuition in 1817, earned a living of sorts into 1821 by pleading the cases sent his way and by writing—for *The Champion,* the *Edinburgh Review,* the *Encyclopaedia Metropolitana,* the *London Magazine,* the *Monthly Repository,* the *New Monthly Magazine* (whose theater section he conducted from February 1820 through March 1831), the *Retrospective Review*—and in February 1821 was called to the bar at the Middle Temple and admitted to the Oxford circuit. Probably in late 1821, certainly by

January 1822, Robinson, to whom Talfourd had come in February 1813 with a letter of introduction from a founder of the *Monthly Repository,* the politician and miscellaneous writer John Towill Rutt (1760–1841), had secured extra employment for Talfourd as a legal reporter on the Oxford circuit and a drama critic for the *Times.* Robinson did so at Talfourd's request in order that Talfourd could afford to be married. In August 1822 he was married, to Rachel, the eldest daughter of Rutt and the former Rachel Pattisson. Talfourd gradually acquired a limited but successful practice before the bar and a sound though not renowned reputation. He was made a serjeant at law in 1833 and elected a member of Parliament for Reading in 1835 and 1837. He lost his seat in Parliament in 1841, lost a celebrated case as well. For then he defended Edward Moxon against the charge of blasphemous libel for having published, in 1840, an edition of the poems of Shelley containing the unexpurgated text of *Queen Mab.* The Crown based its argument largely upon readings from *Queen Mab,* swaying for the Crown the jury but not Lord Chief Justice Thomas Denman, first Baron Denman (1779–1854), the judge in the case, who refused to punish Moxon. On June 28 Talfourd completed revising the argument he had presented—eloquently and conclusively, thought Mary Shelley among others—and permitted Moxon to publish it, as *Speech for the Defendant, in the Prosecution of the Queen v. Moxon, for the Publication of Shelley's Works. Delivered in the Court of Queen's Bench, June 23, 1841, and Revised.* Talfourd was returned to Parliament for Reading in 1847, was elevated to judge of the court of common pleas in 1849, and died of apoplexy, in Stafford, Staffordshire, suffered while charging its grand jury. He was survived by his wife and some of their children, among them Francis (1828–1862), the eldest son, who gained recognition as an author of light dramatic works. Among the children who had predeceased their father was Charles Lamb Talfourd (1829–1835). Several of Thomas Noon Talfourd's works not already mentioned are *Poems on Various Subjects, Including a Poem on the Education of the Poor; an Indian Tale; and the Offering of Isaac, a Sacred Drama* (1811); "Memoir of the Life and Writings of Mrs. Radcliffe," in Ann Radcliffe's *Gaston de Blondeville* (4 vols.; 1826); "Thoughts upon the Intellectual Character of the Late William Hazlitt," in *Literary Remains of the Late William Hazlitt,* edited by Talfourd and the novelist Edward George Earle Lytton Bulwer, later Bulwer-Lytton, first Baron Lytton (2 vols.; 1836); the tragedies *The Athenian Captive* (performed and published in 1838), *Glencoe; or, the Fate of the Macdonalds* (privately printed in 1839; performed and published in 1840), and *The Castilian* (privately printed in 1853); *Vacation Rambles and Thoughts, Comprising the Recollections of Three Continental Tours. In the Vacations of 1841, 1842, and 1843* (2 vols.; 1845); "Prefatory Memoir of the Late William Frederick Deacon," in *Annette, a Tale* (3 vols.; 1852), by Deacon (1799–1845), a journalist primarily, Talfourd's friend. There are numerous editions of the dramatic and of the critical and miscellaneous writings of Talfourd—*The Dramatic Works . . . To Which Are Added, a Few Sonnets and Verses* (11th ed.; London: E. Moxon, 1852), for example, and *Critical and Miscellaneous Writings . . . With Additional Articles Never before Published in This Country* (3d American ed.; New York: D. Appleton, 1864). Further information about him is in the *DNB;* Robert S. Newdick's "Studies in the Literary Works of Sir Thomas Noon Talfourd, D.C.L." (a Master's thesis, containing a bibliography of Talfourd's literary and other works, Harvard University, 1926) and *The First Life and Letters of Charles Lamb: A Study of Thomas Noon Talfourd as Editor and Biographer* (Columbus: Ohio State University, 1935); *H. C. R. on Books and Writers,* esp. I, 119–121 and 277, and II, 738; William S. Ward's "An Early Champion of Wordsworth: Thomas Noon Talfourd," *Publications of the Modern Language Association of America,* 68 (December 1953), 992–1000; Vera Watson's "Thomas Noon Talfourd and His Friends—I [and] II," in the *TLS* of April 20 and 27, 1956; and William A. Coles's

"Magazine and Other Contributions by Mary Russell Mitford and Thomas Noon Talfourd," *Studies in Bibliography: Papers of the Bibliographical Society of the University of Virginia,* 12 (1959), 218–226.

4. An echo of *Twelfth Night, or What You Will,* I, i, 1: "If music be the food of love . . ." Lamb would return to the theme of presents in 1826 and 1833, in "That We Must Not Look a Gift-horse in the Mouth" and "Thoughts on Presents of Game, &c." (*Works,* II, 261–263; and I, 343–344).

5. Thomas Massa Alsager (1779–1846), who had been a friend of Leigh Hunt, Robinson, and the Lambs since about 1813 and had through Lamb become, in 1815, an acquaintance of Wordsworth and Godwin. (See *Hunt's Autobiography,* II, 12, *H. C. R. on Books and Writers,* I, 133 and 167, and *Godwin,* II, 228–229; see also *Shelley and His Circle,* V, 264–266.) Alsager was the owner of the copy of George Chapman's translation of Homer that would, in 1816, inspire Keats to compose "On First Looking into Chapman's Homer" and was the member of the Surrey Institution probably most responsible for Hazlitt's coming, in 1818 and 1819, to deliver there the lectures afterward published as *Lectures on the English Poets* (1818), *Lectures on the English Comic Writers* (1819), and *Lectures Chiefly on the Dramatic Literature of the Age of Elizabeth* (1820). It is noted in *H. C. R.'s Diary,* I, 310, that Alsager "had, at one time, a manufactory and a bleaching-ground near the King's Bench Prison; but he gave this up, and, being a great lover of music, recommended himself to the *Times* as an amateur reporter on musical matters. He became City Correspondent, and wrote the 'State of the Money Market' for many years. He was also a shareholder in the paper till he had a serious misunderstanding with [John] Walter." It is stated of Alsager in *Men of the Reign: A Biographical Dictionary of Eminent Persons of British and Colonial Birth Who Have Died during the Reign of Queen Victoria,* ed. Thomas Humphry Ward (London: George Routledge and Sons, 1885), p. 19, that "besides being what may be called an advocate of music in the abstract, he showed his enthusiasm in a practical manner, playing, it is said, every instrument in the orchestra, and organising a series of important chamber concerts, at which some of the most renowned players first made their appearance before an English audience. He numbered among his friends many of the most celebrated performers of the day, among them Mendelssohn and [the Bohemian pianist Ignaz] Moscheles, and succeeded in placing on a firm footing in this country [England] the quartets and sonatas of Beethoven." By 1825 Alsager was married (his wife has not been identified), had children, and was flourishing. In 1846 he left the *Times* and thus John Walter (see Vol. II, Letter 107, source note) after an association of twenty-eight years, lost his reason, and died from an inflammation of self-inflicted wounds in the throat. Wordsworth expressed his shock over the suicide to Edward Moxon on November 13, 1846, in a letter in *Wordsworths' Letters,* VI, 1299–1300.

6. "The Self-punisher," or "The Self-tormentor"—the title of a comedy by Terence. Referred to below is the letter in the *Morning Chronicle* of August 2 and 3 by the elder Capell Lofft (see above, Letter 286, note 4), in which he argued that detaining Napoleon on an admiralty ship anchored off the British coast preparatory to deporting him was illegal because Napoleon had been brought "within the limits of British *local* allegiance," that Napoleon should in consequence be considered a temporary British subject, that the ship's captain should in consequence be obliged to surrender Napoleon under the writ of habeas corpus. Napoleon with a small suite of officers had come aboard the *Bellerophon,* stationed off the island of Aix, on July 15, 1815, in order to place himself under the protection of the Crown and the laws of England by placing himself in the custody of Frederick, later Sir Frederick, Lewis Maitland (1777–1839), commander of the *Bellerophon.* She reached England about a week later, putting in first in Tor Bay, afterward in Plymouth harbor. On July 31 Napoleon received in

his stateroom Admiral George Keith Elphinstone, Viscount Keith (1746–1823), and Sir Henry Edward Bunbury, later seventh baronet (1778–1860), undersecretary of state for war, who delivered to him the government decree of deportation to St. Helena. On August 5 the *Bellerophon* and the *Northumberland* rendezvoused in an angry sea, and Napoleon made this address:

I hereby solemnly protest, before God and mankind, against the violence that has been done upon me, and against the violation of my most sacred rights, in dealing forcibly with my person and my liberty. I came on board the *Bellerophon* of my own free will. I am not a prisoner; I am the guest of England. I came, moreover, at the instigation of the captain, who said he had instructions from the Government to receive me and to take me to England with my retinue, if that was agreeable to me. I presented myself in good faith to come and put myself under the protection of the laws of England. Once on board the *Bellerophon*, I was at the hearth of the British nation.

If the Government, in instructing the captain of the *Bellerophon* to receive me and my retinue, merely intended to set a trap for me, it has forfeited its honor and disgraced its flag. If this act is consummated, it will be futile for the British to tell Europe of their fairness, their laws, and their liberties. British honor will have been lost in the hospitality of the *Bellerophon*.

I appeal to History: it will say that an enemy who was at war with the English nation for twenty years came voluntarily—in his misfortune—to seek asylum under its laws. What more striking proof could he have offered of his esteem and trust? But does England respond to such magnanimity? She pretended to reach out a hospitable hand to that enemy, and when he had handed himself over in good faith, she immolated him! [André Castelot, *Napoleon,* tr. Guy Daniels (New York: Harper & Row, 1971), p. 573; quoted by permission of Harper & Row, Publishers, Inc.]

On August 7 Napoleon was transferred to the *Northumberland.* On October 15 she arrived at St. Helena. On October 17 he stepped on land for the first time since he had stepped off it at Aix on July 15.

7. The next sentence indicates the work to be August Wilhelm von Schlegel's 1808 Vienna lectures, published originally as *Über dramatische Kunst und Literatur* (2 vols.; Vol. II in two parts; 1809–1811) and in English as *A Course of Lectures on Dramatic Art and Literature* (2 vols.; 1815). The translator was John Black (1783–1855), a translator of foreign correspondence and reporter for the *Morning Chronicle,* from 1817 to 1843 its editor. In Lucas (1935), II, 171, is the conjecture that the asterisks may represent "I know as muc[h] . . . did." Alluded to below are *De la sagesse* (1601), by the French philosopher Pierre Charron (1541–1603), translated in 1612 by the genealogist Samson Lennard (d. 1633) and in 1697 by George Stanhope (1660–1728), dean of Canterbury; *The Parable of the Pilgrim* (1664), by Simon Patrick (1626–1707), bishop, successively, of Chichester and Ely; and *Commentary on the Book of Job* (12 vols., quarto; 1651–1666), by the Independent divine Joseph Caryl (1602–1673). In 1813, in the essay later titled "[Books with One Idea in Them]" (*Works,* I, 153), Lamb had described *De la sagesse*—probably Lennard's translation (see *Works,* I, 442)—as "a cumbrous piece of formality"; in the same place Lamb had characterized the dullness of *The Parable of the Pilgrim* as "freezing, appalling, petrifying" (though there, additionally, Lamb had written of the one good passage contained in each of the two books). He never did publicly attack *Commentary on the Book of Job.*

8. Cf. "Detached Thoughts on Books and Reading" (*Works,* II, 172): "I have no repugnances. . . . I can read any thing which I call a *book.* There are things in that shape which I cannot allow for such. [Examples of such things follow.] With these exceptions, I can read almost any thing. I bless my stars for a taste so

catholic, so unexcluding." Lamb's "make mouths at the invisible event," below, is truly Shakespeare's, in *Hamlet,* IV, iv, 50. "A Clerk I was in London gay," which Lamb would use as one of the epigraphs to "The Superannuated Man" (*Works,* II, 193), is from the younger George Colman's romantic comedy *Inkle and Yarico* (1787), the song at the end of Act III, Scene i. "'Ban, 'Ban, Ca-Caliban" is in *The Tempest,* II, ii, 184.

299. *C. L. to Southey*

[August 9, 1815]

P. S. my kind love to Mrs. S. Mrs. C.[1] & to all. I had not room at the end—

Dear Southey,

Robinson is not on the Circuit, as I erroneously stated in a letter to W. W. which travels with this, but is gone to Brussels, Ostend, Ghent &c. But his friends the Colliers whom I consulted respecting your friend's fate, remember to have heard him say that Father Pardo[2] had effected his escape (the cunning greasy rogue) and to the best of their belief is at present in Paris. To my thinking it is small matter whether there be one fat friar more or Less in the world. I have rather a taste for clerical Executions, imbibed from early recollections of the fate of the excellent Dodd.[3]

I hear Bonaparte has sued his Habeas Corpus, and the Twelve Judges are now sitting upon it at the Rolls—

Your Boutefoy[4] (Bonfire) must be excellent of its kind. Poet Settle presided at the last great thing of the kind in London, when the Pope was burnt in **form**—. Do you provide any verses on this occasion?

Your fear for Hartleys intellectuals is just and rational. Could not the Chancellor be petititioned to remove him?[5] His Lordship took Mr Betty from under the Paternal wing. I think at least he should go thro' a course of matter of fact with some sober man after the mysteries. Could not he spend a week at Poole's before he goes back to Oxford? Tobin[6] is dead. But there is a man in my Office, a Mr Hedges, who proses it away from morning to night, & never gets beyond corporal & material verities. He'd get these crack brain metaphysics out the young gentlemans head as soon as any one I know. When I cant sleep o'nights I imagine a dialogue with Mr Hedges upon any given subject, & go prosing on in fancy with him, till I either laugh or fall asleep. I have literally found it answer

I am going to stand Godfather,[7] I dont like the business, I cannot muster up decorum for these occasions. I shall certainly disgrace the font. I was at Hazlitts marriage & had like to have been turned out several times during the ceremony. Any thing awful makes me laugh. I misbehaved once at a funeral. Yet I can read about these ceremonies with pious & proper feelings—. The realities of life only seem the mockeries. I fear I must get cured along with Hartley, if not too inveterate—

Dont you think Louis the Desirable[8] is in a sort of a quandary?

After all, Bonaparte is a fine fellow, as my Barber says, and I should not mind standing bareheaded at his table to do him service in his fall. They should have given him Hampton Court or Kensington with a tether extending forty miles round London.[9] Qu. would not the People have ejected the Brunswicks some day in his favor? Well, we shall see— —

C Lamb

MS: Mr. W. Hugh Peal. Pub.: Talfourd (1837), II, 9–11; Sala, I, 206–207; Purnell, I, 206–207; Fitzgerald, II, 58–59; Hazlitt, I, 449–451; Ainger (1888), I, 292–294; Ainger (1900), II, 234–236; Macdonald, I, 366–367; Ainger (1904), I, 349–351; Harper, IV, 43–45; Lucas (1905), VI, 467–469; Lucas (1912), V, 493–494; Lucas (1935), II, 166–167. Address: R. Southey Esq/Keswick/Cumberland. Postmark: August 9, 1815.

1. Mrs. Coleridge. The letter to Wordsworth referred to below is the preceding letter: see there at the reference to note 3.

2. Presumably, the journalist and Augustinian priest Manuel Pardo de Andrade. He wrote sometimes under the pseudonym León de Parma; founded, in 1808, the *Diario de la Coruña;* and compiled *Los guerrilleros gallegos en 1809* (2 vols.; 1892). On July 24, 1811, Robinson had remarked on Southey's having read at the Lambs' a selection of Pardo's sonnets; on December 28, 1811, Southey had asked Robinson if he would lend Pardo's sonnets to the theological writer Joseph Blanco White (1775–1841) for publication in *El Español,* a monthly White conducted and the English government, for nationalistic purposes, circulated. See the *Diccionario bibliográfico de la guerra de la independencia Española (1808–1814)* (Madrid: Biosca, 1952), III, 15–16; *H. C. R. on Books and Writers,* I, 41; and *New Southey Letters,* II, 16.

3. William Dodd. (See Vol. II, Letter 134, note 2.) The Rolls, mentioned in the next paragraph, was the name of the complex of buildings, in Chancery Lane, where were preserved the records of the court of chancery—records today in the Public Record Office—and where the master of the rolls, a member of the court, could hear causes and issue decrees.

4. *Boutefeu* must have been meant—an incendiary; a linstock. The French for "bonfire" is *feu de joie.* On August 23, 1815, Southey was to write his brother Henry Herbert of the bonfire and of the cannon set off and large balls of turpen-

tine-soaked tow set aflame on Skiddaw on August 21 in celebration of the victory, of June 18, at Waterloo. (See *Southey's Correspondence,* IV, 121–122.) Elkanah Settle (1648–1724), the poet mentioned in the next sentence, had been the chief organizer of the procession in London of November 17, 1680—the seventy-second anniversary of the accession of the first Elizabeth to the throne—when the pope was burned in effigy.

5. Could not, that is, Lord Chancellor of England John Scott (see Letter 243, note 2) be "petititioned" to remove David Hartley Coleridge (see Vol. I, Letter 7, note 3) from his father? Samuel Taylor Coleridge's poetic and impressionable son, the elder and more dearly beloved, who had trouble distinguishing fact from fancy and would come to retreat too often and too far from fact into fancy, who would fail as a teacher, wander and write (see note 12 to the next letter), and greatly in advance of his death (in the cottage overlooking Rydal Water mentioned in note 2 to Letter 323) become dependent on others and melancholic, had left the Reverend Mr. John Dawes's Ambleside school in June 1814 and, on May 6, 1815, by means of a fund raised for his university education by Southey and Wordsworth, been afforded enrollment at Merton College, Oxford. There he received a small scholarship and, on February 11, 1819, was to receive his degree. Hartley—the David was dropped when, in 1803, he, Derwent, and their sister, Sara, were baptized—was spending his summer vacation with his father at the Morgans' in Calne and seems not to have gone to Thomas Poole of Nether Stowey before going back to his college in the autumn. An expression of Southey's fear for Hartley survives in a letter Southey had written on May 8, 1815, to the clergyman Neville White, a brother of the poet Henry Kirke White (1785–1806), whose remains—*The Remains of Henry Kirke White, of Nottingham, Late of St. John's College, Cambridge; with an Account of His Life, by Robert Southey* (1807 or 1808)—Southey had edited:

> Hartley is by this time at Oxford, and probably settled at Merton. What will his fate be? I hardly dare ask myself the question . . . ; he takes with him a larger stock of Greek than is often carried to college, a powerful intellect, good principles, and good feelings. But with these he has some dangerous accompaniments; for he is headstrong, violent, perilously disposed to justify whatever he may wish to do, eccentric in all his ways, and willing to persuade himself that there is a merit in eccentricity. But his greatest danger arises from a mournful cause, against which it is impossible to protect, or even to caution him,—it arises from his father. Hartley is able to comprehend the powers of his father's mind, and has for it all that veneration which it is both natural and proper that he should feel. The conduct of the father is, of course, a subject on which no one would speak to the son; and Hartley, I believe, contrives to keep it out of his own sight; but if Coleridge should take it in his head to send for the boy to pass any of his vacations with him, there is the most imminent danger of his unsettling his mind upon the most important subjects, and the end would be utter and irremediable ruin. For Coleridge, totally regardless of all consequences, will lead him into all the depths and mazes of metaphysics: he would root up from his mind, without intending it, all established principles; and if he should succeed in establishing others in their place, with one of Hartley's ardour and sincerity, they would never serve for the practical purposes of society, and he would be thrown out from the only profession or way of life for which he is qualified. This you see it is absolutely impossible to prevent. I know but too well, and Coleridge also knows, what an evil it is to be thus as it were cut adrift upon the sea of life; but experience is lost upon him. [*Selections from the Letters of Robert Southey,* ed. John Wood Warter (London: Longman *et al.,* 1856), II, 408–409; good works on Hartley are *Hartley Coleridge* and Grace Evelyn

Griggs and Earl Leslie Griggs's edition of *Letters of Hartley Coleridge* (London: Oxford University Press: Humphrey Milford, 1936).]

Lamb writes below of William Henry West Betty (identified in Vol. II, Letter 208, note 10), who had concluded his career as a boy actor on March 26, 1808, at Bath. After having been tutored by the Reverend Mr. Wollaston of Bath, once a master of the Charterhouse school (in London), Betty, on July 5, 1808, had entered Christ's College, Cambridge. An illness of his father, William Henry Betty (d. 1811), of Pym's Farm, near Wem, Shropshire, caused the younger Betty to withdraw from Christ's College at Christmas 1810. The death of his father caused those concerned about the son to propose, probably in substantial part because of the fortune he had earned as a performer, that he be made a ward of Lord Chancellor Scott. It would appear, however, particularly from Giles Playfair's *The Prodigy; a Study of the Strange Life of Master Betty* (London: Secker & Warburg, 1967), p. 83, and John Peile's *Biographical Register of Christ's College, 1505–1905, and of the Earlier Foundation, God's House, 1448–1505* (Cambridge: Cambridge University Press, 1910), II, 362, that Scott did not become the guardian of Betty, who, on February 15, 1812, returned to the stage at Bath. Donald Missen, archivist of Christ's College, helped greatly with the portion of this note treating of Betty.

6. James Webbe Tobin. (See Vol. II, Letter 146, note 2.) Henry Hedges (1765?–1849), the man Lamb mentions next, was appointed an extra clerk in the East India House in 1781, made an established clerk in its accountant general's office in 1782, and retired in November 1817. Some account of Hedges is in Samuel McKechnie's "Charles Lamb of the India House," *Notes and Queries,* 192 (February 8, 1947), 54 and 55.

7. Probably to the great-nephew of Charles and Mary to whom Mary, as she writes near the end of her share of the next letter, "was godmother the other day." She refers, presumably, to the son of a stepchild of her brother John, who, "after many years of confident bachelorhood, married a widow, a Mrs. Isaac Dowden [d. 1825], with one or more children" (*The Life of Lamb,* II, 82; see II, 149). The sentiment Charles confesses in this paragraph he would publicly confess in a paragraph in "The Wedding," where the occasion recalled is his having given in marriage Sarah (see my Vol. II, Letter 141, note 7), the daughter of the James Burneys:

> I do not know what business I have to be present in solemn places. I cannot divest me of an unseasonable disposition to levity upon the most awful occasions. I was never cut out for a public functionary. Ceremony and I have long shaken hands; but I could not resist the importunities of the young lady's father, whose gout unhappily confined him at home, to act as parent on this occasion, and *give away the bride.* Something ludicrous occurred to me at this most serious of all moments—a sense of my unfitness to have the disposal, even in imagination, of the sweet young creature beside me. I fear I was betrayed to some lightness, for the awful eye of the parson—and the rector's eye of Saint Mildred's in the Poultry [the church, razed in 1872, of St. Mildred the Virgin, Poultry, London] is no trifle of a rebuke—was upon me in an instant, souring my incipient jest to the tristful severities of a funeral. [*Works,* II, 241]

About the marriage ceremony of Hazlitt and Sarah Stoddart see my Vol. II, Letter 225, note 1.

8. Louis XVIII, whom the Royalists called Louis le Désiré. His reign of France, suppressed when the senate, on May 18, 1804, proclaimed Napoleon emperor of the French, had begun its revival following Napoleon's retreat from Moscow and the defeats of 1813. The reign of Louis subsisted, at times thereafter infirmly, to his death, on September 16, 1824.

9. On July 14, 1815, the day before he had come aboard the *Bellerophon,* Napoleon had dictated this statement addressed to her commander, Maitland: "If I am to go to England, I would like to reside in a country house some ten or twelve leagues from London, where I would like to arrive as much incognito as possible" (André Castelot, *Napoleon,* tr. Guy Daniels [New York: Harper & Row, 1971], p. 566). The Brunswicks, mentioned below, are those of the house of Brunswick-Lüneburg, from which have succeeded the hereditary heirs to the throne of the sovereign duchy of Brunswick, Germany. Karl Wilhelm Ferdinand, Duke of Brunswick (1735–1806), and his son and successor, Friedrich Wilhelm (1771–1815), had been favorites of their countrymen and virulent enemies of Napoleon and the Napoleonic domination of Germany.

300. *M. A. L. to Mrs. Morgan, with a note from C. L. to Morgan, Mrs. Morgan, Charlotte Brent, and Coleridge*
Our Thursday [August 17–Sunday or
Monday, August 20 or 21, 1815]

My dear friend

I cannot express what I felt at receiving your letter better than in your own kind words, it was truly "a real comfort to me."[1] Why do we not write often to each other? Whenever you wish to hear how we are going on, and I flatter myself that is not seldom, do pray sit down and treat *us* with a few lines and I will promise you an answer with a week. . *I* am just now interrupted by the coming in of Mrs Reynolds. She desires her love, respects I believe it is and hopes you will remember her, she says she knows Miss Brent will recollect her, why she builds more on her memory than yours I cannot guess and think without foundation, so lively a recollection as you have of our thursdays of which she always makes a part.

Last saturday[2] was the grand feast day of the India House Clerks. I think you must have heard Charles talk of his yearly turtle feast. . He has been lately much wearied with with work, and glad to get rid of all connected with it he used saturday, the feast day being a holiday, and borrowed the monday following, and we set off on the outside of the Cambridge Coach from Fetter Lane at eight Oclock and were driven into Cambridge in great triumph by Hell Fire Dick[3] five minutes before three—Richard is in high reputation— —he is private tutor to the Whip Club. Journeys used to be tedious torments to me but seated out in the open air I enjoyed every mile of the way——the first twenty miles was particularly pleasing to me having been accustomed to go so far on that road in the Ware Stage Coach to visit my Grandmother in the days of other times.

In my life I never spent so many pleasant hours together as I did at Cambridge. We were walking the whole time.—— out of one College into the other. If you ask me which I like best I must make such an answer as your little two years old girl⁴ would being the traditionary unoffending reply to all curious enquirers—"Both." I liked them all best. The little gloomy ones because they were little gloomy ones. I felt as if I could live and die in them and never speak again—and the fine grand Trinity College Oh how fine it was!— and King College Chapel What a place—! I heard the Cathedral service there, and having been no great church-goer of late years *that* and the painted windows and the general effect of the whole thing affected me wonderfully.

I certainly like, St John's College best——I had seen least of it having only been over it once, so, on the morning we returned I got up at six oClock and wandered into it by myself——by myself indeed for there was nothing alive but one cat who followed me all about.* Then I went over Trinity but nothing hailed me there not ever⁵ a cat.

On the sunday we met with a pleasant thing. We had been congratulating each other that we had come alone to enjoy as the miser his feast, all our sights greedily to ourselves, but having seen all we began to grow flat and wish for this and tother body with us when we were accosted by a young gownsman⁶ whose face we knew but where or how we had seen him we could not tell and were obliged to ask his name. He proved to be a youth we had seen twice at a friend's who you do not know. He turned out a very pleasant fellow——. Shewed us the insides of places. We took him home to our Inn to dinner and we drank tea with him in such a delicious college room and then he supped with us, but we made our meals as short as possible to lose no time and walked our young conductor almost off his legs, even when the fried eels were ready for supper and coming up we had a message from a man we had bribed that then we might see Oliver Cromwell⁷ who was *not at home* when we had been to see him and out we went again to make him a visit by candlelight—and so ended our sights. When we were setting out in the morning our new friend came to bid us good-bye and rode to Trompinton with [us]—I never saw a creature so happy as he was the whole time he was with [us], but most especially so when Charles had his pipe in his mouth after supper. He said we had put him in such good spirits he should certainly pass an examination well that he is to go through in six weeks in order to quality[8] himself to get a fellowship.—

Returning home down old Fetter Lane I could hardly keep from crying to think it was all over————Jesus College where Coleridge was——the barbers shop where Manning was——the house Lloyd lived in—the rooms where Charles was with Franklin. I peeped into the window the room was deserted, old chairs standing about in disorder they seemed to have stood there ever since they had sat in them.— I write sad nonsense about these things, but I wish you had heard Charles talk his nonsense over & over again about his first visit to Franklin & how he then first felt himself commencing gentleman & had eggs for breakfast.————

Thank you many times for your kind wishes that I could come & see you. I dare make no promise but I have a notion which almost amounts to a hope that some of these days when I feel very stout I shall surprize you with the sight of me. If ever we do come it will be without giving you notice. I am even thinking if you can lend us Shirts and Che——how do you spell shifts?[9] for the preparation & the very trifling packing up of a poor little trunk aided by the minutely cry of Charles a week beforehand of *"have you got all ready?* **Do you think you can be able to pack up our things?"** has always been the chief thing that has hurt me.

At the *Bolt* & *Tun*[10] in Fleet Street there is always a great board put out with monstrous large letters "A Bath Coach sets out here every day." It always seems a tantalizing invitation to come & see you. How I do wish we could all meet again any how or any wise—. Accept a general love, dearly I love you all. tell dear Charlotte she must be not grateful but Gratidude herself [if] she talks of our attentions to her, we saw in a manner nothing of [her] when she was in town. We never lose a friend in any away without suffering deadly pangs of *Remorse*[11] that we have not made much of our treasure while we had it, and something of this sort I recollect attending the departure of Miss Brent. I wish she was now sitting by me, singing "Jockey to the fair." she was a good girl to buy that song, those are the sort of things I call attentions. I am glad Hartley Coleridge is with you. I should much like to see him. I wonder if I shall ever see Derwent again[12]—I was god-

mother the other day to my great nephew and fill a crying great drops
all over his fine christening robe. I will not say one word for Charles
not even send his love to you for he promised to write a line and if he
does not I will do nothing for him. I have used up all the paper because I thing[13] it will go plain else, for Miss Kelly is going to sing this
evening in a new opera at our little Liceum Threatre and I suspect we
shall go there as soon as we have dined.— Alas we dine not now till
half past four. Pray God bless you and Coleridge & Morgan & Charlotte
and Hartley. Once more love to you all—. Believe me ever to be

Your affectionate friend
M Lamb

Kiss your little two-year-old for me.

pray excuse ruled paper, I write so comfortably upon it

Dear Four,[14]

Your Letter has delighted us, in the vehicle of Mrs. Morgans neat
handwriting. (Morgan might have furnished the sense but not the
sentiment. Miss Brent might have supplied the grammar, but I think
scarcely the spelling. S[. Coleridge (?)] might have furnished sense
sentiment grammar & spelling, but then what characters it would have
been written in? Apropos—this to Mrs. M's especial ear—*V*acation
another time, not *vocation.* when you speak of a young gentleman's
absence from college, vacation is as much as to say cessation from
business or having nothing to do, but vocation is simply a calling to do
or exercise yourself about something. However when you have any
doubt the best way is to leave the second letter dubious as this *vocation,*[15] which may indifferently stand for either as the reader's charity
shall suggest meaning.) When I wrote dear Four at the beginning, It
had slipt me that Mr Hartley (as I suppose he must be call'd now)
had made a **quintuple** alliance of you. Pray our kindest remembrance
to him & our hopes to see him in the great city.[16] Tell Colerge. (the
father) I adjure him by all the delicacies of poetry & friendship that
in the coming selection of his poems he will leave out that exquisite
morceau about the blasted son of a presbyterian bitch. What my
finger recoils from manuscribing, his pen should surely be slow to
print. Tell him it is not wit, it is not anything, but newspaper coarse-
ness. If he will commit the superintendce. to me I will leave out also
fire famine & pestilence, because it is the most popular among a sort of

people I dont care for his pleasing. With these reservations I shall hail his book & preface and wish 'em longer. I fear Xtobel is not in the company.— ⟨As long as Morgan confines himself to a little amateur theatricalship,[17] I have a kind of sympathy with him, but I hope to God he will not take to acting as a profession. So few attain eminence, & of those who do, many like Foote & Kean take to drinking & I cannot bear to think of a st[rolling (?)] life for him.⟩

My dear friends all adieu—

Yours (not very happy in himself)
C Lamb

*We have three black kittens. they are all to be kept. I wish I could send you one or two of them.— [By Mary.—Ed.]

MS: British Museum, London. Pub.: W. Braekman, "Two Hitherto Unpublished Letters of Charles and Mary Lamb to the Morgans," *English Studies*, 44 (1963), 109–111. Address: Mrs Morgan/Calne/Wiltshire. Postmark: August 21, 1815. That postmark, the fourth and eleventh paragraphs in the next letter, and the third sentence in note 13 to this letter bear on the dating of this letter.

1. Presumably, from Mrs. Morgan's letter to Mary. From it she does quote, as the second paragraph in the next letter. Perhaps Mary Lamb should have written "within a week" instead of "with a week" (below); perhaps what she did write is perfect. About Mrs. Elizabeth Reynolds see Vol. I, Introduction, pp. xxviii–xxix.

2. August 12.

3. Richard Vaughan, a notable Cambridge sport once the landlord of The Bell, Cambridge, who, having lost his license to operate the inn because of some improper influence of his on the undergraduates who frequented it, had taken to driving the *Telegraph* stagecoach from Cambridge halfway to London in the mornings and driving it back in the afternoons. The Reverend Mr. J. Richardson wrote of him in *Recollections, Political, Literary, Dramatic, and Miscellaneous, of the Last Half-century* (2 vols. in 1; London: C. Mitchell, 1856), I, 177–180, from which Lucas drew in *At the Shrine of St. Charles,* pp. 80–81. About the Whip Club, mentioned below, see Letter 250, the last two sentences in note 4.

4. Her given name has not been determined. This passage and the first of Mary's postscripts to this letter appear to contain the only references to a child of the Morgans in the literature pertaining to them. Braekman has pointed out on pages 112–113 of the article cited in the source note to this letter that several of the letters Coleridge had written during the autumn of 1813 do, however, show Mrs. Morgan then to have been unwell, possibly as a result of her having borne a child. See *Coleridge's Letters,* III, 443, 453, 457, 458, 461, and 464.

5. For "even," maybe. See the next letter, seventh paragraph.

6. Unidentified. Mary explains in the eighth paragraph in the next letter that she and Lamb had seen him twice at Alsager's.

7. The crayon portrait of Cromwell, confidently attributed to Samuel Cooper (identified in Vol. II, Letter 193, note 5), donated in 1766 to Sidney Sussex College, Cambridge. By "Trompinton," or "Trompinten," below, Mary meant Trumpington, Cambridgeshire.

8. For "qualify." In the eighth paragraph in the next letter Mary gets it right. Near the beginning of the next paragraph in this letter Mary writes of Mr.

Crisp's barber shop, at 3 St. Mary's Passage, above which were lodgings once Manning's; of Mr. Styles's house, presumably, in Jesus Lane, in which the younger Charles Lloyds had lived (see Vol. I, Letter 53, source note, and Letter 10, note 4); and of the rooms where Lamb, probably in the early or middle 1790s, had visited with his former schoolfellow Frederick William Franklin (1774–1836). "Fine, frank-hearted Fr——," as he is designated in "Christ's Hospital Five and Thirty Years Ago" (*Works*, II, 22), the son of Frederick Franklin of Westminster, had proceeded from Christ's Hospital to Pembroke College, Cambridge, in 1793, received his B.A. in 1797 and his M.A. in 1800, and received ordination in London as a priest in 1802. He was an assistant master of Christ's Hospital Junior School in Hertford from 1801 to 1827 and the vicar of Ugley, Essex, in 1816. He was the vicar of Horley, Surrey, from 1817 to 1827 and of Albrighton, Shropshire, from 1827 to 1836. For some unspecified time he was in addition the domestic chaplain to Sir Charles Chetwynd Talbot, second Earl Talbot of Hensol (1777–1849).

9. "Chemises." The Lambs spent a month or so with the Morgans in Calne during June and July 1816. See Letters 318–320 and 322.

10. Properly, The Bolt-in-Tun.

11. An allusion to Coleridge's *Remorse. A Tragedy, in Five Acts* and possibly a deliberate paraphrase of its V, i, 167—". . . one pang of true remorse!" In Coleridge's letter to the Devises, Wiltshire, surgeon R. H. Brabant of June 22, 1815 (*Coleridge's Letters*, IV, 577), is the remark that a traveling company of actors managed by one Mr. Falkner was about to perform the play in Calne; in the portion of Mrs. Morgan's letter to Mary quoted as the second paragraph in the next letter is a comment on the performance. It is not known when Charlotte Brent was last in London. "Jockey to the Fair," mentioned below, is an eighteenth-century folk song. Minnie Earl Sears listed it in *Song Index* (New York: Wilson, 1926), p. 286.

12. Derwent Coleridge (see Vol. I, Letter 75, note 3), who was still a pupil of the Reverend Mr. Dawes in Ambleside, would from the autumn of 1817 to December 1819 be the tutor in the Hopwood family of Lancashire and in May 1820 be entered at St. John's College, Cambridge, where he earned his B.A. in 1824 and his M.A. in 1829. In 1825 he accepted church orders and an appointment as the master of the grammar school in Helston, Cornwall. While there he wrote *The Scriptural Character of the English Church* (1839). In 1841 he left Helston to become the first principal of St. Mark's College, Chelsea. While there he prepared *Poems by Hartley Coleridge, with a Memoir of His Life by His Brother* (*Derwent Coleridge*) (1851) and edited *Essays and Marginalia. By Hartley Coleridge* (1851) and *Lives of Northern Worthies. By Hartley Coleridge* (1852). In 1864 Derwent left Chelsea for the rectorate of Hanwell, Middlesex. He resigned in 1880 and with his wife, the former Mary Pridham, to whom he was married in 1827, retired to Torquay, where he died. Mary intended "fell" for "fill," below.

13. For "think." Frances Maria Kelly (1790–1882), whom Mary names below, was in August 1815 performing at the Lyceum in *My Aunt* and *Sharp and Flat,* both farces, the former by one who has not been identified, the latter by one Lawler; in *Rich and Poor,* a farce or an opera by the singer and composer Charles Edward Horn (1786–1849); and in *The Castle of Andalusia* and *The King's Proxy, or Judge for Yourself,* both comic operas, the former by the actor and dramatist John O'Keeffe (1747–1833), the latter jointly by the dramatist Samuel James Arnold (see Letter 250, note 4) and the vocalist, instrumentalist, and composer Thomas Simpson Cooke (1782–1848). The last of those works, because it is advertised in the *Times* as a "new comic opera" a few days before and on the day of its opening (Saturday, August 19), and noticed as a new work in the review of it in the *Times* (Monday, August 21), would seem to be the opera

to which Mary refers. Miss Kelly was the actress and singer to whom Lamb
would propose marriage, in a letter of July 20, 1819 (in Vol. IV); with whom
the Lambs would maintain a close friendship from about 1819 to 1829, when she
drifted virtually out of their lives; and of whom Lamb, during the period 1813 to
1825, wrote publicly—in "[The New Acting]," "Miss Kelly at Bath," "Richard
Broome's 'Jovial Crew,'" "Isaac Bickerstaff's 'Hypocrite,'" "New Pieces at the
Lyceum" (*Works*, I, 151–152 and 184–191), "Barbara S——" (II, 202–207),
and the sonnets "To Miss Kelly" and "To a Celebrated Female Performer in the
'Blind Boy'" (V, 40 and 55). She was born in Brighton to Mark (1767–1833)
and Mary (1763–1827) Kelly. Miss Kelly's father, the younger son of a Dublin
wine merchant and master of ceremonies at Dublin Castle and the brother of the
singer, actor, and composer Michael (1764?–1826), ran himself extravagantly
into debt and in 1795 deserted his wife and children. Miss Kelly's mother, the
daughter of a Dr. Singleton and the widow of a Mr. Jackson, was the mother of
five. Among them were Lydia Eliza Kelly (b. 1795), who became an actress and
died in America before 1882, and Anne Jackson (1782?–1869). Anne Jackson
became an actress and in 1803 the second wife of the comedian Charles Mathews
(1776–1835). She also became the editor of *Memoirs of Charles Mathews,
Comedian* (4 vols.; 1838 and 1839) and the author of *Anecdotes of Actors: With
Other Desultory Recollections* (1844), *Tea-table Talk, Ennobled Actresses, and
Other Miscellanies* (2 vols.; 1857), and *Friends for the Fireside* (2 vols.; 1860).
She died in Chelsea Villa, Fulham, London. The Lambs came to know the
Mathewses, and Lamb, in 1822 in "The Old Actors" (*Works*, II, 294–295), came
to describe, briefly though enthusiastically, Mathews' collection of from three
hundred to four hundred pictures pertaining to the theater, a collection purchased
in 1836 by The Garrick Club but exhibited when Lamb saw it in a gallery at the
Mathewses' home, Ivy Cottage, Kentish Town, London. Frances Kelly in girlhood
received a little education, played with Edmund Kean—later professionally played
Ophelia to his Hamlet—and, in 1798 at Drury Lane, began her stage career as a
chorister in Michael Kelly's opera *The Dramatick Romance of Blue Beard*. She
was formally taken into the Drury Lane company in 1799 and during the next ten
years performed in a variety of roles, principally at Drury Lane but also at
Glasgow, in the provinces, and in the Italian opera as well, fulfilling the high
promise she had shown in 1800 as Arthur in Shakespeare's *King John* to such as
Sarah Siddons and Richard Brinsley Sheridan. Miss Kelly acted at the Haymarket
and the Lyceum between the burning of the old and the opening of the new
Drury Lane Theatre—between February 24, 1809, and October 10, 1812. Thereafter she acted for the most part at Drury Lane until June 8, 1835, when she
retired from its stage in order to have more time than she had had to fight the
unfavorable prejudices prevailing against actresses. Her plan was to establish a
drama school for women. From 1833 to 1839 she worked toward its establishment
by presenting across England monologues of dramatic recollections fashioned to
persuade her audiences of her qualifications for conducting a school of that kind.
In 1839 she began to have constructed at the rear of her residence, 73 Dean
Street, Soho, the building that became her school and theater, that afterward
became the Royalty Theatre. Both school and theater succeeded from 1840 to
1849 or 1850, when financial and legal troubles caused her to lose the building
and her residence to her landlord and all of her nearly sixteen thousand pounds
of savings. She moved in 1850 to a small house at 30 Moscow Road, Bayswater,
London, and for some years gave readings from Shakespeare and accepted a few
pupils. She moved into Middlesex in the 1870s, to a cottage in Feltham she called
Ross Cottage after her grandaunt Anne Ross, and there died. She left her posses-
sions to Mary Ellen Thatcher Gerbini, later Greville, whom Miss Kelly in a will
of 1830 claimed to be her daughter and to have been born in Edinburgh on or
about April 5, 1829. Whether Miss Greville was Miss Kelly's natural or foster

daughter is not known. For information about Miss Kelly in addition to that in the *DNB* and Frederic Boase's *Modern English Biography* see L. E. Holman's *Lamb's 'Barbara S——': The Life of Frances Maria Kelly, Actress* (London: Methuen, 1935), Basil Francis' *Fanny Kelly of Drury Lane* (London: Rockliff, 1950), and Winifred F. Courtney's query in the *CLSB* of April 1974.

14. From Lamb. The restorations of the canceled passages, below, have been made with the guidance of T. C. Skeat's transcription of Lamb's portion of this letter, in "Letters of Charles and Mary Lamb and Coleridge," *British Museum Quarterly*, 26 (1962–1963), 18–19.

15. Or *"vacation."*

16. Although "great city" is common, Lamb may be quoting from Coleridge's "This Lime-tree Bower My Prison," line 30, or "Frost at Midnight," line 52, or from Wordsworth's "The Farmer of Tilsbury Vale," line 63, or *The Excursion*, II, 216. The "coming selection" of Coleridge's poems, about which Lamb writes below, is *Sibylline Leaves: A Selection of Poems.* Publication of that volume and what Coleridge had originally intended as its preface but was presently developing into *Biographia-literaria; or Biographical Sketches of My Literary Life and Opinions* was delayed until the London firm of Rest Fenner issued both of them, the *Biographia-literaria* in two volumes, in July 1817. (See *Coleridge's Letters*, IV, esp. 579, 584, 657–660, and 754.) Coleridge did include in *Sibylline Leaves* "Recantation: Illustrated in the Story of the Mad Ox," which had first appeared in the *Morning Post* of July 30, 1798, and which Lamb calls "that exquisite morceau about the blasted son of a presbyterian bitch" from its lines 35 and 36— "Od blast you for an *impious* son / Of a Presbyterian wh——re!" Coleridge did also include in *Sibylline Leaves* "Fire, Famine, and Slaughter: A War Eclogue," but did not include "Christabel." It appeared beforehand, in *Christabel; Kubla Khan, a Vision; The Pains of Sleep,* which John Murray published, in three editions, in 1816. (See Letter 313, note 2; Letter 315, note 3; and *Coleridge's Letters*, IV, 634.) The earliest edition of Coleridge's poetical works to contain "Christabel" is that of 1828.

17. In the production at Calne of *Remorse.* (See the next letter, second paragraph.) Samuel Foote, mentioned below, is identified in Vol. II, Letter 189, note 2.

301. *M. A. L. to Sara Hutchinson, with a note from C. L. and a gloss by M. A. L.*

Augst 20[–?21, 1815]

My dear friend

It is less fatigue to me to write upon lines, and I want to fill up as much of my paper as I can in gratitude for the pleasure your very kind letter has given me. I began to think I should not hear from you.[1] knowing you were not fond of letter-writing I quite forgave you but I was very sorry. Do not make a point of conscience of it, but if ever you feel an inclination you cannot think how much a few lines would delight me. I am happy to hear so good an account of your sister & child[2] and sincerely wish her a perfect recovery. I am glad you did not arrive sooner you escaped much anxiety. I have just received a very chearful letter from Mrs Morgan. the following I have picked out as I think it will interest you.

"Hartley Coleridge has been with us for two months. Morgan invited him to pass the long vacation here in the hope that his father would be of great service to him in his studies; he seems to be extremely amiable. I believe he is to spend the next vacation at Lady Beaumont's.[3] Your old friend Coleridge is very hard at work at the preface to a new Edition which he is just going to publish in the same form as Mr Wordsworth's——at first the preface was not to exceed five or six pages it has however grown into a work of great importance. I believe Morgan has already written nearly two hundred pages.[4] the title of it is '*Auto biographia Literaria*': to which are added '*Sybilline Leaves,*' a collection of Poems by the same Author. Calne has lately been much enlivened by an excellent company of Players—last week they performed the "Remorse' to a very crouded & brilliant audience; two of the characters were admirably well supported—at the request of the actors Morgan was behind the scenes all the time and assisted in the music &c."

Thanks to your kind interference we have had a very nice letter from Mr Wordsworth. Of them and of you we think and talk quite with a painful regret that we did not see more of you, and that it may be so long before we meet again.

I am going to do a queer thing—I have wearied myself with writing a long letter[5] to Mrs Morgan a part of which is an incoherent rambling account of a jaunt we have just been taking, I want to tell you all about it for we so seldom do such things that it runs strangely in my head and I feel too tired to give ⟨you more⟩ other than the mere copy of the nonsense I have just been writing.

"Last saturday was the grand feast day of the India House Clerks.— I think you must have heard Charles talk of his yearly turtle feast. He has been lately much wearied with work, and, glad to get rid of all connected with it he *used* saturday, the feast day being a holiday, *borrowed* the monday following, and we set off on the outside of the Cambridge Coach from Fetter Lane at eight o'clock and were driven into Cambridge in great triumph by "Hell Fire Dick," five minutes before three—Richard is in high reputation, he is private tutor to the Whip Club.—— Journeys used to be tedious torments to me but seated out in the open air I enjoyed every mile of the way—the first twenty miles was particularly pleasing to me having been accustomed to go so far on that road in the Ware Stage Coach to visit my Grandmother in the days of other times

In my life I never spent so many pleasant hours together as I did at Cambridge. We were walking the whole time—out of one College into another. If you ask me which I like best I must make the children's traditionary unoffending reply to all curious enquirers *"Both."* I liked them all best. The little gloomy ones, because they were little gloomy ones. I felt as if I could live and die in them and never wish to speak again. And the fine grand Trinity College Oh how fine it was! And King's College Chapel, what a place! I heard the Cathedral service there, and having been no great church goer of late years *that* and the painted windows and the general effect of the whole thing affected me wonderfully.

I certainly like St John's College best—I had seen least of it, having only been over it once, so, on the morning we returned I got up at six o clock and wandered into it by myself—by myself indeed for there was nothing alive to be seen but one cat who followed me about like a dog. Then I went over Trinity but nothing hailed me there, not even a cat.

On the sunday we met with a pleasant thing. We had been congratulating each other that we had come alone to enjoy, as the miser his feast, all our sights greedily to ourselves, but having seen all we began to grow flat and wish for this & tother body with us, when we were accosted by a young gownsman whose face we knew but where or how we had seen him we could not tell and were obliged to ask his name, he proved to be a young man we had seen twice at **Alsager's.** He turned out a very pleasant fellow——shewed us the insides of places—we took him to our Inn to dinner, and drank tea with him in such a delicious college room, and then again he supped with us. We made our meals as short as possible, to lose no time, and walked our young conductor almost off his legs, even when the fried eels were ready for supper and coming up, having a message from a man who we had bribed for the purpose, that then we might see **Oliver Cromwell** who was *not at home* when we called to see him we sallied out again and made him a visit by candlelight——and so ended our sights. When we were setting out in the morning our new friend came to bid us good bye and rode with us as far as Trompington. I never saw a creature so happy as he was the whole time he was with us, he said we had put him in such good spirits that [he] should certainly pass an examination well that he is to go through in six weeks in order to qualify himself to obtain a fellowship.

Returning home down old Fetter Lane I could hardly keep from crying to think it was all over——. With what pleasur[e Charles] shewed me Jesus College where Coleridge was, the barbe[r's shop] where Manning was—the house wher Lloyd lived—Franklin's rooms a young schoolfellow with whom Charles was the first time he went to Cambridge, I peeped in at his window, the room looked quite deserted—old chairs standing about in disorder that seemed to have stood there ever since they had sate in them, I write sad nonsense about these things, but I wish you had heard Charles talk his notsense[6] over & over again about his visit to Franklin and how he then first felt himself commencing gentleman & had eggs for his breakfast." Charles Lamb commencing gentleman!

A lady who is sitting by me seeing what I am doing says I remind her of her husband who acknowledged that the first love letter he wrote to her was a copy of one he had made use of on a former occasion.

This is no letter but if you give me any encouragement to write again you shall have one entirely to yourself, a little encouragement will do, a few lines to say you are well and remember us. I will keep this tomorrow. maybe Charles will put a few lines to it—I always send off a humdrum letter of mine with great satisfaction if I can get him to freshen it up a little at the end. Let me beg my love to your sister Johanna[7] with many thanks. I have much pleasure in looking forward to her nice bacon, the maker of which I long have had a great desire to see.

God bless you my dear Miss Hutchinson. I remain ever
Your affectionate friend
M Lamb

Dear Miss Hutchinson,[8]

I subscribe most willingly to all my sister says of her Enjoyment at Cambridge. She was in silent raptures all the while *there,* and came home riding thro' the air (her 1st long outside journey) triumphing as if she had been *graduated*. I remember one foolish-pretty expression she made use of "Bless the little churches how pretty they are" as those symbols of civilized life opened upon her view one after the other on this side Cambridge. You cannot proceed a mile without starting a steeple, with its little patch of villagery round it, enverduring[9] the waste. I dont know how you will pardon part of her letter being a transcript, but writing to another Lady first (probably as the *easiest task**) it was unnatural not to give you an accot. of what had so freshly delighted her, and would have been a piece of transcendant rhetorick (above her modesty) to have given two different accounts of a simple & univocal pleasure. Bless me how learned I write! but I always forget myself when I write to Ladies. One cannot tame ones erudition down to their merely English apprehensions. But this & all other faults you will excuse from

yours truly

C Lamb

Our kindest loves to Joanna if she will accept it from us who are merely **nominal** to her; & to the child & childs parent.

Yours again

C L

**"easiest task"*   Not the true reason but Charles had so connected Coleridge & Cambridge in my mind by talking so much of him there, and a letter coming so fresh from *him* in a manner *that was the reason* I wrote to them first—. I make this apology perhaps quite unnecessarily, but I am of a very jealous temper myself and more than once recollect having been offended at seeing kind expressions which had particularly pleased me in a friends letter repeated word for word to another.— Farewell once more. [By Mary.—Ed.]

MS: University of Texas Library. Pub.: Harper, IV, 49–55; Lucas (1905), VI, 472–476; Lucas (1912), V, 498–503; Lucas (1935), II, 171–176. Address: Miss S. Hutchinson/Hindwell/Radnor. Postmark: August 21, 181[5]. The second and third sentences in the eleventh paragraph have prompted the dating.

1. This period, which is not in the manuscript, could be placed after "letter-writing," below. My placement of it was determined by the manuscript—"from you" falling at the end of a line; no extraordinary spacing in the locution "letter-writing I"—and by the meaning Mary would seem to have wished conveyed.

2. Mary Hutchinson (Sara's sister-in-law) and Mary and Thomas Hutchinson's child, Thomas. See Letter 298, note 1.

3. Margaret, Lady Beaumont (see Vol. II, Letter 176, note 1), of Stonehall,

Dunmow, in Essex, and of Hall Farm, Coleorton, in Leicestershire. She had contributed to the fund Southey and Wordsworth had raised for Hartley's university education. Hartley spent his summer vacation of 1816 at Keswick, where, as in 1815, he could have seen Sir George and Lady Beaumont. But he stayed, presumably, with his mother and the Southeys. (See *Hartley Coleridge*, p. 68, and *Wordsworths' Letters*, III, 245, 331, and 337.) See the preceding letter, notes 16 and 11, about Samuel Taylor Coleridge's works referred to below.

4. John Morgan was acting as Coleridge's "friendly Amanuensis" (*Coleridge's Letters*, IV, 586). The first two titles, below, are underscored twice.

5. The preceding letter.

6. Mary had originally, it appears, written "nonsense." The lady mentioned in the next paragraph is possibly Elizabeth Reynolds. See the first paragraph in the preceding letter and its note 1.

7. Joanna Hutchinson, who was probably at Hindwell at the time of this letter. (See Vol. I, Letter 98, note 10; *Wordsworths' Letters*, III, 228; and *Sara Hutchinson's Letters*, p. 86.) Joanna ultimately settled with her brother Henry (1769–1839), a mariner, on the Isle of Man.

8. From Lamb.

9. "Making verdurous."

302.   C. L. to Mary Matilda Betham

Wednesday [September 13, 1815]

Dear Miss B.

I am sorry to say that my sister has been taken with one of her violent illnesses,[1] which was so sudden as to have shaken my health a great deal, and made it impossible for me to attend to your letter. I am naturally so indecisive, and this has quite taken all spirit of resolution from me, that I wish you to consult any body else as to your notes & appendix,[2] and beg you to let me transmit them for that purpose. I cannot give attention enough to judge of them. The plain text of the Poem I will chearfully supervise, but I greatly wish you would releive me of the rest. Your Mary[3] is with me but she must go now, as I think of taking lodgings & not returning here till I can get some very good servt. It would never do for us to be left at any time with such a one as she. I told Mary you would get her a country situation

Yours sinceirely

C Lamb

Kind remembes. to all, to Mr Kenny[4]————to Stonham

MS: Mr. W. Hugh Peal. Pub.: Lucas (1935), II, 176. Postmark: September 13, 1[81]5. The addresses on Letters 305 and 306 show Miss Betham to be, presumably with her family (see Vol. II, Letter 222, note 13), in Stonham Aspall, Suffolk.

1. On Thursday, October 19—five weeks and a day from the date of this letter—Lamb would write Sara Hutchinson that "Mary has been ill and gone from home these five weeks yesterday" (Letter 309, first sentence). On November 20, 1815, Robinson would call "late on Lamb to see Miss Lamb" (*H. C. R. on Books and Writers,* I, 177), understanding, rightly, that she had returned home.

2. To Miss Betham's *The Lay of Marie.* See the note to Letter 293.

3. A maid (see the postscript to Letter 306) whose surname is not known. Lamb did not act on his thought (see below) of taking lodgings.

4. James Kenney, I assume, who seems also to be in Stonham Aspall. Miss Betham and her family may have come to know him through his wife when she was still Mrs. Louisa Holcroft. See the next letter and Letter 282, near the reference to note 1.

303. *C. L. to Mary Matilda Betham*

Saturday [September ?16, 1815]

Dear Miss B.

Mr Hunter[1] has this morning put into a Parcel *all I have received from you at various times* including a sheet of notes from the Printer and two fair sheets of Mary. I hope you will receive them safe. The poem I will continue to look over, but must request you to provide for the rest. I cannot attend to any thing but the most simple things. I am very much unhinged indeed. Tell K. I saw Mrs K.[2] yesterday & she was well. You must write to Hunter if you are in a hurry for the notes &c.

Yours sincerely,

C. L.

Shall I direct the Printer to send you fair sheets as they are printed?

MS: unrecovered. Text: *A House of Letters,* p. 163. Also pub.: Hazlitt, II, 397; Harper, IV, 39; Lucas (1935), II, 177. The original of this letter would appear to be the sole Lamb letter among twenty-four autograph letters and other manuscripts inserted into the (unlocated) richly bound extra-illustrated volume of Hazlitt's *The Spirit of the Age: Or Contemporary Portraits* (London, 1825) listed in the American Art Association sales catalogue of November 19–20, 1930, p. 20, item 136. The Lamb letter is there described as an "A. L. s. (initials), 1 p., 12mo, Saturday, n.d., from CHARLES LAMB to '*Dear Miss B.*,' regarding some literary material he is returning to her and a poem which he is reading." I thank Patrick L. Story for sending me a copy of the listing.

1. Rowland Hunter (see Vol. II, Letter 193, note 1), the publisher of *The Lay of Marie.* Its printer, "the Printer . . . of Mary" (below), was Joseph Rogers of 66 Red Lion Street, Clerkenwell, London. His surname and address are in *The Lay of Marie;* his full name, his address, the name of his (junior) partner—Benjamin Knowlden Rogers—are in *A Directory of Printers and Others in Allied Trades, London and Vicinity 1800–1840,* comp. William Burton Todd (London: Printing Historical Society, 1972), p. 164.

2. Presumably, James and Louisa (Mrs. James) Kenney.

304.   *C. L. to Mary Matilda Betham*

[Mid-September 1815]

Dear Miss Betham,—

That accursed word trill[1] has vexed me excessively. I have referred to the M. S. and certainly the printer is exonerated, it is much more like a *tr* than a *k*. But what shall I say of myself?

If you can trust me hereafter, I will be more careful. I will go thro' the Poem, unless you should feel more safe by doing it yourself. In fact a second person looking over a proof is liable to let pass any thing that sounds plausible. The act of looking it over seeming to require only an attention to the words that they have the proper component letters, one scarce thinks then (or but half) of the sense.— You will find one line I have ventured to alter in 3d sheet. You had made hope & yoke rhime, which is intolerable.[2] Every body can see & carp at a bad rhime or no rhime. It strikes as slovenly, like bad spelling.

I found out another *sung* but I could not alter it, & I would not delay the time by writing to you. Besides it is not at all conspicuous— it comes in by the bye 'the strains I sung.'[3] The other obnoxious word was in an eminent place, at the beginning of her Lay, when all ears are upon her.

I must conclude hastily,

dear M. B.

Yours

C. L.

MS: unrecovered. Text: *A House of Letters*, pp. 162–163. Also pub.: Harper, IV, 83–84; Lucas (1912), V, 504; Lucas (1935), II, 177–178.

1. In *The Lay of Marie*, p. 24, line 6. An errata sheet, at the end of the book, corrects "trill" to "kill."

2. Perhaps a reference to what became book page 18, lines 11–12: "Clear'd the maz'd thought for ampler scope, / Sustain'd the flagging wings of hope."

3. On book page 29, in line 16. Lamb in his next sentence writes of what had been "sung" but was altered to and appears in the last line on book page 12 as "sang."

305. *C. L. to Mary Matilda Betham*

London
Thirtieth Septr. 1815

Dr. Miss Bethm

Your letter has found me in such a distressd state of mind owing partly to my situation at home & partly to perplexities at my office, that I am constraind to relinquish any further revision of Marie. The blunders I have alread[y] overlooked have weighed upon me almost insufferably. I have sent the Printer your copy as far as it is clear to 106 page, "happiness too great for me"[1] is the last line of that Page. The rest which I am not in any power to look over being wretchedly ill I send you back. I never was more ashamed of any thing, but my head has a weight in it that forces me to give it up. Pray forgive me, & write to the Printer where you would have it sent in future

Yours truly
C Lamb

I have returnd the printer all the copy of the past sheets
I have altd that line to

That magic laugh **bespeaks thee prest**[2]

You had better consult Rogers about the *expence* of reprinting that sheet. An Erratum there must be about *kill.*

MS: Huntington Library. Pub.: Macdonald, I, 367–368; Harper, IV, 56–57; Lucas (1935), II, 178. Address: Miss Betham/Stoneham/Suffolk. Frank: "Free/ J Rickman." Postmark: [September] 30, 1815. What is in this transcription treated as a heading, the address, and the frank are by John Rickman.
   1. In *The Lay of Marie,* p. 131, line 2. The poem ends on book page 146.
   2. Book page 114, line 5. About the printer, named below, see Letter 303, note 1.

306. *C. L. to Mary Matilda Betham*

[Early October? 1815]

Dr Miss Betham,

All this while I have been tormenting myself with the thought of having been ungracious to you, and you have been all the while accusing yourself. Let us absolve one another & be quiet. My head is in such a state from incapacity for business that I certainly know it to be my duty not to undertake the veriest trifle in addition. I hardly know how I can go on. I have tried to get some redress by explaining my health, but with no great success. No one can tell how ill I am because it does not come out to the exterior of my face but lies in my scull deep & invisible. I wish I was leprous & black jaundiced skin-over and that all was as well within as my cursed **looks.** You must not think me worse than I am. I am determind not to be overset but to give up business rather and get em to allow me a trifle for services past. O that I had been a shoe-maker or a baker, or a man of large independt. fortune. O darling Laziness! heaven of Epicurus! Saints Everlasting Rest! that I could drink vast potations of thee thro immeasured Eternity. **Otium** *cum* **vel** *sine* **dignitate.**[1] Scandalous, dishonerable, any-kind-of *repose.* I stand not upon the *dignified sort.* Accursed damned desks, trade commerce, business——. Inventions of that old original busy-body brainworking Satan, Sabbathless restless Satan——

A curse relieves. Do you ever try it?

A strange Letter to write to a Lady, but more honey'd sentences will not distill. I dare not ask who revises in my stead. I have drawn you into a scrape & am ashamd, but I know no remedy. My unwellness must be my apology. God bless you (tho' he curse the India House & fire it to *the ground*) and may no unkind **Error** creep into Marie, may all its readers like it as well as I do & every body about you like its kind author no worse. Why the devil am I never to have a chance of scribbling my own free thoughts verse or prose again? Why must I write of Tea & Drugs & Piece goods & bales of Indigo———

farewell—

C Lamb

Mary goes to her Place on Sunday—I mean your maid foolish Mary.[2] She wants a very little brains only to be an excellent Servt. She is excellently calculated for the country where nobody has brains—

MS: Mrs. Donald F. Hyde. Pub.: Hazlitt, II, 24–26; Ainger (1888), I, 306–308; Ainger (1900), II, 254–256; Macdonald, I, 368–369; Ainger (1904), I, 363–365; Harper, IV, 57–58; Lucas (1905), VI, 478; Lucas (1912), V, 505–506; Lucas (1935), II, 178–179. Address: Miss Betham/Stoneham/Suffolk. Postmark: [18]15.

1. "Idleness *with* or *without* dignity." The love of idleness and hatred of work **expressed** in this letter Lamb would express in "The Superannuated Man" and

the sonnets "Work" and "Leisure" (*Works,* II, 193–199, and V, 55–56). Particularly comparable, in tone and some language, are parts of this letter and "Work":

> Who first invented work, and bound the free
> And holyday-rejoicing spirit down
> To the ever-haunting importunity
> Of business in the green fields, and the town—
> To plough, loom, anvil, spade—and oh! most sad,
> To that dry drudgery at the desk's dead wood?
> Who but the Being unblest, alien from good,
> Sabbathless Satan! he who his unglad
> Task ever plies 'mid rotatory burnings,
> That round and round incalculably reel—
> For wrath divine hath made him like a wheel—
> In that red realm from which are no returnings;
> Where toiling, and turmoiling, ever and aye
> He, and his thoughts, keep pensive working-day.

Another version of that sonnet is in Lamb's letter to William Marter (identified in Letter 243, note 4), of July 19, 1824 (in Vol. V).

2. See Letter 302, note 3.

307. *C. L. to William Ayrton*

Oct. 4, 1815

Dear Ayrton,

I am confident that the word *air* in your sense does not occur in Spenser or Shakspeare, much less in older writers.[1] The first trace I remember of it is in Milton's sonnet to Lawrence, 'Warble immortal verse and Tuscan air'; where, if the word had not been very newly familiarized, he would doubtless have used *airs* in the plural.

Yours in haste,
C. L.

MS: unrecovered. Text: Lucas (1935), II, 180. Also pub.: Macdonald, I, 369; Harper, IV, 59.

1. According to *The Oxford English Dictionary,* the earliest occurrence of "air" as meaning a melody or a tune is in *A Midsummer Night's Dream* (composed ca. 1595–1596; published in 1600), I, i, 183. Below, Lamb misquotes Milton's Sonnet 20, line 12, the sonnet to a son—probably Edward (1633–1657), a member of Parliament—of the Puritan statesman Henry Lawrence (1600–1664). Lamb had quoted lines 9–12 from the same sonnet in his letter to Manning of August 11, 1800 (Letter 78, in Vol. I). Milton used "Aires" in the title and "aire" in line 8 of Sonnet 13—"*To Mr. H. Lawes, on His Aires.*"

308. *C. L. to Ayrton*

Oct. 14, 1815

Dr A.

  concerning **air**—

  Shakspears Twelfth Night

has

"light airs & giddy recollections"[1]

I am sure I forget whereabouts—

  also you will see another use of it in the Tempest (same sense) in Johnson's Dictiony.—

  Spenser I shall persist in, has it not, much less Chaucers. I have turned to all their places about music——

C L

  No doubt we had it from the Italian *Aria,* now **Aria** is not the latin æra modernized, but **aer,** is it not?[2]

MS: Berg Collection, New York Public Library. Pub.: Macdonald, I, 369; Harper, IV, 59; Lucas (1935), II, 180.

1. *Twelfth Night* (II, iv, 5–6) has, rather, "More than light airs and recollected terms / Of these most brisk and giddy-paced times." Lamb, below, refers Ayrton to *The Tempest,* I, ii, 392–394—"This music crept by me upon the waters, / Allaying both their fury and my passion / With its sweet air . . ."—which is cited in the first, the 1755, edition of Samuel Johnson's *Dictionary of the English Language.*

2. *Webster's Third International Dictionary* tentatively derives "air," in the sense under discussion, through "aria" from the accusative (*aera*) of the Latin *aer* (meaning "air": "the lower atmosphere"). *The Shorter Oxford English Dictionary* considers "air" as an adoption from the French *air,* probably not from the Old French *aire* (meaning "aerie") but as an extension "of the idea of 'atmosphere.' "

309. *C. L. to Sara Hutchinson*

Thursday 19 Oct 1815

Dear Miss H.—

  I am forced to be the replier to your Letter, for Mary has been ill and gone from home these five weeks yesterday.[1] She has left me very lonely and very miserable. I stroll about, but there is no rest but at ones own fireside, and there is no rest for me there now. I look forward to the worse half being past, and keep up as well as I can. She has begun to shew some favorable symptoms. The return of her disorder has been frightfully soon this time, with scarce a six month's interval. I am almost afraid my worry of spirits about the E. I. House was partly the cause of her illness, but one always imputes it to the cause next at hand; more probably it comes from some cause we have no controul ove[r or con]jecture of.— It cuts sad great slices out of the time the lit[tle] time we shall have to live together. I dont know but the recurrence of these illnesses might help me to sustain her death better than if we had had no partial separations. But I wont talk of death. I will imagine us immortal, or forget that we are otherwise, by Gods blessing in a few weeks we may be making our meal together, or sitting in the front row of the Pit at Drury Lane, or taking our evening walk past the theatres, to look at the outside of them at least, if not to be tempted in. Then we forget we are assailable, we are strong for the time as rocks, the wind is tempered to the shorn **Lambs—**.[2] Poor C Lloyd, & poor Priscilla, I feel I hardly feel enough for **him,** my own calamities press about me & involve me in a thick integument not [to] be reached at by other folks misfortunes. But I feel all I can, and all the kindness I can towards **you** all. God bless you. I hear nothing from Coleridge.

Yours truly
C Lamb

my brother is gone to Paris

MS: University of Texas Library. Pub.: Talfourd (1848), I, 184–185; Purnell, II, 71–72; Fitzgerald, II, 430–431; Hazlitt, II, 2; Ainger (1888), I, 297–298; Ainger (1900), II, 240–242; Macdonald, I, 370; Ainger (1904), I, 354–355; Harper, IV, 60–61; Lucas (1905), VI, 479; Lucas (1912), V, 506–507; Lucas (1935), II, 180–181. Address: W Wordsworth Esqr/Rydal Mount/near Kendal/Westmorland/for Miss H——. Postmark: October 19, 1815.

1. See Letter 302, note 1.

2. In Laurence Sterne's *A Sentimental Journey through France and Italy,* the chapter titled simply "Maria." About the younger Charles Lloyd, mentioned following, whose mental health was deteriorating, see Vol. I, Letter 10, note 4. His sister Priscilla (Mrs. Christopher) Wordsworth had died on Saturday, October 7, 1815, about a week after having given birth to a stillborn daughter. See Vol. I, Letter 41, source note, and *Wordsworths' Letters,* III, esp. 251–253.

310. *C. L. to Manning*

Dear Old Friend and Absentee,

This is Christmas-day 1815 with us; what it may be with you I
don't know, the 12th of June next year perhaps; and if it should be
the consecrated season with you, I don't see how you can keep it. You
have no turkeys; you would not desecrate the festival by offering up a
withered Chinese bantam, instead of the savoury grand Norfolcian[1]
holocaust, that smokes all around my nostrils at this moment from a
thousand firesides. Then what puddings have you? Where will you get
holly to stick in your churches, or churches to stick your dried tea-
leaves (that must be the substitute) in? What memorials you can have
of the holy time, I see not. A chopped missionary or two may keep up
the thin idea of Lent and the wilderness; but what standing evidence
have you of the Nativity?—'tis our rosy-cheeked, homestalled divines,
whose faces shine to the tune of *unto us a child;*[2] faces fragrant with
the mince-pies of half a century, that alone can authenticate the cheerful mystery—I feel.

I feel my bowels refreshed with the holy tide—my zeal is great
against the unedified heathen. Down with the Pagodas—down with
the idols—Ching-chong-fo and his foolish priesthood! Come out of
Babylon, O my friend! for her time is come, and the child that is
native, and the Proselyte of her gates, shall kindle and smoke together!
And in sober sense what makes you so long from among us, Manning?
You must not expect to see the same England again which you left.

Empires have been overturned, crowns trodden into dust, the face
of the western world quite changed: your friends have all got old—
those you left blooming—myself (who am one of the few that remember you) those golden hairs which you recollect my taking a pride in,
turned to silvery and grey. Mary has been dead and buried many
years—she desired to be buried in the silk gown you sent her.[3] Rickman, that you remember active and strong, now walks out supported
by a servant-maid and a stick. Martin Burney is a very old man. The
other day an aged woman knocked at my door, and pretended to my
acquaintance; it was long before I had the most distant cognition of

her; but at last together we made her out to be Louisa, the daughter of Mrs. Topham, formerly Mrs. Morton, who had been Mrs. Reynolds, formerly Mrs. Kenney, whose first husband was Holcroft, the dramatic writer of the last century. St. Paul's Church is a heap of ruins; the Monument isn't half so high as you knew it, divers parts being successively taken down which the ravages of time had rendered dangerous; the horse at Charing Cross is gone, no one knows whither,—and all this has taken place while you have been settling whether Ho-hing-tong should be spelt with a —— or a ——. For aught I see you had almost as well remain where you are, and not come like a Struldbug[4] into a world where few were born when you went away. Scarce here and there one will be able to make out your face; all your opinions will be out of date, your jokes obsolete, your puns rejected with fastidiousness as wit of the last age. Your way of mathematics has already given way to a new method, which after all is I believe the old doctrine of Maclaurin,[5] new-vamped up with what he borrowed of the negative quantity of fluxions from Euler.

Poor Godwin! I was passing his tomb the other day in Cripplegate churchyard. There are some verses upon it written by Miss Hayes, which if I thought good enough I would send you. He was one of those who would have hailed your return, not with boisterous shouts and clamours, but with the complacent gratulations of a philosopher anxious to promote knowledge as leading to happiness—but his systems and his theories are ten feet deep in Cripplegate mould. Coleridge is just dead, having lived just long enough to close the eyes of Wordsworth, who paid the debt to nature but a week or two before. Poor Col., but two days before he died he wrote to a bookseller proposing an epic poem on the 'Wanderings of Cain,'[6] in twenty-four books. It is said he has left behind him more than forty thousand treatises in criticism and metaphysics, but few of them in a state of completion. They are now destined, perhaps, to wrap up spices. You see what mutations the busy hand of Time has produced, while you have consumed in foolish voluntary exile that time which might have gladdened your friends—benefited your country; but reproaches are useless. Gather up the wretched reliques, my friend, as fast as you can, and come to your old home. I will rub my eyes and try to recognise you. We will shake withered hands together, and talk of old things—of St. Mary's Church and the barber's opposite, where the young students in mathematics used to assemble. Poor Crisp,[7] that kept it afterwards, set up a fruiterer's shop in Trumpington-street, and for aught I know, resides there still, for I saw the name up in the last journey I took there with my sister just before she died. I suppose you heard that I had left the India House, and gone into the Fishmongers' Almshouses over the bridge. I have a little cabin there, small and homely; but you shall be welcome to it. You like oysters, and to open them yourself; I'll get you some if you come in oyster time. Marshall,[8] Godwin's old friend, is still alive, and talks of the faces you used to make.

Come as soon as you can.

C. Lamb

MS: unrecovered. Text: Lucas (1935), II, 182–184. Also pub.: Talfourd (1837), II, 18–22; Sala, I, 410–413; Purnell, I, 410–413; Fitzgerald, II, 243–246; Hazlitt, II, 11–13; Ainger (1888), I, 298–300; Ainger (1900), II, 242–246; Macdonald, I, 371–373; Ainger (1904), I, 355–357; Harper, IV, 61–65; Lucas (1905), VI, 480–482; Lucas (1912), V, 507–509. Manning was in Canton and would not leave there for England until early in 1817. (See Vol. I, Letter 53, source note.) It is clear from especially the next letter that Lamb had heard, perhaps from Manning's brother Edward (see the first sentence and the third paragraph in that letter and Letter 245, note 7), that Manning was at this time preparing to leave for home. Word from Manning to Lamb on the matter either never existed or has not been preserved: Manning's last and next published letters to him are of October 11, 1810, and May 29, 1819, in the *Manning-Lamb Letters,* pp. 114 and 118–126. Much in this and the next letter of Lamb bears on the concern of "Distant Correspondents: In a Letter to B. F. Esq. at Sydney, New South Wales" (*Works,* II, 104–108).

    1. Of Norfolk, Manning's home and, according to Lucas (1935), II, 184, "the chief source of supply of Christmas turkeys for the London market."

    2. "Unto Us Is Born a Son," a carol listed in Minnie Earl Sears's *Song Index* (New York: Wilson, 1926), p. 583.

    3. Manning had sent Mary a roll of silk from Canton in 1807. See Vol. II, Letter 222 and its note 1, and the first paragraph in the next letter. The surnames Topham, Morton, and Reynolds are fictitious in the genealogy concocted below for Louisa Mercier Holcroft Kenney. About The Monument see Letter 286, note 2. For a jingle on the Charing Cross horse, the equestrian statue of Charles I, see Vol. I, Letter 102, note 9.

    4. *Struldbrugg,* an *immortal* of Luggnagg, in Jonathan Swift's *Gulliver's Travels,* Part III, ch. x.

    5. The Scottish mathematician and natural philosopher Colin Maclaurin (1698–1746). In 1740 he shared with the Swiss and Dutch mathematicians Leonhard Euler (1707–1783) and Daniel Bernoulli (1700–1782) an award of the Académie des sciences for their studies on tides; in 1742 Maclaurin published *A Treatise on Fluxions,* in which he drew on Euler's findings particularly. Mary Hays (see Vol. I, Letter 58, note 1) is the Miss Hayes referred to in the next paragraph.

    6. See Vol. I, Letter 76, note 2.

    7. The barber. About the journey mentioned below see Letter 300, near the reference to note 8 especially.

    8. James Marshal. See Vol. I, Letter 91, source note.

311. *C. L. to Manning*

26th Dec 1815

Dear Manning,

Following your brothers example, I have just ventured one Letter to Canton, and am now hazarding another (not exactly a duplicate) to St. Helena. The first was full of improbable romantic fictions fitting the remoteness of the Mission it goes upon, in the present I mean to confine myself nearer to truth as you come nearer home. A correspondence with the uttermost parts of the earth necesserarily involves in it some heat of fancy, it sets the brain a going, but I can think on the halfway house tranquilly. Your friends then are not all dead or grown forgetful of you thro' old age, as that lying letter asserted, anticipating rather what must happen if you kept tarrying on for ever on the skirts of creation, as there seemed a danger of your doing—but they are all tolerably well and in full and perfect comprehension of what is meant by Manning's coming home again. Mrs. Kenny (cidevant Holcroft) never lets her tongue riot more than in remembrances of you. Fanny[1] expends herself in phrases that can only be justify'd by her romantic nature. Mary reserves a portion of your **Silk,** not to be buried in (as the false nuncio asserts) but to make up spick & span into a new-bran gown to wear **when you come.** I am the same as when you knew me almost to a **surfeiting** identity. This very night I am going to *leave off* **Tobacco!** Surely there must be some other world in which this unconquerable purpose shall be realized. The soul hath not her generous aspirings implanted in her in vain.—

One that you knew and I think the only one of those friends we knew much of in common, has died in earnest. Poor Priscilla wife of Kit Wordsworth. Her brother Robert is also dead, and several of the grown up brothers and sisters in the compass of a very few years.[2] Death has not otherwise meddled much in families that I know. Not but he has his damn'd eye upon us, and is whetting his infernal feathered dart every instant, as you see him truly pictured in that impressive moral picture **The Good Man at the hour of death.**

I have in trust to put in the post four Letters from Diss, and one from Lynn, to St. Helena, which I hope will accompany this safe, and one from Lynn, & the one before spoken of from me, to Canton.³ But we all hope that these latter may be waste paper.

I dont know why I have forborn writing so long. But it is such a forlorn hope to send a scrap of paper straggling over wide oceans. And yet I know when you come home, I shall have you sitting before me at our fireside just as if you had never been away. In such an instant does the Return of a Person dissipate all the weight of imaginary Perplexity from distance of time & space.

I'll promise you good Oysters. **Cory**⁴ is dead that kept the shop opposite St. Dunstans, but the tougher materials of the shop survive the perishing frame of its Keeper. Oysters continue to flourish there under as good auspices. Poor Cory! but if you will absent yourself twenty years together, you must not expect numerically the same population to congratulate your return which wetted the sea beach with their tears when you went away.——

Have you recovered the breathless **stone-staring** astonishment into which you must have been thrown upon learning at landing that an Emperor of France was living in St. Helena.⁵ What an event in the solitude of the seas, like finding a **fishes** bone at the top of Plinlimmon—but these things are nothing in our western world—noveltie[s] cease to affect—. **Come** and try what your presence can—. God bless **you**—

Your old fri[end]

C Lamb

MS: Huntington Library. Pub.: Talfourd (1837), II, 22.–25; Sala, I, 413–416; Purnell, I, 413–416; Fitzgerald, II, 246–249; Hazlitt, II, 13–15; Ainger (1888), I, 300–302; Ainger (1900), II, 246–248; Macdonald, I, 374–375; Ainger (1904), I, 357–359; Harper, I, facsimile, and IV, 65–68; Lucas (1905), VI, 482–484; Lucas (1912), V, 510–511; Lucas (1935), II, 184–186. Address: Thomas Manning Esqr/St. Helena/on his return from China. Postmark: December 27, 1815. See the source note to the preceding letter—"that lying letter" Lamb calls it below.

1. Fanny Holcroft. See Letter 296, note 9; and Vol. II, Letter 133, note 7.

2. See Letter 309, note 2, and Letter 268, note 8. The picture whose title Lamb gives at the end of his paragraph may be some popular print of the day or a fancy arising from Lamb's mental mingling of William Blake's "Death! Great Proprietor of All," where Death is portrayed as hurling a feathered dart, with Blake's "The Death of the Good Old Man," known also as "The Good Old Man Dying" and "The Good Man in the Hour of Death." "Death! Great Proprietor of All" is one in the series of illustrations that the bookseller Richard Edwards (1768–1827) had commissioned Blake to design and engrave for reproduction in Edwards' publication *The Complaint and the Consolation; or, Night Thoughts, by Edward Young, LL.D.* (1797), a work described or listed as both a folio and an atlas quarto. "The Death of the Good Old Man" is one in the series of illustrations—a "moral series"

Henry Fuseli denominated it in the next book listed in this note—that the engraver and publisher Robert Hartley Cromek (1770–1812) had commissioned Blake to design and the line engraver Luigi Schiavonetti (1765–1810) to engrave for reproduction in Cromek's publication *The Grave, a Poem. By Robert Blair. Illustrated by Twelve Etchings Executed from Original Designs* (1808), a work in imperial quarto that the art publisher and bookseller Rudolph Ackermann (1764–1834) reissued, with changes in contents and layout, in both folio and quarto, in 1813. In a letter postmarked May 15, 1824 (in my Vol. V), Lamb would partly identify Blake for Bernard Barton as "a most extraordinary man . . . whose wild designs accompany a splendid folio edition of the Night Thoughts . . . in one of which he pictures the parting of soul & body by a solid mass of human form floating off God knows how from a lumpish mass (fac simile to itself) left behing [sic] on the dying bed." The picture Lamb there describes is not one Blake had done for the 1797 edition of *The Complaint . . . ; or, Night Thoughts,* but one he had done for the 1808 edition of *The Grave*—"The Death of the Good Old Man" or "Death of the Strong Wicked Man" or "The Soul Hovering over the Body Reluctantly Parting with Life." It was probably Robinson, seriously interested in Blake since the spring of 1810, who had introduced Lamb to certain of Blake's creations and had informed Lamb or caused him to inform himself of certain features of Blake's life. "Death! Great Proprietor of All" is reproduced in Archibald G. B. Russell, *The Engravings of William Blake* (London: Richards, 1912), Plate 8, facing p. 74; "The Death of the Good Old Man," "Death of the Strong Wicked Man," and "The Soul Hovering over the Body Reluctantly Parting with Life" are reproduced in S. Foster Damon, *Blake's Grave: A Prophetic Book. Being William Blake's Illustrations for Robert Blair's "The Grave," Arranged as Blake Directed* (Providence, R.I.: Brown University Press, 1963), Plates 5, 4, and 6 (unpaged), and in G. E. Bentley, Jr., *Blake Records* (Oxford: The Clarendon Press, 1969), Plates XX, XXI, and XXVIII, facing pp. 172, 174, and 199. Among the other works consulted in the preparation of this note are Geoffrey Keynes's *Illustrations to Young's "Night Thoughts" Done in Water-colour by William Blake: Thirty Pages, Five Reproduced in Colour and Twenty-five in Monotone, from the Original Water-colours in the Library of William Augustus White* (Cambridge, Mass.: Fogg Museum of Art; London: Oxford University Press, 1927) and Bentley's "The Promotion of Blake's *Grave* Designs," *University of Toronto Quarterly,* 31 (April 1962), 339–353.

3. Lamb refers to letters from Manning's brothers and sister (see Letter 245, note 7) and to the preceding letter.

4. Unidentified beyond what Lamb writes of him here.

5. Manning did land at St. Helena on his way back from China, in 1817, and met with Napoleon in June. For an account of their meeting see Barry E. O'Meara's *Napoleon in Exile; or, a Voice from St. Helena* (2 vols.; New York: Peter Eckler, n.d.), II, 43–46. Plinlimmon, mentioned below, is a mountain in Wales.

312. *C. L. to Leigh Hunt*

Saturday [March 23, 1816]

Dear H.—

We were much gratified by the token of your remembrance, though we had read **Rimini**[1] Previously with great delight, & agree in thinking it superior to your former poems. The third Canto is in particular my favorite. We congratulate you most sincerely on the fruit of your prison hours. Mary joins me in kindest remembrces to yourself to Mrs. H. not forgetting our old grave friend Thornton.

Yours truly

[. . .]

MS: Brewer–Leigh Hunt Collection, The University of Iowa Libraries, Iowa City, Iowa (MsL/L21h/no. 3). Pub.: Lucas (1935), II, 186. Address: L. Hunt Esqr./Vale of Health/Hampstead. Postmark: March 24, 1816. After his release from Horsemonger Lane Jail, in February 1815, Hunt had moved with his family to the Edgware Road and thence to the Vale of Health.
    1. *The Story of Rimini, a Poem* (1816), the greater part of which Hunt had written in jail. About Hunt's wife and son Thornton, remembered below, see Letter 276, near the end of its source note. The signature has been clipped from this letter.

313. *C. L. to William Wordsworth*

Tuesday—9 Apr 1816

Dear Wordsworth—

Thanks for the books[1] you have given me & for all the Books you mean to give me. I will bind up the Political Sonnets & Ode according to your Suggestion. I have not bound the poems yet. I wait till People have done borrowing them. I think I shall get a chain and chain them to my shelves More Bodleiano & people may come & read them at chains length. For of those who borrow, some read slow, some mean to read but dont read, and some neither read nor meant to read, but borrow to leave you an opinion of their sagacity. I must do my money-borrowing friends the justice to say that there is nothing of this caprice or wantonness of alienation in them. When they borrow my money, they never fail to make use of it. Coleridge has been here about a fortninght.[2] His health is tolerable at present, though beset with temptations. In the first place the Cov. Gard. Manager has declined accepting his Tragedy, tho' (having read it) I s[e]e no reason upon earth why it might not have run a very fair chance, tho' it certainly wants a prominent part for a Miss O Neil or a Mr Kean.[3] However he is going to day to write to Lord Byron to get it to Drury. Should you see Mrs. C. who has just written to C. a letter which I have given him, it will be as well to say nothing about its fate till some answer is shaped from Drury. He has two volumes printing together at

Bristol, both finished as far as the composition goes; the latter containing his fugitive Poems, the former his Literary Life.— Nature who conducts every creature by instinct to its best end, has skilfully directed C. to take up his abode at a Chemists Laboratory in Norfolk Street. She might as well have sent a Helluo Librorum[4] for cure to the Vatican.— God keep him inviolate among the traps & pitfalls. He has done pretty well as yet.

Tell Miss H. my Sister is every day wishing to be quietly sitting down to answer her very kind Letter, but while C. stays she can hardly find a quiet time, God bless him—

Tell Mrs. W. her Postscripts are always agreeable. They are so legible too. Your manual graphy is terrible, dark as Lycophron.[5]

Likelihood for instance is thus **typified** ✍ —.
I should not wonder if the constant making out of such Paragraphs is the cause of that weakness in Mrs. W's **Eyes** as she is tenderly pleased to express it. Dorothy I hear has mounted spectacles; So you have **deoculated** two of your dearest relations in life. Well, God bless you & continue to give you power to **write** with a **finger** of power upon **our** hearts what you fail to impress in corresponding lucidness upon our outward **eyesight**—

Mary's Love to all, She is quite well.

I am calle'd off—. to do the deposits on Cotton Wool—but why do I relate this to you who want faculties to comprehend the great mystery of Deposits, of Interest, of Warehouse rent, and Contingent Fund—. Adieu.

C Lamb

A longer Letter when C. is gone back into the Country, relating his success &c——*my* judgment of *your* new Books &c &c——

I am scarce quiet enough while he stays—

Yours again

C L

MS: University of Texas Library. Pub.: Talfourd (1848), I, 185–188; Sala, I, 282–283; Purnell, I, 282–283; Fitzgerald, II, 117–118; Hazlitt, II, 20–21; Ainger (1888), I, 302–304; Ainger (1900), II, 249–251; Macdonald, I, 376–378; Ainger (1904), I, 359–361; Harper, IV, 68–70; Lucas (1905), VI, 484–485; Lucas (1912), V, 511–513; Lucas (1935), II, 186–188. Address: W. Wordsworth Esq/ Rydal Mount/near Grasmere/Kendal/Westmorland. Postmark: April.

1. Proofs, more accurately—Lamb will write Wordsworth on April 26 (Letter 315) of having just finished correcting them—of Wordsworth's *Thanksgiving Ode, January 18, 1816. With Other Short Pieces, Chiefly Referring to Recent Public Events* and of *A Letter to a Friend of Robert Burns: Occasioned by an Intended Republication of the Account of the Life of Burns, by Dr. Currie; and of the Selections Made by Him from His Letters,* both of which Longman's would publish in May. The title poem of the first volume celebrates the day of national thanks-giving declared for the final defeat of Napoleon. The friend of Burns referred to in the title of the second volume is the poet, educator, and chaplain James Gray (d. 1830); about James Currie see my Vol. I, Letter 74, note 3. The passages on book borrowing, below, Lamb would develop, elaborate on, in "The Two Races of Men" (*Works,* II, 22–27). "More Bodleiano" translates, "In the manner of the Bodleian." See Letter 279, note 2.

2. Coleridge had come from Calne to London on about March 23, 1816, in order to submit to the management of Covent Garden his manuscript of the tragic romance or dramatic poem Rest Fenner's company would publish in November 1817, as *Zapolya: A Christmas Tale, in Two Parts: The Prelude Entitled "The Usurper's Fortune"; and the Sequel Entitled "The Usurper's Fate."* Coleridge had found lodgings, first at The Gloucester Coffee House, Piccadilly, and afterward above the shop of the apothecaries Moore and James, 42 Norfolk Street, Strand, and had fallen so ill from having taken massive doses of laudanum as a means of escaping from his anxieties about his own future and Morgan's that he had written Morgan in Calne to attend him in London and had been placed under the care of Morgan's acquaintance Joseph Adams (1756–1818), a physician of Hatton Garden. By April 9, 1816, Coleridge had received from Covent Garden a rejection of *Zapolya.* On April 10 Morgan was to deliver Coleridge's manuscript to Byron, who in March 1815 had consented to read the manuscript of *Sibylline Leaves* with a view to recommending it to a publisher and had also, as a manager of Drury Lane impressed with *Remorse,* encouraged Coleridge to write a tragedy for consideration there. Although the managers of Drury Lane would reject *Zapolya* as a drama for the current season, they would offer Coleridge suggestions for its easy conversion into a melodrama probably acceptable for presentation at Christmas. But months before Christmas a Drury Lane management whose personnel had since changed would mistreat him to the point where he could no longer deal with it; *Zapolya* would go unacted until February 10, 1818, when it was performed at the Surrey Theatre, formerly the Royal Circus, as a melodrama. Perhaps on April 11, 1816, Coleridge managed to leave his bed, call on Byron, and enchant him with a recitation of "Kubla Khan." In the autumn of 1815 Byron had read, with delight, a copy of "Christabel" Coleridge had sent to him. At that time Byron had urged John Murray to see about becoming its publisher. Now Byron spoke to Murray of "Kubla Khan" as well. Apparently on April 12 Murray called on Coleridge and reached the agreement with him that issued in Murray's publishing *Christabel; Kubla Khan, a Vision; The Pains of Sleep,* the first edition on May 25, 1816. Dr. Adams, meanwhile, had come to concur with Coleridge in the belief that Coleridge could be relieved of his dependence on drugs if he were placed under the care of the right man. To that end Adams had written to James Gillman (1782–1839), a son of John Gilman (d. 1821) and his first wife, the former Elizabeth Bracey, of Great Yarmouth, Norfolk. Gillman was a surgeon of the London suburb of Highgate, trained in Norwich, Norfolk, by the surgeon Keymer whose daughter Frances became the second wife of John Gilman, and trained in London at Westminster Hospital and the Royal College of Surgeons. Gillman was to become, in 1838, the author of *The Life of Samuel Taylor Coleridge.* He interviewed Coleridge and, charmed by him, invited him to become a resident patient in his household. The household was settled in 1816 in Moreton House, Highgate Hill, and from November 1823 in Number 3 The Grove, High-

gate. The household comprised Gillman's wife, Anne, or Ann (1779?–1860), a daughter of one James Harding; the Gillmans' only children—James (1808–1877), later a graduate and fellow of St. John's College, Oxford, a minister, Lamb's correspondent; and Henry Anthony (1814?–1858)—and Anne Gillman's sister Lucy Harding. On April 15, 1816, Coleridge arrived at their home, intending to stay with them for a month, but staying for the rest of his life. More on the matters in this note and on the Gillmans is in *Coleridge's Letters*, IV, esp. 559–563, 600–603, 625–636, 721; and Alexander W. Gillman's *The Gillmans of Highgate: With Letters from Samuel Taylor Coleridge, &c., Illustrated with Views and Portraits, Being a Chapter from the History of the Gillman Family* (London: Elliot Stock [1895?]).

3. Eliza O'Neill (see Letter 295, note 2) and Edmund Kean. Coleridge's "two volumes," mentioned below, whose contents were expanded to three volumes (see Letter 300, note 16), are *Sibylline Leaves* and *Biographia-literaria*. They were being printed together at this time in Bristol through the offices of Lamb and Coleridge's old friend John Mathew Gutch—identified in my Vol. I, Introduction, pp. xxxvi–xxxvii.

4. "Devourer of Books." Letter 322 is Mary's next letter that is extant to Sara Hutchinson, referred to in the following paragraph. She was presently dividing her time between the Wordsworths and the Southeys.

5. Born in about 325 B.C., a Greek tragic poet and grammarian known for his tenebrous style. His only work to survive entire is *Alexandra*, or *Cassandra*.

314. *C. L. to Mary Matilda Betham*

[April 20? 1816]

Dear Miss Betham,

I received your present with mixed feelings of gratitude & shame. I look at it set forth so trim & ornate, & reget that I should have shrunk from the task of contributing to its exactness. But you[r] mercy is above my faults. I stole a glance at the Errata & I do not know whether I were glad or sorry that that killing word[1] that must ever stand against my conscience like the handwriting on the wall, did not stand alone. Well, I have nothing to do but to remit my offence as you have done & proceed tho' unworthy to the Perusal. Thanks again. Mary is middling. I am very so so. Dyer shall have his copy forthwith.

I remain, dear Miss B.

Yours truly.

C. Lamb

Hope to talk it over with you soon.

MS: unrecovered. Text: *A House of Letters*, p. 166. Also pub.: Lucas (1935), II, 189. The date is estimated from Southey's letter to Miss Betham of April 20, 1816, published in *A House of Letters*, p. 167: Southey seems to write there of having received a copy of her *The Lay of Marie;* Lamb does write here of having received two copies—one for himself and one he is to pass on to George Dyer.

1. The misprint "trill," for "kill." See Letter 304, first sentence, and Letter 305, last postscript.

315.   *C. L. to William Wordsworth*
SIR,
    PLEASE TO STATE THE WEIGHTS AND AMOUNTS OF THE
FOLLOWING LOTS OF
SOLD   SALE, 181   FOR

                              YOUR OBEDIENT SERVANT,

                              Chas Lamb

ACCOUNTANT'S OFFICE,
    26 apr 1816

Dear W. .

I have just finished the pleasing task of correcting the Revise of the Poems and letter.[1] I hope they will come out faultless. One blunder I saw and shuddered at. The hallucinating rascal had printed **battered** for **battened,** this last not conveying any distinct sense to his gaping soul. The Reader (as they call 'em) had discovered it & given it the marginal brand, but the substitutory **n** had not yet appeared. I accompanied his notice with a most pathetic address to the printer not to neglect the Correction. I know how such a blunder would "batter r at your Peace."[2] With regard to the works, the Letter I read with unabated satisfaction. Such a thing was wanted, called for. The parallel of Cotton with Burns I heartily approve; Iz. Walton hallows any page in which his reverend name appears. "Duty archly bending to purposes of general benevolence" is exquisite. The Poems I endeavored not to understand, but to read them with my eye alone, and I think I succeeded. (Some people will do that when they come out, you'll say.) As if I were to luxuriate tomorrow at some Picture Gallery I was never at before, and going by to day by chance, found the door open, had but 5 minutes to look about me, peeped in, just such a *chastised* peep

I took with my mind at the lines my luxuriating eye was coursing over unrestrained,—not to anticipate another days fuller satisfaction. Coleridge is printing Xtabel by Ld. Byron's recommendation to Murray, with what he calls a vision Kubla Khan—which said vision he repeats so enchantingly that it irradiates & brings heaven & Elysian bowers into my parlour while he sings or says it, but there is an observation Never tell thy dreams, and I am almost afraid that Kubla Khan is an owl that wont bear day light, I fear lest it should be discovered by the lantern of typography & clear reducting to letters, no better than nonsense or no sense.[3] When I was young I used to chant with extacy **mild Arcadians ever blooming,** till somebody told me it was meant to be nonsense. Even yet I have a lingering attachment to it, and think it better than **Windsor forest, Dying Xtians address &c——.** C has sent his Tragedy to D. L. T.[4] it cannot be acted this season, & by their manner of receiving it, I hope he will be able to alter it to make them accept it for next. He is at present under the medical care of a **Mr Gilman (Killman?)** a Highgate Apothecary, where he **plays at leaving off Laud——m.—** I think his essentials not touched, he is very bad, but then he wonderfully picks up another day, and his face when he repeats his verses hath its ancient glory, an Arch angel a little damaged.—[5]

Will Miss H. pardon our not replying at length to her kind Letter? We are not quiet enough. Morgan is with us every day, going betwixt Highgate & the Temple. Coleridge is absent but 4 miles, & the neighborhood of such a man is as exciting as the presence of 50 ordinary Persons. Tis enough to be within the whiff & wind[6] of *his* genius, for us not to possess our souls in quiet. If I lived with him or the *Author of the Excursion,* I should in a very little time lose my own identity, & be dragged along in the current of other peoples thoughts, hampered in a net. How cool I sit in this office, with no possible interruption further than what I may term *material;* there is not as much metaphysics in 36 of the people here as there is in the first page of Lockes treatise on the Human understanding, or as much poetry as in any ten lines of the Pleasure of Hope or more natural Beggars Petitition.[7] I never entangle myself in any of their speculations. Interruption's, if I try to write a letter even, I have dreadful. Just now within 4 lines I was call'd off for ten minutes to consult dusty old books for the settlement of obsolete Errors. I hold you a guinea you dont find the Chasm where I left off, so excellently the wounded sense closed again & was healed.— N. B. Nothing said above to the contrary but that I hold the personal presence of the two mentioned potent spirits at a rate as high as any, but I pay dearer, what amuses others **robs me of my self,** my mind is positively discharged into their greater currents, but flows with a welling violence. As to your question about work, it is far less oppressive to me than it was, from circumstances; it takes all the golden part of the day away, a solid lump from ten to four, but it does not kill my peace as before. Someday or other I shall be in a taking[8] again. My head akes & you have had enough. God bless you.

C Lamb

London

Twenty Sixth April 1816

MS: University of Texas Library. Pub.: Talfourd (1848), I, 219–223; Sala, I, 293–295; Purnell, I, 293–295; Fitzgerald, II, 128–130; Hazlitt, II, 21–24; Ainger (1888), I, 304–306; Ainger (1900), II, 251–254; Macdonald, I, 378–380; Ainger (1904), I, 361–363; Harper, IV, 70–73; Lucas (1905), VI, 486–488; Lucas (1912), V, 513–515; Lucas (1935), II, 189–191. Address: W. Wordsworth Esq/ Rydal Mount/Kendal/Westmorland. Frank: "Free/J Rickman." Postmark: April 28 [or 26], 1816. "London" and the date placed in this transcription at the end of the letter, the address, and the frank are by John Rickman. Lamb writes on his office stationery headed with the printed form here printed in large and small capitals.

1. See Letter 313, note 1. The printer's blunder Lamb below writes of having corrected had occurred in "Ode: The Morning of the Day Appointed for a General Thanksgiving. January 18, 1816," line 114—"Opposed to hopes that battened upon scorn."

2. *Macbeth,* IV, iii, 178. Lamb had used the expression in his letter to Godwin of March 14, 1806 (Vol. II, Letter 199, concluding paragraph). For the parallel drawn between Charles Cotton and Burns, the appearance of Izaak Walton's name, and the passage Lamb misquotes, below, see *A Letter to a Friend of Robert Burns,* in *Wordsworth's Prose Works,* II, 8–9 and 13–14. See, for Lamb's earlier conjoining in one letter references to Cotton, Burns, and Walton, my Vol. II, Letter 142.

3. "Christabel," said Lamb, according to a letter from Godwin's stepdaughter Fanny Imlay (identified initially in Vol. II, Letter 185, note 4) to Mary Shelley of July 29, 1816, "ought never to have been published; that no one understands it; and 'Kubla Khan' is nonsense" (Edward Dowden, *The Life of Percy Bysshe Shelley* [2 vols.; London: Kegan Paul, Trench, 1886], II, 41). But in the *Times* of May 20, 1816, five days before the publication of *Christabel; Kubla Khan, a Vision; The Pains of Sleep* (see Letter 313, note 2), is a favorable review of "Christabel" that Lewis M. Schwartz attributed on strong evidence to Lamb, in "A New Review of Coleridge's *Christabel,*" *Studies in Romanticism,* 9 (Spring 1970), 114–124. Moreover, in the *New Times* of July 19, 1820, is a flattering comment on the lady Christabel in a review of Keats's *Lamia, Isabella, The Eve of Saint Agnes, and Other Poems* (1820) that Lucas assigned on equally strong evidence to Lamb, in *Works,* I, esp. 201 and 470–471. Furthermore, the divine and antiquary John Fuller Russell (1813–1884) recorded, in "Charles Lamb at Home," *Notes and Queries,* 6th Ser., 5 (April 1, 1882), 241, that Lamb—so

Lamb in 1834 told Russell—"regarded the *Ancient Mariner* and *Christabel* as Coleridge's best productions in verse." Other references to "Christabel" in Lamb's letters are in my Vol. I, Letter 66, first postscript, and Letter 75, penultimate paragraph; Vol. II, Letter 146, near the end; Letter 300, near the end, and Letter 317, postscript. Lamb in effect quotes below, as he did quote in his letter to Coleridge of January 2, 1797 (Vol. I, Letter 18, near the reference to note 5), from "Song. By a Person of Quality," line 5 ("mild Arcadians ever blooming"), a poem often ascribed to Pope. In addition to Pope's "Windsor Forest," Lamb refers to Pope's "Adaptations of the Emperor Hadrian: II. The Dying Christian to His Soul, Ode."

4. Coleridge, that is, has sent his manuscript of *Zapolya* to Drury Lane Theatre. See Letter 313, note 2.

5. Satan to his legions in Hell appears so:

> . . . hee above the rest
> In shape and gesture proudly eminent
> Stood like a Towr; his form had yet not lost
> All her Original brightness; nor appeard
> Less then [sic] Arch-Angel ruind, and th' excess   [593]
> Of Glory obscur'd: As when the Sun new ris'n
> Looks through the Horizontal misty Air
> Shorn of his Beams; or from behind the Moon
> In dim Eclips disastrous twilight sheds
> On half the Nations, and with fear of change
> Perplexes Monarchs. . . .

[*Paradise Lost,* I, 589–599, in *The Poetical Works of John Milton: With Translations of the Italian, Latin and Greek Poems from the Columbia University Edition,* ed. Helen Darbishire (1958; rpt. London: Oxford University Press, 1961), p. 20] Sara Hutchinson (see Letter 313, note 4) is the Miss H. mentioned below.

6. *Hamlet,* II, ii, 473; "possess our souls in quiet" (below) is Lamb's adaptation of Luke 21:19. Cf. what Lamb writes of himself in relation to Coleridge and Wordsworth in this and the next paragraph with what he would in 1821 write, surely with Coleridge and Wordsworth in mind, in "The Old and New Schoolmaster" (*Works,* II, 53):

> I would not be domesticated all my days with a person of very superior capacity to my own—not, if I know myself at all, from any considerations of jealousy or self-comparison, for the occasional communion with such minds has constituted the fortune and felicity of my life—but the habit of too constant intercourse with spirits above you, instead of raising you, keeps you down. Too frequent doses of original thinking from others, restrain what lesser portion of that faculty you may possess of your own. You get entangled in another man's mind, even as you lose yourself in another man's grounds. You are walking with a tall varlet, whose strides out-pace yours to lassitude. The constant operation of such potent agency would reduce me, I am convinced, to imbecility. You may derive thoughts from others; your way of thinking, the mould in which your thoughts are cast, must be your own. Intellect may be imparted, but not each man's intellectual frame.—

7. John Locke's *An Essay concerning Human Understanding* (1690); Thomas Campbell's *The Pleasures of Hope* (1799); and Thomas Moss's "The Beggar's Petition," which Moss (d. 1808) included in his *Poems on Several Occasions* (1769) and a manuscript of which Lamb commented on in the original version of "A Complaint of the Decay of Beggars in the Metropolis" (*Works,* II, 387). Lamb had misspelled "petitioned" in Letter 299, near the reference to note 5.

8. A passion.

316. *C. L. to Leigh Hunt*

[May 13, 1816]

Dear Sir,—

I thank you much for the Curious Volume of Southey,[1] which I return, together with Falstaff's Letters, Elgin Stone Report, & a little work of my own, of which perhaps you have no copy & I have a great many.

Yours truly,
C. Lamb

MS: unrecovered. Text: *The Lambs,* p. 136. Also pub.: Harper, IV, 73–74; Lucas (1935), II, 192. Notation: "Received from C. Lamb, 13th May, 1816.— L. H."

1. Possibly one of the two volumes of Southey's *Omniana, or Horae Otiosiores* (1812), to which Coleridge had contributed. Referred to next is James White's *Original Letters, &c. of Sir John Falstaff and His Friends.* (See my Vol. I, Introduction, p. xxxvi.) The House of Commons *Report from the Select Committee . . . on the Earl of Elgin's Collection of Sculptured Marbles* (1816) resulted in the act, passed in July 1816, allowing the British nation to purchase for £35,000 the sculptures and architectural fragments once integral parts of the Parthenon and other classic Athenian buildings—parts in the British Museum since 1816 and celebrated most famously in Keats's "On Seeing the Elgin Marbles for the First Time"—parts that the diplomatist, army officer, and art collector Thomas Bruce, seventh Earl of Elgin and eleventh Earl of Kincardine (1766–1841), had acquired during his tenure (1799–1803) as envoy extraordinary at the Porte. In *The Lambs,* p. 136, Lamb's own "little work" is stated but not shown to be the *John Woodvil* volume.

317. *C. L. to Mary Matilda Betham*

E. I. H.
1 June 1816

Dear Miss Betham,

I have sent your *very pretty lines*[1] to Southey in a frank as you requested. Poor S! what a grievous loss he must have had.— Mary and I rejoyce in the prospect of seeing you soon in Town. Let *us* be among the very first persons you come to see. Believe me that you can have no friends who respect & love you more than ourselves. Pray present our kind remembrances to Barbara, and to all to whom you may think they will be acceptable.

Yours very sincerely

C Lamb

Have you seen Christabel since its publication?—

MS: Huntington Library. Pub.: Hazlitt, II, 26, 396–397, and 455; Ainger (1888), I, 308; Ainger (1900), II, 256; Macdonald, I, 380; Ainger (1904), I, 365; Harper, IV, 74; Lucas (1905), VI, 489–490; Lucas (1912), V, 517; Lucas (1935), II, 193.

1. Unidentified. Southey's "grievous loss" (below) was of his son Herbert (b. 1806), who had died, from an unspecified disease, on April 17, 1816. Remembered by name near the end of this letter is Barbara Betham. See Vol. II, Letter 222, note 13.

318. *C. L. to Henry Dodwell*

Calne——Wilts

Friday, July something [July 5],— —old style

1816——no new style here,

all the styles are old & some of the gates too

For that matter

My Dear fellow—

I have been in a lethargy this long while and forgotten London Westminster Marybone Paddington—they all went clean out of my head, till happening to go to a neighbors[1] in this good borough of Calne, for want of whist players, we fell upon *Commerce,* the word awoke me to a remembrance of my professional avocations and the long-continued strife which I have been these 24 years endeavoring to compose between those grand Irreconcileables **Cash & Commerce; I** instantly call'd for an almanack which with some difficulty was procured at a fortune-tellers in the vicinity (for the happy holyday people here having nothing to do keep no account of time) & found that by dint of duty I must attend in Leadenhall on Wednesd. morning next[2] & shall attend accordingly. Does Master Hennah give macaroons still & does he fetch the Cobbets from my Attic? Perhaps it would'nt be too much trouble for him to drop the inclosed up at my aforesaid Chamber . . & any letters &c with it. but the inclosed should go without delay. N. B. he is'nt to fetch Monday's Cobbett, but it is to wait my Reading when I come back. **Heigh Ho!** Lord have mercy upon me, how many does two & two make? I am afraid I shall make a poor **Clerk** in future, I am spoiled with rambling among hay-cocks & cows & pigs. Bless me I had like to have forgot (the air is so temperate & ob*l*ivious here) to say I have seen your Brother & hope he is doing well in the finest spot of the world——

More of these things when I return, Remember me to the Gentle-men, I forget names——. shall I find all my Letters at my rooms on Tuesday, If you forgot to send e'm never mind, for I dont much care for reading & writing now, I shall come back again by degrees I sup-pose into my former habits——. How is **Bruce de Ponthieu & Porcher & Co.**[3] The tears come into my **Eyes** when I think how long I have neglect[ed them (?).]

Adieu! Ye fields ye shepherds—& herdesses & dairies & creampots & fairies & dances upon the green

I come I come—, Do'nt drag me so hard by the hair of my head Genius of British India! I know my hour is come, **Faustus** must give up his soul, O Lucifer, O Mephostophelies![4] Can you make out what all this Letter is about, I am afraid to look it over——

Ch. Lamb

MS: Berg Collection, New York Public Library. Pub.: Ainger (1888), I, 308–309; Ainger (1900), II, 256–258; Ainger (1904), I, 365–366; Harper, IV, 74–76; Lucas (1935), II, 193–194. Address: H. Dodwell Esqr/India House/London/ In his absence, may be opene'd by Mr Chambers. Postmarks: Calne; July 1816. The remark at the reference to note 2 in this letter and the place of composition and postmark date of the next letter (London, July 9, 1816) establish the date of this letter. The next letter and an unpublished entry in Robinson's diary dis-covered by Gertrude Alison Anderson (see my Vol. I, Introduction, p. lxxxviii) and noted in Lucas (1935), II, 194, stating that Robinson had visited Lamb on Tuesday, June 11, indicate that the Lambs had left London for the John Morgans' in Calne shortly after June 11 and were home again shortly before July 9. (A comment preceding the presentation of this letter in Lucas [1935], II, 193—"It was on the night of 15th June 1816 that Fanny Kelly was fired at by a lunatic named George Barnett during the performance at Covent Garden, some of the shot falling into the lap of Mary Lamb, who was with her brother in the pit"— seems to show that the Lambs had left for Calne after June 15. But the shooting incident, the biographers of Frances Maria Kelly agree, had taken place during the performance, of a farce by John O'Keeffe [see Letter 300, near the beginning of note 13] titled *Modern Antiques; or, the Merry Mourners,* at Drury Lane on February 17, 1816—the date given also in notes about the incident in *Works,* I, 460, and Lucas [1935], II, 240. A few remarks on or relating to the Lambs' vacation are in Letters 319, 320, and 322.) Henry Dodwell (1782?–1837), **the** addressee of this letter and Lamb's East India House crony characterized as

"Do——, mild, slow to move, and gentlemanly," in "The Superannuated Man" (*Works*, II, 197), was the son of the Reverend Mr. Henry Dodwell of Maiden-head, Berkshire. The younger Henry Dodwell was appointed to the accountant general's department of the East India House in 1797, was in receipt of salary as a clerk from 1800 and of a special annual gratuity as the superintendent of the cash and commerce journals, and was retired in 1826. In the course of his service with the East India House he became a captain in the Royal East India Volunteers. He died, according to the *Times* obituary of February 4, 1837, at Pinkney-lodge, Maidenhead. Neither the Mrs. Dodwell mentioned in Lamb's letter to him, at Maidenhead, of October 7, 1827 (in Vol. V), nor his brother mentioned in this letter, near the end of its first paragraph, has been identified. John Chambers (1789?–1862), referred to in the address of this letter and characterized as Lamb's crony "Ch——, dry, sarcastic, and friendly," in "The Superannuated Man" (*Works*, II, 197), had followed Lamb into Christ's Hospital as well as into the East India House. John Chambers was appointed to the accountant general's department in 1805, was in receipt of salary as a clerk from 1808, and was retired in 1834. He died at Lee, Kent, according to the *Times* obituary of September 5, 1862, presumably at his home, Radway Cottage, Lee Green. His elder brother Charles (d. 1857?), the addressee of Letter 330, was at Christ's Hospital with Lamb. Charles Chambers became a surgeon in the royal navy and, afterward, a surgeon in Leamington, Warwickshire. He began to practice in Leamington in 1819—so read the records in the custody of Mr. H. S. Tallamy of the public library and museum of the borough of Royal Leamington Spa—as an assistant to Dr. Henry Jephson, an important contributor to the development of Leamington in the nineteenth century. John and Charles Chambers, like Thomas, Edmund, and Mary, were the children of the Reverend Mr. Thomas Chambers, vicar of Radway-Edgehill, Warwickshire, and the former Miss Miller. Lamb remembered the father in "Thoughts on Presents of Game, &c." (*Works*, I, 343), as "the sensible clergy-man in Warwickshire, whose son's acquaintance has made many hours happy in the life of Elia." Letters from Lamb to members or friends of the Chambers family may be or may have been extant in addition to the letters to John and Charles Chambers in this edition. For in *The Lambs*, pp. 36 and 95, are references to a series of letters—implied is a series of many letters, known but not available to William Carew Hazlitt—from Lamb to members of the Chambers family or its circle. And in G. D. Klingopulos' "Charles Lamb and John Chambers," in the *TLS* of September 5, 1958, is a report of "the theft of the contents of two packages of Lamb's letters during the sale of some of Emily Morriss's effects after her death." Miss Morriss (d. 1893), once the owner of Lamb's letter to Henry Dodwell or John Chambers of August 26, 1819, and of Lamb's "Rules and directions to be observed by Mr [John] Chambers at the end of June 1823" (both in Vol. IV), was John Chambers' adopted daughter. The account of the Chambers family in *The Lambs*, pp. 36–40, is corrected in *Lamb and Hazlitt*, pp. xxxiii–xxxiv. Most helpful in my identifications of Henry Dodwell and John Chambers have been Carl Wood-ring's "Lamb Takes a Holiday," *Harvard Library Bulletin*, 14 (1960), esp. 255–258 and 260; Mr. S. J. McNally of the India Office Library and Records, who time and again has identified or provided the information necessary for the proper identification of Lamb's East India House associates figuring in these letters; and Samuel McKechnie's "Charles Lamb of the India House," *Notes and Queries*, 191 (December 28, 1946), esp. 277 and 278–279, and *Notes and Queries*, 192 (February 8, 1947), 54. The McKechnie article is more substantial than would appear from my citations, here and elsewhere, of what are in fact some of its parts: "Charles Lamb of the India House" is published, serially, in its entirety, in *Notes and Queries*, 191 (November 2, 16, 30, December 14, and 28, 1946), 178–180, 204–206, 225–230, 252–256, and 277–280; in *Notes and Queries*, 192 (January 11, 25, February 8, 15, and March 8, 1947), 9–13, 25–29, 53–56, 72–73, and

103–106; and in the *CLSB* of May, July, and November 1948, and January and May 1949.

1. Possibly to the home of the Reverend Mr. and Mrs. William Money of Whetham, near Calne, or to that of Mr. and Mrs. John Merewether of Blackland, near Calne, families to whom Lamb sends his remembrances in the fifth paragraph in what remains of the next letter. Letters to Money and either to Merewether or to his son John (1797–1850), until 1818 an undergraduate at Queen's College, Oxford, and from 1832 a doctor of divinity and the dean of Hereford, Herefordshire, are in *Coleridge's Letters*, IV, 609–610 and 616–617. *"Commerce"* (below) refers to a card game.

2. July 10. Lamb below inquires after Thomas Richard Buckle Hennah (d. 1843), who had been appointed, presumably as a clerk, to the accountant general's department of the East India House in 1815. The "Cobbets" are issues of *Cobbett's Weekly Political Register* (1802–1835), the successor to William Cobbett's *Porcupine's Gazette* (1797–1799) and *The Porcupine* (1800–1801). (See my Vol. I, Letter 93, note 3.) The enclosure has not been recovered.

3. Samuel McKechnie in "Charles Lamb, Bruce de Ponthieu, and Porcher and Co.," *Notes and Queries,* 186 (January 29, 1944), 71, identified them as East India Houses of Agency, representing "private traders whose commodities were brought to England in the [East India] Company's ships and sold in the Company's Sale Room." McKechnie in "Charles Lamb of the India House," *Notes and Queries,* 192 (February 8, 1947), 54, names the agencies as "Messrs. Bruce, de Ponthieu, Bazett & Co. and Porcher & Co." Lamb's "dances upon the green," concluding the next paragraph, is derived from Sir Walter Scott's *The Lay of the Last Minstrel,* III, 14.

4. Cf. Christopher Marlowe's *The Tragical History of the Life and Death of Doctor Faustus,* V, ii, 141–142, 147, and 187–188.

319. *C. L. to Morgan*

[Tuesday, July 9, 1816]

[. . .] to the Lyceum tonight, all three theatres are shut in consequence of the Duke of Gloster having capriciously altered his mind respecting the Princess Mary[1]—he has seen a cheesemongers daughter in Little Britain he thinks he can be more happy with—

Just as we got to Slough, my heart broke—it frightened every body in the coach—at one corner of it (there are 3, Miss John Wait) at one corner of it was discovered, by help of microscopic glasses the sweet image of—**Old Bendry**——

My kindest love to that worthy old man[—]I never shall forget his civilities—also to Mr. Brooke & the firm

Sheridan is dead, we hear he died worth Two hundred thousand pounds, accumulated in the Manchester & Cotton Trade, which he has been secretly engaged in (to my knowlege) for some years.[2]

Remember me to the Moneys & Mereweathers[—]I shall never forget their hospitality—

I am sorry we did not see the **Waits** & Mr Marsh while we were with you, it was unlucky their being from Town.— Martin Burney is going into the stocking Line,[3] & I have some thoughts of opening a Bazaar. Business is so slack at the India House—

Mary has put in something about somebody coming to town that I am to give up my bed to. I am afraid I shall submit to that with a very ill grace, I get so sleepy of a night after Supper. It is the gauze lettuces.—

How are Charlottes Eyes? she should bathe them in Pump water a mornings & abstain from tragedy-reading &c. God bless her & all of you, I have hardly room to be serious, her allowance of Goosebury is scarcely out of my head yet.

C Lamb

MS: British Museum. Pub.: T. C. Skeat, "Letters of Charles and Mary Lamb and Coleridge," *British Museum Quarterly,* 26 (1962–1963), 20. Address: J. J. Morgan Esqr/Calne/Wilts. Postmark: July 9, 1816. Missing is the first leaf—a bit of it still attached to the second leaf has writing on both sides—of a folio sheet.

1. William Frederick, second Duke of Gloucester of the fifth creation (1776–1834), would, on July 23, 1816, be married to his first cousin Princess Mary—to become in addition Duchess of Gloucester and Edinburgh—the fourth daughter of George III. The ceremony was being delayed until her brother Ernest Augustus, Duke of Cumberland and, later, King of Hanover (1771–1851), could return from Hanover and attend. "Miss John" Wait and the Waits, as well as Bendry, Brooke, and Marsh, mentioned below, apparently Calne acquaintances of the Morgans and Charlotte Brent, have not been identified. Mention of a Mr. Wait of or near Calne for whom Coleridge had in March 1815 drawn up a petition against the Corn Bill addressed to Parliament is in *Coleridge's Letters,* IV, 549. References to Marsh are in IV, 555 and 556, possibly 593 also, though the reference in the last instance could be to Herbert Marsh (1757–1839), bishop of Llandaff from 1816 to 1819 and of Peterborough thereafter, referred to in *Coleridge's Letters,* V, 46. The Moneys and "Mereweathers" are identified in note 1 to the preceding letter in this edition of Lamb letters.

2. Richard Brinsley Sheridan had died on July 7, 1816, from a disease of the brain perhaps partly caused by anxiety over his indebtedness. His income at the end seems to have come solely from his shares in the proprietorship of Drury Lane Theatre.

3. Martin Burney did not go into that line. He continued to pursue a career in the law. The somebody alluded to near the beginning of the next paragraph is probably Charlotte Brent (see Letter 322, seventh paragraph counting the postscript at the head of the letter); by "gauze lettuces" is meant cos lettuce (see Letter 278, at the reference to note 5, and Letter 279, last paragraph not counting the postscript); Miss Brent's eye trouble may have been chronic, for Coleridge had advised Morgan in February 1812 (see *Coleridge's Letters,* III, 370) not to let her rub her eye.

320. *C. L. to William Wordsworth*
from Leadin Hall
Septemr something [September 23] 1816

My dear Wordsworth,

It seems an age since we have corresponded, but indeed the interim
has been stuffd out with more variety than usually checquers my same-
seeming existence—. Mercy on me, what a traveller have I been since
I wrote you last! what foreign wonders have been explored! I have
seen Bath, King Bladuds ancient well,[1] fair Bristol seed-plot of suicidal
Chatterton, Marlbro, Chippenham, Calne, famous for nothing in particular that I know of—but such a vertigo of locomotion has not seized
us for years—. We spent a month with the Morgans at the last named
Borough,—August[2]—and such a change has the change wrought in
us that we could not stomach wholesome Temple air, but are absolutely
rusticating (o the gentility of it) at Dalston, about one mischievous
boy's stone's throw off Kingsland Turnpike, one mile from Shoreditch
church, thence we emanate in various directions to Hackney, Clapton,
Totnam, and such like romantic country. That my lungs should ever
prove so dainty as to fancy they perceive differences of **air!** but so it
is, tho' I am almost ashamed of it, like Milton's devil[3] (turn'd truant
to his old Brimstone) I am purging off the foul air of my once darling
tobacco in this **Eden,** absolutey snuffing up pure gales, **like** old worn
out Sin playing at being innocent which never comes again, for in
spite of good books & good thoughts there is something in a **Pipe** that
virtue cannot give tho' she give her unendowed person for a dowry.
Have you read the review of Coleridges character, person, physiognomy
&c. in the Examiner,—his features even to his *nose*—O horrible license
beyond the old Comedy—.[4] **He** is himself gone to the sea side with his
favorite Apothecary, having left for publication as I hear a prodigious
mass of composition for a Sermon to the middling ranks of people to
persuade them they are not so distressed as is commonly supposed. Methinks he should recite it to a congregation of Bilston Colliers,[5]——
the fate of **Cinna** the **Poet** would instantaneously be his. God bless
him, but certain that rogue-Examiner has beset him in most unman-
nerly strains. Yet there is a kind of respect shines thro' the disrespect

that to those who know the rare compound (that is the subject of it)
almost balances the reproof, but then those who know him but partially
or at a distance are so extremely apt to drop the qualifying part thro'
their fingers. The "after all, Mr Wordsworth is a man of great talents,
if he did not abuse them"[6] comes so dim upon the eyes of an Edinbro'
review reader, that have been gloating-open chuckle-wide upon the
preceding detail of abuses, it scarce strikes the pupil with any consciousness of the letters being there, like letters writ in lemon—. There
was a cut at me a few months back by the same hand, but my agnomen
or agni-nomen[7] not being calculated to strike the popular **ear**, it
dropt anonymous, but it was a pretty compendium of observation
which the author has collected in my disparagement, from some hun-
dreds of social evenings which we had spent together,—however in
spite of all, there is something tough in my attachment to H——
which these violent strainings cannot quite dislocate or sever asunder.
I get no conversation in London that is absolutely worth attending to
but his. There is monstrous little sense in the world, or I am monstrous
clever, or squeamish or something, but there is nobody to talk to—to
talk *with* I should say—and to go talking to ones self all day long is
too much of a good thing, besides subjecting one to the imputation of
being out of ones senses, which does no good to ones temporal interest
at all. By the way, I have seen Colerge. but once this 3 or 4 months,
he is an odd person, when he first comes to town he is quite hot upon
visiting, and then he turns off & absolutely never comes at all, but
seems to forget there are anysuch people in the world. I made one
attempt to visit him (a morning call) at Highgate, but there was something in him or his Apothecary which I found so unattractively-
repulsing-from any temptation to call again, that I stay away as
naturally as a Lover visits. The rogue gives you Love Powders,[8] and
then a strong horse drench to bring 'em off your stomach that they
may'nt hurt you. I was very sorry the printing of your Letter was not
quite to your mind, but I surely did not think but you had arranged
the manner of breaking the paragraphs from some principle known
to your own mind, and for some of the Errors, I am confident that
Note of Admiration, in the middle of two words did not stand so when
I had it, it must have dropt out & been replaced wrong, so odious a
blotch could not have escaped me. Gifford (whom God curse) has
persuaded squinting Murray (whom may God not bless) not to accede

to an offer Field made for me to print 2 vols. of Essays, to include the one on Hogrth. & 1 or 2 more, but most of the matter to be new, but I dare say I should never have found time to make them; **M** would have had 'em, but shewed specimens from the Reflector to **G**—as he acknowledged to Field, & Crispin did for me.[9] "Not on his soal but on his soul damn'd Jew" may the malediction of my eternal antipathy light—. We desire much to hear from you, and of you all, including Miss Hutchinson for not writing to whom Mary feels a weekly (and did for a long time, feel a daily) Pang. How is Southey?— I hope his pen will continue to move many years smoothly & continuously for all the rubs of the rogue Examiner.[10] A pertinacious **foul** mouthed villain it is!—

This is written for a rarity at the seat of business, it is but little time I can generally command from secular calligraphy, the pen seems to know as much and makes letters like figures——an obstinate clerkish thing. It shall make a couplet in spite of its nib before I have done with it,

> "and so I end
> Commending me to your love my dearest **friend**."[11]

C Lamb

MS: University of Texas Library. Pub.: Harper, IV, 76–80; Lucas (1905), VI, 490–492; Lucas (1912), V, 517–520; Lucas (1935), II, 195–197. Address: Wm. Wordsworth Esqr/Rydale Mount/near Kendal/Westmorland. Postmark: September 23, 1816. Leadenhall Street was the site of the East India House.

1. Again Bath: according to the legend Geoffrey of Monmouth (1100?–1154) told in his *Historia regum Britanniæ,* or *Historia Britonum* (1137?), King Bladud, in myth the father of King Lear, founded the city and magically caused its waters to be healing; according to another legend, Bladud founded the city—863 B.C. is the founding date inscribed on his statue in the pump room in Bath—when, wandering in banishment as a leprous swineherd, he discovered that the waters cured his disease. Lamb's next phrase, pertaining to Bristol and Thomas Chatterton, is explained, in effect, in Vol. I, Letter 6, note 2. Marlborough and Chippenham, to the east and northwest of Calne, are, like Calne, old Wiltshire market towns.

2. Parts of June and July, actually. (See Letter 318, source note.) August, the name or the month, may have been so attractive to Lamb that he was lured from fact here and in a letter to Thomas Allsop postmarked September 9, 1823 (in Vol. V), which Lamb dated "9 Aug 23." If the Lambs were "rusticating" (below) at the time of this letter at the address Mary will give in a letter of 1821 to Marianne Ayrton (in Vol. IV), they were at a Mr. Coston's, 14 Kingsland Row, Dalston, a London suburb named in "The South-sea House" (*Works,* II, 1). By "Totnam" is meant Tottenham.

3. In *Paradise Lost*, Books II–IV. Cf. some of Lamb's language or its sense from the end of the parenthesis to the end of the sentence with *Paradise Lost*, II, 399–402—

> . . . and at the brightning Orient beam
> Purge off this gloom; the soft delicious Air,
> To heal the scarr of these corrosive Fires
> Shall breathe her balme . . .

Cf. Lamb's passage also with Coleridge and Southey's "The Devil's Thoughts," line 23—"And the Devil did grin, for his darling sin"; with *The Faerie Queene*, III, v, 870—"There, whether yt divine tobacco were"; with Scott's *The Lady of the Lake*, I, 47—"A moment snuff'd the tainted gale"; and with the proverb "Virtue is her own reward."

4. The review referred to, which is unsigned but by Hazlitt and in *The Examiner* of September 8, 1816—an issue Lamb would forward to Wordsworth, evidently (in Letter 322, in the sentence ending at the reference to note 1, Lamb mentions having received it back)—is titled "A Lay-sermon on the Distresses of the Country, *Addressed to the Middle and Higher Orders. By* S. T. Coleridge, *Esq.* Printed for Gale and Fenner. . . ." The review, so called, is noted to have been "written before the Discourse which it [the 'review'] professes to criticise had appeared in print, or probably existed any where, but in repeated newspaper advertisements." Rather than being a review of Coleridge's work advertised as the title above, a work to be published in November or December 1816, as *The Statesman's Manual; or the Bible the Best Guide to Political Skill and Foresight: A Lay Sermon, Addressed to the Higher Classes of Society, with an Appendix, Containing Comments and Essays Connected with the Study of the Inspired Writings*, Hazlitt's "review" is a poisonous attack on Coleridge. Coleridge to Hazlitt is, among other things, the "Prince of preparatory authors" and the "Dog in the Manger of literature." Coleridge is an "intellectual Mar-Plot" whose notions are "floating and unfixed," whose ideas "seek to avoid all contact with solid substances," to whom truth is "a ceaseless round of contradictions," who "lives in the belief of a perpetual lie," all of whose attempts are marked by "Everlasting inconsequentiality," all of whose impulses are "loose, airy, devious, casual." Coleridge is "the Man in the Moon, the Wandering Jew.—The reason," wrote Hazlitt, "of all this is, that Mr. Coleridge has great powers of thought and fancy, without will or sense. He is without a strong feeling of the existence of any thing out of himself; and he has neither purposes nor passions of his own to make him wish it to be. Mr. Shandy would have settled the question at once:—'You have little or no nose, Sir.' " (That last sentence, incorporating language from Laurence Sterne's *Tristram Shandy*, Vol. III, ch. xxxi, Hazlitt would delete before republishing the "review," in *Political Essays, with Sketches of Public Characters* [1819].) Yet Coleridge is "fit to take up the deep pauses of conversation between Cardinals and Angels—his cue would not be wanting in presence of the beatific vision. Let him talk on for ever in this world and the next; and both worlds will be the better for it. But let him not write, or pretend to write, nonsense. Nobody is the better for it" (*Hazlitt's Works*, VII, 115, 117, 381, and 118; about related attacks of 1816–1817 by Hazlitt and others on Coleridge and others see notes 7 and 10 to this letter, *Hazlitt*, pp. 355–364, and *Coleridge's Letters*, IV, esp. 668). Robinson called on the Lambs in the evening of November 2, 1816, and with them and Martin Burney and Talfourd talked, among other topics, of Hazlitt's present attack on Coleridge. Robinson reported that Lamb thought it "fair enough, between the parties; but he was half angry with Martin Burney for asserting the praise was greater than the abuse. Nobody, said Lamb, will care about or understand the 'taking up the deep pauses of conversation between seraphs and cardinals,' but the satire will be universally felt. Such an article is like saluting a man: 'Sir, you are the greatest man I ever saw,' and then pulling him by the nose" (*H. C. R. on*

Books and Writers, I, 197). "Apothecary," in Lamb's next sentence, alludes to James Gillman.

5. Those employed to work the mines in the vicinity of Bilston, Staffordshire. Lamb below refers to the poet Gaius Helvius Cinna—"Tear him for his bad verses," orders a plebeian mobster in *Julius Caesar,* III, iii, 31—in contradistinction to Lucius Cornelius Cinna, the younger (fl. 44 B.C.), a conspirator against Julius Caesar.

6. Lamb's recollection of something Francis Jeffrey had stated in his review of *The Excursion,* in the *Edinburgh Review* of November 1814 (see Letter 287, note 2): "But the truth is, that Mr. Wordsworth, with all his perversities, is a person of great powers" (p. 16). "Nobody," Jeffrey had also stated, "can be more disposed to do justice to the great powers of Mr. Wordsworth than we are" (p. 29). Cf. the last phrase in Lamb's sentence here with "as words written in lemon come out upon exposure to a friendly warmth," which is in "Mackery End, in Hertfordshire" (*Works,* II, 79) and quoted in context in Letter 296, note 5.

7. A play on *agnomen*—an additional (usually a fourth) name, as in Marcus Porcius Cato Uticensis—and on *agni:* "lamb's." The cut at Lamb is in the last note to a two-part review of Southey's *The Lay of the Laureate. Carmen Nuptiale* (1816), a bitter review, unsigned but by Hazlitt, in *The Examiner* of July 7 and 14, 1816. In that note Hazlitt explained that his review "falls somewhat short of its original destination, by our having been forced to omit two topics, the praise of Bonaparte, and the abuse of poetry. The former we leave to history: the latter," he added, alluding first to Leigh Hunt and then to Lamb, "we have been induced to omit from our regard to two poets of our acquaintance. We must say they have spoiled sport. One of them has tropical blood in his veins, which gives a gay, cordial, vinous spirit to his whole character. The other is a mad wag,— who ought to have lived at the Court of Horwendillus [or Horvendillus, Hamlet's father in the *Historia Danica,* or *Gesta Danorum* (ca. 1200), by Saxo Grammaticus (ca. 1150–1206)], with Yorick and Hamlet,—equally desperate in his mirth and his gravity, who would laugh at a funeral and weep at a wedding, who talks nonsense to prevent the head-ache, who would wag his finger at a skeleton, whose jests scald like tears, who makes a joke of a great man, and a hero of a cat's paw" (*Hazlitt's Works,* VII, 96–97). What follows in Lamb's sentence identifies "H——" (below) as Hazlitt, not Leigh Hunt, the editor of Leigh and John Hunt's *The Examiner.*

8. A paraphrase—another is in Vol. I, Letter 66, at the reference to note 3—of *I Henry IV,* II, ii, 18–19: "If the rascal have not given me medicines to make me love him, I'll be hang'd." Lamb below writes of *A Letter to a Friend of Robert Burns* (see above, Letter 313, note 1) and would seem to refer by "that Note of Admiration . . ." to the misplaced asterisk in the following passage: "The *Edinburgh* reviewer . . . thus writes:* 'The *leading vice* in Burns's character, and the *cardinal deformity,* indeed, of ALL his productions, was his contempt, or affectation of contempt, for prudence, decency, and regularity, and his admiration of thoughtlessness, oddity, and vehement sensibility . . .' " Wordsworth's footnote reads so: "* From Mr. Peterkin's pamphlet [*A Review of the Life of Robert Burns and of Various Criticisms on His Character and Writings* (1815), by the miscellaneous writer Alexander Peterkin (1780–1846)], who vouches for the accuracy of his citations; omitting, however, to apologize for their length" (*Wordsworth's Prose Works,* II, 16). Mary F. Daniels of the Department of Rare Books, Cornell University Library, has been so thoughtful as to scrutinize Cornell's copy of the first edition of Wordsworth's *Letter* and assure me that there are no egregious printer's errors in it.

9. The sentence appears to mean that William Gifford of the *Quarterly Review* has persuaded the publisher John Murray to reject an offer Barron Field had made for Lamb to Murray to publish two volumes of Lamb's essays, volumes to have

contained "On the Genius and Character of Hogarth" (see Letter 291, note 3) and one or two other essays already published or written but to have contained mostly new essays, though Lamb now dares to say he could never have found time to compose them; should Lamb have found time to compose the new ones, Murray would have accepted them and the others for publication, but Murray, as he acknowledged to Field, had shown Gifford specimens of Lamb's essays in *The Reflector,* and Gifford, or St. Crispin (see Letter 287, near the end of the source note), accomplished the defeat of Lamb. Lamb's idea of bringing out an edition of essays changed during the coming months to the plan realized in June 1818, when Charles and James Ollier issued *The Works of Charles Lamb.* Lamb will write about certain of its details in a letter to the Olliers postmarked May 28, 1818 (in Vol. IV), where a note provides information on the edition and its publishers. "Not on thy sole, but on thy soul, harsh Jew" is the line, in *The Merchant of Venice,* IV, i, 123, Lamb appropriates following.

10. Four particularly rancorous rubs against Southey in *The Examiner* were to come and to involve Coleridge: Hazlitt's series of responses to Southey's article headed "Parliamentary Reform" in the *Quarterly Review,* 16 (October 1816), 225–278; to *Wat Tyler; a Dramatic Poem* (1817), a piratical publication of a manuscript advocating sedition for the sake of social reform that Southey had written in 1794; to Coleridge's defenses of Southey in *The Courier* of March 17 and 18, 1817, against the charge William Smith (see my Vol. II, Letter 205, note 1) had made in the House of Commons on March 14, 1817, that *Wat Tyler* revealed its author—the author as well of a *Quarterly Review* article (cited above) denouncing as seditious those persons agitating for reform—to be a renegade after all; and to *A Letter to William Smith, Esq. M.P. from Robert Southey, Esq.* (1817), Southey's defense of himself. Hazlitt's series is in *The Examiner* of March 9 and 30, April 6, and May 4, 11, and 18, 1817; the series is in *Hazlitt's Works,* VII, 168–208, and XIX, 196–198. The affair is discussed, among other places, in *Hazlitt,* pp. 359–362, and *New Southey Letters,* II, 150–151.

11. In Burns's "Man Was Made to Mourn: A Dirge," line 81, is "dearest friend"; in *Hamlet,* I, ii, 182, is "my dearest foe."

321. *C. L. to James and Louisa Holcroft Kenney*

[14? Kingsland Row, Dalston,] **Lonres**
[16?] October month 1816

Dear friends,

it is with infinite regret I inform you that the pleasing privilege of receiving Letters, by which I have for these twenty years gratified my friends and abused the liberality of the Company trading to the Orient, is now at an end. A cruel edict of the Directors has swept it away altogether. The devil sweep away their patronage also. Rascals who think nothing of spunging upon their Employers for their Venison and Turtle and Burgundy five days in a week to the tune of five thousand pounds a year, now find out that the profits of trade will not allow the innocent communication of thought between their underlings and

their friends in distant provinces to proceed untaxed, thus withering
up the heart of friendship and making the news of a friend's good
health worse than indifferent, a tidings to be deprecated as bringing
with it ungracious expences. Adieu gentle correspondence, kindly
conveyance of soul, interchange of love, of opinions, of puns and what
not. Henceforth a friend that does not stand in visible or palpable
distance to me, is nothing to me. They have not left to the bosom of
friendship even that cheap intercourse of sentiment, the twopenny
medium. The upshot is, you must not direct any more letters through
me. . *To* me you may annually or biennially transmit a brief account
of your goings on in single sheet, from ⟨the Expence of⟩ which after I
have deducted as much as the postage comes to, the remainder will be
pure pleasure. But no more of those pretty commissions and counter
commissions, orders & revokings of orders, obscure messages & obscurer
explanations, by which the intellects of Marshall and Fanny[1] used to
be kept in a pleasing perplexity at the moderate rate of six or seven
shillings a week. . In short you must use me no longer as a go-between.
Henceforth I write up **no thoroughfare**——

Well, and how far is Saint **Wallery suresome** from Paris, and do
you get wine and walnuts tolerable, and the vintage does it suffer from
the wet, I take it the wine of this season will be all wine & water, and
have you Plays & Green rooms & Fanny Kellies to chat with of an
Evening, and is the air purer than the old gravel pits, and the bread
so much whiter as they say? Lord what things you see that travel. I
dare say the people are all French wherever you go, what an over-
whelming effect that must have, I have stood one of em at a time, but
two I generally found overpowring, I used to cut and run, but then in
their own vineyards maybe they are endurable enough, they say
marmosets in Senegambia are as pleasant as the days long, jumping
& chattering in the orange twigs, but transport em one by one over
here into England, they turn into monkeys some with tails, some without, and are obliged to be kept in cages. I suppose you know weve
left the Temple pro tempore. By the way this conduct has caused
strange surmises in a good Lady[2] of our acquaintance. She lately sent
for a young gentleman of the India House who lives opposite her at
Monroe's the flute shop in Skinner Street Snowhill, I mention no
names, you shall never get out of me what lady I mean,—on purpose
to ask all he knew about us, I had previously introduced him to her

whist table, her enquiries embraced every possible thing that could be known of me, how I stood in the India house, what was the amount of my salary, what it was likely to be hereafter, whether I was thought clever in business, why I had taken country lodgings, why at Kingsland in particular, had I friends in that road, was any body expected to visit me, did I wish for visitors, would an unexpected call be gratifying or not, would it be better that she sent beforehand, did any body come to see me, was'nt there a Gentleman of the name of Morgan, did he know him, did'nt he come to see me, did he know how Mr Morgan lived, she never could make out how they were maintained, was it true he lived out of the profits of a linen drapers shop in Bishopsgate Street—(there she was a little right & a little wrong—M is a Gentleman tobacconist) in short she multiplied demands upon him till my friend who is neither over modest nor nervous declared he quite shuddered, after laying me as bare to her curiosity as an anatomy he trembled to think what she would ask next, my pursuits, inclinations, aversions, attachments (**some** my dear friends, of a most delicate nature) she lugged 'em out of him or would had he been privy to them, as you pluck a horse bean from its iron stem, not as such tender rose buds should be pulled. The fact is I am come to Kingsland ✳✳✳✳✳✳ ✳✳✳✳✳✳ and that is the real truth of the matter, and nobody but yourselves should have extorted such a confession from me. I suppose you have seen by the Pap[er]s that Manning is arrived in England. He expressed some mortification at not finding Mrs. Kenny in England. He looks a good deal sunburnt, and is got a little reserved, but I hope it will wear off. You will see by the Papers also that Dawe is knighted. He has been painting the Princess of Coborg & her husband.[3] This is all the news I could think of. Write *to* us, but not *by* us, for I have near ten correspondents of this latter description, and one or other comes pouring in every day, till my purse strings and heart strings crack. Bad habits are not all broken at once. I am sure you will excuse the apparent indelicacy of mentioning this, but dear is my shirt, but dearer is my skin,[4] and its too late when the steed is stole to shut the stable door—

Well and does Louisa grown a fine girl, is she likely to have her mothers complexion, and does Tom Polish in french air—Henry I mean—and Kenny is not so fidgety, & *You* sit down sometimes for a quiet halfhour or so, and all is comfortable, no bills (that you call

writs) nor any thing else (that you are equally sure to miscall) to annoy you, **vive la gaite de cœur et la bell pastime vive la beau France et revive ma cher Empreur**

C Lamb

MS: Berg Collection, New York Public Library. Pub.: Macdonald, I, 381–384; Harper, IV, 94–98; Lucas (1905), VI, 503–505; Lucas (1912), V, 530–532; Lucas (1935), II, 213–216. Address: Mr. Kenny/St. Valery Sur Somme/France. Postmark: [October] 16 [1816] or [October 18]16.

1. Probably Godwin's friend James Marshal and either Fanny Imlay or Fanny Holcroft. The fishing and commercial port of St. Valery-sur-Somme (to answer the first question in Lamb's next paragraph) is about one hundred miles northwest of Paris.

2. Mrs. Godwin. The gentleman referred to in the next sentence has not been identified. *Kent's Directory* for 1816 lists a music warehouse of James Monroe at 60 Snow Hill. The Godwins' address was 41 Skinner Street, Snow Hill.

3. Manning had not arrived in England, and George Dawe was never knighted. (See Letter 310, source note, and Letter 233, near the reference to note 5.) Shortly after the marriage, in May 1816, of Princess Charlotte Augusta and Prince Leopold of Saxe-Coburg, however, Dawe did paint "several portraits of the Royal couple in all varieties of costume" (G. D. Leslie and Fred. A. Eaton, "The Royal Academy in the Present Century," *Art Journal* [London: Virtue, 1899], p. 41).

4. An adaptation of the proverb "Close is my shirt, but closer my skin." About those named in the next paragraph see Letter 296, note 9. Lamb's French translates, "long live the heart's mirth and the fine pastime [and] long live beautiful France and restore my beloved Emperor."

322. *M. A. L. to Sara Hutchinson, with two postscripts from C. L.*

Inner Temple
[November? 1816]

Mary has barely left me room to say How d'ye—. I have received back the Examiner containing the delicate enquiry into certain infirm parts of S. T. C's character.[1] What is the general opinion of it. Farewell. My love to all.

C Lamb

My dear friend,

I have procured a frank for this day and having been hindered all the morning have no tim[e] left to frame excuses for my long and inexcusable silence & can only thank you for the very kind way in which you overlook it.

I should certainly have written on the receipt of yours but I had not a frank and also I wished to date my letter from my own home where you expressed so cordial a wish to hear we had arrived.

We have passed ten, I may call them very good weeks at Dalston, for they completely answered the purpose for which we went.— Reckoning our happy month at Calne we have had quite a rural summer & have obtained a very clear idea of the great benifit of quiet—of early hours and time intirely at ones own disposal, and no small advantages these things are, but the return to old friends—the sight of old familiar faces[2] round me has almost reconciled me to occasional headachs and fits of peevish weariness—even London streets, which I sometimes used to think it hard to be eternally doomed to walk through before I could see a green field, seem quite delightful.

Charles smoked but one pipe while we were at Dalston and he has not transgressed much since his return. I hope he will only smoke now with his fellow-smokers which will give him five or six clear days in the week.

Shame on me I did not even write to thank you for the bacon, upon which & some excellent eggs your sister[3] added to her kind present we had so many nice feasts. I have seen Henry Robinson who speaks in raptures of the days he passed with you. He says he never saw a man so happy in *three wives* as Mr Wordsworth is. I long to join you and make a fourth and we cannot help talking of the possibility in some future fortunate summer of venturing to come so far but we generally end in thinking the posibility impossible for I dare not come but by post chaises & the expence would be enormous, yet it was very pleasing to read Mrs Wordsworths kind invitation & to feel a kind of latent hope of what might one day happen.

You ask how Coleridge maintains himself. I know no more than you do. Strange to say I have seen him but once since he has been at Highgate & then I met him in the street. I have just been reading your kind letter over again and find you had some doubt whether we had left the Temple entirely. It was merely a lodging we took to recruit our health and spirits. from the time we left Calne Charles drooped sadly, company became quite irksome, and his anxious desire to leave off smoking and his utter inability to perform his daily resolutions against it became quite a torment to him, so I prevailed with him to try the experiment of change of scene and set out in one of the short stage coaches from Bishop[s]gate street, Miss Brent and I, and we looked over all the little places within three miles and fixed on one quite countrified and not two miles from Shoreditch Church and entered upon it the next day. I thought if we stayed but a week it would be a little rest and respite from our troubles and we made a ten weeks stay and very comfortable we were, so much so that if ever Charles is superannuated on a small pension, which is the great object of his ambition, and we felt our income straitened I do think I could live in the country entirely, at least I thought so while I was there but since I have been at home I wish to live and die in the Temple where I was born. We left the trees so green it looked like early autumn, and can see but one leaf "The last of its clan"[4] on our poor old Hare Court trees. What a rainy summer!—and yet I have been so much out of town and have made so much use of every fine day that I can hardly help thinking it has been a fine summer, we calculated we walked three hundred & fifty miles while we were in our country lodging. One thing I must tell you, Charles came round every morning to a shop[5] near the Temple to get shaved. Last sunday we had such a pleasant day I must tell you of it. We went to Kew and saw the old Palace where the King was was brought up, it was the pleasantest sight I ever saw, I can scarcely tell you why, but a charming old woman shewed it to us she had lived twenty six years there and spoke with such a hearty love of our good old King whom all the world seems to have forgotten that it did me good to hear her—. She was as proud in pointing out the plain furniture, (and I am sure you are now sitting in a larger & better furnished room) of a small room in which the King always dined nay more proud of the simplicity of her royal masters taste, than any shower of Carlton House[6] can be in showing the fine things there, and so she was when she made us remark the smallness of one of the Princesses bedrooms and said she slept & also dressed in that little room. There are a great many good pictures but I was most pleased with one of the king when he was about two years old, such a pretty little white-headed boy.

I cannot express how much pleasure a letter from you gives us. if I could promise myself I should be always as well as I am now I would say I will be a better correspondent in future

If Charles has time to add a line I shall be less ashamed to send this hasty scrawl. Love to all and every one. How much I should like once more to see Miss Wordsworths handwriting if she would but write a postscript to your next which I look to receive in a few days.

Yours affectionately

M Lamb

for[7] a Postscript, see the beginning

MS: University of Texas Library. Pub.: Harper, IV, 81–83; Lucas (1905), VI, 494–496; Lucas (1912), V, 521–523; Lucas (1935), II, 199–201. Watermark: 1815. The date of the letter is estimated from the report, in Mary's fifth paragraph, that the Lambs had seen Robinson: he had gone into the Lake Country in September, returned to London apparently between October 27 and November 2, and remarked in his diary (*H. C. R. on Books and Writers*, I, 196, 197, and 198) on having been with Charles or Charles and Mary on November 2, 7, and 12. The heading of the letter is Mary's.

1. See Letter 320, note 4.
2. From Lamb's poem "The Old Familiar Faces" (*Works*, V, 23–24).
3. Mary Wordsworth, presumably. Wordsworth's *"three wives"* (below) would be Mary and Dorothy Wordsworth and Sara Hutchinson.
4. Coleridge's "Christabel," I, 49.
5. Perhaps that of Lamb's "truly polite and urbane friend, Mr. A——m, of Flower-de-luce-court, in Fleet-street," the barber particularly mentioned in "On the Melancholy of Tailors" (*Works*, I, 174, note). The palace where George III "was was brought up" (below) is Kew Palace, formerly known as Dutch House.
6. Before it was razed, in 1826, in Waterloo Place, Pall Mall. Carlton House, where Princess Charlotte Augusta and Prince Leopold had been married, was the residence of George, Prince of Wales, Prince Regent, afterward George IV, whom Lamb wrote against publicly in "Epigrams: I [and] II," "The Triumph of the Whale," "The Godlike," "On a Projected Journey," "Song for the C[oronatio]n," and "Barrenness of the Imaginative Faculty in the Productions of Modern Art" (*Works*, V, 102–105, 106; and II, 228–229).
7. From Lamb.

323. *M. A. L. and C. L. to Sara Hutchinson*

[November or December 1816?]

My dear Miss Hutchinson

I had intended to write you a long letter but as my frank is dated I must send it off with a bare acknowledgment of the receipt of your kind letter. One question I must hastily ask you. Do you think Mr Wordsworth would have any reluctance to write, (strongly recommending to their patronage) to any of his rich friends in London to solicit employment for Miss Betham as a Mineature Painter?.[1] If you give me hopes that he will not be averse to do this I will write to you more

fully stating the infinite good he would do by performing as irksome a
task as I know asking favours to be. In brief she has contracted debts
for printing her beautiful poem of "Marie" which like all things of
original excellence does not sell at all.

These debts have led to little accidents unbecoming a woman and
a poetess to suffer. Retirement with such should be voluntary. The
Bell rings. I just snatch the Pen out of my sister's hand to finish
rapidly. Wordsw*th* may tell De Q———[2] that Miss B's price for a
Virgin and Child is three guineas.

Yours (all of you) ever
C L

MS: University of Texas Library. Pub.: Harper, IV, 84–85; Lucas (1905), VI,
496–497; Lucas (1912), V, 524; Lucas (1935), II, 202. Watermark: 1815. This
letter—its first paragraph is Mary's, its second is Lamb's—seems to have been
written soon after the preceding one.
    1. If Wordsworth did write letters so recommending Mary Matilda Betham,
they have not been recovered. See Letter 325, near the references to notes 1 and 3.
    2. Thomas De Quincey had been living in Dove Cottage, Grasmere, since
October 1809. On February 15, 1817, he would be married, in the Grasmere
parish church, to Margaret (1796–1837), a daughter of John and Mary Simpson
of Nab Cottage, the cottage overlooking Rydal Water that De Quincey was to own
from 1829 to 1833 and in which Hartley Coleridge was to pass his last years,
those from 1840 to 1849. De Quincey would edit the *Westmorland Gazette* from
July 1818 to November 1819, arrive in Edinburgh by early December 1820, and
during the next several weeks attempt to write for *Blackwood's Edinburgh Magazine*. He would, after having returned to his wife and children in Grasmere, arrive
in London in June 1821, hopeful of becoming connected as an essayist with a
well-paying periodical and carrying a letter of introduction from Wordsworth to
Talfourd, a letter De Quincey characteristically thought proper even though he
had enjoyed Talfourd's company in the Temple seven or eight years earlier. By
renting from the bookseller and publisher Henry George Bohn (1796–1884) a
small back room at 4 York Street, Covent Garden, De Quincey would become a
neighbor of the Lambs, who were to have been settled for nearly four years by
then at 20 Russell Street, Covent Garden. He, Charles, and Mary would renew,
and foster into a friendship, an acquaintance begun when De Quincey had presented himself with a letter of introduction to Lamb at the East India House on
a winter's day in 1804–1805 and accepted an invitation to come that evening to
16 Mitre Court Buildings for tea. It had been an acquaintance half-heartedly
renewed when they had chanced to meet while calling on Coleridge during the
period 1808 to 1814. De Quincey, initially through the kindness of Talfourd and
perhaps that of Lamb, would make the connection he sought in London by becoming acquainted with John Taylor (1781–1864) and James Augustus Hessey
(1785–1870), partners since 1806 in the bookselling and publishing firm of
Taylor and Hessey and proprietors and editors since April 1821 of the *London
Magazine*. They were to serialize, in its numbers for September and October 1821,
"Confessions of an English Opium-eater: Being an Extract from the Life of a
Scholar," the first of De Quincey's contributions to the *London Magazine*. They
were to publish, in 1822, *The Confessions of an English Opium-eater*.

324. *C. L. to Leigh Hunt*

Saturday 7 Dec 1816

Dear Hunt,

It gave me great pain to find that you probably staid at home on Sunday last upon my making a kind of promise to come ⟨in⟩. I thought you were always at home on that day, and did not consider my failing as likely to incoonvenience you at all. The fact is I have been very unwell, suffering from an intense cold, and having grown somewhat effeminate from country hours find myself less able than ever to return to London ones. Night air & late going to bed kill me. I hope you will forgive me & allow me to come when I get a little better, which I hope will not be long. Your kindness expressed towards me in so public & yet so private a way—and **verses** too—make me ashamed of my seeming ingratitude.[1] Believe me they were not lost upon me. You have been often in my recollections. There is not a shadow of misunderstanding left I hope on either side. My sister joins in kind remembes. and means to join me in personal apology soon to you & Mrs. Hunt——

Believe me very kindly
Yours
C Lamb

MS: Brewer–Leigh Hunt Collection, The University of Iowa Libraries (MsL/L21h/no. 1). Pub.: Lucas (1935), II, 202–203. Address: Leigh Hunt Esq/Vale of health/Hampstead. Postmark: December 7, 1816.

1. Hunt as "Harry Brown," imagined as Sir Thomas Browne's descendant, had written of Lamb's thoughtfulness in coming with Mary on a number of occasions to visit him and his wife during his imprisonment. The poem appears as "Harry Brown's Letters to His Friends. Letter VII. To C. L." in *The Examiner* of August 25, 1816; is titled "To Charles Lamb" in *The Poetical Works of Leigh Hunt,* ed. H. S. Milford (London: Humphrey Milford: Oxford University Press, 1923), p. 233; and in its version of 1816 has these as its first two stanzas:

> O thou, whom old Homer would call, were he living,
> Home-lover, thought-feeder, abundant-joke-giving;
> Whose charity springs from deep-knowledge, nor swerves
> Into mere self-reflections, or scornful reserves;
> In short, who were made for two centuries ago,
> When Shakspeare drew men, and to write was to know;—
>
> You'll not be surprised that I can't walk the streets
> Without thinking of you and your visiting feats,

When you call to remembrance how you and one more,
When I wanted it most, used to knock at my door.
For when the sad winds told us rain would come down,
Or snow upon snow fairly clogged up the town,
And dun yellow fogs brooded over its white,
So that scarcely a being was seen towards night,
Then, then said the lady yclept near and dear,
'Now mind what I tell you,—the L.'s will be here.'
So I poked up the flame, and she got out the tea,
And down we both sat, as prepared as could be;
And there, sure as fate, came the knock of you two,
Then the lanthorn, the laugh, and the 'Well, how d'ye do?'

325.   *C. L. to John Rickman*

[December 30, 1816]

Dear R. .

Your goose found her way into our larder with infinite discretion. Judging by her Giblets which we have sacrificed first, she is a most sensible **Bird**. Mary bids me say, first, that she thanks you for your remembrance, next that Mr. Norris and his family are no less indebted to you as the cause of his reverend & amiable visage being perpetuated when his Soul is flown.[1] Finding nothing like a Subscriptn. going on for the Unhappy Lady and not knowing how to press an actual Sum upon her, she hit upon the Expedient of making believe that Mr N. wanted his miniature (which his chops did seem to water after I must confess when twas first proposed, tho' with a **Nolo Pingier**[2] for modesty) and the Likeness being completed Your £5 is to go as from him. This I must confess is robbing Peter, or like the equitable distribution in Alexrs. Feast "Love was crowned" tho' Somebody else "won the Cause." And Love himself, smiling Love he might have sat for, so complacent he sat as he used to sit when in his days of Courtship he ogled thro' his spectacles. I have a shrewd suspicion he has an Eye upon his Spouses picture after this and probably some collateral branches may follow of the Norris or Faint Stock, so that your forerunner may prove a notable **Decoy duck**.[3] The Colliers are going to sit. Item, her Knightly Brother in Ireland is soon coming over apprized of her difficulties & I confidently hope an emergence for her. But **G. Dyer** Executor to a Nobleman. G. D. Residuary Legatee. What Whirligig of Fortune is this. Valet ima Summis. .[4] Strange World, strange Kings, strange composition!— I cant enjoy it sufficiently till

I get a more active belief in it. You've seen the Will of Ld. Stanhope. Conceive his old floor strewd with disjecta membra **Poeseŵs,** now loaden with Codicills, deeds of Trust, Letters of Attorney, Bonds, Obligations, Forfeitures, Excheqrs. Bills, Noverint Universis—Mr Serjeant Best, pray take my Arm Chair, My Lord Holland sit here, Lord Grantly will your Lordship take the other, Mr Jekyll excuse my offering you the Window Seat—We'll now have that Clause read over again—

B. & Fletcher describe a little French Lawyer[5] spoilt by an accidental duel he got thrust into, from a Notable Counseller turned into a Bravo. Here is G. D. more contra naturally metamorphosed. My life on it, henceforth he explodes his old Hobby Horses. No more poring into Cambridge records—

here are other Title deeds to be lookd into——

Now he can make any Joan a Lady.——[6]

And, if he dont get too proud to marry, that long unsolved Problem, G. D's. ⟨q[uickly (?)]⟩ is in danger of being quickly melted. They ca'nt choose but come & make offer of their coy wares. I see Miss H. prim up her Chin, Miss B-n-j-o cock her nose—Miss ———— * *

He throws his dirty Glove—G. D. Iratis Veneribus marries for my life on't.

And tis odds in that case but he leaves off making Love & Verses.

Indeed I look upon our friend as dead, dead to all his desperate fancies, pleasures,—he has lost the dignity of verse, the dignity of poverty, the dignity of digging on in desperation thro' mines of Literature that yielded nothing. Adieu! the wrinkled brow, the chin half shaved, the **Ruined Arm Chair,** the wind-admitting-and-expelling **screen,** the fluttering Pamphlets, the lost Letters, the documents never to be found when wanting——the unserviceable comfortable Landress——[7]

> G. D.'s Occupations oer
> Demptus per vim mentis gratissimus **Error:**
>
> Hæc pauca de amico nostro antiquo accipe pro **Næniis,**
> Exequiis, et ejusdem generis aliis
>
> **Vale noster G. D——**
>
> from Yours as he was, unchanged by Fortune
> C L

MS: Huntington Library. Pub.: Ainger (1904), I, 366–368; Harper, IV, 85–88; Lucas (1935), II, 203–205. Address: J. Rickman Esqr/New Palace Yard/ Westminster. Postmark: December 30, 1816.

1. Mary Matilda Betham—Lamb refers to her and Mary Lamb in the following sentence—had just painted the miniature of Randal Norris reproduced in *At the Shrine of St. Charles,* facing p. 14.

2. "Paint me not." Lamb quotes below from John Dryden's "Alexander's Feast: Or, the Power of Music; an Ode in Honor of St. Cecilia's Day," line 108: "So Love was crown'd, but Music won the cause."

3. "Decoy-ducks" is used in Vol. II, Letter 192, below Lamb's itemization. No record appears to exist of Mary Matilda Betham's having completed paintings of Mrs. Norris, née Faint; of any of the "collateral branches" of her or her husband's family; or of the Colliers, mentioned following. (See Vol. I, Introduction, p. xxix, about Randal and Elizabeth Norris; and Vol. II, Letter 224, source note, about John D., Jane, and John P. Collier.) About Sir William Betham, Miss Betham's "Knightly Brother in Ireland," see Vol. II, Letter 222, note 13. Charles Stanhope, third Earl Stanhope (see Vol. I, Letter 5, note 5; Vol. II, Letter 123, note 2, and Letter 124, notes 4 and 5), had died, of dropsy at Chevening, Kent, on December 15, 1816, and (according to the *DNB*) had left most of his disposable estate to ten executors named in a will made in 1805. Lamb's expressed reaction here to learning that George Dyer is among them is complemented, as it were, by an anecdote of Robinson (who refers to Anna Letitia Barbauld and her brother John Aikin; Charles James Fox; and Philip Henry Stanhope, fourth Earl Stanhope—persons identified in Vol. II, Letter 114, note 1; Letter 137, note 4; and Letter 124, note 4): "One day Mrs. Barbauld said to me: 'Have you heard whom Lord Stanhope has made executor?' 'No! Your brother?' 'No, there would have been nothing in that. The very worst, imaginable.' 'Oh, then, it was Buonaparte.' 'No! Guess again.' 'George Dyer.' 'You are right.' Lord Stanhope was clearly insane. Dyer was one of six executors, Charles Fox another. They were also residuary legatees. Dyer was one of the first to declare that he rejected the legacy and renounced the executorship. But the heir insisted on granting him a small annuity" (*H. C. R. on Books and Writers,* I, 5). The executors and legatees Lamb names near the end of his paragraph are, in addition to Dyer, William Draper Best, from 1829 first Baron Wynford (1767–1845), serjeant at law since 1799; the statesman and man of letters Henry Richard Vassall Fox, third Baron Holland (1773–1840), a nephew of Charles James Fox; William Norton, second Baron Grantley (1742–1822), the king's minister to the Swiss cantons; and the wit and politician Joseph Jekyll (1753?–1837), a friend of the Norrises and Dyer and Lamb, and the "J——ll, ever ready to be delivered of a jest," of "The Old Benchers of the Inner Temple" (*Works,* II, 85). Jekyll, the only son of Captain Edward Jekyll of the royal navy, had earned a B.A. in 1774, an M.A. in 1777, at Christ Church, Oxford, and in 1778 been called to the bar at Lincoln's Inn. He had transferred to the Inner Temple in 1795 and there become a bencher in 1795, a reader in 1814, and the treasurer in 1816. He had represented Calne in Parliament from 1787 to 1816, received appointments as solicitor general to the Prince of Wales and as king's counsel in 1805, and received an appointment as a master in chancery—one of the twelve assistants to the lord chancellor—in 1815. Jekyll was a contributor to the *Morning Chronicle* and *Evening Statesman* and the author of *Facts and Observations Relating to the Temple Church and the Monuments Contained in It* (1811). He was married, in 1801, to the former Maria Sloane, a woman of wealth by whom he had two sons. He kept chambers at 6 King's Bench Walk, Inner Temple, and by 1833 was living at 22 New Street, Spring Gardens, London. A letter from him thanking Lamb for a copy of *The Last Essays of Elia: Being a Sequel to Essays Published under That Name* (1833) Lamb will transcribe in his letter to Mrs. Norris postmarked July 6 and 10, 1833 (in my Vol. VI).

4. Horace, *Odes,* I, xxxiv, 12–16:

> . . . valet ima summis

> > mutare et insignem attenuat deus,
> > obscura promens; hinc apicem rapax
> > fortuna cum stridore acuto
> > sustulit, hic posuisse gaudet.

Margaret Ralston Gest, in her *The Odes of Horace, with Five Prefacing Epodes, Translated in Their Original Meters,* ed. Miriam M. H. Thrall (Kutztown, Pa.: Kutztown Publishing, 1973), p. 111, so translated the lines:

> . . . Oh, the god can change all:

> > the famed he pulls down, lifting the lowly man
> > instead to high state. Fortune can seize the crown
> > from one, with wings' sharp hiss, can speed it,
> > straight to the head of a man just chosen.

Lamb's next sentence is an adulteration of Shakespeare's *King John,* II, i, 561—"Mad world, mad kings, mad composition!" The "disjecta membra Poesew̄s," in imitation of Horace's *disiecti membra poetœ* (*Satires,* I, iv, 62), may be rendered as "sundered remains of Poetry." With "Noverint Universis" Lamb perhaps intends to suggest the legalism *Noverint universi per presentes*—"Know all men by these presents."

5. Monsieur La Writt, in *The Little French Lawyer,* a comedy on which Francis Beaumont and John Fletcher probably collaborated with Philip Massinger. With regard to the concluding sentence in Lamb's paragraph see Vol. I, Letter 86, note 11.

6. Cf. *Love's Labour's Lost,* III, i, 205—"Some men must love my lady, and some Joan." The first two of the women alluded to below are probably Mary Hays and Elizabeth Ogilvy Benger. (See Vol. I, Letter 58, note 1, and Letter 66, note 2; see also Vol. II, Letter 119, note 2.) In the 1728 version of Jonathan Swift's "The Country Life," or "The Journal," line 81, is "cocks his Nose." In *Timon of Athens,* V, iv, 49, is "Throw thy glove." A translation of "Iratis Veneribus" is "Despite the Wrath of his Loves."

7. To his "Landress," Mrs. Honour Mather, Dyer in 1824 would be married. (See Vol. I, Letter 5, near the end of note 5.) From "Adieu" (above) through "oer" (below) Lamb parodies *Othello,* III, iii, 347–357:

> . . . O now, for ever
> Farewell the tranquil mind! farewell content!
> Farewell the plumed troops and the big wars
> That makes ambition virtue! O, farewell!
> Farewell the neighing steed and the shrill trump,
> The spirit-stirring drum, th' ear-piercing fife,
> The royal banner, and all quality,
> Pride, pomp, and circumstance of glorious war!
> And O you mortal engines, whose rude throats
> Th' immortal Jove's dread clamors counterfeit,
> Farewell! Othello's occupation's gone.

The Latin remaining, the first line of it from Horace's *Epistles,* II, ii, 140, translates so:

> A most charming Delusion has been forced away:

> Accept these few words about our old friend in place of Dirges, Obsequies, and other things of that kind

> Farewell our G. D——

326. *C. L. to Ayrton*

Sir,

IN OBEDIENCE TO THE ORDERS OF THE HONOURABLE COM-
MITTEE OF ACCOUNTS, I HAVE TO REQUEST THAT YOU WILL SETTLE
THE FOLLOWING ERROR IN IN PAYMENT OF

I AM,

YOUR HUMBLE SERVANT,

Ch Lamb

ACCOUNTANT'S OFFICE,
EAST-INDIA HOUSE.

Friday aft the *18* 18*

SALE 18   FOLIO   LOT

Dear A.

I am in your debt for a very delightful evening—I should say two—
but Don Giovanni in particular was exquisite, & I am almost inclined
to allow **Music** to be one of the Liberal Arts which before I
doubted.—[1] **Could you** let me have 3 Gallery Tickets—dont be
startled—they shall positively be the last—or 2 or 1—for the same
for tomorrow or Tuesday—. They will be of no use for tomorrow if
not put in the post *this day* addrest to me **Mr Lamb India House;** if
for any other evening, your usual blundering direction No. 3 Middle
Temple instead of 4 Inner Temp. Lane will do.

MS: Huntington Library. Pub.: Macdonald, I, 384; Harper, IV, 88; Lucas
(1935), II, 205–206. Address: Wm Ayrton Esqr/James Street/Westminster. Postmark: April 18, 1817. Lamb writes on his office stationery headed with the
printed form here printed in large and small capitals.
1. Ayrton's production of *Don Giovanni*, the first production of Mozart's opera
in England, was playing at the King's Theatre. See Letter 250, note 4.

327. *C. L. to Ayrton*

Temple 12 May (1817)

My dear friend——
   Before I end——
   Have you any
More orders for Don Giovanni
     To give
   Him that doth live
   Your faithful Zany?

     Without raillery
      I mean Gallery
        ones.

For I am a person that shuns
    All ostentation
And being at the top of the fashion,
    And seldom go to operas
      But in formâ Pauperis.[1]

I go to the Play
In a very economical sort of a way,
    Rather to see ⟨than⟩
    Than be seen.[2]
Though I'm no ill sight
    Neither
    By candle light
And in some kinds of weather.
    You might pit me
      For height
    Against Kean.[3]

But in a grand tragic scene
    I'm nothing.
It would create a kind of loathing
    To see me act Hamlet.
      There'd be many a damn let
      Fly

At my presumption
If I should try
Being a fellow of no gumption—

By the way tell me candidly how you relish
This which they call the lapidary
Style?
Opinions vary.
The late Mr. Mellish[4]
Could never abide it.
He thought it vile,
And coxcombical.
My friend the Poet Laureat
Who is a great lawyer at
Any thing comical
Was the first who tried it
But Mellish could never abide it.
But it signifies very little what Mellish said,
Because he is dead.

For who can confute
A body that's mute?
Or who would fight
With a senseless sprite?
Or think of troubling
An impenetrable old goblin
That's dead and gone
And stiff as a stone—

To convince him with arguments pro & con
As if he were some live logician
Bred up at Merton[5]
Or Mr. Hazlitt the Metaphysician—.
Ha! Mr. Ayrton——
With all your rare **tone**——

For tell me . . . how should an Apparition
List to your call,
Though you talk'd for ever
Ever so **clever**,

When his ear itself
By which he must hear or not hear at all
    Is laid on the shelf?
      Or put the case
      (For more grace)
It[6] were a female spectre—
    How could you expect her
      To take much gust
        In long speeches
With her tongue as dry as dust
    In a sandy place
      Where no peaches
Nor lemons nor limes nor oranges hang
To drop on the drouth of an arid harangue,
    Or quench
With their sweet drench
The fiery pangs which the worms inflict
    With their endless nibblings[7]
      Like quibblings
Which the corpse may dislike but can ne'er contradict[?]
    Ha! Mr Ayrton!—
    With all your rare **tone**——

    I am
    C. Lamb

MS: Berg Collection, New York Public Library. Pub.: Talfourd (1837), II, 31–33; Fitzgerald, VI, 428–431; Hazlitt, II, 26–28; Ainger (1888), II, 1–3; Ainger (1900), III, 1–4; Macdonald, I, 384–387; Ainger (1904), II, 1–3; Harper, IV, 89–91; Lucas (1905), VI, 497–499; Lucas (1912), V, 525–527; Lucas (1935), II, 206–208. Address: Wm Ayrton Esqr./James Street/Westminstr. Postmark: May 13, 1817. Lucas in effect explained in *Works*, V (*Poems and Plays*), viii, that he decided not to include this rhyming letter in that volume.

1. "But 'as a Pauper.' " Four canceled lines follow.
2. Unlike the fashionable women in Ovid's *The Art of Love*, I, 99: "They come to see, come that they may themselves be seen" (*Spectatum veniunt, veniunt spectentur ut ipsæ*). English renditions of the expression, become proverbial, are in Chaucer's Prologue to "The Wife of Bath's Tale," line 558 in some editions and line 552 in others, and Ben Jonson's "Epithalamion, or a Song, Celebrating the Nuptials of That Noble Gentleman, Mr. Hierome Weston . . . with the Lady Frances Stewart . . . ," line 20.
3. Edmund Kean, like Lamb, was short.
4. Possibly the Joseph Charles Mellish who prepared *Paläophron and Neoterpe*.

A Masque for the Festival of the 24th of October 1800. From the German of Goethe, by the Translator of Goethe's Herrmann and Dorothea (1801); possibly, provided Lamb is mistaken or is not serious about this man's being dead, Joseph Charles Mellish (1768–1823), the British consul at Hamburg who translated selections from and edited Schiller's works and compiled and translated the offerings forming *Specimens of the German Lyric Poets . . .* (1822). Southey, since 1813 "Poet Laureat" (below), had employed the lapidary style at greatest length in *Thalaba the Destroyer.* He was hardly the first to have tried it. *The Shorter Oxford English Dictionary* shows "lapidary" as an adjective modifying "style" to mean "Characteristic of or suitable for monumental inscriptions" in use since 1724.

    5. Merton College, Oxford.
    6. "If it" is meant.
    7. A canceled line follows.

328. *C. L. to John Chambers*

[East India House
Late May or early June 1817]

Dear C.—

    I steal a few minutes from a painful and laborious avocation, aggravated by the absence of some that should assist me, to say how extremely happy we should be to see you return clean as the cripple out of the pool of Bethesda.[1] That damn'd scorbutic—how came you by it? . . . You are now fairly a damaged lot; as Venn would say, One Scratched. You might play Scrub in the *Beaux' Stratagem.* The best post your friends could promote you to would be a scrubbing post. "Aye, there's the rub." I generally get tired after the third rubber. But you, I suppose, tire twice the number every day. First, there's your mother, she begins after breakfast; then your little sister takes it up about Nuncheon[2] time, till her bones crack, and some kind neighbour comes in to lend a hand, scrub, scrub, scrub, and nothing will get the intolerable itch (for I am persuaded it is the itch) out of your penance-doing bones. A cursed thing just at this time, when everybody wants to get out of town as well as yourself. Of course, I don't mean to reproach you. You can't help it, the whoreson tingling in your blood.[3] I dare say you would if you could. But don't you think you could do a little work, if you came? as much as D—— does before 12 o'Clock. Hang him, there he sits at that cursed *Times*—and latterly he has had the *Berkshire Chronicle* sent him every Tuesday and Friday to get at the County news. Why, that letter which you favored him with, appears to me to be very well and clearly written. The man that wrote that might make out warrants, or write Committees. There was as much in quantity written as would have filled four volumes of the Indigo appendix; and when we are so busy as we are, every little helps. But I throw out these observations merely as innuendos. By the way there's a Doctor Lamert[4] in Leadenhall Street, who sells a mixture to purify the blood. No. 114 Leadenhall Street, near the market. But it is necessary that his Patients should be on the spot, that he may see them every day. There's a sale of Indigo advertised for July, forty thousand lots—10,000 chests only, but they sell them in quarter chests which makes 40,000. By the bye a droll accident happened here on Thursday, Wadd[5] and Plumley got quarrelling about a kneebuckle of Hyde's which the latter affirmed not to be standard; Wadd was nettled at this, and said something reflecting on tradesmen and shopkeepers, and Plumley struck him. . . . Friend is married; he has married a Roman Catholic, which has offended his family, but they have come to an agreement, that the boys (if they have children) shall be bred up in the father's religion, and the girls in the mother's, which I think equitable enough. . . . I am determined my children shall be brought up in their father's religion, if they can find out what it is. Bye[6] is about publishing a volume of poems which he means to dedicate to Matthie. Methinks he might have found a better Mecænas. They are chiefly amatory, others of them stupid, the greater part very far below mediocrity; but they discover much tender feeling; they are most like Petrarch of any foreign Poet, or what we might have supposed Petrarch would have written if Petrarch had been born a fool! Grinwallows[7] is made master of the ceremonies at Dandelion, near Margate; of course he gives up the office. "My Harry" makes so many faces that it is impossible to sit opposite him without smiling. Dowley danced a Quadrille at Court on the Queen's birthday with Lady Thynne, Lady Desbrow, and Lady Louisa Manners. It is said his performance was graceful and airy. Cabel[8] has taken an unaccountable fancy into his head that he is Fuller, member for Sussex. He imitates his blunt way of speaking. I remain much the same as you remember, very universally beloved and esteemed, possessing everybody's good-will, and trying at least to deserve it; the same steady adherence to principle, and correct regard for truth, which always marked my conduct, marks it still. If I am singular in anything it is in too great a squeamishness to anything that

remotely looks like a falsehood. I am call'd Old Honesty; sometimes
Upright Telltruth, Esq., and I own it tickles my vanity a little. The
Committee have formally abolish'd all holydays whatsoever—for which
may the Devil, who keeps no holydays, have them in his eternal burn-
ing workshop. When I say holydays, I mean Calendar holydays, for at
Medley's instigation[9] they have agreed to a sort of scale by which the
Chief has power to give leave of absence, viz.:—

Those who have been 50 years and upwards to be absent 4 days in
the year, but not without leave of the Chief.

35 years and upward, 3 days,

25 years and upward, 2 days,

18 years and upward, 1 day,

which I think very Liberal. We are also to sign our name when we *go*
as well as when we *come,* and every quarter of an hour we sign, to
show that we are here. Mins[10] and Gardner take it in turn to bring
round the book—O here *is* Mins with the Book—no, it's Gardner—
"What's that, G.?" "The appearance book, Sir" (with a gentle inclination of his head, and smiling). "What the devil, is the quarter
come again?" It annoys Dodwell amazingly; he sometimes has to sign
six or seven times while he is reading the Newspaper—[. . . (?)][11]

MS: unrecovered. Text: Ainger (1888), II, 17–20. Also pub.: Hazlitt, II, 42;
Ainger (1900), III, 24–28; Ainger (1904), II, 17–20; Harper, IV, 115–119;
Lucas (1935), II, 230–232. Address, from Ainger (1888), II, 307: Mr. John
Chambers, Leamington, Warwick. The date is estimated from Lamb's remarks
(near the references to notes 4, 7, and 9) on "a sale of Indigo advertised for
July"; on the birthday of Charlotte Sophia (May 19, 1744–November 17, 1818),
queen of George III; and on an action by the East India House committee of
accounts, constituted to inquire into ways of saving money for the East India
Company, that resulted in the abolishment of "all . . . Calendar holydays":
company records show that on May 14, 1817, its court of directors resolved
henceforth to allow only Christmas Day and Good Friday and general fast and
thanksgiving days as holidays to persons employed in the East India House and
the company warehouses, to require such persons to report for work on even those
days if the amount of work to be done should be heavy, and to increase to ten
pounds per year the compensation of such of those persons already entitled to
receive five shillings per holiday worked. John Chambers and his family are
identified in Letter 318, source note.
1. The healing pool, in Jerusalem, named in John 5:2. "Scorbutic," as Lamb
uses the word in his next sentence, is properly an adjective meaning, for instance,
of or pertaining to scurvy. Venn is identified in Ainger (1888), II, 307, as an
auctioneer; although the London directories do not list him, they do list Ventom
and Sons, a firm of auctioneers at 117 Whitechapel Road. *The Beaux'* [or *Beaux*]
Stratagem is one of George Farquhar's comedies. The quotation is from *Hamlet,*
III, i, 64.

2. A between-meals refreshment, originally of a little liquor taken in the afternoon; a lunch.

3. *II Henry IV*, I, ii, 111–113: "This apoplexy . . . is a kind of lethargy . . . , a kind of sleeping in the blood, a whoreson tingling." Alluded to below is Henry Dodwell: see the last sentence in this letter and the source note to Letter 318.

4. A name that does not appear in the London directories for the period or in the indexes to the personnel records of the Society of Apothecaries or in the freedoms and apprenticeship records of the Barber-surgeons' Company. *Johnstone's London and Commercial Guide and Street Directory* for 1817 lists John Clarke, a hat manufacturer, at 114 Leadenhall Street, the address Lamb gives (below) for Lamert. Thus Lamert may be Lamb's invention. For all of that information and for some of that provided in the third sentence in note 1, above, I thank Mr. Godfrey Thompson of the Guildhall Library, City of London Libraries.

5. Henry Wadd (1784?–1834) was a son of the surgeon Solomon Wadd of Basinghall Street, London, and a brother of William (1776–1829). William was a member of the Royal College of Surgeons and of the council of the College of Surgeons of England, the author and illustrator of several medical books, and, from 1821, surgeon extraordinary to George IV. Henry, about whom Lamb wrote the epigram "What Wawd knows, God knows; / But God knows *what* Wawd knows!" (*Works*, V, 344), who in July 1811 had by accident "nearly put . . . [Lamb's] eye out by throwing a pen full of ink into it" (*H. C. R. on Books and Writers*, I, 40), was appointed to the accountant general's office of the East India House in 1799, in receipt of salary as a clerk from 1802, and retired in 1830. He rose, in the course of his employment, from an ensign to a lieutenant in the Royal East India Volunteers. William Dawson Plumley (1787?–1848), named next, Lamb's East India House crony characterized as "Pl——, officious to do, and to volunteer, good services," in "The Superannuated Man" (*Works*, II, 197), was a son of William Plumley, a silversmith and clockmaker and watchmaker of Ludgate Hill, London. William Dawson Plumley was appointed to the accountant general's office in 1804, in receipt of salary as a clerk from 1807 and of a special annual gratuity as an assayer of silver and gold bullion, and retired in 1834. James Chicheley Hyde (1761?–1838), who claimed to be a relative of Lord Chancellor Edward Hyde, first Earl of Clarendon (1609–1647), was appointed as a clerk in the accountant general's office in 1780, in receipt of salary from 1784, advanced to chief clerk by 1821, acting briefly as deputy accountant general in 1821, and retired, as chief clerk, in 1825. George Friend (d. 1873), whose bride and family have not been identified, was still in his teens, not yet in receipt of salary, and the junior clerk in service time to all except two clerks in the office at the time of this letter. He had received his appointment in 1815, was elevated to accountant general in 1858—when the administration of England's territories in India passed from the East India Company to the Crown—and was retired, on a pension equal to his full salary, in 1866.

6. Thomas Bye (d. 1848) was appointed to the accountant general's department of the East India House in 1783, in receipt of salary as a clerk from 1786, caused to suffer a reduction in salary in 1819 from £600 to £100 annually for coming to work drunk—Lamb writes of Bye's trouble in letters to Manning and Wordsworth postmarked May 28 and June 7, 1819 (both in Vol. IV)—and retired, on a pension of £300 annually, in 1820. No record of publication appears to exist of the volume of poems, mentioned below, Bye meant to dedicate to John Matthie (d. 1836). Matthie, whose security bonds at the East India House were signed by the former prime minister Sir William Petty (see Vol. II, Letter 193, note 2), was employed as an extra clerk in the accountant general's department in 1788, resigned in 1789, was employed as an established clerk in the same department in 1793, promoted to second auctioneer in 1797 and to auctioneer, possibly to

inspector of indigo as well, in 1815, and retired in 1834. Gaius Cilnius Maecenas is identified in Vol. I, Letter 34, note 5.

7. Charles Greenwollers (1764?–1831), who was hired as a writer, or clerk, in the Bengal and Coast warehouse of the East India Company in 1805, made an extra clerk in the accountant general's office of the East India House in 1815, and retired in 1826. "Dandelion" (below), properly Daundelyon, or Dent de Lion, is the manor house, located between Margate and Westgate, of a thirteenth-century manor once the seat of the family of Sir John Daundelyon (d. 1443?). "My Harry," here a reference probably to Henry Dodwell, is in *II Henry IV,* IV, v, 212, the king's form of address to Prince Henry, afterward Henry V. Thomas Dowley (d. 1833) was appointed to the accountant general's office of the East India House in 1791, in receipt of salary as a clerk from 1794, and retired in 1832. The ladies with whom Lamb imagines him as having danced are, presumably, altogether imaginary, the name of the last being the same as that of the seven-year-old narrator of "The Farmhouse," in *Mrs. Leicester's School (Works,* III, 283–288).

8. Thomas Scutt Cabell (1788?–1847) was employed as a clerk in the accountant general's department of the East India House in 1803, made assistant to the accountant general and his deputy in 1821 or 1822, promoted to deputy accountant general in 1824 and to accountant general in 1832, and retired in 1834. Lamb writes below that Cabell is imitating the blunt speaking manner of John Fuller (1757?–1834), who had been a member of Parliament for Southampton from 1780 to 1784 and for Sussex from 1801 to 1812. Fuller is listed in Gerrit Parmele Judd's *Members of Parliament, 1734–1832* (1955; rpt. Hamden, Conn.: Archon Books, 1972); his obituary is in the *Gentleman's Magazine,* N.S. 2 (July 1834), 106–107.

9. That of George Medley (1784?–1827), who was appointed as a clerk in the accountant general's office of the East India House in 1799, serving at the time of this letter as clerk to the committee of accounts (see the source note to this letter), and retired in 1825. By "the Chief" (below) Lamb probably means the accountant general, Charles Cartwright. See Vol. I, Letter 5, note 9.

10. Martin Minns, who entered the service of the East India House as a porter in the accountant general's department in 1807, was advanced to doorkeeper in a year not known, and remained at least into December 1824, when the record about him leaves off. John Gardner, mentioned next, entered the service of the East India House as a laborer in 1806, became a porter in the accountant general's department in 1813, and was retired in 1834. Most of the details noted here about Lamb's office associates mentioned in this letter I have taken from information Mr. S. J. McNally of the India Office Library and Records sent to me. Some of the details I have drawn or derived from Ainger (1888), II, 307, about Hyde and Plumley; from Mrs. G. A. Anderson's "On the Dating of Lamb's Letters," *London Mercury,* 18 (August 1928), 394, about Bye; from Samuel McKechnie's "Charles Lamb of the India House" in *Notes and Queries,* 191 (November 30, December 14, and 28, 1946), 226, 255, and 277–278, about Matthie, Wadd, and (again) Plumley; and from McKechnie's "Charles Lamb of the India House" in *Notes and Queries,* 192 (February 8, 15, and March 8, 1947), 56, 73, and 103–104 and 106, about Friend and Greenwollers and (again) Matthie, Medley, and Cabell and (again) Hyde and (again) Medley and (again) Wadd.

11. "[*Unfinished.*]" is the notation below or at the end of this letter in Ainger (1888) and other editions. But in Ainger (1888), II, 306 and 307, are these statements: "This letter, from the original in the possession of Mr. George Bentley [(1828–1895), the publisher and author] . . . , is now for the first time printed by his most kind permission. . . . The few notes that follow are taken from some memoranda supplied by the late Mr. H. G. Bohn [see Letter 323, note 2], from

whose collection the letter passed into the hands of Mr. Bentley. . . . Mr. Bohn adds that 'this letter is evidently complete although it ends abruptly and is not signed.' "

329. *C. L. to Barron Field*

Aug. 31st, 1817

My dear Barron,—

The bearer of this letter so far across the seas is Mr Lawrey,[1] who comes out to you as a missionary, and whom I have been strongly importuned to recommend to you as a most worthy creature by Mr Fenwick, a very old, honest friend of mine; of whom, if my memory does not deceive me, you have had some knowledge heretofore as editor of the *Statesman;* a man of talent, and patriotic. If you can show him any facilities in his arduous undertaking, you will oblige us much. Well, and how does the land of thieves[2] use you? and how do you pass your time, in your extra-judicial intervals? Going about the streets with a lantern, like Diogenes, looking for an honest man? You may look long enough, I fancy. Do give me some notion of the manners of the inhabitants where you are. They don't thieve all day long do they? No human property could stand such continuous battery. And what do they do when they an't stealing?

Have you got a theatre? What pieces are performed? Shakspeare's, I suppose; not so much for the poetry, as for his having once been in danger of leaving his country on account of certain "small deer."[3]

Have you poets among you? Damn'd plagiarists, I fancy, if you have any. I would not trust an idea, or a pocket-handkerchief of mine, among 'em. You are almost competent to answer Lord Bacon's problem, whether a nation of atheists can subsist together. You are practically in one:

> "So thievish 'tis, that the eighth commandment itself
> Scarce seemeth there to be."

Our old honest world goes on with little perceptible variation. Of course you have heard of poor Mitchell's death,[4] and that G. Dyer is one of Lord Stanhope's residuaries. I am afraid he has not touched much of the residue yet. He is positively as lean as Cassius. Barnes is going to Demerara, or Essequibo, I am not quite certain which. Alsager is turned actor. He came out in genteel comedy at Cheltenham this season, and has hopes of a London engagement.

For my own history, I am just in the same spot, doing the same thing, (videlicet, little or nothing,) as when you left me; only I have positive hopes that I shall be able to conquer that inveterate habit of smoking which you may remember I indulged in. I think of making a beginning this evening, *viz.* Sunday, 31st Aug., 1817, not Wednesday, 2nd Feb., 1818, as it will be perhaps when you read this for the first time. There is the difficulty of writing from one end of the globe (hemispheres I call 'em) to another! Why, half the truths I have sent you in this letter will become lies before they reach you, and some of the lies (which I have mixed for variety's sake, and to exercise your judgment in the finding of them out) may be turned into sad realities before you shall be called upon to detect them. Such are the defects of going by different chronologies. Your "now" is not my "now"; and again, your "then," is not my "then"; but my "now" may be your "then," and vice versa. Whose head is competent to these things?

How does Mrs Field get on in her geography? Does she know where she is by this time? I am not sure sometimes you are not in another planet; but then I don't like to ask Capt. Burney, or any of those that know any thing about it, for fear of exposing my ignorance.

Our kindest remembrances, however, to Mrs F., if she will accept of reminiscences from another planet, or at least another hemisphere.

C. L.

MS: unrecovered. Text: Macdonald, I, 387–389. Also pub.: Talfourd (1837), II, 34–36; Purnell, II, 93–95; Fitzgerald, III, 14–16; Hazlitt, II, 28–30; Ainger (1888), II, 4–5; Ainger (1900), III, 5–7; Ainger (1904), II, 4–5; Harper, IV, 91–94; Lucas (1905), VI, 500–501; Lucas (1912), V, 528–529; Lucas (1935), II, 209–210. Barron and Jane Field had been in New South Wales, which Governor Lachlan Macquarie (d. 1824) was transforming from a penal settlement into a colony, since February 1817. See Letter 296, note 1.

1. Identified in Ainger (1900), III, 228, as the Reverend Mr. Walter Lawry, a Wesleyan minister. About John Fenwick and *The Statesman,* mentioned below, see my Vol. II, Letter 108, note 1.

2. Called *"Hades of Thieves"* in "Distant Correspondents: In a Letter to B. F. Esq. at Sydney, New South Wales" (*Works,* II, 107), the essay into which Lamb will elaborate this letter.

3. From *King Lear,* III, iv, 138, and to be used in Lamb's "In *re* Squirrels" (*Works,* I, 306). Most of Lamb's sentence here alludes to Shakespeare's alleged prosecution, in perhaps 1585 by Sir Thomas Lucy (1532–1600) of Charlecote, Warwickshire, for poaching deer on Lucy's estates, and flight from Stratford-on-Avon and punishment. Lucas, who stated (in Lucas [1935], II, 210) that he had not seen the original of this letter, followed Talfourd and printed "Cursed

plagiarists" rather than "Damn'd plagiarists," below. What Lamb calls "Lord Bacon's problem, whether a nation of atheists can subsist together," Bacon implied in his essay "Of Atheism." The lines indented are Lamb's corruption of Coleridge's "The Rime of the Ancient Mariner," lines 599–600: "So lonely 'twas, that God himself / Scarce seeméd there to be."

4. One of the lies in this letter: the classical scholar Thomas Mitchell (b. 1783), who had been a schoolfellow of Leigh Hunt at Christ's Hospital and, with Lamb and Field, a contributor to *The Reflector,* did not die until 1845. Lamb and Mitchell had met on or by April 29, 1812, when Robinson recorded having attended a party at Field's that included Lamb, Mitchell, and Hunt. (See *H. C. R. on Books and Writers,* I, 70.) In Letter 325, note 3, are comments on the news Lamb next conveys. In *Julius Caesar,* I, ii, 194, is Caesar's remark on the leanness of Gaius Cassius Longinus (fl. 53–44 B.C.). Thomas Barnes (1785–1841), the editor of the *Times* from 1817 to 1841, once another of Hunt's schoolfellows and of the contributors to *The Reflector,* was not going to Demerara or Essequibo, districts of British Guiana. Lamb and Barnes had met on or by March 16, 1812, when Robinson recorded having called on Lamb and found Barnes, Field, and Hunt with him. (See *H. C. R. on Books and Writers,* I, 66; for biographical sketches of Mitchell and Barnes containing accounts of their contributions to *The Reflector* see Hunt's *"Reflector,"* pp. 107–112 and 91–98.) See Letter 298, note 5, and *Sara Hutchinson's Letters,* p. 111, about Thomas Alsager, who had been the guest of the Wordsworths at Rydal Mount shortly before the time of this letter and had not turned actor. Talfourd printed "A——," Lucas printed "A[lsager]" rather than "Alsager."

330. *C. L. to Charles Chambers*

[September 1, 1817]

with regard to a **John Dory,** which you desire to be particularly informed about——I honour the fish, but it is rather on account of **Quin**[1] who patronized it, and whose taste (of a *dead* man) I had as lieve go by as any body's, (**Apicius** and **Heliogabulus** excepted—this latter started nightingales brains and peacock's tongues as a garnish—)

Else, in *itself,* and trusting to my own poor single judgment, it hath not that moist mellow oleaginous gliding smooth descent from the tongue to the palate, thence to the stomach &c. as your Brighton[2] Turbot hath, which I take to be the most friendly and familiar flavor of any that swims—most genial & at home to the palate—

nor has it on the other hand that fine falling off flakiness, that obsequious peeling off (as it were like a **sea onion**) which endears your cods head & shoulders to some appitites, that manly firmness combined with a sort of womanish coming-in-pieces which the same cods head & shoulders hath—where the *whole* is easily separable, pliant to a knife or a spoon, but each *individual flake* presents a pleas-

ing resistance to the opposed tooth—you understand me—these delicate subjects are necessarily obscure—

but it has a third flavor of its own, totally distinct from Cod or
Turbot, which it must be owned may to some not injudicious palates
render it acceptable—but to my unpractised tooth it presented rather
a crude river-fish-flavor, like your Pike or Carp, and perhaps like them
should have been tamed & corrected by some laborious & well chosen
sauce. Still, I always suspect a fish which requires so much of artificial settings off. Your choicest relishes (like native loveliness) need
not the foreign aid of ornament, but are when unadorned (that is,
with nothing but a little plain anchovy & a squeeze of lemon) are
then adorned the most.³ However, I shall go to Brighton again, next
Summer, and shall have an opportunity of correcting my judgment,
if it is not sufficiently informed. I can only say that when **Nature** was
pleased to make the **John Dory so** notoriously deficient in outward
graces (as to be sure **he** is the very **Rhinoceros** of fishes, the ugliest
dog that swims, except perhaps the **Sea Satyr** which I never saw, but
which they say is terrible) when she formed him with so few external
advantages, she might have bestowed a more elaborate finish on his
parts internal, & have given him a **relish,** a **sapor,** to recommend him;
as she made **Pope** a **Poet** to make up for making him crooked.⁴

I am sorry to find that you have got a knack of saying things which
are not true, to shew your wit. If I had no wit, but what I must shew
at the expence of my virtue or my modesty, I had as lieve be as stupid
as ✱✱✱⁵ at the **Tea Warehouse.** Depend upon it, [m]y dea[r] Chambers,
that an ounce of integrity at our death bed will stand us in more avail
than all the Wit of Congreve or ✱✱✱✱. For instance you tell me a fine
story about Truss, and his playing at Leamington, which I know to be
false, because I have advice from Derby that he was whipt through the
Town on that very day you say he appeared in some character or
other, for robbing an old woman at church of a seal ring. And Dr.
Parr has been two months dead.⁶ So it wont do to scatter these random
stories about **among people** that **know** any thing. Besides, your forte
is not invention. It is *judgment,* particularly shewn in your choice of
dishes. We seem in that instance born under one star. I like you for
liking hare. I esteem you for disrelishing minced veal. Liking is too
cold a word, I **love** you for your noble attachment to the fat unctuous
juices of **deers** flesh & the **green unspeakable** of turtle.⁷ I honor you

for your endeavors to esteem and approve of my favorite which I ventured to recommend to you, as substitute for hare, bullock's heart; and I am not offended that you cannot taste it with *my* palate. A true son of Epicurus should reserve one taste peculiar to himself. For a long time I kept the secret about the exceeding deliciousness of the **marrow** of boiled knuckle of veal, till my tongue weakly run out in its praises, and now it is prostitute & common.— But I have made one discovery, which I will not impart till my dying scene is over, perhaps it will be my last mouthful in this world, delicious thought, enough to sweeten (or rather make savoury) the hour of death. It is a little square bit about this size in or near the huckle bone of a fried joint of ✳✳✳✳✳✳ fat I cant call it, nor lean neither altogether, it is that beautiful compound which Nature must have made in Para- dise Park venison, before she separated the two substances, the dry & the oleaginous, to punish sinful mankind; Adam ate them entire & inseparate, and this little taste of Eden in the huckle bone of a fried ✳✳✳✳ seems the only relique of a Paradisaical state. When I die, an exact description of its topography shall be left in a cupboard with a key, ins[c]ribed on which these words, "C. Lamb—dying imparts this to C. Chambers as the only worthy depositary of such a secret." You'll drop a tear— — —

— — —

MS: Mr. W. Hugh Peal. Pub.: Fitzgerald (Enfield and Temple editions only— see my Vol. I, Introduction, pp. lxix and lxx), III, Supplemental Letters; Hazlitt, II, 30–31; Macdonald, I, 389–391; Harper, IV, 327–330; Lucas (1905), VII, 680–682; Lucas (1912), VI, 727–729; Lucas (1935), II, 211–213. Address: Mr. C. Chambers/Leamington/near/Warwick. Postmark: September 1, 1817. Charles Chambers is identified in Letter 318, source note.

1. The actor James Quin (1693–1766), whom Tobias Smollett in *The Expedition of Humphry Clinker* had Jeremy Medford partly portray in his letter to Sir Watkin Phillips of April 30 as desiring to send for the head of the cook who "had committed felony, on the person of that John Dory, which is mangled in a cruel manner, and even presented without sauce—*O tempora! O mores!*" See my Vol. I, Letter 34, near the reference to note 7, for an instance of Lamb's use of that expression originally Cicero's, and Vol. II, Letter 200, near the reference to note 3, for Lamb's naming together elsewhere the epicures named together below; Heliogabalus is mentioned, without Apicius, in "Edax on Appetite" and "Grace before Meat" (*Works,* I, 121, and II, 94).

2. Where, Mary remarks near the end of her share of the letter to Dorothy Wordsworth postmarked November 21, 1817 (in Vol. IV), the Lambs and Mrs. Morgan had vacationed the past summer.

3. James Thomson, *The Seasons,* "Autumn," lines 202–204:
. . . For loveliness
Needs not the foreign aid of ornament,
But is when unadorned adorned the most.

4. Pope was about twelve years old when tuberculosis of the spine deformed him.

5. Thomas Bye has been suggested as the person to whom Lamb alludes. But Bye worked in the East India House. (See Letter 328, note 6.) Below, after mentioning the wit of the dramatist William Congreve and of the person (perhaps Lamb himself) represented by four asterisks, Lamb fabricates his own fine story about William Henry Truss, who was appointed as an extra clerk in the accountant general's department of the East India House in 1800, was advanced to an established clerk in the auditor's department in 1806, was in receipt of salary from 1808, and resigned in 1829. Samuel McKechnie stated in "Charles Lamb of the India House" in the *CLSB* of November 1948 that William Truss "was to be appointed one of the Managers of the Savings Bank established by the India House for the use of the staff." Mr. S. J. McNally of the India Office Library and Records has informed me that he has not found in the minutes from 1819 to 1834 of the East India Company's Bank for Savings, established in April 1819, any reference to William Truss. McKechnie also stated that at "an earlier period [earlier than the period of Lamb's present letter] Lamb had had for some ten years, as an Accountant Office colleague, a clerk named John Truss." John Truss was appointed to the East India Company's Home Service in 1801, was (as a clerk, presumably) in receipt of salary in the accountant general's office of the East India House from 1803, and resigned in 1810.

6. Dr. Samuel Parr of Hatton, Warwickshire (see Vol. II, Letter 117, note 1)— the pedagogue, priest, political writer, Latin scholar, friend of Joseph Priestley, Samuel Rogers, Thomas Moore, Walter Savage Landor—would not be two months dead until May 6, 1825.

7. Lamb will write in "Grace before Meat" that a man "shall confess a perturbation of mind, inconsistent with the purposes of the grace, at the presence of venison or turtle" (*Works,* II, 92); that "unctuous morsels of deer's flesh were not made to be received with dispassionate services"; that Elia "shrink[s] instinctively from one who professes to like minced veal" (II, 95). (J. Milton French has pointed out in "A Chip from Elia's Workshop," *Studies in Philology,* 37 [January 1940], 93, that the manuscript of "Grace before Meat" in the Harvard College Library shows "unctuous morsels" to be a revision of "unctuous juices," the phrase used in this letter.) In "Thoughts on Presents of Game, &c." (*Works,* I, 343–344) Lamb will at some length express his appreciation of hare.

331. *C. L. to T. Hill*

[October 1817?]

Dr Sir,

It is necessary *I see you sign,* can you step up to me 4 Inner Temple Lane this Eveng

I shall wait at home

Yours &—
C Lamb

MS: British Museum. Pub.: Hazlitt, I, 399; Lucas (1905), VII, 710; Lucas (1912), VI, 757; Lucas (1935), III, 51. Address: T Hill Esqr. The addressee of Lamb's present note and one dated March 3, 1825 (in my Vol. V), may be the drysalter and book collector Thomas Hill (1760–1840), a busybody who sought the acceptance of theatrical and literary celebrities and was or was to become a patron of the poets Robert Bloomfield and Henry Kirke White, a friend of Theodore Edward Hook and the model for Hull in Hook's novel *Gilbert Gurney* (1836), and, perhaps—the suggestion is in Lucas (1935), III, 51–52—the original of the subject of Lamb's "Tom Pry" (*Works,* I, 276–277). Lamb will name Thomas Hill in a letter to John Bates Dibdin postmarked June 30, 1826 (in my Vol. V). Lamb could have written his present note on any day between June 3, 1809, the date he and Mary had moved to 4 Inner Temple Lane, and probably late October 1817, about the time they moved to 20 Russell Street, Covent Garden. (In *The Life of Lamb,* I, 390, is the statement that they "moved to Great Russell Street," Covent Garden. The statement is incorrect, as Basil Savage shows in "Charles and Mary Lamb in Russell Street," in the *CLSB* of July 1977.) On November 1, 1817, Robinson called on the Lambs at their new address: "I found them," he wrote, "comfortably situated, their apartments neat, and to them not unpleasant from the noise" (*H. C. R. on Books and Writers,* I, 210).

INDEX OF NAMES

Boldface numbers refer to key pages.

The Letters of
Charles and Mary Anne Lamb

Designed by R. E. Rosenbaum.
Composed by York Composition Company, Inc.,
in 11 point Intertype Baskerville, 2 points leaded,
with display lines in monotype Baskerville.
Printed letterpress from type by York Composition Company
on Warren's Olde Style, 60 pound basis.
Illustrations printed offset by Art Craft of Ithaca.
Bound by Vail-Ballou Press
in Joanna bookcloth
and stamped in All-Purpose foil.